A History of American Privateers

Edgar Stanton Maclay

Overawing the enemy.

The *Paul Jones* and the *Hassan*.

(See page 12.)

A HISTORY OF
AMERICAN PRIVATEERS

EDGAR STANTON MACLAY, A.M.

A HISTORY OF
AMERICAN PRIVATEERS

BY

EDGAR STANTON MACLAY, A. M.

AUTHOR OF

A HISTORY OF THE UNITED STATES NAVY,
REMINISCENCES OF THE OLD NAVY

EDITOR OF

THE JOURNAL OF WILLIAM MACLAY
(U. S. Senator from Pennsylvania, 1789-1791)

ILLUSTRATED

LONDON
SAMPSON LOW, MARSTON & CO. (LIMITED)
1900

PRINTED AT THE APPLETON PRESS.
NEW YORK, U. S. A.

TO

THEODORE ROOSEVELT,

PIONEER OF
THE MODERN SCHOOL OF NAVAL WRITERS,

THIS WORK
IS RESPECTFULLY DEDICATED.

April, 1898.

PREFACE.

THE history of the United States navy is so intimately connected with that of our privateers that the story of one would be incomplete without a full record of the other. In each of our wars with Great Britain many of the captains in the navy assumed command of privateers, in which they frequently rendered services of national importance, while the privateersmen furnished the navy with a large number of officers, many of whom became famous. In our struggle for independence more than sixty American craft armed by private enterprise were commanded by men who had been, or soon became, officers in the regular service; and in more than one instance, notably that of the officers and men of the *Ranger*—Captain John Paul Jones' famous ship, then commanded by Captain William Simpson —almost the entire ship's company of a Continental cruiser turned to privateering. Many of our most distinguished naval officers have pointed with pride to their probationary career in privateers. The mere mention of such names as Truxtun, Porter, Biddle, Decatur, Barney, Talbot, Barry, Perry, Murray, Rodgers, Cassin, Little, Robinson, Smith, and Hopkins will show how closely related were the two arms of our maritime service.

In his History of the United States Navy the author endeavored to show that our maritime forces were a powerful factor not only in attaining American independence, but in maintaining it.

A few general statements will show that in both wars with England our privateers were a most important if not predominating feature of our early sea power.   In our first struggle the Government war vessels—built, purchased, or hired—numbered forty-seven, or, including the flotilla on Lake Champlain, sixty-four vessels of all descriptions, carrying a total of one thousand two hundred and forty-two guns and swivels.   This force captured one hundred and ninety-six vessels.   Of the privateers there were seven hundred and ninety-two, carrying more than thirteen thousand guns and swivels. These vessels captured or destroyed about six hundred British vessels.   In the War of 1812 the regular navy of the United States on the ocean numbered only twenty-three vessels, carrying in all five hundred and fifty-six guns.   This force captured two hundred and fifty-four of the enemy's craft.   In the same period we had five hundred and seventeen privateers, aggregating two thousand eight hundred and ninety-three guns, which took no fewer than one thousand three hundred prizes.

The following table will show, in a most striking manner, the importance of the part taken by our privateers in the struggle for independence:

Comparative List of American-armed Vessels (1776–1782).

CLASS OF CRUISERS.	1776.	1777.	1778.	1779.	1780.	1781.	1782.
Continental	31	34	21	20	13	9	7
Privateers.............	136	73	115	167	228	449	323

Comparative Number of Guns carried by the above Vessels.

CLASS OF CRUISERS.	1776.	1777.	1778.	1779.	1780.	1781.	1782.
Continental	586	412	680	462	266	164	198
Privateers.............	1,360	730	1,150	2,505	3,420	6,735	4,845

Looking at it from a financial point of view, we find that the money value of the prizes and cargoes taken by Government cruisers during the Revolution, allowing an average of thirty thousand dollars for each, to be less than six million dollars, and, allowing the same average for the privateers, we have a total of eighteen million dollars. In the second war with Great Britain we find, on the same basis of calculation, the money value of Government prizes to be six million six hundred thousand dollars, while that of the privateers was thirty-nine million dollars. Taking the entire maritime forces of the United States—both navy and privateers—into consideration, we find that about eight hundred vessels were captured from the English in the war for independence, valued at twenty-three million eight hundred and eighty thousand dollars, while the prisoners could not have been short of sixteen thousand; and in the second war against Great Britain the value of the prizes was forty-five million six hundred thousand dollars, while there were no fewer than thirty thousand prisoners. Against these figures we have some twenty-two thousand prisoners taken by our land forces during the Revolution, and about six thousand in the War of 1812.

To the American people, who for generations have been taught that our independence was achieved almost entirely by the efforts of our land forces, and that the War of 1812 was brought to a creditable close principally by the operations of our armies, these statements of the comparative values and amount of work done on sea and land will prove a matter of surprise. Every reader of American history is familiar with the capture of Stony Point and its British garrison of five hundred and forty-three men; of Ticonderoga, with its garrison of fifty men; of the battle of Trenton, with nearly one thousand prisoners. But it is doubtful if many have heard of the capture of three hundred British soldiers, with their colonel, in two transports, by the little State cruiser *Lee*, of the two hundred Highlanders and twenty army officers of the Seventy-first Regiment by our *Andrea Doria*, of twenty-four British army officers by Captain John Burroughs Hopkins' squadron, of the two hundred and forty Hessians captured by the privateer *Mars*, of the company of dragoons taken by the privateer *Massachusetts*, of the sixty-three Hessian chasseurs made prisoners by the privateer *Tyrannicide*, of the capture of a colonel, four lieutenant colonels, and three majors by the privateer *Vengeance*, and of the capture of one hundred soldiers by the privateer *Warren*. We all know that Washington took about one thousand men at Trenton, that Gates made some eight thousand prisoners at Saratoga, and that the Americans and French secured about seven thousand at Yorktown; but it is not so generally known that in the same period fully sixteen thousand prisoners were made by our sea forces. While fewer than six thousand prisoners were taken by our land forces in the War of 1812, fully thirty thousand were taken by our sea forces.

A careful review of British newspapers, periodicals, speeches in Parliament, and public addresses for the periods covered by these two wars will show that our land forces, in the estimation of the British, played a very insignificant part, while our sea forces were constantly in their minds when "the American war" was under discussion. When England determined to coerce the refractory Americans, she little thought that she was inviting danger to her own doors. Her idea of an American war was a somewhat expensive transportation of German mercenaries across the Atlantic, where the dispute would be settled in a wilderness, far removed from any possible chance of interference with British interests in other parts of the world. The British merchant looked forward to the war with no small degree of complacency; for, in spite of the provisions of the Navigation Acts, which were designed especially to protect him from colonial competition, he keenly felt American rivalry for the carrying trade of the world. It would cost several million pounds annually to send Hessians to America, but this would be more than offset by the British merchant securing the colonist's share of commerce.

This was the view generally taken by Englishmen before hostilities began. But had they anticipated that American cruisers and privateers would cross the Atlantic and throw their coasts into continual alarm; that their shipping, even in their own harbors, would be in danger; that it would be unsafe for peers of the realm to remain at their country seats; that British commerce would be almost annihilated; that sixteen thousand seamen and eight hundred vessels would be taken from them—they would have entered upon a coercive policy with far greater hesitancy. Without her ships and sailors England would be reduced to one of the least of the European powers, and, while she could afford to lose a few thousand Hessians, the loss of her maritime ascendency touched her to the quick. It was this attack on England's commerce that struck the mortal blows to British supremacy in America—not Saratoga nor Yorktown.

Dr. Franklin early saw the great importance our marine forces would play in this struggle. Writing from Paris, May 26, 1777, to the Committee on Foreign Affairs, he said: " I have not the least doubt but that two or three of the Continental frigates sent into the German Ocean, with some less swift-sailing craft, might intercept and seize a great part of the Baltic and Northern trade. One frigate would be sufficient to destroy the whole of the Greenland fisheries and take the Hudson Bay ships returning." Not having the frigates available, the Marine Committee sent the cruisers *Reprisal* and *Lexington*; and in June these little vessels, with the 10-gun cutter *Dolphin*, made two complete circuits of Ireland, occasioning the greatest alarm, and after securing fifteen prizes they returned to France, where the prizes were sold to French merchants. The proceeds thus realized afforded much needed pecuniary assistance to the American commissioners who were pleading the cause of the colonists in European courts. The two celebrated expeditions of Captain John Paul Jones are equaled in the annals of marine history only by the daring and success of our privateers.

So great was the alarm occasioned by the exploits of the American maritime forces that Silas Dean, writing to the Marine Committee in 1777, said: "It effectually alarmed England, prevented the great fair at Chester, occasioned insurance to rise, and even deterred the English merchants from shipping goods in English vessels at any rate of insurance. So that in a few weeks forty French ships were loaded in London on freight—an instance never before known." Not only did the British merchants ask for the protection of war ships for their merchantmen on distant voyages, but they even demanded escorts for linen ships from Ireland to England. "In no former war," said a contemporary English newspaper, "not even in any of the wars with France and Spain, were the linen vessels from Ireland to England escorted by war ships."

The following letter, written from Jamaica in 1777 by an Englishman, shows what havoc was created in British commerce by our privateers: "Within one week upward of fourteen sail of our ships have been carried into Martinique by American privateers." Another Englishman, writing from Grenada in the same year, says: "Everything continues exceedingly dear, and we are happy if we can get anything for money, by reason of the quantity of vessels taken by the Americans. A fleet of vessels came from Ireland a few days ago. From sixty vessels that departed from Ireland not above twenty-five arrived in this and neighboring islands, the others,

it is thought, being all taken by American privateers. God knows, if this American war continues
much longer we shall all die with hunger. There
was a ship from Africa with four hundred and fifty
negroes, some thousand weight of gold dust, and a
great many elephant teeth—the whole cargo being
computed to be worth twenty thousand pounds—also
taken by an American privateer, a brig mounting
fourteen cannon." So loud were the protests of the
British mercantile classes against carrying on the
American war that every pressure was brought to
bear on Parliament for its discontinuance.

It will be interesting to note that in all the memo-
rials presented to Parliament the arguments used
to bring about peace with America was the unprecedented destruction of British commerce. On the
6th of February, 1778, Alderman Woodbridge testified at the bar of the House of Lords that " the number of ships lost by capture or destroyed by American privateers since the beginning of the war was
seven hundred and thirty-three, whose cargoes were
computed to be worth over ten million dollars. That
insurance before the war was two per cent. to America and two and one half to North Carolina, Jamaica,
etc., but now that insurance had more than doubled,
even with a strong escort, and, without an escort,
fifteen per cent."

William Creighton, who also appeared before
their lordships, said that " the losses suffered by
British merchants in consequence of captures made
by American privateers up to October, 1777, could
not be short of eleven million dollars." In 1776 Captain Bucklon, of the 16-gun privateer *Montgomery*,
from Rhode Island, reported that the rate of insurance in England had risen to thirty per cent. on vessels sailing in convoy, and to fifty per cent. for those
sailing without convoy. Bucklon made this report
on his return from a cruise in the English Channel.

When the War of 1812 was about to break out

the English carried a vivid recollection of the damages our maritime forces had occasioned in the first
war, and seemed to be more concerned with what
American sea power might do in the impending
war than what our land forces could do. The London Statesman said: " Every one must recollect what
they did in the latter part of the American war. The
books at Lloyd's will recount it, and the rate of
assurances at that time will clearly prove what their
diminutive strength was able to effect in the face
of our navy, and that when nearly one hundred pen-
nants were flying on their coast. Were we able to
prevent their going in and out, or stop them from
taking our trade and our storeships, even in sight of
our own garrisons? Besides, were they not in the
English and Irish Channels picking up our homeward-
bound trade, sending their prizes into French and
Spanish ports, to the great terror and annoyance of
our merchants and shipowners?

" These are facts which can be traced to a period
when America was in her infancy, without ships,
without money, and at a time when our navy was
not much less in strength than at present. The
Americans will be found to be a different sort of
enemy by sea than the French. They possess nautical knowledge, with equal enterprise to ourselves.
They will be found attempting deeds which a Frenchman would never think of, and they will have all the
ports of our enemy open, in which they can make
good their retreat with their booty. In a predatory
war on commerce Great Britain would have more to
lose than to gain, because the Americans would retire within themselves, having everything they want
for supplies, and what foreign commerce they might
have would be carried on in fast-sailing, armed vessels, which, as heretofore, would be able to fight or
run, as best suited their force or inclination."

Such was the opinion of an intelligent English
writer as to the potency of American maritime en-

terprise in the pending war. About the same time Mr. Niles, of Baltimore, wrote: "How far will the revenue [of Great Britain] be touched by the irresistible activity and enterprise of one hundred thousand American seamen, prepared or preparing themselves, to assail British commerce in every sea—to cut off supplies from abroad and forbid exportation with safety! The Americans will prove themselves' an enemy more destructive than Great Britain ever had on the ocean—they will do deeds that other sailors would not dare to reflect on. Witness their exploits in the Revolutionary War and at Tripoli, in which, perhaps, not a single instance occurred of their being defeated by an equal force, though many cases to the contrary are numerous. What part of the enemy's trade will be safe? France, duly estimating the capacity of America to injure a common enemy, will open all the ports of the continent as places of refuge and deposit for our privateers, and all the fleets of England cannot confine them to their harbors, at home or abroad. The British Channel will be vexed by their enterprises, and one hundred sail of armed vessels will be inadequate to the protection of the trade passing through it. For the probability of these things let Lloyd's lists from 1777 to 1783 be referred to. Terror will pervade the commercial mind and mighty bankruptcies follow, to all which will be superadded the great privations of the manufacturers and the increased distresses of the poor."

Toward the close of the War of 1812 English newspapers were full of articles recounting the vast amount of damage that had been inflicted on British commerce by American privateers. The master of one English vessel, who had been captured three times by American privateers and as many times recaptured, reported that he had seen no less than ten Yankee privateers in his voyage. In June, 1813, flour in Great Britain was fifty-eight dollars a bar-

the direct ... of the naval power
... first ... nation, whose flag, till of late, waved
... sea and triumphed over every rival. That
... reason to believe that in the short space
of ... than twenty-four months above eight hun-
... have been captured by that power whose
... strength we have hitherto, impolitically,
... contempt. That, at a time when we were at
peace with all the world, when the maintenance of

our marine costs so large a sum to the country, when the mercantile and shipping interests pay a tax for protection under the form of convoy duty, and when in the plenitude of our power we have declared the whole American coast under blockade, *it is equally distressing and mortifying that our ships can not with safety traverse our own channels*,[1] that insurance cannot be effected but at an excessive premium, and that a horde of American cruisers should be allowed, unheeded, unresisted, and unmolested, to take, burn, or sink our own vessels in our own inlets, and almost in sight of our own harbors.

"That the ports of the Clyde have sustained severe loss from the depredations already committed, and there is reason to apprehend still more serious suffering, not only from the extent of the coasting trade and the number of vessels yet to arrive from abroad, but as the time is fast approaching when the outward-bound ships must proceed to Cork for convoys, and when, during the winter season, the opportunities of the enemy will be increased both to capture with ease and escape with impunity. That the system of burning and destroying every article which there is fear of losing—a system pursued by all the cruisers and encouraged by their own Governments—diminishes the chances of recapture and renders the necessity of prevention more urgent."

From the foregoing it is seen that the English themselves regarded our maritime forces, rather than our land forces, as the dominant factors in both these wars. We do not hear of any high municipal officers testifying at the bar of the House of Lords as to the vast amount of damage caused by American armies, or as to the danger menacing Great Britain from any movements of our land forces. We

---

[1] The italics are the author's.

2

hear of no petitions direct to the throne asking protection for British interests from our soldiers. We do not come across notices of meetings held to protest against the ravages caused by our troops. On the contrary, the British public seemed to have ignored our land forces altogether, or, when they were mentioned, it was only to speak of them with contempt, as the following extract from the London Times will show. Speaking of the *Wasp–Reindeer* action, it says: "It seems fated that the ignorance, incapacity, and cowardice of the Americans by land should be continually relieved in point of effect on the public mind by their successes at sea. To the list of their captures, which we can never peruse without the most painful emotions, is now to be added that of His Majesty's ship *Reindeer*, taken after a short but most desperate action by the United States sloop of war *Wasp*."

We do not find the English studying our army tactics, with a view of profiting by any superior arrangements which American ingenuity and forethought may have suggested; but we do find them examining most minutely into the construction and discipline in our war ships, and frankly acknowledging our superiority in many important details. When the London Times learned of the result of the *Enterprise–Boxer* fight, it said: "The fact seems to be but too clearly established that the Americans have some superior mode of firing, and that we can not be too anxiously employed in discerning to what circumstance that superiority is owing." We do not find English military officers changing their methods of army management after models devised by Americans, but we do find the Admiralty adopting American naval ideas in a most radical and sweeping manner. We introduced 24-pounders in our frigates, which at first the enemy ridiculed, but before the war was over they were compelled to imitate, and finally they paid us the compliment of building and fitting out cruisers on the "exact lines" of the American 44-gun frigates. In the introduction to a new edition of Mr. James' History of the British Navy, the editor remarks: "It is but justice, in regard to America, to mention that England has benefited by her [America's] example, and that the large classes of frigates now employed in the British service (1826) are modeled after those of the United States." Our frigates were called "terrible nondescripts," and one of the English 74-gun line of battle ships actually sailed from Cadiz for the North American station *disguised* as a frigate. The London Courier of January 4, 1813, notes that some of the most famous British line of battle ships—some of them having been under Nelson's orders—including the *Culloden, Monarch, Thunderer,* and *Resolution,* were selected to be cut down as frigates to cope with our *Constitution, President,* and *United States.*

An English naval expert, speaking of the *Goliath* (1898) as the latest and most powerful battle ship ever constructed in Great Britain, says: "It is of historic interest that the modern ironclad, with its turrets and massive plates, had its root idea in the famous monitors first designed for the United States Government by Ericsson, who sought to combine invulnerability with very heavy ordnance. The earliest monitors had decks almost level with the water, revolving turrets, and cannon that threw round shot one hundred and fifty pounds and upward in weight. But even under favorable conditions they could fire only one round in three minutes; and, although that measure of offensive capacity was capable of destroying any other contemporary man-of-war, it would be of no account at the present day. Ericsson, however, gave the cue to naval designers all over the world, and his elementary principle has only been developed and modified during the years that have elapsed."

For capturing the *Chesapeake* Captain Broke received a sword from the city of London, the Tower guns were fired in honor of the victory, and the freedom of the city was presented to him—honors seldom granted. When the news of the *Chesapeake's* defeat reached London Parliament was in session and Lord Cochrane was severely criticising the Government's naval administration of the war. Mr. Croker "rose to answer him with the announcement that the *Shannon* had captured the *Chesapeake*. This was received with the loudest and most cordial acclamations from every part of the House"—simply because an English ship had captured an American of equal force.

It is in vain that we search the English newspapers for those expressions of fear and humiliation on the report of their land reverses which they so freely indulged in on hearing of the loss of their ships. When the London Times learned of the loss of the first British frigate in 1812 it said: "We know not any calamity of twenty times its amount that might have been attended with more serious consequences to the worsted party had it not been counterbalanced by a contemporaneous advantage [alluding to Wellington's successes in Spain] of a much greater magnitude. As it was, the loss of the *Guerrière* spread a degree of gloom through the town which it was painful to observe."

The news of the second naval defeat was at first discredited: "There is a report that another English frigate, the *Macedonian*, has been captured by an American. We shall certainly be very backward in believing a second recurrence of such a national disgrace. . . . Certainly there was a time when it would not have been believed that the American navy could have appeared upon the high seas after a six months' war with England; much less that it could, within that period, have been twice victorious. *Sed tempora mutantur.*" On the following day, when the news was confirmed, the Times exclaimed: " In the name of God, what was done with this immense superiority of force!" And the next day it says: "Oh, what a charm is hereby dissolved! What hopes will be excited in the breasts of our enemies! The land spell of the French is broken [alluding to Napoleon's disastrous retreat from Moscow], and so is our sea spell." The London Chronicle asked: "Is it not sickening to see that no experience has been sufficient to rouse our Admiralty to take such measures that may protect the British flag from such disgrace."

The news of the loss of the third British frigate, the *Java*, was commented upon by the Times as follows: "The public will learn, with sentiments which we shall not presume to anticipate, that a third British frigate has struck to an American. . . . This is an occurrence that calls for serious reflection—this and the fact stated in our paper of yesterday, that Lloyd's list contains notices of upward of five hundred British vessels captured in seven months by the Americans. Five hundred merchantmen and three frigates! Can these statements be true? And can the English people hear them unmoved? Any one who had predicted such a result of an American war this time last year would have been treated as a madman or a traitor. He would have been told, if his opponents had condescended to argue with him, that long ere seven months had elapsed the American flag would have been swept from the seas, the contemptible navy of the United States annihilated, and their marine arsenals rendered a heap of ruins. Yet down to this moment not a single American frigate has struck her flag."

It is interesting to note, in connection with this subject, that James' History of the British Navy was inspired by the naval occurrences between the United States and Great Britain. James first wrote a small pamphlet, entitled An Inquiry into the Merits of the Principal Actions between Great Britain and the United States. This work met with

such encouragement that he wrote his Naval Occurrences of the Late War between Great Britain
and the United States, a single octavo volume. The
reception given to these two works induced him
to write his History of the British Navy, which for
more than half a century has been regarded as the
standard work on that subject—the result, as the
author himself declares, of the naval operations of
the United States maritime forces.[1]

In summing up the results of this war, the Times
for December 30, 1814, says: "We have retired from
the combat with the stripes yet bleeding on our
backs. Even yet, however, if we could but close the
war with some great naval triumph, the reputation
of our maritime greatness might be partially restored. But to say that it has not suffered in the
estimation of all Europe, and, what is worse, of
America herself, is to belie common sense and uni-
versal experience. 'Two or three of our ships have
struck to a force vastly inferior!' No, not two or
three, but many on the ocean and whole squadrons
on the lakes, and the numbers are to be viewed with
relation to the comparative magnitude of the two
navies. Scarcely is there an American ship of war
which has not to boast a victory over the British
flag; scarcely one British ship in thirty or forty that
has beaten an American. With the bravest seamen
and the most powerful navy in the world, we retire
from the contest when the balance of defeat is so
heavy against us." And it may be added that this
was written before the Times had heard of the capture of the *Cyane* and the *Levant* by the *Constitution*
—the most brilliant naval victory of the war—or
the disabling of the *Endymion* by the *President*, or
the capture of the *Nautilus* by the *Peacock*, or the

---

[1] Lord Nelson's first prize was an American privateer, and his first
command, the 14-gun schooner *Hichinbrook*, was captured at sea by an
American privateer shortly after Nelson had left her.

capture of the *Penguin* by the *Hornet*, or the disastrous and humiliating repulse of armed boats from a British squadron by the American privateer *General Armstrong* at Fayal.

From the foregoing it will be seen that, so far as the British were concerned, it was our maritime forces, rather than our armies, that played the dominating part in both the war for our independence and in the War of 1812. The object of all wars is to operate on the mind of the enemy to the extent of bringing him to the desired terms. That our maritime forces were vastly more efficient in this effort is seen by the unbiased testimony of the English themselves.

Such being the importance of the part played by our sea power in these two wars, it is fitting that our privateers should be properly recognized in the history of our navy, inasmuch as they formed the largest section of our maritime forces in those struggles. It is not the author's purpose to defend privateering. The Declaration of Paris in 1856 sealed the fate of that style of warfare, so far as civilized countries are concerned; for, although the United States and Spain did not ratify the Declaration, yet the course pursued by both nations in the Hispano-American War, and the propositions made by our delegates to the Peace Conference at The Hague in 1899, showed plainly enough that they had renounced old-time privateering. Privateering—in its proper form, however—exists to-day. The essential feature of privateering is commerce destroying. Our commerce destroyers of the navy to-day, like the *Columbia, Minneapolis,* and *Olympia,* take the place of our early privateers, and are capable of doing the work far more effectively, while—as we have seen in the case of the *Olympia* at Manila—they are equally efficient when needed for the regular service.

There are many well-meaning people in the United States who believe that the old style of pri-

vateering should be maintained. A few facts will
show the fallacies of their arguments. One of the
great defects in old-time privateering was lack of
organization. Each ship was a free lance, at liberty
to roam the seas as she willed, having no central
organization or concert of movement. The *Olympia*
showed what commerce destroyers can do when
properly governed. There are a few instances where
our early privateers rendered assistance to the regular navy; but then there are more instances where
they were a positive hindrance. Had the Penobscot
expedition in 1779 been organized with the Government vessels and privateers under one management,
it might have resulted in a glorious victory instead
of a disastrous defeat.

There have been many instances of American privateers running away from each other and throwing
overboard their guns, under the impression that they
were in the presence of an enemy, because there was
no efficient code of signaling between the regular
war craft and the privateers, or among the private
armed craft themselves. In one case the American
privateer *Anaconda* maintained a action with the
United States cruiser *Commodore Hull*, Lieutenant
Newcomb, near Boston, in which the American commander and several men were seriously wounded.
On March 9, 1813, Master-Commandant Arthur Sinclair, of the *Argus*, by mistake had an action with
the privateer *Fox*, Captain Jack, of Baltimore, in
Chesapeake Bay. Sinclair says: "In consequence of
silencing her I ceased my fire, believing that she had
struck; but although she fired on me first, after
being told who we were and never would answer
who she was, yet so much did I fear that it was some
of my imprudent, headstrong countrymen that I
took every opportunity to spare her, and to try and
find out who she was. I much fear they were all
lost, as she could not have a whole boat left, and we
found pieces torn out of her by our shot ten or twelve

feet long on the shore the next morning. I judge
her to be upward of two hundred tons by the 9½-inch
cable and the seven-hundred or eight-hundred weight
anchors we got next day. She was crowded with
men, as we could see by the light of her guns. I
was sure she would sink, as we were within one
hundred and fifty yards of her and I pointed myself
seven long 18-pounders, double and trebled shotted,
just amidships between wind and water and could
plainly hear the shots strike her." [1]

Many such instances could be cited to show that
privateering as practiced in our early wars is undesirable. Commerce destroying, under the exclusive
control of the navy, is the privateering of to-day, and
in this form is a legitimate and most potent factor
in warfare.

In venturing upon a history of American privateers the author realizes that he has, in truth, entered upon a new and most difficult field of historical
research. No complete record of American privateers has ever been published; the nearest approach being Captain George Coggeshall's History
of American Privateers, which is limited to the operations of our amateur cruisers in the War of 1812,
and, aside from the highly interesting narrative of
the part Captain Coggeshall played as commander
of the *David Porter* and the *Leo*, is far short of a
standard history. In writing his History of the
United States Navy, the author had the official
reports and other reliable records on which to base
his work; but in attempting a history of American
privateers he found himself entirely cut off from
this solid basis, and was dependent on the fragmentary and scattered records which are to be found
in the periodicals of that day and on the private
letters, logs, and traditions that have been preserved by the descendants of our privateersmen.

---

[1] Sinclair, in a private letter.

These valuable records have been scattered all over the United States, and had it not been for the generous co-operation of the persons having them in their possession this work never could have been given in its present complete form.

The author desires to acknowledge the assistance he has received in the preparation of this work from the Hon. Henry Cabot Lodge, United States Senator from Massachusetts; from Rear-Admiral Montgomery Sicard, U. S. N.; from Captain Arent Schuyler Crowninshield, U. S. N.; and from Rear-Admiral John Francis Higginson, U. S. N., and his brother James J. Higginson, of New York. To Miss Annetta O'Brien Walker, a lineal descendant of Captain Jeremiah O'Brien of Revolutionary fame, the author is indebted for many valuable details concerning the first sea fight in the struggle for independence, which have thrown much light upon, and rectified some inaccuracies relative to, that memorable fight. Interesting data bearing on our early privateersmen have been received from Bowden Bradlee Crowninshield, of Boston; Charles Thomas Harbeck, of New York; Benjamin I. Cohen, of Portland, Oregon; Samuel C. Clarke, of Marietta, Georgia; Thomas Wentworth Higginson, of Cambridge, Massachusetts; Arthur Curtiss Stott, of Stottsville, New York; Edward Trenchard, of New York; Franklin Eyre, of Philadelphia; Charles Albert Hazlett, of Portsmouth, New Hampshire; Otis Burr Dauchy, of Chicago; Mr. and Mrs. Samuel Dodge, of Portsmouth, New Hampshire; John C. Crowninshield, of Andover, Massachusetts; W. H. Osborne, of Boston; and Judge Addison Brown, of New York.

The officers of the following historical societies and libraries have given the author every possible aid in prosecuting his researches: John Robinson, Secretary of the Salem Peabody Academy of Science; Robert S. Rantoul, President of the Essex Institute, Salem, Massachusetts; William T. Peoples, of the

Mercantile Library, New York; Amos Perry, Secretary of the Rhode Island Historical Society; and Orville Burnell Ackerly, Secretary of the Suffolk Historical Society, of Riverhead, New York. Valuable records and suggestions have also been received from Professor Wilfred H. Munro, of Brown University, Providence, Rhode Island; Ripley Hitchcock, of New York; William Edward Silsbee, a grandson of Nathaniel Silsbee, who commanded the privateer *Herald* in her fight against the French letter of marque *Gloire* in 1800, and who afterward became a colleague of Daniel Webster in the United States Senate. The author will be glad to receive any further facts of interest bearing on our privateers for insertion in future editions of this work.

E. S. M.

OLD FIELD POINT,
SETAUKET, LONG ISLAND, N. Y.,
October, 1899.

CONTENTS.

PART FIRST.

THE WAR OF THE REVOLUTION.

CHAPTER I.

PRIVATEERS AND PRIVATEERSMEN.

CHAPTER II.

DANGERS PECULIAR TO PRIVATEERING.

CHAPTER III.

COLONIAL PRIVATEERS.

CHAPTER IV.

BEGINNING HOSTILITIES.

PART SECOND.

THE WAR OF 1812.

CHAPTER I.

FIRST VENTURES.

3

CHAPTER VI.

A DISTINGUISHED PRIVATEERSMAN.

CHAPTER VII.

DECATUR-DOMINICA FIGHT.

CHAPTER VIII.

SOUTHERN PRIVATEERS.

CHAPTER IX.

CAREER OF THE AMERICA.

CHAPTER X.

A TYPICAL PRIVATEERSMAN.

CHAPTER XI.

AN ESCAPE FROM GIBRALTAR.

CHAPTER XII.

IN BRITISH PRISONS.

CHAPTER XIII.

THE PRINCE DE NEUCHÂTEL.

CHAPTER XIV.

CRUISES OF THE GRAND TURK.

CHAPTER XXV.

CONCLUSION.

LIST OF ILLUSTRATIONS.

For the use of the three illustrations by Mr. George Gibbs mentioned in this list Messrs. D. Appleton and Company desire to acknowledge the courtesy of the Curtis Publishing Company, publishers of the Saturday Evening Post. Acknowledgment should also be made to Charles T. Harbeck, Esq., for his loans of rare prints and documents.

PART FIRST.

THE WAR OF THE REVOLUTION.

CHAPTER I.

PRIVATEERS AND PRIVATEERSMEN.

THERE seems to be much confusion in the minds of some people as to what a privateer is. With many, Government cruisers, privateers, and even pirates, have been classed under one head—namely, a vessel intended for fighting; and, as will be seen in the chapter on Colonial Privateers, there was a time when there was little to distinguish the privateer from the rover of the sea. In some instances, notably that of Captain Kidd, officers of the Royal Navy turned to piracy. In one of the first records we have of privateering, that in which a ship belonging to Sir Thomas Stanley, son of the Earl of Derby, brought a prize into the Mersey amid " great rejoicing," the opinion was expressed that, after all, the capture might have been an act of piracy.

Mr. Pepys, who is a recognized authority on matters pertaining to the early history of the British navy, notes: " The *Constant-Warwick* was the first frigate built in England. She was built in 1649 by Mr. Peter Pett for a privateer for the Earl of War-wick, and was sold by him to the States. Mr. Pett took his model of a frigate from a French frigate which he had seen in the Thames; as his son, Sir Phineas Pett, acknowledged." This admission, taken in connection with the fact just noted—namely, that the son of the Earl of Derby owned a privateer— would seem to indicate that the British peerage, if not the originators of the practice of privateering, were at

8

least deeply engaged in it at this time. The *Constant-Warwick* was a formidable craft for her day. She measured about four hundred tons and carried twenty-six guns, divided as follows: Eighteen light demi-culverins, or short 10-pounders, on the main deck; six light sakers, or short 5-pounders, and two minions.

It was not very long before the American colonies had secured their independence of Great Britain that privateering had come into vogue as a recognized profession. During the reign of George II privateers began to play a prominent part in the sea power of England, and then the Britons seem to have been driven to it only because of the disastrous activity displayed by their Continental rivals. On the outbreak of the Seven-Years War, 1756, French privateers hovered about the coasts of Great Britain and almost annihilated her commerce, that of Liverpool being especially exposed. French privateers found their way into the Irish Sea, and at one time actually blockaded the port of Liverpool, then England's greatest shipping center. Insurance rose to prohibitive rates, while trade was at a standstill. The "black ivory" trade at that time had been especially profitable and the British merchant had the alternative of sitting idly with folded hands or engaging in the same amateur warfare that his French brother was so vigorously waging. Acting with his usual energy, when once the plan was decided upon, the British merchant not only equipped his useless traders as armed cruisers, but began the construction of many swift-sailing vessels designed especially for privateering. These craft were sent out, and not only succeeded in making it dangerous for the enemy to venture near the coast, but captured a large number of merchantmen.

One of the first of these privateers to leave Liverpool returned in a few weeks with a French West Indiaman as a prize, which was computed to be worth twenty thousand pounds. Other captures of equal value quickly followed; and "then," records an English writer, "the whole country became mad after privateering and the mania even spread to the colonies"—meaning America. Certain it is that about this time privateering became extremely active in these colonies. On the whole, however, the Liverpool merchant was opposed to this kind of warfare. It was strictly as a business venture that he was induced to engage in it, in the first instance; for, notwithstanding the fact that his privateersmen were eminently successful, having taken in the first four years one hundred and forty-three prizes, he found that the final results were disastrous to trade. When the war with the American colonies broke out the British merchant was loath to resort to privateering, and while the Americans were sending out dozens of these craft the Liverpool people did little. In fact, it was not till the French had joined in the war that the Liverpool merchant bestirred himself in this line —the only paying occupation left to him.

One of the most celebrated of Liverpool's privateersmen was Captain Fortunatus Wright. As early as 1744, shortly after the outbreak of the war with France, this man, with the assistance of some English merchants residing in Leghorn, fitted out a privateer, which they called the *Fame*, for the purpose of preying on the enemy's commerce. According to the Gentleman's Magazine of 1776 the *Fame*, while under the command of Captain Wright, captured sixteen French ships in the Levant, the cargoes and craft being valued at four hundred thousand pounds.

When, in 1756, the merchants of Liverpool determined to go into privateering on their own account, Wright was again at Leghorn. Believing a renewal of hostilities with France to be inevitable, he caused a small vessel, which he called the *St. George*, to be built and fitted out for the express purpose of cruising against the enemy. His plans became known to the French, and a xebec mounting sixteen guns was stationed at the entrance of the harbor to nip his mischievous project in the bud. As the xebec carried a complement of two hundred and eighty men, which was more than Wright could hope to bring together, the chances of his getting to sea were small, especially as it was well known that the French king had promised a reward of three thousand livres a year for life, the honor of knighthood, and the command of a sloop of war to whomsoever brought this particular Wright, dead or alive, into France. The prodigality of these offers for the head of the doughty Englishman is sufficient evidence of the vast amount of harm he had occasioned French commerce.

Stimulated by the prospect of these glittering rewards, the people in the xebec maintained a successful watch on the *St. George.* At that time the Tuscan Government was in sympathy with that of France, and it added to the critical position of Wright by insisting that he must leave port with no more than four guns and twenty-five men. In keeping with these instructions Wright sailed from Leghorn, July 25, 1756, in the *St. George,* having in company three small merchantmen. When clear of the harbor he took on board eight guns which he had concealed in his convoys. Wright also had induced some fifty-five volunteers, consisting for the most part of Slavonians, Venetians, Italians, Swiss, and a few Englishmen, to enter his convoys in the same way, and they also were transferred to the *St. George.* With this armament and complement he awaited the attack of the xebec.

The action was begun about noon in full view of thousands of spectators, nearly all of them sympathizers of the French. In three quarters of an hour the xebec had her commander, lieutenant, and eighty-eight men killed, some seventy more wounded, and the ship herself was so cut up that the survivors were glad to make their escape toward the shore. Wright had only five men killed, one of them his lieutenant, and eight wounded. The result of this action so angered the Tuscan authorities that they seized the *St. George*, and in all probability would have detained her indefinitely had not Admiral Hawke, with two ships of the line, appeared off Leghorn shortly afterward and brought them into a more friendly state of mind. In March of the following year Wright was lost at sea while on a voyage from Leghorn to Malta.

The privateer, as understood at the outbreak of the war for American independence, was a ship armed and fitted out at private expense for the purpose of preying on the enemy's commerce to the profit of her owners, and bearing a commission, or letter of marque, authorizing her to do so, from the Government. Usually the Government claimed a portion of the money realized from the sales of prizes and their cargoes. The owners, of course, had the lion's share, though a considerable portion was divided among the officers and crew as an additional incentive to securing prizes. In fact, it was this division of the spoils, rather than the wages, that induced many of our best seamen to enter this peculiarly dangerous service. It frequently happened that even the common sailors received as their share, in one cruise, over and above their wages, one thousand dollars—a small fortune in those days for a mariner.

This opportunity to get rich suddenly gave rise to a peculiar class of seamen, who became known as "gentlemen sailors." All seaports sending out privateers were thronged with these tars of exalted degree, and, in many cases, of long pedigree. Usually they were of highly respectable parentage, and in some instances belonged to well-known families. They went to sea, not as common seamen, but as adventurers to whom the chances of making prize money were sufficient inducement to undergo the hardships and perils

of the sea. Being better educated and well trained
to the use of arms—especially excelling the ordinary
sailor in the latter accomplishment—they were welcomed in the privateer, and the commander was glad
to give them unusual privileges. They were not
assigned to the ordinary work of the seaman, but
formed a sort of a marine guard, standing between
the officers and the regular crew. This arrangement
came to be understood when the "gentleman sailor"
shipped. The common seamen were to do the real
drudgery of ship work, while these privileged tars
were to be on hand when fighting was to be done.

It seems that the "gentlemen sailors" were not
confined to the male sex, for when our schooner
Revenge was captured by the British privateer *Belle
Poole* the American prisoners were ordered to Portsmouth prison, upon which one of the prisoners announced "himself" to be a woman. Her love for
adventure had induced her to don male attire, and
she had been serving many months without her sex
having been known.

The officers and crews of our Government war
ships also received a proportion of the money resulting from taking a prize, and even when they
failed to bring the vessel to port, and in some cases
where they lost their own ship, they received their
share of prize money. According to a law made April
13, 1800, the following rule for distribution of prize
money was made for Government cruisers: "When
the prize is of equal or superior force to the vessel making the capture, it shall be the sole property of the captors. If of inferior force, it shall be
divided equally between the United States and the
officers and men making the capture." The act regu-
lates the proportion in which the officers and men
shall divide the prize money. "All public ships in
sight at the time of making prize shall share equally.
Twenty dollars to be paid by the United States for
each person on board an enemy's ship at the com-

mencement of an engagement which shall be burned, sunk, or destroyed by any United States vessel of equal or inferior force. All prize money accruing to the United States is solemnly pledged as a fund for payment of pensions and half pay should the same be hereafter granted. If this fund be insufficient, the faith of the United States is pledged for the deficiency; if more than sufficient, the surplus is to go to the comfort of disabled mariners, or such as may deserve the gratitude of their country."

By an act made June 26, 1812, the prize money from captures made by private armed craft was to go only to their owners, the officers and crew, " to be distributed according to any written engagement between them; and, if there be none, then one moiety to the owners, and the other to the officers and crew. Two per cent. on the net amount of the prizes to be paid over to the collectors as a fund for widows and orphans and disabled seamen." The Government also paid twenty dollars bounty for every man in the captured vessel at the beginning of the engagement.

Congress voted fifty thousand dollars to the officers and crew of the *Constitution* when they captured the *Guerrière,* and the same amount when she took the *Java,* notwithstanding the fact that each craft was destroyed at sea. The same sum was given to the captors of the *Macedonian.* The rule for distributing prize money in the navy was to divide the total amount into twenty equal parts. Where the sum was fifty thousand dollars the result was as follows: Three parts, or seven thousand five hundred dollars, to the captain; two parts, or five thousand dollars, to the sea lieutenants and sailing master; two parts, or five thousand dollars, to the marine officers, surgeon, purser, boatswain, gunner, carpenter, master's mates, and chaplain; three parts, or seven thousand five hundred dollars, to the midshipmen, surgeon's mates, captain's clerk, schoolmaster, boatswain's mates, steward, sailmaker, master-at-arms,

4

armorer, and coxswain; three parts, or seven thousand five hundred dollars, to the gunner's yeomen, boatswain's yeomen, quartermasters, quarter gunners, coopers, sailmaker's mates, sergeants and corporals of the marines, drummer, fifer, and extra petty officers; seven parts, or seventeen thousand five hundred dollars, to the seamen, ordinary seamen, marines, and boys. As the last item, seventeen thousand five hundred dollars, was divided among some two hundred men and boys, it gave about eighty-seven dollars to each man, or nearly an equivalent to a year's wages. To the commander, whose pay varied from six hundred dollars to twelve hundred dollars, the sum of seven thousand five hundred dollars was a snug fortune. Each of the sea lieutenants got a little less than one thousand dollars, their regular pay being four hundred and eighty dollars.

In case of actions between sloops of war Congress generally allowed twenty-five thousand dollars to our officers and crews if victorious, even in the case of Master-Commandant Jacob Jones, where he lost not only his prize, the *Frolic*, but his own ship. For the battle of Lake Erie Captain Chauncey, being the superior officer on the Great Lakes—although taking no part in the action—received twelve thousand seven hundred and fifty dollars; Master-Commandant Perry, twelve thousand one hundred and forty dollars, his pay being only seven hundred and twenty dollars; Master-Commandant Elliott, seven thousand one hundred and forty dollars; each commander of a gunboat, lieutenant, sailing master, and lieutenant of marines, two thousand two hundred and ninety-five dollars; each midshipman, eight hundred and eleven dollars, the pay of a midshipman being only two hundred and twenty-eight dollars; each petty officer, four hundred and forty-seven dollars; marines and sailors each two hundred and nine dollars.

These, however, were comparatively insignificant

instances of prize moneys. In a cruise lasting only a few weeks in 1779 the United States cruisers, *Queen of France*, Captain John P. Rathbourne; the *Providence*, Captain Abraham Whipple, who was in command in the first overt act of resistance against British authority in America; and the *Ranger*, Captain William Simpson, brought eight merchantmen into Boston, their cargoes being valued at over a million dollars. One of the boys in the *Ranger*, fourteen years old, who less than a month before had left a farm to ship in this cruiser, received as his share one ton of sugar, from thirty to forty gallons of fourth proof Jamaica rum, some twenty pounds of cotton, and about the same quantity of ginger, logwood, and allspice, besides seven hundred dollars in money. In many instances during the War of 1812 American cruisers took prizes valued at over a million dollars. The *Chesapeake* has been credited with being one of the unlucky cruisers in that war, yet in the cruise just before her meeting with the *Shannon* she captured one ship, the *Volunteer*, the cargo of which was valued at seven hundred thousand dollars; and in the same cruise she took the *Ellen*, whose cargo was sold in Boston for seventeen thousand five hundred and sixty dollars. The little sloop *Peacock*, Master-Commandant Lewis Warrington, in one cruise took prizes valued at six hundred and thirty-five thousand dollars.

The Government usually allowed a bounty for each prisoner brought into port. This bounty amounted to about twenty dollars a head, but in most cases the privateersman preferred to rid himself of prisoners at the earliest possible moment. There were several reasons for this. Even had the bounty been as high as one hundred dollars a man, it would not have paid the successful privateersman to accumulate prisoners, especially when on a long voyage—and there could be no telling how long a cruise would last—for the cost of feeding amounted to a large sum. Then the danger of having too many prisoners was shown dozens of times when the captured rose on their captors, and not only recovered their own vessel, but made prisoners of the privateersmen. On August 2, 1813, a law was enacted providing a bounty of twenty-five dollars on each prisoner.

The first and greatest element of success with a privateersman was audacity. Without that, above all other things, he was doomed to ignominious failure. The regular man-of-warsman might go and come on his cruises without meeting an enemy or taking a prize and yet suffer little in the estimation of the department. In fact, in our first essays against the mistress of the ocean, both at the time of the Revolution and in the War of 1812, the naval commander who put to sea and regained port with a whole skin was regarded, by our then overtimid naval administrators, as being a singularly fortunate and capable officer. Not so with a privateersman. To return to port empty-handed was to commit the greatest sin of the profession. Hence we find that the privateersman was preëminently a bold and daring man, and when such qualities were combined with skillful seamanship we have the ideal privateersman.

A good illustration of the "audacious impudence" of our privateersmen is had in the case of the *Paul Jones*, of New York. This vessel put to sea at the outbreak of the War of 1812 with a complement of one hundred and twenty men, but with only three guns. Almost her first prize was the heavily armed British merchantman *Hassan*, carrying fourteen guns and a crew of twenty men, while her cargo was worth some two hundred thousand dollars. The *Paul Jones*, though carrying only three guns, was pierced for seventeen. It is said that the commander of the *Paul Jones* sawed off some spare masts to the length of guns, painted them black, and, being mounted on buckets, rolled them out of his empty ports as effective imitations of heavy ordnance. Then filling his rigging with his superfluous force of men, so far overawed the enemy that they surrendered as soon as the privateer, with her dummy guns, got fairly alongside. The Americans then helped themselves to such of the *Hassan's* guns and ammunition as they needed and went on their way rejoicing.

The English privateersmen of 1778 are described by one of their countrymen of that period as " a reckless, dreadnaught, dare-devil collection of human beings, half disciplined, but yet ready to obey every order. The service was popular; the men shipping in privateers, being safe from impressment, the most dashing and daring of the sailors came out of their hiding holes to enter in them. Your true privateersman was a sort of half horse, half alligator, with a streak of lightning in his composition—something like a man-of-warsman, but much more like a pirate —with a superabundance of whisker, as if he held, with Samson, that his strength was in the quantity of his hair." So far as the " dare-devil " and " dreadnaught " qualities of this description go, they fit the American privateersmen well enough; but so far as the " whisker," " half horse, half alligator," and " pirate " parts of it are concerned the author is satisfied that they are widely shy of the mark. We can readily believe, however, after reading the following account of a battle between an English and a French privateer, published over a century ago, that the foregoing description of the British privateersman is not overdrawn: " December 23, 1777, Captain Death, of the privateer *Terrible*, of London, was killed in an engagement with the *Vengeance*, a privateer of St. Malo. The annals of mankind can not show an effort of more desperate courage than was exerted under the command of Captain Death. He had in the beginning of his cruise made a prize of a rich merchantman with which he was returning to England in triumph when he had the fortune to fall in with the *Vengeance,* much his superior in force, thirty-six to twenty-six guns. The *Terrible's* prize was soon taken and converted against her; but so unequally matched, Captain Death maintained a furious engagement. The French captain and his second in command were killed with two thirds of his company, but much more dreadful was the slaughter on board the *Terrible.* When the enemy boarded they only found one scene of slaughter, silence and desolation. Of two hundred men only sixteen were found remaining, and the ship so shattered as scarcely to be kept above water. The following are the remarkable names of the officers of the *Terrible*: Captain Death, Lieutenants Spirit and Ghost, Boatswain Butcher, Quartermaster Debble; launched out of Execution Dock, London."

In general, the conduct of American privateersmen on the high seas was most commendable. They showed themselves to be not only daring, but gentlemanly. When the schooner *Industry,* Captain Renneaux, a prize to the privateer *Benjamin Franklin,* Captain Ingersol, of New York, reached that port, August 24, 1812, it was learned that the craft belonged to a widow whose only dependence was on the earnings of that vessel. Although the *Industry* had two thousand dollars' worth of goods aboard, the Americans restored her and her cargo to the widow. Many of our privateersmen were men engaged in the Newfoundland fisheries, and a hardier or more daring set of men would be difficult to find. An American periodical, of the date August 8, 1812, notes: "About thirty fishing vessels have arrived at Marblehead (Mass.), from the Banks within a few days, and only three remained absent. These hardy and patriotic citizens will generally become *fishers of ships.*"

Soon after the outbreak of the War of 1812, Niles, in his Register, notes: "The enemies of the United States have used many efforts to discredit the business of privateering in proclaiming, magnifying, and reiterating, under many new shapes, any enormity that may have been committed by any of our private armed vessels, and some must be expected. But it confounds these wretches, and affords great satisfaction to the people at large, to observe that our privateers, in general, have conducted themselves with remarkable propriety, in many cases receiving the public thanks of the captured. We trust this good name will be sustained, though the enemy, through his friends here, may strive to blast it."

The humanity of Americans who were engaged in the "business of privateering" early in the century is amusingly brought out in a notice which appeared in a London paper, published in December, 1814: "Mr. Editor: You will please a great number of your readers in Great Britain, who are zealous in spreading the Divine Gospel all over the earth, by showing them that there are some American citizens who are willing to unite with us in sending missionaries to all parts of the globe. The Rev. Mr. Benson read the following note, which was transmitted to him by one of his brethren in Wales: 'A few weeks since a trading vessel laden with corn [wheat] from Cardigan, in Wales, was taken in the channel by an American privateer. When the captain of the latter entered the cabin to survey the prize he espied a small box with a hole in the top—similar to that which tradesmen have in their counters through which they drop their money—on which the words "Missionary box" were inscribed. On seeing this the American captain seemed not a little astounded and addressed the Welsh captain as follows:

"'"Captain, what is this?" pointing to the box with his stick.

"'"Oh," replied the honest Cambrian, heaving a sigh, "'tis all over now."

"'"What?" said the American captain.

"'"Why, the truth is," said the Welshman, "that

I and my poor fellows have been accustomed every Monday morning to drop a penny each into that box for the purpose of sending out missionaries to preach the Gospel to the heathen; but it is all over now."

" ' " Indeed," answered the American captain, " that is very good."

" ' After pausing a few minutes he said: " Captain, I'll not hurt a hair of your head, nor touch your vessel," and he immediately departed, leaving the owner to pursue his course to his destined port.' "

That all the religious qualities of American privateersmen were not confined to skippers from New York is seen in the following account of the capture of the brig *Falcon* by the *America:* " Among the goods of the valuable prize brig *Falcon* sent into Bath by the *America* of Salem were about nine hundred Bibles in the English and Dutch languages and five hundred Testaments forwarded for distribution at the Cape of Good Hope by the British and Foreign Bible Society.   The Messrs. Crowninshield, to whom the privateer belonged, permitted a purchase of them to be made by the Bible Society of Massachusetts at a price hardly sufficient to legalize the sale—say about twenty cents to the pound sterling.   The conduct of those gentlemen is highly spoken of in the Eastern papers."

Another instance of the gallantry of the American privateersman is had in the following:

A Mrs. Elizabeth Bell, of Nova Scotia, happened to be a passenger in the schooner *Ann*, Captain Kelly, of Halifax, when captured by the American privateer *Dolphin*, Captain Endicott.   Reaching Salem Mrs. Bell caused a notice to be published in a newspaper acknowledging " with much gratitude the gentlemanly and humane treatment of the captain and prize master of the *Dolphin* in returning to her nine hundred dollars, together with her personal effects."

A still more forcible illustration of the humanity of American privateersmen is had early in 1782, when the private armed sloop *Lively*, Captain D. Adams, of Massachusetts, rescued the officers and crew of the British frigate *Blonde* which had been wrecked on a barren and desolate island.   The treatment which all American prisoners, and especially privateers-men, had received at the hands of the British would have almost justified the commander of the *Lively* in leaving these shipwrecked mariners to their fate. But the American jack tar is a generous fellow, and nothing appeals so strongly to his compassion as a fellow-seaman in distress, and on this occasion the people of the *Lively* extended every assistance to their enemies and brought them safely into port.

So widespread had become the practice of priva-teering that by the outbreak of the Revolution Brit-ish merchantmen had two, and only two, well-defined methods of going to sea: First as a part of a fleet con-voyed by a suitable force of war ships, or as strongly armed " running ships."   Fleet sailing with the Brit-ish was the favorite practice and grew to enormous proportions, a fleet of one hundred merchantmen not being unusual, and it is recorded that as many as six hundred have sailed at one time.   On some occasions several months were spent in collecting the fleet at a port convenient to the English or Irish Channels —generally at Portsmouth or Dublin—and on a stated day they sailed for the East or West Indies, escorted by a number of war ships.

Of course, in the case of such a large fleet sailing its departure and destination were widely advertised in England several months before, so that American agents had every opportunity to inform their friends across the Atlantic of the facts.   The result was that as soon as a fleet sailed American cruisers or priva-teers were in waiting on the course the fleet must take, and were ready to pounce upon any stray mer-chantman that had the ill-luck to be separated from the convoy.   If it was a large fleet, the flagship of the convoy usually was a line of battle ship commanded

by an admiral, and was accompanied by one or two
frigates and a number of sloops of war or brigs. If a
small fleet, a frigate with one or two sloops of war
was considered sufficient. When ready for sea the
admiral signaled for all commanders to come aboard,
when written instructions or "sailing orders" were
given as to the meaning of the various signals that
might be used in the course of the voyage, and also
such other information as might conduce to their
safety.

On leaving port the flagship usually took the lead,
and was known as the vanship, while a fast-sailing frigate took her position in the rear so as to tow
up any dull-sailing merchantman that otherwise
might be left behind. The sloops and brigs of war did
guard duty on each flank. One of the most rigid
rules of fleet sailing was that no merchantman
should go ahead of the vanship, which vessel was
to be constantly watched for signals. Another
equally rigid rule, and the one most frequently en-
forced, was for the headmost ships to shorten sail
when signaled to do so by the flagship, and for the
sternmost vessels to make all sail to catch up; and
frequently a frigate or a sloop of war was ordered
to tow up some dull sailer so as to keep the fleet as
compact as possible. In order to do this a hawser
was made fast to the foremast of the merchantman,
and she was towed ahead of all the other merchantmen, or just under the vanship's stern. At nightfall
the signal "close order" was given from the flagship,
and the merchantmen huddled together as closely as
possible under the stern of the vanship and did not
spread out again until daylight.

This cumbersome arrangement of fleet sailing had
its disadvantages. When such a fleet homeward
bound was being collected in the West Indies, it was
impossible to keep the fact concealed from the vigilant privateersmen, and they took advantage of it
by placing their vessels in the course the fleet was

obliged to take. These merchantmen usually were laden with sugar and coffee, the most desirable cargoes for privateersmen, who not infrequently dogged a convoy across the Atlantic in the hope of picking up some stray craft. On such occasions two privateers acting in concert stood a much better chance than one—especially if it was a small fleet, escorted by only one vessel; for, while the "bull-dog" was furiously chasing one of the swift-sailing privateers, the other managed to pounce upon the prey unseen by the escort. In such cases the quick-est kind of work was necessary, for although the prizes were rich and easily made, the "bulldog" might be back at any moment. For this reason prize crews were ready, at the word, to be thrown aboard the prize, run her to leeward, and then steer in differ-ent directions so as to divide the enemy's attention.

In these attacks the privateersman operated al-most without danger of capture, for the war ships dared not pursue too far away from their convoy. It has happened on more than one occasion that cap-tured merchantmen have been so hard pressed by the escort that the prize crew were obliged to abandon the prize and return to the privateer in their boats, the war ship usually being content with recovering the prize. In dogging a merchant fleet across the Atlantic the privateersman usually can do nothing in the way of taking prizes if the weather is fine, but should it come on thick, or a strong gale, he has a golden opportunity. At such times the merchantmen become widely scattered, and the deft privateer runs from one to the other, making easy capture. As a rule, the specie and most valuable goods are hastily transferred to the privateer, a prize crew placed aboard the merchantman and ordered to some port, while the privateer hastens to other conquests.

The second method of sailing in war time was to procure swift-sailing vessels, heavily armed and

manned, which could rely on their own speed or
strength to avoid the clutches of a privateer. These
vessels usually had rich cargoes, and several American privateers were fitted out for the express purpose of capturing them, with the result that many
a hard-fought action took place.

Early in the War of 1812 most of the American
privateers were small pilot boats, but it was soon
found that they were too weak to capture the average trader, as most of the English merchantmen
were heavily armed. This led to the construction
of powerful, swift-sailing craft, mounting 12-, 18-,
24-, and even 36-pounders, and manned by one hundred and twenty to one hundred and sixty men—
veritable corvettes—which were sent to sea at private expense. Of this class were the privateers *Paul
Jones, Rosamond, Saratoga, General Armstrong, Yorktown, Anaconda, Revenge, Volunteer, Rossie, Reindeer,
Avon,* and *Blakeley.* Perhaps the most formidable
of all was the frigate-built ship *America,* a privateer
which was purchased in France in 1795 by George
Crowninshield and was commissioned as a privateer
in 1802.

Many of our merchant vessels, transformed into
privateers, proved to be formidable craft. In fact,
a large proportion of them were built with a view
to speed; for, thanks to British interference in
our mercantile affairs, the American shipowner
had found it preferable to sacrifice a little carrying space in his ships to additional speed, as it
would enable him to outsail the British cruiser and
thus avoid disastrous delays and degrading impressment. Speed in the American merchant marine had
been fostered also by the forced running trade to
France and the West Indies, so that when the War
of 1812 broke out the American merchantman found
himself abundantly supplied with swift-sailing vessels. It was just this circumstance that proved to
be the foundation stone of the marvelous success of

American privateers in this war. The ordinary channels of commercial enterprise being closed by hostilities, the American merchant was quick to turn his
energies to mounting his fast-sailing vessels with a
few cannon, and, after manning them with a large
complement of officers and seamen, sending them out
in quest of his cousin's ships. Thus it was that ag-
gressive British impressment on the high seas, several
years before the war, had caused the development of
a fleet of American merchant ships which soon proved
to be a terrible scourge in the hands of the daring and
skillful American skipper.

CHAPTER II.

DANGERS PECULIAR TO PRIVATEERING.

ORDINARILY there was little glory or sympathy for the privateersman. The navy man went to sea knowing that if he made a good fight, even though defeated, his professional standing would in no way be impaired; on the contrary, decidedly improved. He knew that if he fell he, at least, would have the grateful record of history. Almost any man can be brave if he be conscious that the eye of the world is upon him. The average man can perform deeds of heroism when he knows that substantial rewards and professional advancement are in store for him. But it requires a man of unusual bravery to face danger unflinchingly when he realizes that no one will be cognizant of his deeds save the immediate participants, and when loss of life or limb will be regarded merely as his own personal misfortune.

Our privateersmen did not have the stimulus and advantages of an organized service. They left port with the avowed intention of plundering the enemy. If they were successful, their only reward was a division of the spoils; if failure attended them, they were kicked about like the under dog in the fight. " Served them right," said their envious brothers on land. " They wanted to get rich too fast, while we poor fellows are obliged to plod along in the usual slow, poking way." If the officers and men sacrificed life or limb to secure a prize, no pension awaited them or their families. If they came out unscathed

22

they were rewarded, perhaps, with a cold "thank you," and received their share of the profits calculated down to the last cent with mathematical exactness. There was no generous Congress to vote fifty thousand dollars to them if they sank their prize in the effort to capture her, as was the case with the captors of the *Guerrière* and *Java*; neither could they expect twenty-five thousand dollars if they lost both prize and their own ship, as was the case in the *Wasp–Frolic* fight.

In no light does the daring of our privateersmen shine more resplendently than in this. They went to sea, it is true, for mere pelf, but in many instances they performed services of national importance. Scores of American seamen, like Reuben James, John Cheever, Bartlett Laffey, and John McFarland won imperishable fame by acts of heroism because they were performed in an organized service and under the national colors. But the privateersman, although materially assisting in the defense of the flag, could die at his post and the fact might easily pass unrecorded. A commander of a privateer could capture the king's cruisers, thereby inflicting unprecedented shame and humiliation on the Royal Navy, and the incident scarcely would be known; while the owners of the privateer would not thank him for the unwarranted risk he ran, as, ordinarily, there was nothing to be got out of a war ship except hard knocks and empty holds. Had the capture been made by an officer of the navy in the Government service it would have been heralded abroad, while substantial rewards and rapid promotion would have followed.

Under these circumstances it is truly surprising that we discover acts of such superb bravery among the American privateersmen, yet a careful research into the history of that most important branch of our maritime power shows that it is replete with deeds of heroism. An instance of the daring of American privateersmen is related with characteristic frankness in a London periodical of the year 1777: "An American privateer of twelve guns came into one of the ports of the Jersey Islands, in the English Channel, yesterday morning, tacked about on the firing of the guns from the castle, and just off the island took a large brig bound for this port, which they have since carried into Cherbourg. The American privateer had the impudence to send her boat in the dusk of the evening to a little island off here called Jetto, and unluckily carried off the lieutenant of Northley's Independent Company with the garrison adjutant, who were shooting rabbits for their diversion. The brig they took is valued at thirty-five thousand dollars."

Charles W. Goldsborough, who during the first twenty years of the navy's existence as a separate department acted as its chief clerk, relates that during one of the many battles between British cruisers and American privateers a cannon ball came aboard the latter, and, after spending its force in smashing things up indiscriminately, rolled along the deck not quite decided what to do next. An American sailor picked it up and wrote on it with a piece of chalk, "Postpaid and returned with the compliments of Yankee Doodle;" then putting the shot in a cannon fired it back to its owners.

In privateers speed was a great and ruling consideration, and in their efforts to attain it the builders—having no Government or public opinion to check them—were apt to get their craft dangerously top-heavy. This eagerness to acquire speed resulted disastrously in the case of the privateer *Arrow*, Captain E. Conkling, of New York. She is described as a beautiful brig mounting fourteen guns and carrying a complement of one hundred and fifty men. Sailing from New York January 14, 1815, she cruised some time in the West Indies. After leaving one of those ports she was never heard of, and, being heavily spared, the opinion was generally expressed that she was capsized, either in a squall or during a chase.

Another danger to which we may allude as being peculiar to privateersmen was that of prisoners rising and overpowering their captors. This danger was especially great during long and prosperous voyages, when the privateer's complement was weakened by drafts for prize crews, and when usually there was a larger number of prisoners in the ship than there was of the crew. A striking illustration of this is had in the case of the privateer sloop *Eagle*, of Connecticut. This vessel carried six guns and thirty men, also commanded by a Captain E. Conkling. In a single cruise she captured six vessels, "one to every gun," that being the acme of privateering luck as expressed by the tars of that day. A privateer that made more prizes than the number of guns she carried was regarded as sailing in very dangerous waters, and was, perhaps, quite as objectionable as one that had made fewer captures. So that by capturing six vessels, or one for every gun in the sloop, it will be seen that the *Eagle*, on this venture, had reached the climax of privateering success.

It was unfortunate for her that she took so many prizes, for by manning them all she had reduced her complement to fifteen men, besides which were a large number of prisoners aboard. Taking advantage of a favorable opportunity, these prisoners rose on their captors, overpowered them, and, putting all but two boys to death, made away with the ship. They had not gone far, however, before they were recaptured by the American privateer *Hancock*. In the following year the *Eagle* was blown up in New York.

A case somewhat similar to this was that of the privateeer *Yankee*, Captain Johnson, of Massachusetts. This craft carried nine guns, sixteen swivels, and forty-three men. She was one of the first to get to sea in the war for American independence. Leaving port she made directly for English waters, and in July captured the merchant ships *Creighton* and *Zachara* laden with rum and sugar. , Placing prize crews in these vessels, Captain Johnson was continuing his cruise in their company when the prisoners in the prizes rose, secured their captors and their vessel, and then joined in an attack on the *Yankee*. Being short-handed, through manning his prizes, Captain Johnson was compelled to surrender. He was taken to Dover with his men and imprisoned.

Our privateersmen were especially exposed to the anger of British naval officers, and there were but few instances in which they were treated much better than pirates. On December 1, 1812, the privateer *Jack's Favorite*, Captain Miller, of New York, put into St. Barts for provisions. A few days later the British 12-gun war schooner *Subtle*, Captain Brown, entered the same port, and her commander boasted, in the presence of a number of merchants and others, that he would " follow and take the damned Yankee privateer if he went to hell for her." When Captain Miller sailed out of the harbor, the *Subtle* followed and gave chase. Not wishing to engage a man-of-war, the Americans carried a press of sail, and the Englishmen also spread all the canvas their craft could stand under. While the two vessels were staggering under the pressure, a squall came up. The Americans adroitly took in their canvas so as to receive the brunt of the blow under bare poles, but their pursuer was capsized. In a few minutes the squall blew over, and Captain Miller, failing to discover the slightest trace of his foe, was moved by motives of humanity to retrace his course. On reaching the spot where the *Subtle* was last seen he found a few caps and hammocks floating in the water. This was all that was left of the *Subtle*, all of her people having gone down with her.

Little or nothing was done to pension or assist the families of unfortunate privateers in our war for independence, but on June 5, 1813, the Navy Department issued the following order: "To enable those who may be wounded or disabled in any engagement with the enemy to obtain certificates entitling them to pensions, the like regulations and restrictions as are used in relation to the navy of the United States are to be observed, to wit: That the commanding officer of every vessel having a commission, or letters of marque or reprisal, cause to be given to any officer or seaman who, during his cruise, shall have been wounded or disabled as aforesaid, a certificate of the surgeon on board, to be approved and signed by such commanding officer, describing the nature and degree, as far as practicable, of such wound or disability, naming his place of residence and the rate of wages, if any, to which he was entitled at the time of receiving such wound or disability; and that such certificate be transmitted to this department.

"The widows (or orphans, where the wife is dead) of those persons who may be slain in any engagement with the enemy, on board such vessels, will be entitled to pension certificates upon forwarding to this office proof from the commanding officer of the vessel to which such persons were attached of their having been slain as aforesaid, and the certificate of a justice of the peace for the county in which such widows or orphans may reside that they actually stand in that relation to the deceased."

CHAPTER III.

COLONIAL PRIVATEERS.

THE first American sea fight of which we have record was in the nature of a private enterprise. In May, 1636, Mr. Oldham, while sailing in Long Island Sound, near Plum Island, in a trading vessel, was murdered by the Narragansett Indians and his vessel seized. Scarcely had the savages taken possession of their prize when John Gallop, who also was cruising in that vicinity in a twenty-ton sloop, came upon the scene and recognized the vessel as Mr. Oldham's, the latter having sailed only a few days before with a crew of two white boys and two Narragansett Indians. Approaching Oldham's vessel Gallop hailed, and receiving no answer he ran close alongside and discovered fourteen Indians lying on the deck apparently endeavoring to avoid detection.

Noticing that a canoe manned by Indians and loaded with goods was leaving the craft, Gallop was convinced that something was wrong. This belief was strengthened when the savages in the vessel slipped the cable and attempted to make off in the direction of Narragansett Bay. Gallop now fired a volley from his small arms into the vessel. The savages being armed, for the most part, with spears, knives, and tomahawks, were quickly driven below, only the few possessing firearms making any show of fight, and these also quickly sought the protection of the hold. Fearing to board in the presence of so many enemies Gallop maneuvered so as to run the vessel down, and in a few minutes succeeded in giving her a blow with his prow that sent her careening on her beam ends. Thinking that their prize was about to capsize, six of the Indians ran on deck, threw themselves into the sea, and were drowned.

Gallop now rigged his anchor over the bow in such a manner that the fluke would act as a spur which might pierce the thin sides of Oldham's vessel. Filling away Gallop again rammed, the anchor fluke crashing through the side of the prize. The white men then began firing down the hold, but, finding that this did not dislodge the remaining natives, Gallop sheered off and prepared to bunt again. Before this could be done, three or four more Indians rushed to the deck and jumped into the sea, where they also perished. One Indian now appeared and made signs of submission. He was taken aboard the sloop, and, being bound, was placed in the hold. Then another Indian offered to submit. He was taken aboard, but fearing that the savages might arrange some plan for overpowering him Gallop caused him to be thrown into the sea.

There were now only a few Indians remaining aboard the prize, but they were armed, and occupying a small apartment below, where they could not be easily reached, they prepared to sell their lives dearly. Removing all the goods in the prize to his ship, Gallop hauled up for the Connecticut shore with the sloop in tow. As the wind increased soon afterward, the tow was cut adrift, and finally went ashore somewhere in Narragansett Bay. Oldham's body, horribly mutilated and still warm, had been discovered by Gallop. When the news of this affair reached the authorities in Massachusetts an expedition was sent out under Mr. Endicott, and the Narragansett Indians were severely punished.

In 1645 a colonial ship carrying fourteen guns and thirty men had an all-day fight with a rover of Barbary which is said to have carried twenty guns and

seventy men. The action took place near the Straits
of Gibraltar. Night put an end to the struggle and
the vessels separated, the rover with a loss of her
rudder. The American ship was built at Cambridge,
Massachusetts, and had been trading in the Canaries.

For the first hundred years and more after the
establishing of the colonies in the New World, the distinction between privateers, slavers, pirates, and even
Government cruisers was vague, and at times obliter-
ated altogether. It was a period in which, on the
high seas, might was right; and when their home
Governments were at war with each other—and sometimes when at peace—the colonial seaman seized
whatever he could, whether he was a pirate, privateersman, or a king's officer. The astonishing growth
of commerce in the New World made it a tempting
field for depredations of every kind, and the result
was that high-handed proceedings on the open sea
was the rule rather than the exception. As a result
of this chaotic state, the colonists found themselves
compelled to maintain cruisers at their own expense,
while traders were as carefully prepared for fighting
as for carrying merchandise.

In some seaports there was a general connivance
on the part of the people at this state of affairs so
long as the depredations were directed against
" others." At Charleston, South Carolina, pirates of
all degrees walked the streets with impunity. Men
well known for their participation in piratical deeds
were welcomed by those among whom they spent
their ill-gotten gains. In some cases they were tried,
but the juries always managed to return a negative
verdict.

One authority says: " It is true that as long as
the pirates preyed on Spanish ships, and were free in
spending Spanish gold and silver in Charleston, they
were welcomed there, at least by those who were
beneficiaries. The authorities frowned, not very
darkly, it is true, and made feeble efforts to suppress

these visitors; but the juries were made up of the people, and then, as now, public sentiment ruled, the law to the contrary notwithstanding. Of course, piracy was illegal whether the colonists were the sufferers or not; but it was difficult for the authorities to obtain proof of the guilt of these men, and they could not be punished on suspicion—a provision of the law which the public commended. Many of the pirates came and went without question; others against whom charges were made gave security for good behavior till the Lords Proprietors could grant a general pardon. And no trouble was taken to observe how they behaved themselves when away from Charleston. Governor Ludwell was ordered to change the manner of securing juries so as to enable the authorities to convict the pirates, and the Proprietors ordered that they be tried under the laws of England, which were more severe than those of Carolina. But by lavish expenditure of money the sea robbers made so many friends that it was difficult even to bring them to trial and impossible to convict. They secured the best legal talent in the colony, and their strong defense by the prominent and influential men who were the lawyers in those days had its effect upon that class which made up the juries.

"Many of the pirates retired on their fortunes, purchased lands in the colony about Charleston, and made their homes there, becoming subjects of King George, and doubtless leading honest lives. While it is now impossible to ascertain those among the law-abiding citizens of South Carolina whose paternal ancestors harassed the Spanish shipowners two hundred years ago, it is quite certain that many of the taxpayers in this State could claim that distinction. But the condition of piracy can not be measured by present lights. In those times of almost incessant war, when one Government commissioned individuals to rove the seas and rob its enemies' ships of commerce, the step from the privateer to the pirate was natural, and the moral difference not very marked. Men of very good family became pirates because they loved adventure; it was profitable if they were not hanged, and they had nothing to do at home except fight."

We can better understand this leniency toward the outlaws when we remember that in the Spanish attack on Charleston in 1706 the authorities did not scruple calling on these " desperate " men to enlist in the vessels hastily prepared for defense of the town. The Spanish force, commanded by a French admiral, consisted of four war ships and a galley. To oppose them Lieutenant-Colonel Rhett, with a commission of vice-admiral, collected all the armed vessels in port and offered battle, but the enemy, having suffered reverses on shore, fled precipitately. A few days afterward the colonists learned that a large ship belonging to the enemy was on the coast. Going out with two of his vessels, Rhett captured her.[1]

It was when these rovers of the seas began to plunder the colonists themselves that real steps were taken to put a stop to their unlawful practices. In 1699 the culture of rice in Carolina had developed to such proportions that there were not enough ships available to transport the commodity to England. In that year a piratical ship was fitted in the West Indies and captured several vessels bound for Charleston, their crews being sent ashore in boats. Owing to a quarrel over the division of booty nine of the pirates were set on shore, and, making their way to Charleston, were recognized by some of the men captured in the merchant vessels. The enormity of piracy was then apparent to the colonists, and these men were seized and seven of them were hanged, while the other two were imprisoned.

---

[1] For the several expeditions against the French in Canada see Maclay's History of the Navy, vol. i, pp. 7-18.

Early in the eighteenth century a nest of pirates was established on the island of Providence, in the Bahamas, from which place they sent out ships to prey on commerce. Another headquarters of the sea robbers was opened near the mouth of Cape Fear River, and for many years these parts of the Atlantic were completely in their possession. Shipowners in England in 1718 appealed to the Crown, and Captain Woods Rogers sailed against Providence with several war ships. At that time it was estimated that there were several hundred men on the island, and all but one hundred of them accepted the king's pardon and gave up the unlawful practice. The remainder, under the leadership of Captain Vane, escaped in a vessel, and, sailing up the coast, captured two merchantmen from Charleston bound for London.

Learning that two piratical ships had put into Cape Fear River, Governor Johnson commissioned Colonel Rhett to command a war ship fitted up for the purpose and sail against these outlaws. One of the two piratical craft was a sloop carrying ten guns and commanded by Captain Steed Bonnett, " a handsome young fellow," who was said to be a member of an old English family. Being reckless and wild he had chosen to be a pirate chief. The second vessel, commanded by Richard Worley, carried only six guns. These two rovers had been in the habit of boldly cruising off Charleston harbor for days at a time and in plain sight of the town, waiting for the first merchantman that might venture out.

At the time Rhett sailed, Steed Bonnett was doing duty in the blockading vessel. On making out the force of Rhett's ship Bonnett sailed for Cape Fear River, hotly pursued. When within the entrance of the river Rhett came up with the pirate, and after firing a few shots induced the freebooter to haul down his flag. Before consenting to give themselves up, however, the pirates stipulated, under threats of blowing up their ship and involving their captors in the explosion, that they should receive no punishment for their offenses. Rhett could only promise that he would use his influence in their behalf, upon which the pirates, to the number of forty, were brought into Charleston with their sloop.

Governor Johnson then sailed in search of Worley, taking command of the colonial cruiser in person. He met the piratical craft about seventy-five miles north of Charleston and a desperate action immediately was begun. The pirates fought with the ferocity of despair, well knowing the fate that awaited them in case of capture. Although much inferior in force they inflicted great damage in the colonial cruiser, killing a number of men and wounding more. Finally, every man in the piratical craft was killed or disabled, saving Worley himself and his second in command. These two fought a gun until desperately wounded, when they surrendered. They were taken into Charleston and hanged.

In the case of Steed Bonnett there were the old-time delays and legal hitches, so that it was about a year after his capture before he was hanged. His forty companions, however, were promptly executed after conviction, which was a few days after their arrival in port. They were all hanged on the same day, on the spot where the beautiful Battery now is, and their bodies were buried a few yards away, below high water, in the Ashley River.

As early as 1646 the colony of New Haven caused a vessel of one hundred and fifty tons to be built at Rhode Island for the purpose of protecting her commerce. This craft was lost at sea on her first cruise. Soon afterward the settlements of Hartford and New Haven united in fitting out a vessel carrying ten guns and forty men to cruise in Long Island Sound for protection against the Dutch and against " all other evil-doers." Connecticut, in 1665-'66, maintained an armed vessel at Watch Hill to prevent the Narragansett Indians from crossing and attacking the Montauk

The pirates fought with the ferocity of despair.

tribe. In view of the fact that by 1676 Massachusetts alone had constructed over seven hundred vessels, varying in tonnage from six to two hundred and fifty tons, and Connecticut boasted of one thousand tons of shipping, it is not strange that we find the colonial governments fitting out war craft at their own expense, and that merchants armed their vessels with cannon.

It was not long before buccaneers began to scent this rich booty. This class of sea rovers seems to have originated in the West Indies. They were outlaws who swarmed around Tortugas, and at first contented themselves by attacking vessels from the shore. Rendered bold by their first successes they increased in numbers, and gradually ventured farther, until they began to infest the entire North American coast. Less than a dozen years after the landing of the Pilgrims, one David Bull, with a crew of fifteen Englishmen, committed acts of piracy on New England fishermen, and even attacked settlements. With a view to capturing him and guarding against other freebooters the *Blessing of the Bay*, a bark of thirty tons, in 1632, was launched. Before this boat could get to sea, however, the fishermen themselves had manned several pinnaces and shallops, in which they made three expeditions in search of the marauders, but without success.

It is probable, however, that the charges against Bull were somewhat exaggerated, as the stern Puritans were apt to regard levity of any kind as something akin to crime. It is stated that one of the " serious accusations " against Bull and his men was that when the New England fishermen assembled on deck at the hour of prayer Bull caused his men to sing boisterous songs and shout meaningless phrases, which might well horrify the strict Puritan, who has been known to condemn women to death on the mere suspicion of witchcraft. A certain Stone also was seized by the New Englanders in 1633 and bounden to appear at the Admiralty courts in England, as being somehow connected with piracy. The grand jury discharged him, and it is believed that the real cause of his arrest was a charge of adultery.

The case of Captain William Kidd is a good illustration of the general looseness on the high seas at this time. A large number of privateers had been fitted out at New York, and there were reasons to believe that they did not always confine their attentions to the enemy's commerce, but appropriated goods of the colonists. With a view to checking these depredations a privateer was fitted out, with sanction of the Government, and Captain Kidd was placed in command of her. In this enterprise the High Lord Chancellor and several other distinguished noblemen had shares, while one tenth of the profits were to revert to the Crown. The vessel sailed from Plymouth, England, in 1696, but instead of directing his energies against the lawless privateers and pirates on the American coast Kidd spent three years in the Indian Ocean plundering the commerce of all nations. He finally turned his prow toward America, and, anchoring in Gardiner's Bay, buried some of his treasures on Gardiner's Island, which for many years has been owned by a family of that name. Kidd intrusted Mr. Gardiner with his secret and then sailed away, burying other treasures at different points along the shore.

Kidd then paid and discharged his crew, and, appearing in Boston in 1699, was arrested. Among his papers was found a list of his buried treasures, and when the officials presented themselves to Mr. Gardiner the rover's box of booty.was recovered. The plunder consisted of bags of gold dust, gold and silver bars, jewelry, lamps, etc.; in all valued at about twenty thousand dollars. Kidd was sent to England and tried, and it is a curious commentary on the times to note that, on May 9, 1701, he was executed, not for piracy, but on the charge of killing one of his own crew.

We can easily believe that such a career as that of
Captain Kidd's was possible—and that many other
similar depredations, on a smaller scale, were perpetrated—when we come to investigate the condition
of society in the colonies during this period, for it
appears that not only were the privateersmen lawless
on the high seas, but were quite as unruly when in
port. Many murders in which this class of mariners
acted as principals were committed in the streets of
New York, so that it was unsafe for citizens to appear
when any considerable number of these craft were in
port.

On the night of September 19, 1705, an unusually
large number of privateers happened to be in the harbor, many of them recently returned from successful
voyages, and as a consequence the ale and wine
houses were crowded and the streets were filled with
drunken, boisterous, and dangerous gangs of seamen
ready for any mischief in which to engage their
whipped-up energies. One of the many disturbances
took place in front of a house in which the sheriff of
New York lived. As he was endeavoring to disperse
the mob that official was set upon and beaten, while
several citizens who came to his assistance were seriously wounded. In a short time privateersmen from
various parts of the town met in front of the sheriff's
house and assumed such a threatening tone that
troops from the fort were sent to repress them. At
the same time the sheriff, together with some men belonging to the British war ships in port, hastened to
the scene of trouble.

Unfortunately, before these several bodies repre-
senting law and order could get together, the privateersmen met Lieutenant Wharton Featherstone
Hough and Ensign Alcock, two officers of Colonel
Livesay's regiment, which had just arrived in the
Jamaica fleet. These men were peaceably returning
to their lodgings when they fell in with the rioting
seamen. The ensign was knocked down several times

and badly bruised. His sword was taken from him, and it is believed that this was the weapon which was thrust through Lieutenant Hough's heart a moment later, killing him instantly.

At this juncture the privateersmen were set upon by the sheriff's posse and by the man-of-warsmen, and a general fight took place. The discipline of the trained seamen soon prevailed over the unorganized gang of rioters, and in a few minutes the latter were fleeing in all directions, leaving a number of their comrades dead in the street, besides several wounded and a number as prisoners. Most of these privateersmen were from the private armed brigantine *Dragon*, Captain Ginks.

The behavior of the American privateersman while in port, however, was no worse than that of his cousin across the sea. English accounts state that even as late as 1778 there was great difficulty in maintaining order in the city of Liverpool when any considerable number of privateersmen was in port. One record says: " The privateersmen, when they came into port, were the terror of the town, and committed many excesses. So outrageous did their conduct become that in 1778 the mayor of Liverpool issued a proclamation cautioning these lawless persons that he would in future call in the aid of the military for the protection of the lives and property of the peaceable inhabitants."

Piracy increased rather than diminished on the North American coast after the peace of 1713; the ship *Whidah*, of twenty-three guns and one hundred and thirty men, under the command of Captain Samuel Bellamy, seizing vessels off the New England coast as late as 1717. His career was cut short by a storm, in which his vessel was wrecked off Cape Cod, more than one hundred bodies being washed ashore. Six of his men who escaped the sea were seized, tried in Boston, and executed. These drastic measures did much toward clearing the coast of freebooters, but did not exterminate them entirely, for we find that in 1723 a British sloop of war entered Newport with twenty-five pirates who were sentenced to be hanged.

After the peace of Utrecht most of the colonies maintained small armed vessels for the protection of their coasts and commerce, some of their commanders afterward entering the Royal Navy. One of these officers was Captain Wooster, of Massachusetts, who was killed in the Revolution, at Danbury, while holding the rank of brigadier-general. When England declared war against Spain in 1739 many American armed vessels were employed as transports.

It was in the war against France, which broke out in 1744, that American privateers first began seriously to assert themselves as a distinctive sea force. Besides the highly important part they played in the expedition against Louisburg,[1] a large number of privateers put to sea on their own responsibility and made independent cruises against the enemy. The profits resulting from some of these ventures were enormous, it frequently happening that a single cruise netted a common sailor one hundred pounds, while in one instance it is recorded that one hundred and sixty pounds were realized by each seaman—a respectable fortune for a sailor in those days.

After the 20-gun ship *Shirley*, Captain Rouse, had completed her work in the Louisburg expedition, May, 1745, she separated from her consorts and captured eight French vessels, two of which made a determined resistance. For this service Captain Rouse received a captain's commission in the king's service.

In June, 1744, the privateers *Hester* and *Polly* entered New York harbor with a prize, a new brig laden with cocoa, the share of each American sailor being eleven thousand pounds of the cargo.

In August of the following year the privateer

---

[1] See Maclay's History of the Navy, vol. i, pp. 10-13.

Clinton brought into the same port *La Pomona*, a sloop of one hundred and eighty tons, carrying fourteen guns and forty-three men. This craft was taken without loss. Her cargo consisted of eighty-eight casks of sugar, two hundred and thirty-seven casks of indigo (or eighty-seven thousand five hundred pounds of that commodity), and fifteen bales of cotton. In the capture of this vessel the commander of the *Clinton* is reported as having acted in a highly honorable manner. After *La Pomona* had been boarded, the American sailors were requested by their commander to "desist" from plundering the passengers, officers, and sailors of the prize. The tars acquiesced, and the master of *La Pomona* was so affected by the delicacy shown that on his arrival in New York he gave the officers and crew of the *Clinton* "a very handsome treat of a hogshead of punch and an ox roasted whole."

A large, heavily armed French ship, the *Rising Sun*, was taken by a clever stratagem in 1746. This vessel belonged to a fleet of merchantmen convoyed by three men-of-war, and for several days the American privateer *Prince Charles*, Captain Tingley, hung on the outskirts of the convoy in the hope of an opportunity to attack. The *Prince Charles* herself had been a French craft taken by an American privateer, and, on being refitted, was "reckoned the stoutest vessel fitted out of North America." She was of three hundred and eighty tons burden, carried twenty-four carriage guns (mostly 9-pounders) and thirty-four swivels, besides a complement of two hundred men. The *Rising Sun* also was a formidable vessel for a private armed craft, carrying twenty-two heavy guns and a corresponding complement. Had the two vessels met squarely, a desperate battle, with a doubtful outcome, would have resulted. Not that Captain Tingley had any objections to a fair yardarm and yardarm fight, but, like the shrewd, calculating American that he was, he did not see the use of shedding blood when the prize might be taken by a stratagem.

After dogging the fleet three days he came upon the *Rising Sun* separated from the other vessels. Putting on a bold front, the American commander affected to be a regular man-of-war and demanded the surrender of the *Rising Sun*. To assist him in the deception Captain Tingley armed a number of his men like marines and placed grenadier caps on their heads, and arranged to have those imposing headpieces appear just above his bulwarks, where the enemy could see them. The trick worked admirably, and the Frenchmen surrendered with no more resistance than emphatic protests. The *Rising Sun* arrived off Sandy Hook early in April. Her cargo consisted of one thousand one hundred and seventeen hogsheads of sugar, four hundred and fifty-eight casks of coffee, and other goods, besides specie. She drew eighteen feet of water, so that some difficulty was experienced in getting her over the bar.

Early in June, 1746, the privateers *Dragon* and *Greyhound* appeared in New York harbor in a sorry plight. They had with them as a prize the Spanish privateer *Grande Diablo*, which they had manned and used as a consort. The three vessels subsequently, while cruising in the Gulf of Mexico, fell in with a Spanish war ship mounting thirty-six guns and manned by three hundred men. The privateers began an attack on the cruiser and kept it up for two days. By that time the four ships had been reduced to wrecks, and the Americans, having exhausted their ammunition, hauled off. The Spaniard had her flag shot away in the course of the engagement, but rehoisted it on the withdrawal of her assailants.

That the line between privateering and piracy was not very distinctly drawn by the middle of the eighteenth century is shown in an item published in one of the " newspapers " of New York in 1747: " Captain Troup, in the privateer brig *Royal Hester*, of this port,

6

lately met with a Danish vessel that had a Spanish merchantman with eight thousand pieces of money on board. Captain Troup thought proper to accept of the money, and, paying the Dane his freight, very civilly dismissed him."

Captain Troup also commanded the privateer *Sturdy Beggar*, a ship carrying twenty-six guns and credited with a complement of two hundred men. In fact, a majority of the colonial privateers carried heavy armaments and large complements, the average probably being not far from eighteen guns and one hundred and thirty men, making them really more formidable than the average cruiser of that day. Keeping this fact in mind, it will not be difficult to believe the statement made in the Weekly Post Boy of September 3, 1744: "'Tis computed there will be before winter one hundred and thirteen sail of privateers at sea from the British-American colonies, most stout vessels and well manned. A naval force, some say, equal that of Great Britain in the time of Queen Elizabeth."

In January, 1758, the 14-gun privateer *Thruloe*, Captain Mantle, having a complement of eighty-four men, had a hard-fought action with the French private armed ship *Les Deux Amis*, Captain Félix. The Frenchmen carried only ten guns, but had a complement of ninety-eight men, who, as the battle was fought at close quarters, made good use of their small arms. This was the principal, if not the most obstinately contested, sea fight between privateers in this war. The action lasted over two hours, and "it was not," so an old-time record declares, "until three hundred powderflasks and seventy-two stinkpots" had been thrown aboard *Les Deux Amis* that the enemy was induced to yield. The Americans had thirty-seven men killed or wounded, while the French are credited with a loss of eighty.

CHAPTER IV.

BEGINNING HOSTILITIES.

IT was on water—not on land, as has been so generally believed—that the first overt act of resistance to British authority in the North American colonies was made. It appears that an illicit trade had long been carried by the English colonists, and in endeavoring to suppress it the commissioners of customs, as early as 1764, had stationed armed vessels along the coast from Casco Bay to Cape Henlopen. The vessel cruising off Rhode Island in 1764 was the *St. John*, Lieutenant Hill, which made herself so obnoxious to the colonists that an armed sloop was fitted out to destroy her, and was deterred from the attempt only by the arrival in Newport of the British man-of-war *Squirrel*. The colonists, however, ventured so far as to land on Goat Island, seize the battery, and open a " fire of defiance " on the war ship.

In the same year the British frigate *Maidstone* appeared at Newport, and for several months greatly exasperated the townsfolk by impressing seamen from vessels entering the harbor, and in taking men from boats and other small craft plying in the bay. The climax of these outrages was reached when a brig from Africa, entering Newport harbor, was stopped by the *Maidstone* and her entire crew impressed. That night a crowd of about five hundred men and boys seized one of the *Maidstone's* boats lying at the wharf, and, dragging it through the

43

streets to the Common, burned it in front of the courthouse amid the derisive shouts of the people. "This affair was so suddenly concocted and carried into effect that the authorities had no time to interfere." [1]

Five years after this occurrence, or in 1769, the commissioners of customs sent Captain Reid to Newport, in the armed sloop *Liberty*, who exhibited extraordinary zeal and unnecessary arrogance in carrying out his instructions. While cruising in Long Island Sound, July 17, 1769, Reid seized a brig and a sloop belonging to Connecticut and brought them into Newport. Captain Packwood, of the brig, had duly reported his cargo, and had conformed to all the requirements of law. After waiting two days, and finding that no proceedings had been instituted against him, he went aboard the *Liberty*, and—Captain Reid being ashore at the time—some difficulty took place between Packwood and the men in the *Liberty* which resulted in several musket shots being fired at Packwood's boat as it was returning shoreward. Exasperated by this unwarrantable proceeding the people of Newport boarded the *Liberty*, cut her cables, and allowed her to drift ashore near Long Wharf. At that place they again boarded her, cut away her masts, and threw her armament overboard. On the returning high tide she drifted to Goat Island, and on the following night a party from Newport burned her. [2]

In March, 1772, Lieutenant William Dudingston, in the armed schooner *Gaspé*, made his appearance in Narragansett Bay, and soon proved himself to be even more exacting than his predecessors. "He stopped all vessels, including small market boats, without showing his authority for doing so; and even sent the property he had illegally seized to Boston for trial, contrary to an act of Parliament

[1] John Russell Bartlett.   [2] For map see page 96.

which required such trials to be held in the colonies where the seizures were made." [1] Suit was begun against Dudingston by the owners of one of these cargoes, Jacob Greene & Co., of Warwick, in July, 1772, which resulted in a judgment against the British officer. Complaints of these proceedings were duly made, and Joseph Wanton, colonial Governor of Rhode Island, sent a number of letters to Rear-Admiral John Montagu, at Boston, protesting against the outrages, which, however, only elicited an arrogant reply from the admiral, who said: " I shall report your two insolent letters to my officer [Lieutenant Dudingston] to his majesty's secretaries of state, and leave to them to determine what right you have to demand a sight of all orders I shall give to officers of my squadron; and I would advise you not to send your sheriff on board the king's ship again on such ridiculous errands. . . . I am also informed the people of Newport talk of fitting out an armed vessel to rescue any vessel the king's schooner may take carrying on an illicit trade. Let them be cautious what they do, for as sure as they attempt it, and any of them are taken, I will hang them as pirates." Dudingston evidently realized that many of his seizures were illegal, for he feared to venture ashore, as many suits at law were threatened against him by the owners of goods and vessels he had taken. The suit brought by Jacob Greene & Co. was instituted after Dudingston had been taken ashore by the captors of the *Gaspé*.

Affairs were in this critical state when, on June 9, 1772, the packet *Hannah*, Captain Benjamin Lindsey, left Newport for Providence. Soon after meridian the *Gaspé* gave chase and ordered the packet to come to. Lindsey refused, and, favored by the wind, led the schooner a 25-mile race up the bay. When off " Namquit Point, which runs off from the

---

[1] John Russell Bartlett.

farm in Warwick, about seven miles below Providence, now owned by Mr. John Brown Francis, our late Governor,"[1] the *Hannah* stood westward, while the *Gaspé*, in close pursuit, changed her course and grounded on the Point. "Lindsey continued on his course up the river and arrived at Providence about sunset, when he immediately informed Mr. John Brown, one of our first and most respectable merchants, of the situation of the *Gaspé*. He [Brown] immediately concluded that she would remain immovable until after midnight [as the tide was beginning to ebb], and that now an opportunity offered of putting an end to the trouble and vexation she daily caused. Mr. Brown immediately resolved on her destruction, and he forthwith directed one of his trusty shipmasters to collect eight of the largest longboats in the harbor, with five oars each; to have the oars and rowlocks well muffled, to prevent noise, and to place them at Fenner's Wharf, directly opposite the dwelling of Mr. James Sabin, who kept a house of board and entertainment for gentlemen. . . . About the time of shutting-up of shops, soon after sunset, a man pased along the main street beating a drum, and informing the inhabitants of the fact that the *Gaspé* was aground on Namquit Point and would not float off until three o'clock the next morning, and inviting those persons who felt disposed to go and destroy that troublesome vessel to repair in the evening to Mr. James Sabin's house. About nine o'clock, I took my father's gun and my powderhorn and bullets and went to Mr. Sabin's and found the southeast room full of people, where I loaded my gun, and all remained there till about ten o'clock, some casting bullets in the kitchen and others making arrangements for departure, when orders were given to cross the street to Fenner's

[1] Account of Colonel Ephraim Bowen, the last survivor of the men who made the attack on the *Gaspé*, written August 29, 1839.

Wharf and embark, which soon took place, and a
sea captain acted as steersman of each boat." [1]

Abraham Whipple was chosen commander of the
enterprise, having as his lieutenant John Burroughs

Captain Abraham Whipple.
From a painting in possession of the R. I. Historical Society.

Hopkins, both of whom afterward became captains
in the Continental navy.   Others known to have
taken part in the attempt were John Brown, Ben-

---

[1] Account of Ephraim Bowen.

jamin Dunn, Samuel Dunn, Joseph Bucklin, Dr. John
Mawney, —— Dickenson, Benjamin Page, Turpin Smith, Joseph Tillinghast, and Simeon H. Olney.
Dr. Mawney wrote, in 1826: " I went to Corlis's
Wharf with Captain Joseph Tillinghast, who commanded the barge, it being the last boat that put
off. In going down we stopped at Captain Cooke's
Wharf, where we took in staves and paving stones;
which done, we followed our commander [Whipple],
and came up with them a considerable distance
down the river."

When the party came in sight of the *Gaspé*, Whipple formed his boats in a line abreast, taking the
immediate command on the right, while Hopkins
had charge of the left. Whipple arranged his attack
so as to approach directly upon the bow of the *Gaspé*,
where she could not bring a gun to bear. " We
rowed gently along," continues Dr. Mawney, " till
we got near the schooner, when we were hailed from
on board with the words:

" ' Who comes there?'

" Captain Whipple replied:

" ' I want to come on board.'

" The reply was:

" ' Stand off! You can't come on board.'

" On which Whipple roared out:

" ' I am the sheriff of the County of Kent; I am
come for the commander of this vessel, and I will
have him, dead or alive. Men, spring to your oars!' "

According to other reliable accounts Whipple, in
this brief parley, emphasized his words with a remarkable amount of real sailor-like profanity, possibly with a view of concealing his identity. By this
time Dudingston had appeared on deck in his shirt
sleeves and ordered the boats to keep away, and on
their persistent approach discharged his pistol,
while several of his men also fired. Colonel Bowen
says: " I took my seat on the main thwart, near the
larboard [port] rowlock, with my gun by my right

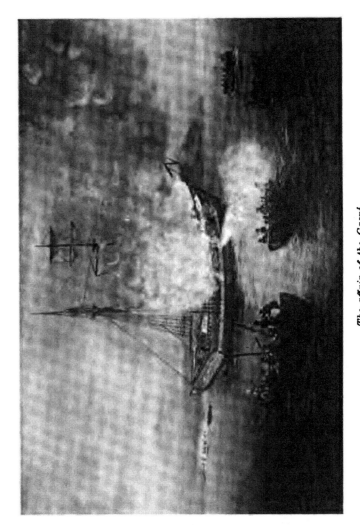

The affair of the Gaspé.

From a painting in the possession of the Rhode Island Historical Society.

side, facing forward. As soon as Dudingston began
to hail, Joseph Bucklin, who was standing on the
main thwart, by my right side, said to me: 'Ephe,
reach me your gun and I can kill that fellow.' I
reached it to him accordingly, when, during Captain
Whipple's replying, Bucklin fired and Dudingston
fell, and Bucklin exclaimed: 'I have killed the
rascal!' [The ball shattered the lieutenant's arm
and lodged in his groin.] In less than a minute
after Captain Whipple's reply the boats were alongside the *Gaspé* and [we] boarded without opposition. The men on deck retreated below as Dudingston entered the cabin."

Dr. Mawney thus describes the boarding of the
Gaspé: "We were in an instant under her bows. I
was then sitting with Captain Tillinghast in the
stern of the barge and sprang immediately forward,
and seeing a rope hang down her bows seized it to
help myself in. The rope slipping, I fell almost to
my waist in the water, but being nimble and active I
recovered, and was the first of our crew on deck,
when Simeon H. Olney handed me a stave, with
which, seeing one [man] that I took to be of the
crew of the schooner floundering below the windlass, I was in the attitude of a leveling stroke, when
he cried out: 'John, don't strike!' Being very intimately acquainted with Captain Samuel Dunn, I
knew his voice, left him, and sprang back of the
windlass, where there was commotion and noise,
but which soon subsided. The crew jumping down
the hold, I immediately followed, when I ordered
them to bring cords to tie their hands with, and
told them they should not be hurt, but be sent on
shore. They brought some tarred strings, with
which I tied the hands of two, when John Brown,
Esq., called to me, saying I was wanted immediately on deck, where I was instantly helped. When
I asked Mr. Brown what the matter was he replied, 'Don't call names, but go immediately into

the cabin; there is one wounded and will bleed to death.' I hastened into the cabin and found Lieutenant Dudingston in a sitting posture, gently reclining to the left, bleeding profusely, with a thin white woolen blanket loose about him, which I threw aside, and discovered the effect of a musket ball in his left groin.   Thinking the femoral artery was cut, I threw open my waistcoat, and taking my shirt by the collar tore it to my waistband.   Mr. Dudingston said: ' Pray, sir, don't tear your clothes; there is linen in that trunk.'   Upon which I requested Joseph Bucklin to break open the trunk and tear the linen and scrape lint, which he immediately attempted, but, finding the linen new and strong, could not make lint."   Discovering that dawn was rapidly aproaching Dr. Mawney tore the linen into strips, and, bandaging Dudingston as well as he could, placed him in one of the boats where the other prisoners had been collected.   After setting fire to the *Gaspé* so that she burned to the water's edge and blew up, the boats returned to Providence, landing the prisoners at Pawtuxet.

This affair caused great excitement, the British Government offering a reward of one thousand pounds for the apprehension of the leader of the attack and five hundred pounds for any of the participants, at the same time promising pardon to any one who would make disclosures.   No one was found willing to give the desired information, although a special commission sat for this purpose from January to June, 1773.   All those taking part in the affair were more or less disguised at the time.

This spirited attack was followed, in June, 1773, by the famous " Boston Tea Party."   This was somewhat in the nature of a private maritime enterprise.   One of the measures adopted by England to coerce the colonists was to place a heavy tax on tea.   The latter evaded it by agreeing not to import or use the article, the result being that the merchandise soon accumulated in the warehouses of the East India Company. At Charleston the people caused the tea to be stored in damp cellars, where it spoiled, while the New York-

The "Boston Tea Party."
From an old print.

ers and Philadelphians compelled some ships to return without unloading.

Three cargoes arrived at Boston which the people endeavored also to send back, but the Crown officials refused to give the necessary clearances. Determined to prevent the landing of the offensive article, a number of the inhabitants, disguised as Indians, on the night of December 17, 1773, suddenly appeared on the wharf, took possession of the ships, and, opening the hatches, broke open the chests and poured the tea into the bay. Three hundred and forty-two chests of tea were destroyed in this way.

The first sea fight after the battle of Bunker Hill was that between the captured schooner *Unity* and the British armed cutter *Margaretta*, Lieutenant Moore. The rapid concentration of troops in Boston made it necessary for the enemy to provide additional barracks, and for the purpose of securing lumber for these buildings the British ordered two small vessels, about eighty tons each, belonging to Ichabod Jones, of Boston, under the convoy of the *Margaretta*, to Machias,[1] "the extreme easterly outpost of the

Birthplace of Colonel Jeremiah O'Brien, near Machias, Maine.
From a photograph.

colonists; and being the only point in all the region beyond the Penobscot, and between it and the St. Croix, at which any considerable number of white men have found lodgment, in a region which had lately become safe from aboriginal and French incursions, they were in many respects seemingly un-

---

[1] According to the account of John O'Brien, one of the participants, the lumber wanted was " pickets and planks, to be used by the English in the defense of Boston."

recognized, and apparently almost without the pale of colonial jurisdiction." [1]

The *Margaretta*, with her convoy, arrived at the mouth of the Machias River June 2, 1775, and on June 3d Lieutenant Moore circulated a paper among the inhabitants for signatures " as a prequisite to their obtaining supplies of any provisions," [2] of which the people were in great need. According to the terms of this paper, or contract, the inhabitants were to " indulge Captain Jones in carrying lumber to Boston, and to protect him and his property at all events." On June 6th the people held a meeting and decided not to grant his request for lumber, upon which Jones reported the matter to Moore, who caused the sloop and the *Margaretta* to anchor near the village, where his guns would command the houses. This had the effect of changing the attitude of the inhabitants, to the extent that a majority voted to allow Jones to get the lumber and to permit the citizens individually to purchase provisions. But there were many who voted against this resolution.

Upon learning of this decision Jones brought his lumber vessels up to the wharf and distributed the provisions only among those who had voted in his favor. This gave offense to those who were denied provisions, and they determined to seize Jones and put a stop to his mission of securing lumber.[3] Vague rumors of the fight at Lexington had reached this outpost of civilization, and the arrival of these vessels in quest of this particular kind of lumber confirmed the news in the minds of the townsfolk. But Lieutenant Moore, under the impression that these people were ignorant of that occurrence, was careful to con-

---

[1] G. W. Balch. [2] Official report of the Machias Committee of Safety.

[3] Nearly all the popular accounts of the *Margaretta* fight have omitted these important preliminary details, leaving it to be inferred that the Crown vessels, with their convoy, arrived at Machias June 10th or 11th. The above account is taken from the official report of the Machias Committee of Safety.

ceal all information on the subject. Soon after his arrival he assumed an arrogant tone, and took exception to the liberty pole which the inhabitants had erected on the village green. " He said it must be taken down or the town would be fired upon. A Mr. Stephen Jones was present, and, owning a store in Machias, had considerable weight with the people.

O'Brien's Brook, near Machias, Maine, where the patriots held
their secret meetings.
From a photograph.

He advised Moore to suspend his determination until the people could assemble a town meeting; perhaps the town would agree to take down the liberty pole. The town met, as was proposed, and voted not to take it down. Mr. Jones, who was in considerable favor with the English commander, persuaded him to defer execution of his threat until a second town meeting could be called, it being stated that the first was not fully attended." [1]

Anticipating that there would be trouble over the liberty pole the inhabitants of Machias secretly sent word to Pleasant River village, about twenty miles distant, and to a few other settlements within reach, asking for reënforcements. Before this aid could

---

[1] Account of John O'Brien, one of the participants in the affair.

come the people had held another meeting—a secret
one—on Sunday, June 11th, in the woods at the back
of the settlement, at which the project of capturing
the Crown boat and her convoy was discussed. After
some talk Benjamin Foster, of East Falls, Machias—
Pizarro-like—stepped across a brook near by and
called upon all, who would take part in an attempt,
to follow him. He was promptly supported by the
sturdy men at the gathering, and Foster was dele-
gated to proceed to East Machias to secure a
schooner lying there, which was well adapted for the
undertaking.

Meantime Moore and Ichabod Jones, with several
of their men, ignorant of the fact that a secret meeting
was being held, had attended religious service in the
meetinghouse. Some of the villagers, in anticipation
of trouble, carried their guns to church, but took care
to keep them out of sight, John O'Brien concealing
his under a board. He observed Moore when the
latter entered the edifice, and took a seat directly behind the British officer. In the course of the service
Moore happened to look out of the open window, and
he saw up the river, at a distance of about half a mile,
a number of men crossing the stream on logs, holding
guns in their hands.[1] These were the reënforcements
coming from Pleasant River village. The English
commander at once surmised their object and realized
the peril of his situation. At that time the meetinghouse was unfinished and there were no pews, the con-
gregation using temporary benches.[2] Making his
way over these seats Moore reached a window, jumped
out, and managed to make his way to his vessel, then
anchored at White's Point. Ichabod Jones took to
the woods, where he secreted himself several days.
Stephen Jones, who also was at the meeting, was
taken prisoner and held under guard.

[1] Account of John O'Brien, one of the participants.
[2] Collections of the Maine Historical Society.

The temper of these Maine people is touchingly shown by an incident that occurred the following day. The men who came from Pleasant River were short of powder, having only two or three charges each. It appears that one of them, Josiah Weston, of Jonesboro, forgot his powderhorn. His wife Hannah, after his departure, noticed the oversight, and, following the trail through the woods, reached Machias on the next day with the precious article. In this plucky tramp through the woods, Mrs. Weston was accompanied by her husband's sister, Miss Rebecca Weston, a frail girl fifteen years old. Mrs. Weston herself was in her seventeenth year and had been married five months. The powder, which was carried in a bag, weighed forty pounds. "There were no roads or bridges, and the two girls followed spots on trees, coming out on Machias River, where Whitneyville now is, and followed the river to Machias."[1]

After sending word to the inhabitants that he would burn the town if they persisted in their hostile demonstrations, Moore dropped the *Margaretta* below the Narrows. Notwithstanding his threat the Americans seized the sloop *Unity*, and forty of the men of Machias went aboard her, while another party took the second sloop and brought her up to the wharf. "On examining their equipments of warfare, only twenty guns could be produced, many of which were mere fowling pieces, carrying scatter shot, and of powder, ball, and shot there were no more than three rounds to each firearm. The remaining weapons consisted of thirteen pitchforks, a few scythes, and ten or twelve axes."[2] The *Margaretta* was armed with four 3-pounders and fourteen swivels. Only two of the Machias men had ever seen military service; they were Morris O'Brien and Benjamin Foster, both of whom had served in the expedition against Louis-

---

[1] Collections of the Maine Historical Society.
[2] G. W. Balch, a descendant of Morris O'Brien.

burg.   Morris was now incapacitated by extreme
age.   Jeremiah O'Brien, then thirty-one years old,
a son of Morris O'Brien, was chosen commander
of the *Unity*, and Edmund Stevens was made his
lieutenant.

While this had been going on a number of the inhabitants had gathered on the highland overlooking
the *Margaretta's* refuge near the Narrows, and threatened to attack if she did not surrender.   Receiving
for answer " fire and be damned," they opened fire,
which Moore returned, but finding himself at a disad-
vantage again got under way, and, running into a bay,
anchored near the confluence of two streams.   Here
he lashed the *Margaretta* alongside a small sloop commanded by a Mr. Toby, whom Moore compelled to
come aboard the Crown cutter and act as pilot.

It was not until Monday morning, June 12th, that
the patriots were ready to make sail in pursuit, when
the *Unity*, followed by the second lumber craft having twenty men under the command of Benjamin Foster aboard, got under way.   Observing the approach
of the Americans, Moore again weighed anchor and
maneuvered so as to avoid a collision.   In this effort
his vessel lost her boom and gaff, whereupon he ran
into Holmes Bay, and, taking a spar and all the provisions, together with Robert Avery, of Norwich, Connecticut, out of a craft he met coming in from the
Bay of Fundy, repaired his injury.

While this work was going on the Americans
again drew near, and to avoid them Moore stood out
to sea.   " During the chase our people built their
breastworks [bulwarks] of pine boards, and anything they could find in the vessels that would screen
them from the enemy's fire." [1]   Finding that the
Americans were not only following him, but were
rapidly gaining, Lieutenant Moore cut away his

---

[1] Letter of Machias Committee of Safety to the " Honorable Congress
of Massachusetts Bay," June 14, 1775.

7

boats, and as this did not enable him to hold his distance he, when "at the entrance of our harbor,"[1] began firing, one of his shots killing an American. This fire was answered by one of the volunteers named Knight, who discharged his "wall piece" —a musket too heavy to fire offhand, needing the support of a "wall," but in this instance probably the "breastwork" or bulwark—killing the English helmsman, an impressed seaman, and clearing the poop of men. The two craft quickly came together, when a sharp fire of small arms was opened. Moore made a gallant defense, throwing personally a number of hand grenades and with great effect, until he was shot through the breast with a brace of musket balls. The unfortunate Mr. Avery also was killed. A British midshipman named Stillingfleet became terrified and secreted himself below.

The Americans now boarded and soon obtained possession of the cutter, the action having lasted "for near the space of an hour." The first man to board was John O'Brien, brother of Jeremiah, and the second was Joseph Getchell. On the part of the Americans one was killed and six were wounded,[2] one of the latter afterward dying. The enemy had four men killed and about ten wounded,[3] one mortally, her commander, who died in the village the next day. For this brilliant affair the Colonial Council, then in session at Cambridge, tendered Jeremiah O'Brien a vote of thanks and gave him the custody of his prizes. The *Margaretta* was brought back to port and her armament was transferred to the *Unity*. "We purpose," wrote the Machias Committee of Safety, "to convey the prisoners to Pownalborough Gaol as soon as possible."

---

[1] Massachusetts Archives.

[2] Official report of the Machias Committee of Safety.

[3] Letter of Joseph Wheaton to John O'Brien. Wheaton was one of the Americans participating.

There has been confusion in some accounts of this affair as to which O'Brien commanded the *Unity*. Inquiring of Miss Annetta O'Brien Walker, a descendant of Morris O'Brien, the author learns that it unquestionably was Jeremiah who had the honor. The confusion very naturally arises from the fact that there were six O'Briens in the fight, three of them having the letter "J" as their initial. As many of the early records give only the first letter, "J," to the commander, doubt easily arose as to which O'Brien was intended. The six brothers were Jeremiah, Gideon, Joseph, Dennis, John, and William. Their father, Morris, came from Dublin, Ireland, in 1740, and settled in Scarboro',[1] then in Massachusetts. About 1760 the family moved to Machias on account of the facilities there offered in the lumber business.[2] They built and owned sawmills. The gunboat *Machias*, of our present navy, was named for the town where the fight took place.

The news of this fight greatly enraged British navy officials, and about a month later they sent two armed sloops, the *Diligence* and the *Tapanagouche*, or *Tapuaquish*, from Halifax to punish the audacious Yankees. These sloops carried eight guns and fifty men for the first and sixteen swivels for the last. Hearing of their approach, O'Brien sailed from Machias with the *Unity* and the coasting vessel *Portland Packet*, commanded by Benjamin Foster, to anticipate them. They met July 12, 1775, in the Bay of Fundy, and by attacking them separately the Americans took both and brought them in triumph to Watertown. For this truly brilliant affair O'Brien was made a captain in the Massachusetts State marine, and with his last two prizes, which he named *Machias Liberty* and *Diligence*, he went out to cruise after British transports, O'Brien commanding the *Machias Liberty*

---

[1] Maine Historical Society collections.
[2] Annetta O'Brien Walker to the author.

and a Mr. Lambert the *Diligence*. Under their new commanders these vessels were highly successful. On August 9, 1775, they recaptured a schooner that had fallen into the hands of the enemy, and also a cutter and two barges, with thirty-five men, under the command of a lieutenant of the British sloop of war *Falcon*, that were operating in Gloucester Bay. In this capture the Americans had one man killed and two wounded.

These maritime successes so exasperated Admiral Graves, then commander on the North American

Edward Preble

station, that he sent out a squadron of four war vessels under Captain Mowatt to "overawe" the colonists. Mowatt destroyed the town of Falmouth, Maine (now Portland), in October, compelling many women and children to seek cover in hastily constructed huts at the beginning of the severe northern winter. Among these children was Edward Preble, then only fourteen years old. Later in life he became famous as a captain in our navy. The *Machias Liberty* and *Diligence* continued to cruise off the New England coast for a year and a half, when they were laid up. Captain O'Brien afterward entered the privateer service, commanding the armed ships *Little Vincent*, *Cyrus*, and *Tiger*, of New Hampshire. Late in September, 1777, he captured off Cape Negro a vessel from Ireland laden with pork for the British army. This craft had been taken by an American privateer, was recaptured by the British cruiser *Scarborough*, and was again seized by Captain O'Brien.[1]

---

[1] Kidder's Eastern Maine.

Later in the war Jeremiah, with his brother John and several others, built at Newburyport a ship called the *Hannibal*, carrying twenty guns and a complement of one hundred and thirty men. On her first cruise, to Port au Prince, she was commanded by John O'Brien. Returning from this voyage with several prizes, the *Hannibal* was under the command of Jeremiah O'Brien. Meeting with varied success in a cruise of considerable length the *Hannibal*, in 1780, was captured, after a chase of forty-eight hours, by two British frigates which were escorting a fleet of merchantmen in the vicinity of New York. Captain O'Brien and his men were taken into that port and were confined in the ill-famed prison ship *Jersey*, where they were subjected to great hardship. After six months of imprisonment the *Hannibal's* crew was exchanged, with the exception of Captain O'Brien, who it seems, by orders from England, was reserved for the special malice of the British Government. He was transported to England and thrown into Mill Prison, and made the object of personal ill treatment.

Notwithstanding the careful watch kept on him, O'Brien managed to effect his escape. The story of this exploit, as told by his brother John, is as follows: " He purposely neglected his dress and whole personal appearance for a month. The afternoon before making his escape he shaved and dressed in decent clothes, so as to alter very much his personal appearance, and walked out with the other prisoners in the jail yard. Having secreted himself under a platform in the yard, and thus escaping the notice of the keepers at the evening round-up, he was left out of the cells after they were locked for the night. He escaped from the yard by passing through the principal keeper's house in the dusk of the evening. Although he made a little stay in the barroom of the house, he was not detected, being taken for a British soldier. In company with a Captain Lyon and an-

other American who also had escaped from the prison
and were concealed somewhere in the vicinity, he
crossed the English Channel to France in a boat and
thence came to America," just about the time hostilities ceased.   He lived to see the second war with
Great Britain, but at that time was too old to become
an active participant.   One of our new torpedo boats
is named *O'Brien* in honor of Jeremiah O'Brien.

While his brother was confined in British prisons,
John O'Brien had purchased the fast-sailing brig
Hibernia, carrying six 3-pounders and sixty men. He
sailed from Newburyport in this vessel June 9, 1779,
and on the 21st captured an English brig and sent
her into port. About noon, June 25th, Captain John
O'Brien discovered a large ship, and rapidly coming
up with her opened fire about three o'clock in the
afternoon.   The stranger was the British cruiser
General Pattison, Lieutenant Chiene, from New York
for England, carrying, besides her regular complement, a number of British officers homeward bound.
She was armed with 6- and 9-pounders. After a desultory cannonading, lasting from three to five o'clock
in the afternoon, Captain O'Brien drew off, feeling
satisfied that the enemy was too strong to be taken.
In this affair the Americans had three men killed and
several wounded,[1] the loss of the enemy being unknown.

Scarcely had the *Hibernia* hauled off from the
General Pattison when a British frigate hove in sight
and gave the Americans a hard chase until midnight,
when she desisted.   Continuing her cruise, the *Hibernia*, on July 7th, took a schooner which was sent
into Newburyport. Three days later she fell in with
the 12-gun privateer *Polly*, of Salem, Massachusetts,
Captain J. Leach. Leach was a successful privateersman throughout the war. In September, 1776, while
in command of the private armed schooner *Dolphin*,

---

[1] Log of the *Hibernia*.

carrying only eight swivels and twenty-five men, he
captured the brig *Royal George*, with a cargo of provisions, and also a sloop laden with fish.   Before
Leach got the *Dolphin* she was commanded by Captain Daniel Waters.   In September, 1778, Leach was
captain of the 6-gun sloop *Happy Return*.   That vessel captured one brig and two sloops laden with fustic
and rum.

At the time Captain Leach fell in with the
Hibernia, July 10, 1779, he was in command of the
fine 12-gun sloop *Polly*, carrying, besides her main
guns, eight swivels and one hundred men. The *Polly*
had been hanging on the outskirts of a fleet of merchantmen, and shortly after the two privateers came
together the fleet hove in sight, convoyed by a small
cruiser.   The American privateers, after some adroit
maneuvering, captured a ship carrying thirteen 4-
pounders, a brig, and a schooner laden with molasses.
On the following day the *Hibernia* took a hermaphro-
dite brig in ballast, and being incumbered with
prisoners Captain John O'Brien placed them aboard
her, with permission to make their most convenient
port.   On the same day, July 11th, he gave chase to
another brig and captured her.   " Had not Captain
Leach been parted from me in the fog we could have
taken the whole fleet." [1] The *Hibernia* then returned
to port with her rich prizes. The *Polly*, in the following month, took a brig laden with tobacco.   In 1782
Captain Leach commanded the privateer *St. Mary's*,
a brig of one hundred and twenty-eight men.

A number of spirited affairs like that of the *Margaretta* took place at the outbreak of the Revolution,
the result of private enterprise.   From an English
source we get the following account of an audacious
attack on British transports by an American privateer: " On the 23d of November, 1775, a small fleet
of transports under the convoy of the frigate *Tartar*

---

[1] Journal of Captain John O'Brien.

arrived off Boston, and, with the exception of two, safely entered the port. The ship *Hunter* and a brig, owing to a shift in the wind, were obliged to anchor outside the harbor, which, being observed by two American privateers that had been following the convoy, they, in the most daring manner, attacked and boarded them, setting them on fire. A signal was immediately made for the *Raven* to weigh anchor and go in chase, but Lieutenant John Bourmaster, who had been appointed to protect Boston Lighthouse, then under repair, and who was in command of an armed transport, on observing the privateers fire upon the *Hunter*, set sail and reached the transports in time to save them from destruction."

In April, 1775, several whaleboats under the command of one N. Smith captured the British schooner *Volante* in Martha's Vineyard. The *Volante* was a tender to the British frigate *Scarborough*, one of whose prizes, as we have just seen, was captured by Captain Jeremiah O'Brien. In December of the same year four boats under the command of James Barron, afterward a captain in the navy, captured a British tender in Chesapeake Bay. A whaleboat carrying three swivels and twenty-two men, under the command of one B. Bormer, in the same year seized an English sloop mounting six guns, and afterward recaptured two prizes off Ocracoke Inlet, North Carolina.

From November 13, 1775, to the evacuation of Boston by the British, March 17, 1776, thirty-one English vessels, while endeavoring to gain port, were captured by the vigilant Americans. In this period there were only a few State cruisers in commission off Boston, so that a good share of these captures must be credited to private enterprise. General Washington, on his own responsibility, borrowed two vessels from Massachusetts and sent them into the Gulf of St. Lawrence to intercept military supplies consigned to the enemy. These were the schooners *Lynch* and

Franklin, the first carrying six guns, ten swivels, and seventy men, under the command of Captain Nicholas Broughton; and the second carrying four guns, ten swivels, and sixty men, commanded by Captain John Selman. When first commissioned the *Lynch* was commanded by Captain John Ayres, her first and second officers being John Roche and John Tiley. From the circumstance of all her officers bearing the same first name, this craft was jokingly dubbed *The Three Johns*. Ayres soon was succeeded by John Selman as commander, so that the nickname of the boat was in no way disturbed.

The *Lynch* and *Franklin* were highly successful, notwithstanding the fact that their commanders missed their way to the St. Lawrence and brought up in the Bay of Fundy. In the fall of 1775 they made ten prizes and captured Governor Wright, of St. John's. " All of the vessels were released, however," wrote Elbridge Gerry to John Adams, " as we had waged a ministerial war, and not one against our most gracious Sovereign." In the spring of 1776 the *Franklin*, then commanded by Captain James Mugford, captured the ship *Hope* and brought her safely into port. She was laden with fifteen hundred barrels of gunpowder, a large quantity of intrenching tools, gun carriages, and other stores which were intended for the British army, all of which were duly forwarded to the troops under Washington—a sufficient commentary on his wisdom in sending such craft to sea.

The American commander in chief also sent out the little cruisers *Lee* and *Harrison*, issuing their commissions with his own hand. The *Lee* was commanded by Captain Daniel Waters, her first and second officers being Richard Stiles and Nicholas Ogilby; while the *Harrison* was under the orders of Captain Charles Dyar, her first and second officers being Thomas Dote and John Wigglesworth. The *Lee* belonged to the State of Massachusetts, and while under the command of Captain John Manly made one of the most important captures of the war. On November 29, 1775, she entered Cape Ann Roads with her prize, the *Nancy*, the latter being laden with two thousand muskets and bayonets, eight thousand fuses, thirty-one tons of musket shots, three thousand rounds of shot for 12-pounders, a 13-inch mortar, two 6-pounders, several barrels of powder, and fifty "carcasses," or great frames for combustibles, designed for the purpose of setting buildings on fire.

On December 8th this cruiser captured three vessels: the *Jenny*, carrying two guns, a crew of twenty men, and a cargo of provisions; the *Concord*, with a cargo of dry goods, and the *Hannah*, a brig, with a cargo of rum. These vessels were not taken without a fierce struggle with a fourth, the convoying ship, which, though mounting eight guns, was finally beaten off. The prizes were brought into port, and the *Hannah's* cargo alone netted twenty-five thousand dollars to her captors. On the same day the *Harrison* captured the schooner *Industry* and the sloop *Polly*. Soon after this lucky stroke she was chased into Gloucester by the British cruiser *Falcon*. By running close inshore the *Lee* inflicted considerable injury on her pursuer and escaped. This is the second unlucky experience we have noted the *Falcon* as having with Americans, for in this same bay the *Falcon's* boats were repulsed in an attempt to take one of Captain Jeremiah O'Brien's prizes. For these valuable services Manly received a commission, April 17, 1776, as captain in the Continental navy, and the command of the 32-gun frigate *Hancock* was given to him.[1]

On the retirement of Manly from the command of the *Lee*, Captain Waters, as has been noted, assumed charge of that cruiser. Early on the morning of June 17, 1776, the *Lee*, in company with three small privateers out of New England ports, fell in with two

---

[1] For Manly's subsequent brilliant career in this war see Chapter XV, "Captain John Manly."

heavily armed British transports, the *Annabella* and the *Howe*, and immediately began a running fight with them, the enemy putting on all sail to escape. They finally evaded the Americans by running into Nantasket Roads.

Toward evening the Americans met the Massachusetts State cruiser *Defense*, Captain Seth Harding, which had sailed from Plymouth that morning, and, being attracted by the heavy firing, drew toward the scene of hostilities. An arrangement was soon made between Harding, Waters, and the privateersmen, and about eleven o'clock the *Defense* boldly ran into the Roads, and getting between the two transports, within pistol-shot distance, Harding called upon the British to strike their colors. A voice from one of the troopships was heard, in reply, " Ay, ay—I'll strike," and a broadside was poured into the *Defense*. The Americans promptly responded, and after an hour of heavy firing the British called for quarter. The transports were found to have on board about two hundred regulars of the Seventy-first Regiment. Among the prisoners was Lieutenant Campbell. Eighteen of the Englishmen had been killed in the action and a larger number were wounded. On the part of the Americans not one was killed and only nine were injured. Among the British dead was Major Menzies, who had answered the summons to surrender with " Ay, ay—I'll strike." Lieutenant Campbell afterward was exchanged, was again captured by our sea forces, and finally, having attained the rank of lieutenant-colonel, distinguished himself in the southern campaigns against Greene.

On the following morning the Americans discovered another sail in the offing, which was chased, and on being captured proved to be the transport *John and George*, carrying six guns and having on board one hundred soldiers of the same regiment. By this daring stroke the private armed vessels captured three hundred men of one of the best English regiments in America. The *Defense*, in 1779, was lost in the ill-fated Penobscot expedition.

Some of the other States also fitted out cruisers at the outbreak of hostilities. On November 14, 1775, Clement Lemprière was placed in command of the South Carolina ship *Prosper*. On the 11th of the same month the armed schooner *Defense*, also belonging to that State, while sinking some hulks in Hog Island Creek, Charleston harbor, was fired on by the British 16-gun ship *Tamar* and the 6-gun schooner *Cherokee*. On December 21, 1775, North Carolina authorized the equipment of three armed vessels for the protection of her coast trade. She also armed the sloop *Sally* for river defense. Virginia early established a board of commissioners to superintend her naval affairs.

That all our private maritime enterprises were not successful is shown by British records. From 1774 to 1776 the enemy claim to have captured the following vessels belonging to the rebelling colonies: The *Belisarius*, of twenty guns; the *Hussar*, of twenty-four guns; the *Sullivan*, of eighteen guns; the *Tobago*, of twelve guns, and the *Warren*. These vessels nowhere appear in American records; but although some of them, while classed in British accounts under the general head " American," doubtless belonged to other North American colonies aside from the thirteen in revolt, yet one or two of them may have been correctly traced. The fact that this list includes vessels taken as early as 1774 also leaves room for the supposition that some of them may have been unarmed coasting vessels arbitrarily detained by the British blockading ships.

The private armed brig *Washington*, Captain Martindale, carrying ten guns, ten swivels, and eighty men, was captured off the coast of North Carolina by the British frigate *Fowey* and carried into Boston. This vessel, together with four other ships seized by the enemy, were left in Boston in a dismantled state after they evacuated that city.

CHAPTER V.

WHEN the American colonists finally realized that they must resort to open hostilities in order to maintain their rights, they became extremely active in fitting out vessels at private expense. Every seaport soon had its quota of privateers scouring the seas or hovering on the coasts of the enemy. Merchant ships that were no longer able to ply their usual trade were hastily fitted with a few guns and were sent to sea with a commission. Fishing smacks were divested of their cargoes and were transformed into belligerent craft, while even whaleboats ventured out, and in many cases succeeded in making valuable prizes.

In the first two years of the war New Hampshire, although pretending to only one considerable seaport, sent out eight privateers, while her powerful neighbor, Massachusetts, had in commission fifty-three. Little Rhode Island and Connecticut had six and twenty-two, respectively, and even New York, whose principal seaport was held by the British through most of the war, managed to secure seven commissions. New Jersey, in the first two years, had only one privateer credited to her, but Pennsylvania had thirteen and Maryland twenty-one, while six were sent out from South Carolina and three from North Carolina, making a total of one hundred and forty-two privateers fitted out by the colonists in the first two full years of the war. "The people have gone mad a-privateering," said one of the writers of the day, and in some cases the expression "the enemy's coasts are swarming with our armed ships" was literally true. This was especially the case off Halifax and in the Gulf of St. Lawrence, where so many American privateers had collected that they, in truth, very much interfered with one another. In reading over the personal narratives of privateersmen concerned in that period, it is surprising in how many instances we find American privateers chased by their own countrymen, and in some instances guns, provisions, and other equipage were thrown away in frantic effort to escape from friends.

Among the first of these privateers to get to sea were the *Yankee*, the *Yankee Hero*, and the *Yankee Ranger*, all of Massachusetts. Like the vessels bearing the name "Yankee" in the War of 1812, this trio of Revolutionary Yankees had singularly exciting and varied experiences. The *Yankee* was a large sloop, carrying nine guns and a complement of sixteen men, under the command of Captain Johnson. She got to sea early in the war, and in July, 1776, captured the valuable British merchantmen *Creighton* and *Zachara*, laden with rum and sugar. Johnson detailed prize crews to man these vessels, and then proceeded to escort them to an American port. Before gaining a place of safety, however, the prisoners in the prizes rose on their captors, retook the ships, and then united in an attack on the *Yankee*. Captain Johnson, as we have noted, had only sixteen men, which number had been seriously reduced by the drafts for prize crews. Each of the British crews numbered more than the entire crew of the *Yankee*, and, as the merchantmen were well armed, the prisoners soon compelled the privateer to surrender. The *Creighton* and *Zachara* arrived at Dover, England, with their prize, the *Yankee*, and Captain Johnson, with his men, was thrown into Mill Prison.

Scarcely less unfortunate than the *Yankee* was the

Yankee Hero, Captain J. Tracy, a brig of fourteen guns, with a crew of forty men. In June, 1776, this privateer was chased by the English frigate *Lively*. Captain Tracy did his best to outsail his powerful pursuer, but the Englishman managed to get alongside and compelled the Americans to surrender; not, however, until the latter had made a desperate resistance, in which four of their number were killed and thirteen were wounded. The *Yankee Ranger* was more fortunate than either of her sisters. In August, 1776, she made prizes of three brigs laden with cotton, coffee, and oil.

Some of the other successful privateers from Massachusetts were the 10-gun schooner *America*, Captain McNeil, which in October, 1777, captured a ship laden with rum, sugar, wine, and logwood. The 12-gun brig *Charming Peggy*, Captain J. Jauncey, in October, 1776, seized a small vessel having a cargo of provisions, and the schooner *Dolphin*, Captain Leach, in September, 1776, captured the brig *Royal George* (also laden with provisions) and a sloop loaded with fish. The brig *Hannah and Molly*, Captain Crabtree, in the same year took a ship mounting four guns and eight swivels, one brig, two schooners, and a sloop— a very successful cruise for that day. These vessels were taken by a stratagem in the harbor of Liverpool, Nova Scotia. The 6-gun schooner *Independence*, Captain Nichols, in September, 1776, captured six vessels; while the *Independency*, Captain Gill, in the same month took a brig, but it was retaken by the prisoners.

In September, 1776, the 8-gun brig *Joseph*, Captain C. Babbidge, afterward commanded by Captains Field and West, made a prize of a schooner in ballast, and two months later took a valuable ship. In September, 1776, the 16-gun brig *Massachusetts*, Captain D. Souther, captured a brig of six guns and twenty-eight men, having on board a company of dragoons. About the same time the 12-gun sloop *Republic*, Captain John

Foster Williams,[1] captured two valuable ships, one named *Julius Cæsar*, and sent them into Boston. The *Retaliation*, a 10-gun brig commanded by a Mr. Giles, took, in the same year, after a severe action of two hours' duration, a ship armed with two guns.

Most successful of all the privateers commissioned from Massachusetts in the first two years of the war was the 12-gun sloop *Revenge*, Captain J. White. In August, 1776, this vessel captured the ships *Anna Maria* and *Polly* (the former with a cargo of rum and sugar, and the latter laden with wine), the brigs *Harlequin* and *Fanny*, laden with rum and sugar; the sloop *Betsey*, and one other that was given up to the prisoners. Prizes also were taken in this year by the Massachusetts privateers *Rover*, Captain Forrester, a sloop of eight guns, and the 8-gun sloop *Speedwell*, Captain Greely. The *Rover* had an action with the British merchant ship *Africa*, which was maintained with much obstinacy until a shot ignited the *Africa's* magazine, blowing the craft to pieces, only three of her complement of twenty-six men being saved. The *Rover* also took the brigs *Mary and James*, *Sarah Ann*, and *Good Intent*, besides the snow *Lively*.

On October 14, 1776, the 6-gun schooner *General Gates*, Captain B. Tatem, captured a schooner, but shortly afterward, while off Portsmouth, New Hampshire, was herself taken by the English brig *Hope*. The American commander and his men escaped by swimming ashore. While cruising off Boston, June, 1776, the sloop *Lady Washington*, Captain Cunningham, was attacked by four armed barges from British war ships. The privateer beat the boats off, killing several of the Englishmen. In October the *Lady Washington*, again cruising near Boston, captured a ship with a cargo of rum, sugar, and cotton. In the same month the 6-gun schooner *Liberty*, Captain

---

[1] Afterward a successful commander in the service of Massachusetts. See vol. i, p. 99, Maclay's History of the Navy.

Pierce, seized a ship with a cargo of fish and lumber.

The *Baltimore Hero* was one of the first privateers to leave the waters of Maryland. She was a schooner carrying from six to fourteen guns, and was commanded at first by Captain T. Waters, and in 1779 by Captain J. Earle. Under Earle she had an action with a British privateer schooner of fourteen guns in Chesapeake Bay and captured her. About the same time the *Baltimore Hero* put to sea the *Betsey*, Captain B. Dashiell, sailed from the Chesapeake. She was a sloop of ten guns. A private armed brig of the same name sailed from Maryland waters under the command of Captain J. Brice in 1777, and under Captain B. Brudhurst in 1778. *Betsey* seems to have been a favorite name for privateers in this war, New York, Massachusetts, Pennsylvania, Rhode Island, and Connecticut each being credited with a *Betsey*.

The 6-gun sloop *Beaver*, Captain S. Dean, sailed from New York in 1776, 1779, and again in 1781. In June, 1779, she captured a sloop. A privateer schooner of this name, but carrying twice the number of guns, was commissioned from Connecticut in 1778, under the command of Captain D. Scoville, and one from Pennsylvania, commanded by Captain W. Harris. Between August 3 and 6, 1776, the 10-gun sloop *Broom*, Captain W. Knott, of Connecticut, captured the ship *Charles and Sally*, the snow *Ann*, and the brigs *Caroline* and *John*. These vessels were laden with rum, sugar, and fustic. Of the other private armed vessels sailing from Connecticut the *Washington*, *Warren*, *Spy*, and *Shark* were the most successful. In September, 1776, the *Washington*, Captain Odiorne, took the brig *Georgia* and a schooner, both laden with rum and sugar, besides making prize of a snow having a cargo of cannon aboard.

The *Warren*, Captain Coas, in April took the sloop *Betsey and Polly*, and in the following June, while under the command of Captain Phillips, seized a

8

transport armed with four guns and having on board
one hundred soldiers. Several weeks later this privateer captured the ship *Isaac and Picary*, and in August she captured a brig carrying three guns and ten
swivels.   In this prize was a quantity of gold dust
and ivory.   Before the close of the year the *Warren*
herself fell into the hands of the British frigate *Liverpool*. The *Spy* and *Shark* cruised for some time with
Captain Hopkins' squadron, and in August, 1776, the
former took the ship *Hope*, and in the following
month the schooner *Mary and Elizabeth*, both prizes
being laden with coffee and sugar.   In 1779 the *Shark*
made four prizes.

Of the privateers that put to sea early in the war
those from Pennsylvania seem to have met with the
greatest success. The *Chance*, a little sloop mounting
four guns, under the command of Captain J. Adams,
in May, 1776, took the valuable ship *Lady Juliana*.
The 24-gun privateer *Cornet*, about the same time,
while off St. Kitts, fell in with a heavily armed British merchantman, and for three hours engaged her at
close quarters, when the Englishmen managed to
escape with the loss of their mizzenmast.

The audacity of Captain S. Cleaveland, of the brig
Despatch, is typical.   This vessel left Philadelphia
without a gun aboard, her commander taking his
chances of capturing some kind of an armament on
the passage across the Atlantic or of purchasing guns
in France. Captain Cleaveland had not been to sea
many days before he captured a vessel, and, transferring the guns to his own ship, continued his cruise.

The 12-gun brig *General Mifflin*, Captain J. Hamilton, in 1776 made directly for British waters, where
she took several valuable vessels, one of them being a
ship with a cargo of wine. On her return passage
the *General Mifflin* fell in with a British privateer
carrying eighteen guns and eighty men. An action
was immediately begun, and the Englishmen, after
having sustained a loss of twenty-two killed or

wounded, including their commander, surrendered. The American casualties were thirteen.

In October of the same year the *General Montgomery*, a brig of twelve guns and one hundred men, under Captain Montgomery, came across a fleet of one hundred merchantmen, convoyed by several British war ships. By adroit maneuvering the privateer managed to cut out one of the merchantmen, the ship *Thetis*, with a cargo of rum and sugar.

Other privateers commissioned from Pennsylvania that got to sea early in the war were the 6-gun brig *Nancy*, the 14-gun snow *Ranger*, and the 14-gun brig *Sturdy Beggar*. The *Nancy*, on June 29, 1776, was chased ashore near Cape Henry by a British cruiser. After getting a portion of their cargo and powder on land the Americans blew the *Nancy* up. The *Ranger*, Captain Hudson, captured two storeships laden with military supplies. The *Sturdy Beggar*, in May, 1778, was captured, with eight other American vessels, in Croswell Creek by an English force consisting of two schooners, four gunboats, four galleys, and about twenty flatboats, under the command of Captain Henry, of the Royal Navy, and Major Maitland.

Besides her privateers Pennsylvania had a number of galleys built especially for river defense. They were armed with two or three guns each and carried from twenty to fifty men. These boats were constructed under a resolution passed by the Pennsylvania Council of Safety, July 6, 1775, under which Robert White and Owen Biddle were appointed a committee to attend to the construction of these gunboats and to prepare machines for the defense of the Delaware. The first of these boats to be launched was the *Bull Dog*, built by the Messrs. Manuel, Jehu, and Benjamin George Eyre, for half a century well-known shipbuilders in Philadelphia. The *Bull Dog*, Captain Henderson, took the water July 26, 1775, and the others followed in rapid succession. They were the *Burke*, Captain Blair; the *Camden*, Captain Nicholas Biddle, afterward famous in the navy; the *Chatham*, Captain J. Montgomery; the *Congress*, Captain Hamilton; the *Convention*, Captain J. Rice; the *Delaware*, Captain Doughty; the *Dickinson*, Captain Rice; the *Effingham*, Captain Mears; the *Experiment*, Captain Thompson; the *Franklin*, Captain Biddle; the *Hancock*, Captain Moore; the *Spitfire*, Captain Grimes;

Colonel Jehu Eyre of the Philadelphia firm of ship-builders.

From a silhouette.

and the *Warren*. The *Spitfire*, on August 3, 1776, took part in the attack on the British war ships *Rose* and *Phœnix* in Hudson River. In this affair the *Spitfire* had one man killed and three wounded. Pennsylvania also had a fire ship called the *Ætna*, commanded by William Gamble. The *Ranger*, a craft hastily fitted for harbor defense, in October, 1775, under the orders of Captain Hume, captured a West India privateer. The vessel was carried by boarding, the English having some forty men killed or wounded before they surrendered.

Among the first privateers to get to sea from South Carolina was the 14-gun brig *Cornet*, Captain J. Turpin. This vessel sailed on her first cruise without instructions. On November 2, 1776, she captured the ship *Clarissa*, the schooner *Maria*, and the sloop *George*. The *Clarissa* was laden with lumber and had on board forty negroes.

New York, having her most available seaport in the hands of the enemy during the greater part of the war, did not send out her usual quota of armed craft. Some of her ships put to sea, however, and were successful. The sloop *Montgomery*, Captain William Rodgers, in 1776 captured two brigs, one schooner, and one sloop; while the privateer *Schuyler*, Captain J. Smith, in June took a ship having on board twenty prisoners. In August the *Schuyler* seized five other vessels and recaptured the *Nancy*. The galley *Whiting*, Captain McCleave, on August 3, 1776, took part in the attack on the British war ships *Rose* and *Phœnix*, the galley having one man killed and four wounded.

The only privateer from New Jersey that succeeded in getting to sea early in the war was the schooner *Enterprise*, Captain J. Campbell. In July and August, 1776, she captured the ship *Lancaster*, carrying four guns and sixteen men; the ship *Black Snake*, with a cargo of rum and sugar; the snow *James*, having twenty-three men and a cargo of molasses and rum, and the ship *Modesty*, laden with sugar. On July 22d the *Enterprise* captured the ship *Earl of Errol*, mounting six guns and having a cargo valued at one hundred thousand dollars. On the same day the *Enterprise* took the ship *Nevis* after a spirited action of one hour.

New Hampshire, in 1776, sent out the 12-gun brig *Putnam*, Captain J. Harman, which in one cruise captured a ship and four schooners. Other private armed craft sent out from Portsmouth in this year were the brig *Enterprise*, Captain D. Jackson; the 14-gun sloop *Harlequin*, Captain D. Shaw; the 6-gun schooner *McClary*, Captain R. Parker; and the 20-gun ship *Portsmouth*.

The privateers sent out from Rhode Island in 1776 were highly successful. Between July 1st and August 30th the *Diamond*, Captain N. Chase, captured the ships *Jane*, *Star and Garter*, and *Friendship*, the brig *Mars*, and the snow *Portland*. These vessels had cargoes of cocoa, fustic, rum, and sugar. In August the privateer *Eagle*, Captain Paine, took the ship *Venus*, with a cargo of mahogany, shells, etc. She also seized another ship (name not given) laden with rum, sugar, cotton, and the brig *Virginia*, with a cargo of tobacco. In the following October the brig *Favorite*, Captain Coffin, captured a ship and a schooner, with cargoes of pimento, rum, and sugar. Two years later the same privateer, while under the orders of Captain Lamb, captured a ship armed with sixteen guns having a cargo of logwood. The 10-gun brig *Industry*, Captain Child, in 1776, captured a brig, and then had a drawn battle with a ship of ten guns. The action lasted two hours, with a loss of two killed and six wounded on the part of the American. In October the 16-gun ship *Montgomery*, Captain Bucklon, captured the ships *Rover*, *Isabella*, and *Harlequin* and the brigs *Devonshire* and *Henry*. The 12-gun brig *Putnam*, Captain Ferguson, took four ships; and the same vessel, while under the command of Captain C. Whipple, captured two snows, one brig, and had a severe action with an armed ship. The *Independence*, of ten guns, also made a cruise under Captain Thomas Whipple.

CHAPTER VI.

NAVY OFFICERS IN PRIVATEERS.

WE can better appreciate the high plane to which privateering had been raised, at the hands of American seamen in the war for independence, when we remember that some sixty of our most formidable privateers were commanded by men who were, or soon afterward became, captains in the navy. In fact, the privateer service became the training school of our embryo navy, not only in supplying officers, but seamen. The conditions of early privateering were such as to develop an exceptionally capable group of officers, and not a little of the marvelous success attained by the infant navy of the United States is directly traceable to this circumstance.

Among the first of our navy officers to engage in privateering was Lieutenant Joshua Barney.[1] Barney had been taken prisoner early in the war, and after a confinement of nearly five months in the

---

[1] For Barney's brilliant services in the War of 1812 see Maclay's History of the Navy, vol. i, pp. 583–585.

prison ships at New York he was exchanged for an English officer of equal rank—the first lieutenant of the British frigate *Mermaid*, which had been compelled, by the approach of the French fleet, in July, 1778, to run ashore on the Jersey side of the Delaware. Making his way to Baltimore, Barney secured the command of a trading vessel, which was described as " a fine little schooner, armed with two guns and eight men," having a cargo of tobacco bound for St. Eustatia. This craft had a short and unfortunate career. In going down Chesapeake Bay she fell in with an English privateer carrying four guns and sixty men, and after a running fight of a few minutes was overtaken and carried by boarding, the Americans having one man killed and two wounded. As the Englishman had no desire to incumber himself with prisoners, he landed them at Cinapuxent, on the eastern shore of the Chesapeake, and sailed away with the prize.

Lieutenant Barney returned to Baltimore, where, after several weeks spent in a vain endeavor to secure another vessel, he met his old commander, Captain Isaiah Robinson, whose creditable career in the navy also has been recorded.[1] These two officers soon came to an agreement by which Robinson was to secure the command of a privateer and Barney was to serve in her as first officer. Much difficulty was found in securing a suitable vessel, and still more in getting the necessary arms, ammunition, and men, so that it was not until February, 1779, that they were able to leave Alexandria on a private cruise. The craft they secured was the brig *Pomona*, carrying twelve guns, of varying calibers, and a crew of thirty-five men. She was loaded with tobacco consigned to Bordeaux.

The adventures of these two navy officers began on the third day after clearing the Capes, when they

---

[1] See Maclay's History of the Navy, vol. i, p. 45.

were discovered by a vessel and chased. As Captain Robinson's first object was to get the cargo of tobacco safely to France, he made every endeavor to avoid the stranger, but she proved to be a remarkably fast sailer. At eight o'clock in the evening, a full, unclouded moon giving the chase every opportunity, the stranger came within hailing distance, and, running up English colors, asked, " What ship is that? " The only answer Robinson made was to show his flag, which the Englishman immediately ordered down.

The *Pomona* then delivered her broadside, which brought down the enemy's fore-topsail, cut away some of their rigging, and apparently caused much surprise and confusion on board. The Englishman responded with his battery, and a running fight was kept up until nearly midnight. Early in the fight the enemy discovered that the Americans had no stern gun ports, and availing themselves of this they maneuvered for positions off the *Pomona's* stern and quarters where she could not return their fire. As an evidence of the confusion into which the enemy had been thrown by the first broadside from the *Pomona*, it was noted that, with all their advantage of position, the English gunners were able to fire only one or two shots every half hour. Noting this, Robinson caused a port to be cut in his stern and a long 3-pounder whipped up from the gun deck and run out of it.

This was accomplished about midnight, when the Englishmen were drawing near for another shot. Apparently they had not discovered the shift in the *Pomona's* armament, for they drew quite near, and received such a discharge of grape that they hauled off and did not again come within gunshot that night.

The light of day showed the Americans that the stranger was a brig of sixteen guns, and as several officers could be seen through her ports wearing

uniforms, it was believed that she was a regular
cruiser. Afterward it was learned the stranger was
only a privateer, and her officers had resorted to the
trick of donning uniform and displaying themselves
in conspicuous places, so as to lead the Americans
to believe that they were contending against one of
the king's cruisers. This, the English thought, would
show the Americans the hopelessness of the struggle,
and would induce them to surrender without further
resistance. But Captain Robinson was not to be
frightened by gold buttons and epaulets, and when
about sunrise the stranger ran close under the
Pomona's stern for the purpose of boarding the
Americans made every preparation for giving her a
warm reception. The solitary 3-pounder in the stern
was loaded with grapeshot, and the charge was
topped off by a crowbar stuck into the muzzle.

Just as the English were about to board Barney,
with his own hand, discharged this gun, and with
such accurate aim that the British were completely
baffled in their attempt, their foresails and all their
weather foreshrouds being cut away. The loss of
these supports compelled the Englishman to wear in
order to save his foremast from going by the board.
This maneuver gave the Americans an excellent
chance for raking, and promptly going about Robinson delivered an effective broadside. The enemy did
not again return to the attack, so the *Pomona* resumed
her course, arriving in Bordeaux without further incident.

Captain Robinson afterward learned that his antagonist was the privateer *Rosebud*, Captain Duncan,
with a crew of one hundred men, of whom forty-seven
were killed or wounded. The *Rosebud* made her way
to New York, where Duncan "charged" the Americans with "unfair fighting in using langrage." The
only langrage Captain Robinson used on this occasion was the crowbar referred to.

No better illustration of the dare-devil spirit of

our privateersmen can be had than in the manner
many of them put to sea. Any old tub of a craft, if
nothing better offered, would do them, and if there
were no cannon the junk shops were ransacked for
old muskets, pistols, blunderbusses, swords, hand-
spikes, and knives, and the commander went to sea in
the hope of capturing merchantmen and transferring
their armaments to his ship. Many of our privateers
put to sea in this condition and met with astonishing success.

The *Pomona* sailed from the Chesapeake with guns,
it is true, but with less than she was pierced for, and
the cannon she did carry were of varying and small
calibers, which made it difficult to secure the proper-
sized shot. She also started out with only half her
complement, hoping to make up the full number
from prospective prisoners. As we have seen, she
did not succeed in making any prizes on her way
across the Atlantic, but on reaching Bordeaux Captain Robinson sold his cargo of tobacco, and from
the proceeds loaded with brandy and purchased
eighteen 6-pounders, the regular armament of the
brig, and a sufficient quantity of powder and shot.
He also succeeded in enlisting thirty-five additional
men, raising his complement to seventy. Sailing from
Bordeaux in the early part of August, 1779, in this
much-improved condition, the *Pomona* shaped her
course for the return passage to America.

One morning at daylight, when about halfway
across the ocean, Captain Robinson made a sail which,
from her peculiar maneuvers, seemed to be " feeling " the *Pomona's* strength. By the time the sun rose
the vessels had come within gunshot and several
broadsides were exchanged, but at the end of the first
half hour the stranger crowded on sail before the wind
to escape. The Americans were promptly in chase,
but being heavily laden the *Pomona* steadily fell behind, although she managed to keep the enemy in
sight all that day.

Toward evening a squall of wind and rain came on. Availing himself of this Captain Robinson crowded on canvas, and on again coming up with the stranger exchanged several more broadsides, the Englishman still endeavoring to escape. During the night the chase was lost sight of, but on the following morning she was made out, in the somewhat thick weather, four or five miles ahead, it then being calm. Captain Robinson now got out his sweeps, and by dint of hard rowing managed to get alongside of his foe for the third time, when the stranger, without waiting for another broadside, surrendered at the

John Barry

first summons. The prize was found to be an English privateer carrying sixteen guns, 6- and 9-pounders, and a crew of seventy men. Twelve of her people had been killed and a number wounded, besides which she had been seriously injured in her hull, rigging, and spars. The only man killed in the *Pomona* was a lad who had shipped at Bordeaux as a passenger. Two of the Americans were wounded. Lieutenant Barney, with a prize crew, took possession of the privateer, and both vessels arrived safely at Philadelphia in the following October. Both Captain Robinson and Lieutenant Barney realized a handsome fortune in this audacious venture.[1]

One of the most successful commanders in the

---

[1] For the continuation of Barney's brilliant career in the privateer service, see chapters xii and xiv, Part First.

navy of the Revolution was Captain John Barry.[1]
This enterprising officer, like most of his brothers in
the service, at times was unable to get a command
in the navy, and employed the interim by privateering. Some of the armed vessels placed under his
orders were the 10-gun brig *Delaware*, the 6-gun brig
General Montgomery, and the 24-gun ship *Rover*. A
packet ship mounting six guns, called the *Rover*, was
captured by an American privateer in 1779 under the
command of Captain Sweet.

Equally successful was Alexander Murray, who
served with such distinction as a captain in the navy
during the wars with France and Tripoli.[2] While
commanding the privateer *Prosperity*, a brig carrying
five 6-pounders and twenty-five men, Captain Murray, in 1781, sailed for St. Croix with a cargo of tobacco. When a few days out he fell in with a British
privateer of fourteen guns, and after two hours of
hard fighting drove her off. The enemy made several
attempts to board, but were repelled with great loss.
The *Prosperity* was so injured in this action that soon
afterward she lost her masts, and it was only with
great difficulty that Murray reached St. Thomas.
Here he refitted, and taking on board a full armament
of fourteen guns, he sailed for the United States.
When off Port Royal he captured a British packet
ship.

Captain Murray also commanded the privateers
Columbus, the *General Mercer*, the *Revenge*, each of ten
guns, and the 12-gun brig *Saratoga*. In the *Saratoga*
Murray captured an English cutter of ten guns and
fifty-two men. On this occasion Captain Murray was
assisted by Silas Talbot, of the navy. The *Saratoga*,
in 1779, had just taken the English brig *Chance*, when
the *Argo*, Captain Talbot, hove in sight, and after closing upon the cutter carried her by boarding, the Amer-

---

[1] For Barry's naval career, see Maclay's History of the Navy, vol. i,
pp. 39, 42, 43, 92-94, 145-147.

[2] See Maclay's History of the Navy, vol. i, pp. 165, 167, 187, 197, 235.

icans having four killed and several wounded. In the
following year Murray, then commanding the *Revenge*, cut out a brig from a convoy of fifty sail. Arm-
ing his prize and placing a good crew aboard, Captain
Murray continued his cruise in company with his
prize as a "commodore." Soon afterward he fell in
with another American privateer, when the little
squadron was attacked by three English privateer
schooners in company with an armed ship and a brig,
one of the first instances of a "fleet action" we have
in which privateers were the sole participants. Soon
realizing that they were dealing with ships better
stored with shot and powder than with rich merchandise, the American and British privateersmen desisted and resumed their search for more tempting
prizes. While cruising on the Newfoundland Banks
the *Revenge* captured a British privateer. Then
standing for the English coast, Captain Murray was
chased and captured by a frigate.

Perhaps the most successful of all the navy officers who served their apprenticeship in the privateers of the Revolution was Thomas Truxtun, whose
battles with two French frigates, a few years later,
won for him imperishable renown.[1] We first note
Truxtun in the 10-gun ship *Independence*, of Pennsylvania. In 1777 he captured a ship having a cargo of
sugar. This merchantman was armed with sixteen
guns, and did not surrender without a stout resistance. While in the *Independence* Truxtun also captured a brig and a sloop with cargoes of rum, etc.
Two years later we find him in command of the
armed ship *Andrew Caldwell*, of ten guns, which craft
he shortly exchanged for the fine 24-gun ship *Mars*.
In the latter Truxtun cruised some time in the British Channel, making a number of prizes which were
sent into Quiberon Bay, France.

[1] See Maclay's History of the Navy, vol. i, pp. 160, 165, 176, 177-183,
193-197, 233.

So great had been the success of Captain Truxtun that in 1781 he was intrusted with the perilous task of convoying across the Atlantic Mr. Barclay, our consul-general to France. The splendid 20-gun privateer *St. James*, having a complement of one hundred men, was placed under his command, William Jones, afterward the Secretary of the Navy, serving in her as third officer. It seems that the British had learned of the proposed sailing of Mr. Barclay for France, and being especially anxious to intercept him they sent out a sloop of war from New York for the express purpose of capturing him. How accurately informed the enemy were of our secret movements is shown by the fact that this sloop of war fell in with the *St. James* a short time after she cleared land. A severe action was immediately begun, which resulted in the Englishman

being forced to haul off, while the privateer continued her way to France. Having successfully performed this hazardous service, Truxtun assumed the command of the 14-gun ship *Commerce*, with a crew of fifty men. In December, 1782, the *Commerce*, while at sea, had an action with a British brig of sixteen guns and seventy-five men and a schooner of fourteen guns and eighty men. Notwithstanding the disparity of forces, Truxtun prepared to give battle, and had been sharply engaged with one of these vessels for twenty minutes, when a frigate hove in sight and compelled the *Commerce* to make all sail to escape. In this battle the Americans had one man killed and two wounded, while the loss of the British is placed at fourteen killed and twenty-four wounded.

Stephen Decatur, Sr., the father of one of the heroes of the War of 1812, commanded five different privateers in the Revolution. The younger Decatur also served in some of these craft, and received that training which in later years did so much to make our naval officers respected and feared the world over. The vessels commanded by the elder Decatur were the *Comet, Fair American, Retaliation, Rising Sun,* and *Royal Louis.* It was in the last ship that Decatur made his greatest reputation as a sea warrior. The *Royal Louis* carried twenty-two guns, and is credited with a complement of two hundred men—a veritable

corvette. In July, 1781, the *Royal Louis* had a desperate action with the British cruiser *Active,* and took her only after heavy loss of life on both sides. This was only one of the many instances in which our privateers attacked and captured the king's cruisers.[1] For these brilliant services Stephen Decatur, Sr., was taken into the navy as a captain.

Daniel McNeil, noted alike for his eccentricities of character and bravery as an officer, had the honor, in 1778, while in command of the 20-gun privateer *General Mifflin,* to receive a salute from the French admiral at Brest. This so offended the British ambassador that he threatened to leave the country. The *General Mifflin* then made several captures near the British coast, one of her prizes being a ship laden with wine. On her homeward passage from France the *General*

[1] For the subsequent career of Stephen Decatur, Sr., see Maclay's History of the Navy, vol. i, pp. 165, 169, 385.

Mifflin had a severe action with a British privateer of eighteen guns and eighty men. The Englishmen finally surrendered, having had their commander and twenty-two men killed or injured. McNiell's next command in the privateer service was the 10-gun ship *Ulysses*. In 1782 we find him in command of the 6-gun brig *Wasp*, with a complement of twenty men.

Two other navy officers who served in privateers must be specially noticed, Daniel Waters and George Little. Waters, in 1778, commanded the 16-gun ship *Thorn*, in which vessel he gave battle to the British 16-gun brig *Governor Tryon*, Captain Stebbins, a Government craft. She had in company the 18-gun brig *Sir William Erskine*, Captain Hamilton, another king's ship. Waters had received his commission because of his extraordinary attack on the British troopship *Defense* in 1776,[1] and in the present instance he showed himself to be a privateersman of true mettle. He closed on both the British vessels at the same time, and after a spirited action of two hours compelled them to surrender, Captain Stebbins being among the many killed. On his homeward passage Waters, after an action of fifty minutes, captured the English ship *Spartan*, mounting eighteen guns and having a complement of ninety-seven men. Just before gaining Boston harbor with his three prizes, Waters had the misfortune to lose the *Governor Tryon*, that vessel escaping under cover of night. The *Sir William Erskine* and *Spartan*, however, were brought safely into port.

George Little, who commanded the *Boston* in her remarkable action with the French corvette *Berceau*, 1800,[2] was in charge of the 13-gun privateer sloop *Winthrop* during the latter part of the war for independence. In his first cruise in this vessel Little

---

[1] See Maclay's History of the Navy, vol. i, pp. 49, 50.

[2] Ibid., vol. i, pp. 208-213.

9

captured two English privateers, and soon after cut
out the British armed brig *Meriam* that was lying in
the Penobscot with a prize sloop. The *Winthrop* made
several other considerable prizes before the close of
the war, among them being an 8-gun schooner which
had first been chased ashore. Captain Little had as
his first officer in the *Winthrop* Edward Preble, who
afterward took part in our
early operations in the Mediterranean.

Some other navy officers
who commanded privateers
in this struggle were David
Porter, in the *Aurora* and the
Delight; Nicholas Biddle, in
the *Camden* and *General Moul-
trie*; Dudley Saltonstall, in
the *Minerva*; Charles Alexander, in the *Active* and *Elizabeth*; Hoysted Hacker, in the
Buccaneer; John Rodgers, in
the *General Smallwood*; John
Burroughs Hopkins, in the *Lee* and the *Success*;
Samuel Tucker, in the *Live Oak* and *Thorn*; James
Sever, in the *Pluto* and the *Rambler*; and Stephen
Cassin, in the *Rising Sun* and the *Vengeance*.

CHAPTER VII.

CAPTAIN SILAS TALBOT.

FEW privateersmen of the Revolution had a more distinguished career than Silas Talbot. Born of poor parents in Dighton, Massachusetts, young Talbot, at the age of twelve, engaged in a small coasting vessel as a cabin boy, and rapidly rose in his profession, until, in 1772, when twenty-one years old, he had accumulated enough money to build for himself a house in Providence, Rhode Island. On June 28, 1775, he was commissioned a captain in a Rhode Island regiment commanded by Colonel Hitchcock, and took part in the operations before Boston which led to the evacuation of that place by the British, March 17, 1776. While on his way to New York with the American army, Talbot stopped

Esek Hopkins.

at New London, at which port Captain Esek Hopkins had just arrived after his successful expedition to the Bahamas. Hopkins applied to Washington for two hundred volunteers to assist his squadron in reaching Providence, and Talbot was one of the first to offer himself. He proceeded in the squadron to the desired haven, and then, with his men, rejoined the army before New York.

At that time several fire ships were in course of

construction, which it was hoped would destroy some of the vessels of the British fleet then at anchor near New York. When these vessels were nearly ready, Captain Talbot and Ensign Thomas, of the same regiment—the latter also having been a seaman—applied for and were placed in command of two of these fire craft. When Washington retreated to Harlem Heights, the British fleet moved up Hudson River, the American fire ships keeping just ahead of them and anchoring above Fort Washington. Here they remained three days, when Talbot received a letter from Major Anderson directing him to take the first opportunity to destroy the British vessels with his fire ships. About this time three of the enemy's vessels anchored seven miles above the city, with the view of turning the right wing of the American army.

The following night proving fair, Captain Talbot, about two o'clock in the morning, weighed anchor, and, standing toward one of the ships, spread fresh priming on all the trains leading to the fire barrels and sprinkled quantities of turpentine over the combustible material that had been placed aboard. It was intended to set fire to the mass from the cabin, but in order that the flames might spread more readily Talbot prevailed upon one of his men, named Priestly—an expert swimmer—to lie down on the forecastle with a lighted match so as to fire the trains the instant they fouled the enemy's ship. Selecting the largest of the three ships, the 64-gun ship of the line *Asia*, Talbot availed himself of the darkest hour, just before daylight, and moved directly upon her. The British were found to be on the alert, and when the approaching fire ship was still some distance off a boy aboard the *Asia* discovered her and gave the alarm. The enemy promptly opened a rapid fire, and, although several shots passed through the fire ship, no serious damage was done. In a few minutes the vessels fouled, matches were applied to the fore and aft trains at the same instant, and so rapid was the progress of the flames that they burst forth from all sides, while Talbot himself was compelled to grope around in the fire and received severe burns before he found the sally port through which he and his men were to escape. The brave Priestly, who had undertaken the perilous task of giving direct fire to the trains, was compelled to jump overboard, but was rescued by the boat.

The greatest confusion prevailed aboard the *Asia*. Guns were fired while boats from the other British war craft put off to her assistance and to intercept the daring adventurers. The brilliant flames from the fire ship soon illuminated the river for miles, rendering the little boat containing the Americans a fair target. All the English ships opened on her with round and grape shot, but owing to the excitement of the moment only two small shot passed through the frail craft. After great efforts the British succeeded in extinguishing the flames, but the enterprise had made such an impression upon their commanders that they immediately slipped their cables, and, falling down the river, anchored below New York. Captain Talbot and his men reached the Jersey shore in safety, but he was so burned and blistered by the fire as to be blinded, and his men led him through the woods to English Neighborhood. " Accommodations were solicited for him there at several houses, but to no purpose, the people alleging generally that his appearance was so horrible he would frighten their children. At last a poor widow who lived in a small log hut that had but one room in it took him in, where he was laid on the floor and covered with a blanket, and his poor hostess procured for him every consolation in her power. But in the course of the day General Knox and Dr. Eustis, passing that way and hearing of his distressing situation—for he was at that time deprived of his sight—they called in to see him, and the doctor gave directions for his more proper treatment. When the captain was a little recovered he left this poor but hospitable abode and went to Hackensack, where he remained till he was able to join his regiment."[1] For this gallant affair Congress promoted Talbot to the rank of major. Ensign Thomas brought his fire ship alongside a British tender of fourteen guns in Tappan Bay and destroyed her, but the gallant officer himself perished in the flames of his vessel.

In the British attack on Fort Mifflin in November, 1777, where Talbot was stationed, he received a musket ball through his left wrist. Notwithstanding the excruciating pain, he continued at his post with a handkerchief tied round the injured part. Soon afterward a ball penetrated his hip, and, being totally disabled, Talbot was placed in a boat and transferred to Red Bank, and thence to the hospital at Princeton. Receiving permission from General Washington to return to his home in Rhode Island until his wounds were healed, Talbot proceeded to Providence.

In the campaign of 1778 a French fleet, under Count d'Estaing, appeared on the American coast, and an expedition was planned to drive the British out of Rhode Island. In this effort the Americans were commanded by General Sullivan, while the English garrison was under the orders of Sir Robert Pigot. The first step to be taken by the Americans was to construct a large number of flat-bottom boats, in which the army could be transferred from the

---

[1] Caritat's Life of Silas Talbot.

mainland to Rhode Island. Major Talbot was ordered to superintend this work, and in a short time
had eighty-six boats in readiness, sixteen of which
were built in one day, and calked by candlelight
in an open field the following night. "Major Talbot, by the middle of the night, put everything
in train for having all ready by the next morning;
and then, being worn out with fatigue and want
of rest for several days, laid down under one of the
boats, that the dew might not fall upon him, and
slept soundly, notwithstanding the calkers worked
over his head part of the time to finish the boat." [1]
The embarkation of the American army began August 9th, and on gaining the island began its march
southward toward the British garrison at Newport.
Being ordered to ride ahead so as to reconnoiter,
our gallant major came in sight of the enemy's fort,
when he discovered three British artillerymen in a
garden foraging. He leaped his horse over the wall
and threatened the men with instant death if they
attempted to move. The soldiers, mistaking Talbot
for a British officer, began apologizing for their absence from the fort, and begged that they might not
be punished, diplomatically offering to share their
forage with him. Taking their side arms, Talbot
marched them up the road before him into the
American lines.

Owing to the failure of the French fleet to co-
operate with the Americans, the attack on Newport
was not made, and on August 28th our army began
its retreat to the mainland. When the French ships
first appeared off Newport, July 25th, the English
burned several of their men-of-war and sank the
frigate *Flora*, at that time heaved down on the beach
for cleaning. This step opened to the Americans the
water passages on each side of Rhode Island, which
were of inestimable advantage. With a view of

---

[1] Caritat's Life of Silas Talbot.

again closing these channels, the British, after the departure of the French vessels for Boston, converted a stout brig of some two hundred tons into a galley. Her upper deck was removed, and on the

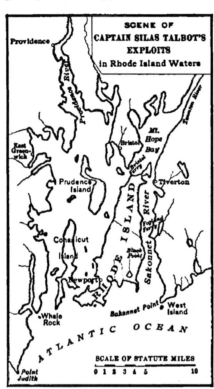

lower deck eight 12-pounders from the *Flora* were mounted, besides ten swivels, and being provided with strong boarding nettings, and manned by forty-five men, she became a formidable auxiliary to the British land forces. This craft, named in honor of the British commanding general, Sir Robert Pigot, was placed in charge of Lieutenant Dunlop, of the British navy, and on taking a station in the eastern passage succeeded in completely interrupting the important commerce carried on through that channel.

Determined to capture or destroy this mischievous vessel, Talbot early in October obtained General Sullivan's permission to fit out a craft and call for volunteers. The small coasting schooner *Hawk*, of seventy tons, was secured, and in two days was prepared for the enterprise with two 3-pounders and sixty men under Talbot, Lieutenant Baker being second in command. These daring men promptly made sail, and had proceeded about eight miles below Providence when the wind failed, so that they were obliged to remain at anchor all that night and the following day. In order to reach the *Pigot*, Talbot was compelled to run past two British earthworks, one of which was erected on the south side of the passage at Bristol Ferry, while the other was on the west side of Fogland Ferry. The channel opposite these batteries is about three quarters of a mile wide.

On the following night Talbot, favored with a good breeze, got under way, and by keeping as near as possible to the opposite shore passed the fort at Bristol Ferry. He was discovered and fired upon, but fortunately all the enemy's missiles fell wide of the *Hawk*, and she ran about six miles up Taunton River, anchoring on the west side of Mount Hope Bay, some fifteen miles from the *Pigot*, the direction of the wind at that time rendering it impracticable to approach Fogland Ferry. As the breeze failed to serve on the following morning, Talbot, leaving Baker in charge of the *Hawk*, proceeded in his boat to the east side of Sakonnet River. He landed alone, and securing a horse rode down the shore to a point opposite the galley, where with a good glass he reconnoitered her at his leisure. This intrepid officer soon discovered that she was a far more formidable craft than he had been led to believe, her boarding nettings being very high, and were carried entirely around, making it exceeding difficult to take her by boarding—the main reliance of the Americans in the proposed attack. Yet, in spite of the unexpected difficulties involved in the attempt, Talbot determined to move against the *Pigot* that evening. Returning to the *Hawk*, he asked for and received from Brigadier-General Cornell a reënforcement of fifteen men under Lieutenant Helm, of Rhode Island. When the men had got aboard, Major Talbot called all hands, and for the first time fully explained his plans for taking the *Pigot*, concluding his remarks with an exhortation, urging the men to keep cool, and making a considerable personal reward for the man who first gained the galley's deck. The men responded to the harangue with cheers, and promptly at nine o'clock the *Hawk* got under way and proceeded down the river.

In making his preparations for the attack, Talbot showed true Yankee ingenuity by lashing a kedge anchor fast to the end of his jib boom, so that when the *Hawk* ran against the *Pigot* the kedge would tear a wide chasm in the nettings. A grapnel also was held in readiness to throw aboard the enemy so as to hold the vessels together. As the Americans approached the fort at Fogland Ferry, Talbot lowered his sails so that the *Hawk* would drift past under bare poles, thereby reducing the chances of discovery. On the successful passage of this fort undiscovered largely depended the ultimate success of the enterprise; for the *Pigot* lay only four miles below, near Black Point, and would have been warned of the approaching danger by the sound of guns. So onward in the darkness glided the silent *Hawk*, with every sound hushed and every light carefully screened, and though she drew so near the earthworks as to enable her people to clearly distinguish the sentinels every time they passed the light at the window of the barrack she continued on her way down stream undetected.

Having safely passed the fort, Talbot again set his sails, and stood swiftly down the river with all hands at quarters. Owing to a possible overanxiety Talbot did not gain a view of the *Pigot* as soon as he had expected, and, fearing that he had passed her in the darkness, he came to anchor, and, getting into his boat, pulled with muffled oars down the stream and went in search of his enemy. He had not proceeded far when the galley suddenly loomed up directly ahead. To make absolutely sure of success this discreet officer, instead of exhibiting undue haste by pulling immediately back to his craft, moved closer to the *Pigot*, and having satisfied himself as to how she rode with the tide and wind, returned to the *Hawk*. Getting his schooner under way again, Talbot bore directly down on the galley. Soon her dark outlines were distinguished in the surrounding gloom, and almost at the same instant a challenge was heard across the water. The hail was repeated several times, and as no answer was made a small volley of musketry was delivered at the Americans, which occasioned little or no injury, as the crew had been ordered to lie down behind the bulwarks.

Before the British could discharge a single cannon the *Hawk* had fouled them, the kedge tearing a great hole in the boarding nettings, while the grapnel, being promptly swung aboard, held the two craft together. The Americans then rose, and, giving a volley of small arms, followed Lieutenant Helm's lead in boarding the galley. In a short time every Englishman was driven below excepting their gallant commander, Lieutenant Dunlop, who appeared on deck in his underclothing, and began preparations for a desperate resistance. He was soon overpowered, however, and when informed that his craft had been taken by a small sloop carrying only two 3-pounders, manned exclusively by soldiers—though many of them had been seamen—burst into tears, saying that he "fancied himself to stand as fair for promotion as any lieutenant in the navy, but that now all those agreeable hopes were swept away." Major Talbot, in a magnanimous spirit, endeavored to console the crestfallen officer. Having ascertained that not a man on either side had been killed, Talbot sent his prisoners below, where they were secured by coiling the cables over the gratings, and, getting both vessels under way, ran into Stonington that evening, where the prisoners were

landed and marched to Providence on the following day.

"The good effects resulting from this well-
planned and bravely executed enterprise," said a
contemporary writer, "were numerous and extensive. The spirit of the people, which by the failure
of the late attempt on the English garrison at Newport had been greatly depressed, was raised, and
the intercourse by sea, which, to the immense preju-
dice of this part of the country, had long been shut
up, was now opened." For this handsome exploit
Congress promoted Talbot to the rank of lieutenant
colonel, while the General Assembly of Rhode Island
presented both Talbot and Helm with a sword.

Stimulated by his successes against the *Asia* and
Pigot, Talbot soon formed a plan for destroying the
50-gun ship *Renown*, which the enemy, late in 1778,
stationed off Rhode Island. An old, high-sided merchant ship, of about four hundred tons, was carried
down the river a few miles below Providence, and a
stage was built on her deck, as if for carrying cattle.
"This stage was calculated to be about seven feet
higher above the surface of the water than the upper tier of guns in the *Renown*, and was spread out
over the sides in order to facilitate boarding when
the two vessels lay close together, and its height
would not only enable the men to command the
decks of the enemy, but place them above the
fire of their guns. To drive the enemy from their
upper decks, the colonel provided a great number of
stout earthen pots, each of which held three pounds
of dry gunpowder and three hand grenades ready
charged. These fire pots were securely closed, and,
then, to preserve them from any accidental wet, covered with sheep or lamb skin, with the wool on the
outside. Over all were laid two pieces of slow match
that were so long that when lashed on with a cord
made a handle to hold it by, while the ends of the
match hung below the pot as much as twelve inches.

By repeated experiments the colonel found that any man of common strength could throw these pots to a distance of forty feet with considerable certainty. Their fall on the deck would infallibly break them and scatter the contents, when the fire of the slow match would communicate with the loose powder, and in an instant with the grenades. It was the colonel's design, in real action, to station one hundred men in a convenient part of his ship with one of these fire pots in each hand. He conceived that the explosion on the enemy's decks of two hundred pots, containing together six hundred pounds of dry powder, and the successive bursting of six hundred hand grenades, would in the night, when assisted by musketry fire from two hundred men and the shouts and huzzas of all, produce a terrible scene of destruction and alarm at the first outset, drive the enemy from their quarters, so that the boarding party might, without great difficulty, succeed in getting possession of the quarter-deck of the man-of-war."[1] Talbot also counted on, as a considerable item in the success of this enterprise, the reported lack of discipline aboard the *Renown*, he having learned from some prisoners who had been detained aboard this craft that her officers were especially negligent at night. On the evening selected for the attempt, the American vessel dropped six miles farther down the river, while a body of nearly four hundred men marched along the shore, abreast of her, ready to embark and take part in the attempt when all was ready. Unfortunately for the projectors of this daring scheme, the weather that night suddenly came on very cold, the ice forming so rapidly in the river as to prevent the land force from getting aboard, and when morning dawned it was found that the river was frozen over, holding both the *Renown* and the merchantman immovable all that winter.

[1] Carltat's Life of Silas Talbot.

To guard against any attack on the *Renown* over the ice, the British placed a large detachment of soldiers aboard her. When navigation opened in the spring the *Renown* was ordered from this station, her place being taken by a 44-gun ship, which anchored under the guns of the fort in Newport harbor. The fact of this vessel being anchored in a safer place induced Talbot to make an attempt upon her, as he reasoned that her people would be less vigilant than when stationed farther up the river. This enterprising officer again prepared the old merchantman, and with three hundred and fifty volunteers moved down Providence River. Unfortunately the pilot ran the ship hard-and-fast aground, and as she could not be floated again until the enemy would have been warned of the danger Talbot was obliged to return.

Observing the great success of privateers fitted out by the rebelling colonists, a number of Tories in New York transformed some of their merchantmen in that port into private cruisers and sent them out to prey on the coastwise trade, with the result that in a short time American commerce in the vicinity of New York was almost annihilated. This was especially the case in Long Island Sound and in the waters of Rhode Island. The effect of this Tory privateering, aided by the regular cruisers of the Royal Navy, was so injurious to the American cause that General Gates, commanding the Continental army in the northern department, reported to Washington that it was almost impossible to secure provisions. At Washington's suggestion Gates prepared the captured *Pigot* as a coast guard, while the little sloop *Argo*, of one hundred tons, was fitted with twelve 6-pounders, and being placed under the command of Colonel Talbot, with sixty volunteers from the army—most of whom had been seamen—sailed from Providence, in May, 1779, to cruise after the mischievous Tories. The *Argo* "was steered with a long tiller, but had no wheel; had a high bulkhead.

Her bulwarks also were very high. She had a wide stern, and her appearance altogether was like a clumsy Albany sloop."[1] Proceeding round the east end of Long Island, Talbot fell in with the privateer *Lively*, Captain Stout, of New York, mounting twelve 6-pounders. This craft was made out early in the morning, the *Argo* promptly giving chase. After a hard run of five hours, in which the Tory made every effort to avoid a fight, Talbot succeeded in getting up with her and compelled her to strike. She was sent into port. Three or four days after this the *Argo* sighted two English privateers, which proved to be from the West Indies, heavily laden and bound for New York. Both of them surrendered after the Americans were fairly alongside, and prize crews being thrown aboard they were carried into Boston.

Not only were the Tories in New York active in fitting out privateers, but those in Newport also sent out the stout brig *King George*, Captain Hazard, mounting fourteen 6-pounders and manned by eighty men. As this craft hailed from his native State, and had taken many American vessels, Talbot naturally was anxious to meet her, though he knew that she was more formidable than the sloop he commanded. " Captain Hazard was a native of Rhode Island, and had been universally esteemed till he took command of this privateer for the base purpose of plundering his neighbors and old friends. Whenever the *Argo* went out from Providence, Stonington, New London, or any other port in that quarter, where she occasionally ran in for the night, it was the common wish of the inhabitants that she might take or sink Captain Hazard."[2]

Captain Talbot soon had the satisfaction of gratifying this patriotic desire of the New Englanders; for on his second cruise, when about one hundred

---

[1] Caritat's Life of Silas Talbot.   [2] Ibid.

and twenty miles south of Long Island, the day
being exceptional, beautiful and calm, a vessel was
sighted about noon, which was discovered to be the
King George. The vessels gradually approached each
other, and when within a short distance Talbot
hailed, and to his great pleasure found his hail answered by Captain Hazard in person. The *Argo* was
promptly run alongside, and, delivering their broadside, the Americans boarded, and soon drove their

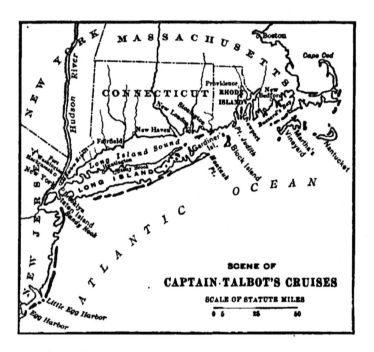

enemies below, not a man on either side being killed.
Placing a prize crew aboard the *King George*, Talbot
ordered her into New London, where she arrived
amid the cheers of the population—"even the
women, both old and young, expressed the greatest
joy." Soon after this most gratifying success the
Argo seized an American privateer which was in the
hands of a British crew and sent her into New Bed-

ford. In the same cruise Talbot captured the British merchant brig *Elliott*, from London for New
York, mounting six guns, and sent her into New
London. She had a valuable cargo of dry goods and
provisions.

This " army privateer " had now taken five vessels without serious fighting. Talbot had developed
his crew to the highest state of efficiency, and they
were anxious to test their mettle against that of a
worthy foe. Early one morning in August, when the
sloop was at sea, a sail was discovered, which soon
gave promise of a struggle. She was quickly made
out to be a large ship, armed and full of men. As
the stranger showed no disposition to avoid the *Argo*,
the two craft were soon within gunshot of each
other, the Americans at their cannon ready for action. After exchanging hails, and finding that they
were enemies, both vessels opened an animated fire
from their guns. The battle was fought within pistol shot, and lasted four hours and a half. At one
time the speaking trumpet which Colonel Talbot
held to his mouth was pierced by shot in two places,
and about the same time a cannon ball took off the
skirt of his coat. Evidently the *Argo* was getting
a real taste of a sea fight, for after the action had
lasted several hours nearly all the men stationed on
her quarter-deck were killed or wounded. Talbot
pluckily continued the fight, notwithstanding his
severe losses, and finally had the satisfaction of observing his opponent's mainmast fall. Upon this
the Englishmen surrendered and announced their
ship to be the privateer *Dragon*, of three hundred
tons, mounting fourteen 6-pounders and manned by
eighty men.

Just as the enemy's colors came down Talbot was
informed by one of his officers who had been stationed in the magazine below that the *Argo* was
sinking, the water in her hold having reached the
gun deck. At this alarming report Talbot promptly
10

ordered the sides of his sloop to be inspected, believing the cause of the inrushing waters to be shot holes. His surmise proved to be correct, and in a short time men were swung over the sides, who plugged the holes, after which all hands manned the pumps and succeeded in clearing the sloop of water. The *Dragon* was then manned and sent into New Bedford.

Scarcely had the American repaired damages when another sail was reported. This was the English privateer brig *Hannah*, of two hundred tons, armed with twelve 12-pounders and two 6-pounders. Although a vessel twice the size and force of the *Argo*, Colonel Talbot did not hesitate to attack her. Soon after the action began the American privateer *Macaroni*, Captain D. Keybold, of Pennsylvania, a brig of six guns and twenty men, drew near, upon which the *Hannah* surrendered. She was sent into New Bedford in company with the *Dragon*. "When the *Argo* returned to port with these last prizes she was so much shivered in her hull and rigging by the shot which had pierced her in the last two engagements that all who beheld her were astonished that a vessel of her diminutive size could suffer so much and yet get safely to port. The country people came down from a considerable distance, only to see Captain Talbot and his prizes and to count the shot marks about the *Argo*." [1] On September 17, 1779, Congress gave Talbot a commission as captain in the navy, and further declared that his pay as lieutenant colonel should continue until he could be employed by the marine committee.

After refitting, the *Argo* put to sea, and, skirting the southern coast of Long Island, appeared off Sandy Hook, where she fell in with the privateer *Saratoga*, Captain Munroe, of Providence. While these two vessels were cruising in company off this

---

[1] A contemporary account.

port, on a clear moonlight night, the English privateer *Dublin*, Captain Fagan, fitted out by the Tories
in New York, was discovered coming out. After a
short consultation between the American commanders, it was agreed that, in order to induce the *Dublin*
to give battle, the little *Argo* should boldly approach
Sandy Hook and challenge the Tories to action, the
Dublin carrying two more guns than the Rhode
Island sloop.   In accordance with this programme,
Talbot stood close in, and, after exchanging hails
with Captain Fagan, engaged him in a spirited fight.
For two hours the crews fought with great determination, the Americans wondering greatly at the
failure of their consort, the *Saratoga*, to come up to
their assistance as agreed upon. This circumstance
is explained as follows:

"The *Saratoga* was steered with a long wooden
tiller on common occasions, but in time of action
the wooden tiller was unshipped and put out of the
way, and she was then steered with an iron one
that was shipped into the rudder head from the
cabin. In the hurry of preparing for battle, this
iron tiller had been shoved into the opening of the
rudder case, but had not entered its mortise in the
rudder head at all, and the *Saratoga* went away
with the wind at a smart rate, to the surprise of
Captain Talbot and the still greater surprise of Captain Munroe, who repeatedly called to the helmsman:

" ' Hard a-weather, hard up there!'

" ' It is hard up, sir.'

" ' You lie, you blackguard! She goes away lask-
ing. Hard a-weather, I say again.'

" ' It is hard a-weather, indeed, sir,' was the only
reply the helmsman could make.

"Captain Munroe was astonished, and could not
conceive 'what the devil was the matter with his
vessel.' He took in the after-sails and made all
the headsail in his power. 'All' would not do, and

away she went. He was in the utmost vexation lest Captain Talbot should think him actually running away. At last one of his under officers suggested that possibly the iron tiller had not entered the rudder head, which on examination was found to be the case. The blunder was soon corrected, and the *Saratoga* was made to stand toward the enemy; and that some satisfaction might be made for his long absence Captain Munroe determined, as soon as he got up, to give them a whole broadside at once. He did so, and the *Dublin* immediately struck her colors." [1] The privateers carried their prize into Egg Harbor. The day following the capture of the *Dublin* the *Argo* seized the British merchant brig *Chance*, from London for New York, laden with a valuable cargo of stores for the English army. She was of about two hundred tons, and was carried into Egg Harbor.

A few days after this successful cruise the boy at the *Argo's* masthead reported a ship on the horizon. This was about ten o'clock in the morning, and, it being a clear day, the stranger was a great distance off when first noticed. Talbot made all sail in chase of the ship, when, discovering the sloop, the stranger made every effort to get away. All that day the pursuit was maintained, and by nightfall the Americans had gained only slightly. A clear night enabled the *Argo* to keep the stranger in sight, and early on the following morning she had her within long gunshot. Talbot now believed that she was a large transport bound for the West Indies, and, as he could not discover any guns or gun ports, he was extremely anxious to get up to her. The stranger was running dead before the wind, which was her best point of sailing, but about ten o'clock the wind died away. Being within gunshot the Americans made every preparation for battle, the

---

[1] Caritat's Life of Silas Talbot.

stranger all the time keeping her stern toward her pursuer, so that it was impossible to ascertain her force.

Just as the *Argo* was getting ready to open fire, the people in the chase were observed getting out their sweeps, and in a few minutes they had brought their broadside to bear, and to the astonishment of the Americans the stranger ran out thirty guns and delivered a terrific broadside. The little *Argo* had been chasing a ship of the line, and was now becalmed under her guns! Captain Talbot promptly set all hands at his sweeps. Fortunately the Englishmen fired with more haste than accuracy, though several of their shots hulled the sloop, killing one of the crew and wounding another in his right arm. By great exertions the Americans gradually worked their sloop to a position on the Englishman's quarter, and in the course of several hours managed to get beyond the reach of his guns, when the Americans, utterly exhausted, threw themselves on the deck and rested. Soon afterward a breeze sprang up and the *Argo* effected her escape. The stranger proved to be the *Raisonable*, which had been sent from New York with all possible speed to join the British fleet in the West Indies. Had it not been for this circumstance, the *Raisonable* might have captured the *Argo*. One of the English shots, a 32-pounder, penetrated the *Argo's* bulwark, smashed a boat, and spent itself on the deck.

Early in September, shortly after his adventure with the ship of the line, Captain Talbot discovered a sail standing toward him which was believed to be a British privateer. Soon the sail was made out to be a brig of considerable force, apparently using her utmost endeavor to overhaul the little sloop. Talbot allowed her to approach within pistol shot, when he exchanged hails. The brig then showed English colors, upon which Talbot displayed the Stars and Stripes, calling out:

"You must now haul down those British colors, my friend."

The commander of the brig, a Scotchman, coolly replied with a dignity and elaborateness worthy of a Chesterfield:

"Notwithstanding I find you an enemy, as I suspected, yet, sir, I believe I shall let them hang a little bit longer—with your permission—so fire away, Flanagan."

This was the signal for both vessels to open, and for nearly an hour a spirited cannonade was maintained, when the Scotchman, having all of his officers and many of his men killed or wounded, surrendered. The brig was the *Betsey*, a privateer pierced for sixteen guns, but mounting only twelve 6-pounders, with a crew of thirty-eight men. She was bound for New York, and had on board two hundred and fourteen puncheons of rum. Shortly after this Talbot captured a sloop from New Providence for New York, with a cargo of stores for the British army.

When Captain Talbot returned to Providence after this cruise he found orders awaiting him there from Congress to surrender the *Argo* to her owner, Nicholas Low, of New York. The sloop, when first fitted up as an "army privateer," belonged to Mr. Low, who, being in New York at the time, could not be reached by the American authorities, and the sloop was seized without his permission. This little vessel had taken, while under Talbot's command, twelve prizes, and had rendered inestimable service to the American cause, not only in ridding the southern part of the New England coast of Tory privateers and in taking valuable prizes, with three hundred prisoners, but in opening navigation so that the army under General Gates could receive much-needed supplies.

After his relinquishment of the command of the *Argo* every effort was made by the authorities to

secure another vessel for this successful privateersman.   In the summer of 1780 the private cruiser
General Washington, of Providence, mounting twenty
6-pounders and manned by one hundred and twenty
men, was fitted out and placed under Talbot's orders.
In his first cruise in this formidable vessel Talbot
captured a valuable merchantman from Charleston
for London, which was sent into Boston. Afterward
he took a British ship from the West Indies for Ireland, but this prize was recaptured before reaching
port.   Running up to Sandy Hook after this capture, Talbot inadvertently ran into the British fleet
under Admiral Arbuthnot. He made sail to escape,
hotly pursued. The wind soon came on to a strong
gale, and one of the Englishmen, a 74-gun ship of the
line, carried away her foreyard and dropped astern.
The ship of the line *Culloden*, however, continued the
chase, and finally captured the privateer. Captain
Talbot was taken aboard the *Robuste*, Captain Cosby
—afterward admiral—and was treated with courtesy. From this vessel Talbot was transferred to
a tender and taken to New York, and was confined in
the *Jersey*, where he received the usual ill treatment.
Toward the close of the year 1780, Talbot, with a
number of other American officers and seamen, was
placed in the ship of the line *Yarmouth*, Captain Lutwidge—afterward admiral—and taken to England.
The barbarous treatment of the prisoners aboard the
Yarmouth is narrated in the chapter " An Escape
from Old Mill Prison." After being incarcerated in
Plymouth Prison some months, Talbot, in October,
1781, was released and made his way to France.
Early in February, 1782, he sailed from Nantes for
Rhode Island in a brig commanded by Captain Fol-
ger. When fifteen days out the vessel was captured
by the British privateer *Jupiter*, Captain Craig, who
treated his prisoners with kindness. Falling in with
a British brig from Lisbon for New York, Captain
Craig placed Talbot aboard her, remarking that Tal-

bot had been a prisoner so long, and had suffered so much, that he ought to have the earliest opportunity to reach home. Arriving at New York, Talbot took passage in a lumber boat to Stony Brook, Long Island, from which place he walked some fifteen miles to a tavern kept by one Munroe, at Huntington. Remaining here a week, he crossed the Sound at night in a boat and landed at Fairfield, Connecticut, from which place he made his way overland to Providence. After the war Talbot was regularly attached to the navy, and commanded the famous frigate *Constitution* in 1799, when she had her merry race with a British war ship of the same class.[1] One of the torpedo boats of our new navy has been named after Silas Talbot.

---

[1] See Maclay's History of the Navy, vol. i, pp. 173, 174.

CHAPTER VIII.

RAPID GROWTH OF PRIVATEERING.

THAT our privateers were a powerful agency in bringing about the successful termination of the war for independence is seen in the marvelous development of that form of maritime warfare. While our Government war vessels steadily diminished in number and force, from thirty-one vessels, with five hundred and eighty-six guns, in 1776, to seven ships, with one hundred and ninety-eight guns, in 1782, our privateers increased at the following remarkable rate: One hundred and thirty-six vessels, with thirteen hundred and sixty guns, for the years 1775 and 1776; seventy-three vessels, with seven hundred and thirty guns, in 1777; one hundred and fifteen vessels, with eleven hundred and fifty guns, in 1778; one hundred and sixty-seven vessels, with two thousand five hundred and five guns, in 1779; two hundred and twenty-eight vessels, with three thousand four hundred and twenty guns, in 1780; four hundred and forty-nine vessels, with six thousand seven hundred and thirty-five guns, in 1781; and three hundred and twenty-three vessels, with four thousand eight hundred and forty-five guns, in 1782.

Another interesting feature of this extraordinary development of privateering was the rapid increase in the size and efficiency of the craft thus engaged. In the earlier part of the war any vessel, old or new, that could possibly be converted into a war craft was eagerly seized, a few guns mounted on her, and she was sent to sea with, in some cases, the most curious assemblage of men imaginable. Physicians, lawyers, army officers, politicians, staid merchants, and even ministers of the Gospel, were found in their complements; all seemingly carried away by the " craze for privateering."

As the war progressed, and as the profits from prizes enriched the owners of these craft, new, swifter, and better vessels were built expressly for this service, so that when, on the outbreak of hostilities, ten guns was considered a large armament for a privateer, and thirty to sixty men were deemed sufficient to man each, toward the latter part of the war vessels mounting twenty, and even twenty-six guns, and having complements of one hundred and fifty to two hundred men, were the rule rather than the exception. As the Government cruisers one by one fell into the hands of the enemy, or were lost by shipwreck, or were blockaded in our ports, their number rapidly diminished, and Congress frequently called upon our privateers to perform missions of national importance.

One of the first privateers to get to sea in 1778 was the 16-gun brig *Hazard*, Captain John Foster Williams, of Massachusetts. She captured a brig and a schooner. On the 16th of March, 1779, the *Hazard*, while cruising off St. Thomas, fell in with the English brig *Active*, Captain Sims, carrying eighteen guns, with sixteen swivels, and a complement of one hundred men. An action quickly followed, and after thirty-seven minutes of spirited fighting the enemy surrendered, having thirteen men killed and twenty wounded; the loss of the Americans being three killed and five wounded.

Soon after this the *Hazard* had a battle with an English bomb ship of fourteen guns and eighty men, the *Hazard's* original complement of ninety men having by this time been reduced to about fifty men. Realizing their advantage in numbers, the British made several attempts to board, when, after being repelled each time with heavy loss, they sheered off. In the summer of 1779 the *Hazard* joined the Penobscot expedition, and in August was burned to prevent her falling into the hands of the enemy.

Some time in 1778 the privateers *Bennington* and *Bunker Hill* got to sea and made fairly successful cruises. The former, commanded by Captain W. Newton, and afterward by Captain R. Craig, was a sloop mounting six guns and four swivels, and was manned by fifteen men. She was commissioned from Maryland and captured a valuable ship. In the following year she took a British privateer of twelve guns. The *Bunker Hill*, a schooner of ten guns, with a complement of forty-five men, under Captain S. Thompson, from Connecticut, in 1778 made one prize.

The privateer brigs *Columbus* and *Favorite* also made cruises in 1778, in which they captured one vessel each. The *Columbus*, carrying twelve guns and thirty men, under Captain T. Moore, took the sloop *St. Peter*, while the *Favorite*, Captain Lamb, captured a ship armed with sixteen guns, having a cargo of logwood.

The 6-gun sloop *Eagle*, Captain E. Conkling, had a more exciting experience. She went to sea with only thirty men, and in one cruise made six prizes. In manning these vessels Captain Conkling reduced his own crew to fifteen men, who, besides having the work of handling the sails, were compelled to guard the large number of prisoners taken aboard. It was not long before the British prisoners realized the critical position in which the Americans had been placed, and, seizing a favorable opportunity, they rose on their captors, and killing all except two boys took possession of the *Eagle* and endeavored to run her into a British port. Before reaching a place of safety, however, the *Eagle* fell in with the American privateer *Hancock* and was retaken. In 1779 the *Eagle*, while in New York, was blown up.

The splendid privateer ships *General Putnam* and *Marlborough* got to sea in the spring of 1778. The former, carrying twenty guns and one hundred and fifty men, under Captain T. Allen, from Connecticut, captured a brig with a cargo of provisions. The *Marlborough*, Captain Babcock, from Massachusetts, was one of the most successful privateers in this war, having made, in all, twenty-eight prizes; one of them a slaver with three hundred negroes aboard.

Perhaps next to the *Marlborough* in point of number of prizes was a mere boat armed with only two guns and manned by twenty men. In spite of her unprepossessing name this boat, called the *Skunk*, commissioned in New Jersey, is reported to have sent in no less than nineteen prizes, many of them of considerable value.

In June, 1778, the armed sloop *Volante*, Captain Daniel, of Connecticut, captured the sloop *Ranger*, carrying eight guns and thirty-five men; and about the same time the 18-gun ship *Minerva*, Captain J. Earle—afterward commanded by Captain J. Angus—from Pennsylvania, made a prize of a schooner. The *Minerva* had a complement of sixty men.

The 6-gun brig *Monmouth*, of Massachusetts, Captain D. Ingersol, captured one vessel in 1778, but afterward the prize was lost by shipwreck near Portsmouth, her crew of eleven men perishing. In the following year the *Monmouth* made a cruise in which she took two brigs, a schooner, and a sloop. The last was in charge of a midshipman in the Royal Navy, who had four men with him.

For American privateersmen September seems to have been the luckiest month in the year 1778. On September 6th the 10-gun brig *Gerard*, Captain J. Josiah, of Pennsylvania, while cruising in company with the American privateer *Convention*, met a sail which immediately aroused suspicions. Chase was promptly given, and in spite of the utmost endeavors of the people in the chase the American privateers soon had her under their guns. On investigation the stranger proved to be an American privateer, the sloop *Active*, which, having made several prizes, had taken aboard a number of prisoners. These prisoners, as in the case of the sloop *Eagle*, just noticed, had risen on their captors and made themselves masters of the sloop. To make sure that there would be no repetition of this experience, Captain Josiah escorted the *Active* into Philadelphia.

On September 17th the 18-gun brig *Vengeance*, Captain Newman, of Massachusetts, having a complement of one hundred men, fell in with the British packet ship *Harriet*, mounting sixteen guns and manned by forty-five men. Although the *Harriet* was a packet ship, selected for that service especially because of her great speed, she was unable to keep her lead on the American privateer, which, after a hard chase of several hours, overhauled her and forced a battle. Newman reserved his fire until within musket shot, when he delivered his broadside, the Englishmen responding with spirit. In fifteen minutes, however, the superiority of American gunnery asserted itself and the enemy surrendered, having a number killed or wounded. On the part of the Americans one man was killed.

Four days after this Captain Newman had the good fortune to fall in with another packet ship, the *Eagle*, of fourteen guns, having a crew of sixty men. Again were the superior sailing qualities of the American privateer emphatically shown, for after a long chase the *Vengeance* overtook the swift *Eagle* and brought her into action. As in his engagement with the *Harriet*, Captain Newman reserved his shot until within the closest range, when he delivered his fire with great effect. The Englishmen fought with their usual bravery, but in twenty minutes were compelled to haul down their colors, having several of their number killed or wounded—among the former a colonel. Aboard the prize were four lieutenant colonels and three majors who had taken passage in the *Eagle* so as to join their regiments in America. On August 14, 1779, while under the command of Captain Thomas, the *Vengeance* was destroyed in the Penobscot expedition. Another armed vessel, mounting sixteen guns, called *Vengeance*, while under the command of Captain Deane, in October, 1779, had a well-contested action with the British brig *Defiance*, carrying fourteen guns and seventy-two men. The Englishmen finally were overcome, having fifteen of their number killed or wounded, while the American loss was eight.

It was on September 19, 1778, that one of the most dramatic actions in which an American privateer was concerned took place. Readers of American naval history are familiar with the tragic fate of the United States 32-gun frigate *Randolph*, which on March 7, 1778, gave battle to the British 74-gun ship of the line *Yarmouth* in order to save a convoy of merchantmen which was under the *Randolph's* protection. An unlucky shot from the *Yarmouth* ignited the *Randolph's* magazine and blew her to pieces, only four of her complement of three hundred and fifteen men being saved. Only a few months after this, or on September 19th, this sea tragedy was repeated, with the difference that this time it was the British, not the American, that was blown up.

On the day mentioned the privateer *General Hancock*, Captain Hardy, of Massachusetts, carrying twenty guns and a crew of one hundred and fifty men, fell in with the British 32-gun ship *Levant*, Captain J. Martin, manned by over one hundred men. After an action of about three hours a shot from the *General Hancock* reached the *Levant's* magazine and blew her up, all on board perishing excepting the boatswain and seventeen men. It is a singular coincidence that both the ill-starred *Randolph* and *Levant* carried the same number of guns.

Soon after this Captain Hardy came across a fleet

of twenty-one sail under the protection of several war vessels. By adroit maneuvering Hardy managed to cut out the 8-gun ship *Lady Erskine*. In this affair the *General Hancock* was assisted by the American privateer *Beaver*.

The little privateer sloop *Providence*, Captain J. Conner, of Pennsylvania, made several successful ventures in 1778 and in 1779, capturing the ship *Nancy*, the brigs *Chase* and *Bella*, and the schooner *Friendship*. Captain Conner placed a prize crew aboard the *Nancy*, with orders to make for the most available American port. When the privateer had disappeared below the horizon, the British prisoners in the *Nancy*, seizing a favorable opportunity, suddenly fell upon their captors, overpowered them, and regained possession of their ship. Before they had proceeded far on their new course, however, the *Nancy* again fell in with the *Providence* and was recaptured.

It was some time in 1778 that the American 12-gun privateer *True American*, Captain Buffington, of Massachusetts, had a severe engagement with a West India letter of marque. Unfortunately the details of this affair have not been preserved.

Perhaps one of the most formidable privateers that put to sea in the year 1778 was the *Black Prince*, of Massachusetts, Captain West. This vessel was built expressly for privateering, being among the first of this class of formidable war craft to get to sea. She is said to have been an exceptionally handsome specimen of naval architecture. Carrying eighteen guns, with a complement of one hundred and sixty men, this fine ship put to sea in October, 1778, and captured a snow and two brigs. In the following year she was attached to the Penobscot expedition and was destroyed.

CHAPTER IX.

A BOY PRIVATEERSMAN.

In following the career of Andrew Sherburne, a boy privateersman in the Revolution, the reader will become familiar with a phase of privateering of which too little is known. Sherburne began his sea life at the age of fourteen by entering the United States cruiser *Ranger* soon after her return from her celebrated cruise in the Irish Sea under Captain John Paul Jones. The *Ranger* sailed from Boston in June, 1779, under the command of Captain Simpson, one of her lieutenants in her fight with the *Drake*. After a successful career in the West Indies the *Ranger* returned to Boston in August refitted, and, getting to sea again, made a short cruise, and then put into Charleston, where she was captured by the British, together with several Continental cruisers.

As the *Ranger* had been built at Portsmouth, New Hampshire, the patriotic citizens of that place, on learning of her loss, built another ship, which they called the *Alexander*, to be used as a privateersman, the command of her also being given to Captain Simpson. Young Sherburne, with most of the officers and men of the *Ranger*, enlisted in her. The *Alexander* got to sea in December, 1780, and returned to port after a profitless cruise of several weeks. Sherburne had intended to sail in her again, but he happened to meet a stranger in the streets of Portsmouth one day who persuaded him to go aboard the fishing schooner *Greyhound*, that Captain Jacob Willis, of Kennebunk, was fitting out as a privateersman. Sailors at that time were very scarce, and peculiar methods were employed to fill out complements. Sherburne was taken into the cabin and introduced to the officers, who made themselves extremely agreeable to the budding privateersman, patting him on the head, saying that he was a fine-looking youngster, etc., and finally asking him to sing. Even this elaborate flattery did not secure the boy, who still held off, but promised to consider the offer. He remained aboard the *Greyhound* while she ran down to Old York, a small port nine miles east of Portsmouth, in the hope of enticing more seamen aboard. The officers of the *Greyhound* went ashore, put up at a tavern, and gave what they called " a jovial evening," to which all seafaring men were invited. When the company had become sufficiently " jolly," the officers went among the men endeavoring to induce them to enlist. Several were shipped in this manner.

Stopping at several other ports for the same purpose the *Greyhound* put to sea and appeared off Halifax. Here, during a gale of wind, she was chased by a large schooner and overtaken, but the stranger proved to be an American privateer. Running close into Halifax harbor, Captain Willis discovered a ship that appeared to be in distress, and believing that she might prove a rich prize he ran down, and did not realize that she was a British cruiser until within gunshot. The *Greyhound* turned in flight, with the " crippled merchantman " in full chase. In a few minutes it was seen that the stranger was neither crippled nor a dull sailer, for she rapidly overhauled the American and would have captured her had not a heavy fog rolled over, completely enveloping both vessels and enabling the *Greyhound*, by changing her course, to escape.

After this adventure Captain Willis changed his cruising ground to the mouth of the St. Lawrence. A large number of sails were seen, but they all proved to
11

be Americans on the same business as the *Greyhound*. Touching at a small group of islands, where the privateer took aboard several dozen bushels of wild bird eggs, Captain Willis fell in with "an independent English fisherman"—that is, one who was not in the employ of the British company that had a monopoly of fishing in those waters—from whom he learned that an English brig had recently entered Fortune Bay with supplies for the fishing stations. The *Greyhound* did not find the brig, but captured several fishing shallops, two of which were manned and ordered to the United States.

Young Sherburne was placed in one of these, the *Greyhound* meantime making for Salem. While endeavoring to cross the Gulf of St. Lawrence the shallop in which Sherburne had been placed met heavy weather, and in a few days sighted a strange vessel. Sherburne says: "We sometimes thought whether it might not be another prize that the privateer had taken. Shortly, however, most of us were rather inclined to think it was the enemy. She continued to gain upon us and we discovered that her crew were rowing. . . . They soon began to fire upon us with long buccaneer pieces, into which they put eight or ten common musket balls for a charge. The first time they fired they did not strike us, but we heard their bullets whistle over our heads. The second time their charge went through the head of the mainsail, and the third time it went through the middle of our mainsail. We now heaved to. In a few minutes they were alongside of us and twenty men sprang aboard with these long guns in their hands, loaded, cocked, and primed, and presented two or three at each of our breasts without ceremony, cursing us bitterly and threatening our lives. We pleaded for quarter, but they, with violence, reprimanded us, and seemed determined to take our lives, after they had sufficiently gratified themselves with the most bitter imprecations that language could afford. There were one or

two who interceded for us. One of these was their
commander, but their entreaties seemed to increase
the rage of some of the others. We stood trembling
and awaiting their decisions, not presuming to re-
monstrate, for some of them seemed to be perfect
furies. At length their captain and several others,
who seemed more rational, prevailed on those heady
fellows to forbear their rashness.

"Their first business was to get the prizes
under way for their own port, which was called
Grand Bank. By this time, say two or three o'clock,
there was quite a pleasant breeze. The Newfound-
landers (for I am inclined, for the present, to forbear calling them English or the Irish) made it their
business to go into particular inquiries as to what
had transpired with us since we left the bay. One
of us had a copy of the *Greyhound's* commission as a
privateer. The wind being fair, we arrived at
Grand Bank before night, and almost the whole village were collected to see the Yankee prisoners.
We were taken on shore and soon surrounded, perhaps by a hundred people. Among them was an
old English lady of distinction who appeared to
have an excellent education, and to whose opinion
and instructions they all seemed to pay an especial
deference. She was the only person among them
who inquired after papers. I presented the commissions. This lady took them and commenced reading them audibly and without interruption until
she came to the clause in the privateer's letter of
marque and reprisal which authorized to 'burn,
sink, or destroy,' etc. Many of the people became
so exceedingly exasperated that they swore that we
ought to be killed outright. They were chiefly west
countrymen and Irishmen, rough and quite uncul-
tivated, and were in a state of complete anarchy.
There was neither magistrate nor minister among
them. They appeared very loyal, however, to his
majesty. The old lady interposed, and soon called

them to order. She informed them that we were prisoners of war and ought to be treated with humanity and conveyed to a British armed station. She then went on with her reading, and closed without further interruption. This good woman gave directions, and they began to prepare some refreshment for us. They hung on a pot and boiled some corned codfish and salted pork. When it was boiled sufficiently, they took the pot out of doors, where there was a square piece of board which had a cleat on each edge, the corners being open. They then turned the pot upside down upon the board, and when the water was sufficiently drained away the board was set on a table, or rather a bench, something higher than a common table, and the company stood around this table without plates or forks. They had fish knives to cut their pork, but generally picked up the fish with their fingers, and had hard baked biscuit for bread. Having taken our refreshment, we were conducted into a cooper shop and locked up, the windows secured, and a guard placed outside."

On the following morning the prisoners were placed aboard a shallop and locked in the fish room —a dark, noisome place, where they had everything taken from them except the clothes they wore. Even their shoes were appropriated. In this filthy hole they were conveyed to a little harbor called Cornish, where they found the owner of the "independent fishing boat," who treated them kindly, offering them a loaf of bread and a plate of butter. The Americans were locked up overnight in this place in the warehouse, and on the following morning they were taken six miles up the river and landed so as to strike across the land to Cape Placentia Bay. In this march of twenty miles the privateersmen suffered greatly, as, being without shoes, their feet soon became lacerated. About five miles from their destination they met an old Jerseyman who owned a number of shallops, several of which had been captured by American privateers. When the old man discovered who the prisoners were, he became highly exasperated, and insisted that they ought to be put to death, and, had it not been for the guard of seven sturdy men, he might have carried out his wishes with his own hands. Refusing to give food or shelter to the prisoners overnight, the irascible Jerseyman slammed the door in the faces of the travelers and went into the house. Thereupon the guard took possession of his brewhouse, which, although wet and muddy, made a fairly good shelter for the night.

Arriving at a small port called Morteer, where the inhabitants fired a gun in celebration of the advent of " Yankee prisoners," our adventurers were placed aboard a fishing boat and taken to Placentia, the largest fishing station in that part of Newfoundland. It was now May, 1781, and in September the British sloop of war *Duchess of Cumberland*, Captain Samuel Marsh—formerly the American privateer *Congress*, built at Beverly, Massachusetts, which had recently been captured and taken into the English service—came into port, and, taking the Americans aboard, sailed for St. John's, Newfoundland, where there was a prison ship in which a number of our seamen had been confined.

On the night of September 19th, while the *Duchess of Cumberland* was on her passage to St. John's, she was wrecked on a desert island, and twenty of her one hundred and seventy people were lost. After enduring great hardships, the survivors regained Placentia, where our privateersmen were again placed in the garrison house. About the end of the following October the British sloop of war *Fairy*, Captain Yeo, came into the harbor, and, taking the Americans aboard, carried them to Plymouth, England, where they were confined in Old Mill Prison.

Captain Yeo was the father of Sir James Lucas Yeo, who became notorious in our naval war with Great Britain in 1812, and it is probable that James was aboard the *Fairy* in 1781, as Captain Yeo is known to have had his son with him. It was Sir James who wrote, in September, 1812: " Sir James Yeo presents his compliments to Captain Porter, of the American frigate *Essex*, and would be glad to have a *tête-à-tête* anywhere between the Capes of Delaware and Havana, where he would have the pleasure to break his sword over his damned head and put him down forward in irons." We now get our first insight into the character of the Yeos. Young Sherburne describes Captain Yeo as a " complete tyrant." He writes: " Willis and myself were called upon the quarter-deck, and, after being asked a few questions by Captain Yeo, he turned to his officers and said: ' They are a couple of fine lads for his majesty's service. Mr. Gray, see that they do their duty, one in the foretop and the other in the maintop.' I said that I was a prisoner of war, and that I could not consent to serve against my country. With very hard words and several threats we were ordered off the quarter-deck and commanded to do our duty in the waist. . . . While lying at St. John's we had an opportunity of seeing some of Captain Yeo's character exhibited. It was contrary to orders to bring any spirituous liquors aboard. It was the custom to hoist in the boat at night, lest any of the men should elude the guard, steal the boat, and run away. One evening, as the boat was hoisted in, there was a bottle of rum discovered in the boat. No one of the boat's crew would own the bottle, and the next morning the whole crew, six in number, were seized up to the gangway, with their shirts stripped off, and each received a dozen lashes. It was very common for this captain to have his men thus whipped for very trifling faults, and sometimes when faultless. At a certain hour the cook gives out word to the men and officers' waiters that they may have hot water to wash their dishes, etc. One day a midshipman's boy called on the cook for hot water. The cook had none, and reprimanded the lad for not coming in proper season. The boy complained to his master, whose rank on board was no higher than the cook's, and who was himself but a boy. The midshipman came forward and began to reprimand the cook, who told him, that had the boy come at the proper time he would have had hot water enough, but that he should not now furnish him or any one else. This young blood made his complaint to the captain that he was insulted by the cook, who was a man in years, and who for this affront, offered to a gentleman's son, must be brought to the gangway and take his dozen lashes. I believe that the laws of the navy do not admit of a warrant officer being punished without he is first tried and condemned by a court-martial. I understand that the captain had violated the laws of the navy in a number of instances. He had a number of men in irons on the whole passage to England." On arrival in Plymouth, Captain Yeo was superseded in the command of the *Fairy* by a new captain. Young Sherburne notes the change of commanders as follows: "Captain Yeo took leave of his ship without any ceremony of respect being shown him from the crew. Shortly after the new captain came on board, and was saluted with three cheers from the crew."

In striking contrast to the brutal temperament of Captain Yeo, we have that of the *Fairy's* carpenter. Two days after Yeo had compelled the two American lads to serve against their country, all hands were called. Sherburne and Willis went to the cable tier, the proper place for prisoners of war, and on the boatswain approaching them and demanding why they refused to obey the call for all hands the boys said that they considered themselves prisoners. "Tell me nothing about prisoners," he said. "Upon deck immediately!" "We still kept our stations and remonstrated," records Sherburne. "He uttered a number of most horrid imprecations, and at the same time commenced a most furious attack upon us with his rattan. We for a while sternly adhered to our purpose, while he alternately thrashed the one and the other. He became more and more enraged, and we, not daring to resist, thought it best to clear out. We mounted the deck, with him at our heels repeating his strokes. . . . The carpenter, whose name was Fox, was sitting in his berth looking on. After we returned from quarters Fox called me and said: 'I see, my lad, that you are obliged to do duty. It is wrong, but it would not do for me to interfere; yet I was thinking in your favor. His majesty allows me two boys. If you will come into my berth and take a little care here, I will excuse your keeping watch and all other duty. You will be much less exposed if you stay with me than you will be if you have to do your duty before the mast, and it is in vain for you to think to escape that, for Captain Yeo is a very arbitrary man; he is not liked by the crew, and his officers do not set much by him. I intend to leave the ship myself when we get home.'" Arriving at Plymouth, Fox gave further evidence of his kindness by offering to adopt the American boys. He said that he did not intend to follow the sea; that he had a wife, but no child. On the boys declining this generous offer, the carpenter took pains to put them in a way of becoming prisoners of war again. "In a day or two after he [the new commander] had come on board, Mr. Fox came into his cabin where I was and said to me: 'Sherburne, the captain is walking alone on the quarter-deck. I think it is a good time for you to speak to him. It may be that he will consider you as a prisoner of war.'" The two boys timidly approached the new commander and stated their position, and in an hour they were sent aboard the prison ship *Dunkirk*.

From that place the boys were taken to Old Mill Prison, where they were confined several months, until exchanged and sent to America in a cartel. Young Sherburne had been in his native land only a few weeks when he entered a privateer—the *Scorpion*, Captain R. Salter—and made a cruise in the West Indies.   On the homeward passage the *Scorpion* was captured by the British frigate *Amphion*, and for a third time Sherburne found himself a prisoner of war.   This time he was taken to New York and placed in the infamous ship *Jersey*, where he experienced the usual brutal treatment accorded to Americans confined there.   After an imprisonment of several weeks he was released in an exchange of prisoners, and made his way home, the war by that time having ended.

CHAPTER X.

THE WORK OF 1779.

THE winter of 1777–'78, during which the American army, under the immediate command of Washington, had its headquarters at Valley Forge, has been popularly accepted as the darkest hour in our struggle for independence. The American army had been driven out of New York, the most important city in the rebelling colonies, the British had occupied Rhode Island and had undisputed possession of Philadelphia, and as the only material offset to these disasters we have the capture of Burgoyne's army of some eight thousand men in Northern New York. In the light of these reverses, the hope for independence was indeed forlorn. Congress, being largely influenced by foreign adventures, was impotent, and really did more to hamper than to assist the American arms. So far as our operations on land were concerned, therefore, it might almost be said that the winter of 1777–'78 was the "darkest hour of the Revolution."

When we consider the work of our maritime forces down to this period, however, we find that some of the heaviest blows at British supremacy in the North American colonies had been delivered—blows that were felt by the ministry across the ocean more keenly than any reverses English arms had suffered on land. At the time the Continental army was encamped at Valley Forge, American cruisers, and especially privateers, were scouring the seas,

capturing great numbers of the enemy's war craft
and merchantmen, harassing English trade in all
parts of the then known world, hovering on the
coast of the British Isles, throwing their ports into
frequent alarm, and, what is perhaps most important of all, maintaining communications between the
colonies and the outside world, by means of which
news of the victories gained by the Americans was
carried to the French court, and specie and munitions of war were brought into the country.

So disastrous had been the operations of our
maritime forces on the high seas to British commerce that Parliament, early in 1778, made special
inquiries.   On February 6, 1778, Alderman Woodbridge testified at the bar of the House of Lords that
" the number of ships lost by capture or destroyed
by American privateers since the commencement of
the war was seven hundred and thirty-three, of
which, after deducting for those retaken and restored, there remained five hundred and fifty-nine."
William Creighton, Esq., " not only corroborated the
alderman in the most material points, but added
many new facts which had fallen within his own
knowledge.   He stated the losses suffered by merchantmen in consequence of the captures made by
the American privateers to have amounted to at
least two million pounds sterling in October last
[1777], and that by this time they could not be less
than two million two hundred thousand pounds." [1]

Seven hundred and thirty-three ships taken from
the enemy by American privateers in the first two
full years of the war! Truly an astonishing record,
and one that might well justify posterity in regard-
ing the winter of 1777-'78 as far from being the
" darkest hour of the Revolution!"   But the most
astonishing feature of these achievements is that
these vessels were captured by a comparatively

---

[1] Records of Parliament, vol. xix, pp. 707-711.

small number of men and ships. Down to the close
of 1777 there had been commissioned from the various ports of the colonies, in all, one hundred and
seventy-four private armed craft, mounting one
thousand eight hundred and thirty-eight guns and
manned by nine thousand two hundred and thirty-
six men and boys. Some of these privateers did not
succeed in getting to sea, while others returned to
port without making a prize, and a number were captured by the enemy. On the other hand, some of
these private armed craft took as many as twenty in
a single cruise, and on one occasion twenty-eight
prizes. But, admitting that one hundred and seventy-four of our privateers got to sea, we find that,
taking the aggregate of seven hundred and thirty-
three vessels, our amateur man-of-warsmen averaged
more than four prizes each. Allowing the moderate
estimate of fifteen men to each captured British
merchantmen, we have a total of ten thousand nine
hundred and ninety-five prisoners made on the high
seas by our enterprising and daring privateersmen,
or fully as many prisoners as our land forces took
in the same time, with this important difference—
namely, that many of the prisoners taken by our
land forces were foreign mercenaries, who could be
replaced so long as the stock of Hessians lasted,
while the men captured by our privateers were sailors, a class of men absolutely necessary to England's existence as a great power, and a class she
could not afford to lose.

The year 1779 opened inauspiciously for American privateers. On January 7th one of the newest
and best of our armed craft, the 20-gun brig *General Arnold*, Captain J. Magee, of Massachusetts,
was driven ashore near Plymouth, and seventy-five
of her complement of one hundred and twenty
men perished. In the same month the 6-gun
sloop *General Stark*, with twenty men aboard, was
wrecked on Nantucket Shoals, and all hands lost.

IN CONGRESS,

WEDNESDAY, APRIL 3, 1776.

INSTRUCTIONS *to the* COMMANDERS *of Private Ships or Vessels of War, which shall have Commissions or Letters of Marque and Reprisal, authorising them to make Captures of British Vessels and Cargoes.*

I.

YOU may, by Force of Arms, attack, subdue, and take all Ships and other Vessels belonging to the Inhabitants of Great-Britain, on the High Seas, or between high-water and low-water Marks, except Ships and Vessels bringing Persons who intend to settle and reside in the United Colonies, or bringing Arms, Ammunition or Warlike Stores to the said Colonies, for the Use of such Inhabitants thereof as are Friends to the American Cause, which you shall suffer to pass unmolested, the Commanders thereof permitting a peaceable Search, and giving satisfactory Information of the Contents of the Ladings, and Destinations of the Voyages.

II.

You may, by Force of Arms, attack, subdue, and take all Ships and other Vessels whatsoever carrying Soldiers, Arms, Gun-powder, Ammunition, Provisions, or any other contraband Goods, to any of the British Armies or Ships of War employed against these Colonies.

III.

You shall bring such Ships and Vessels as you shall take, with their Guns, Rigging, Tackle, Apparel, Furniture and Ladings, to some convenient Port or Ports of the United Colonies, that Proceedings may thereupon be had in due Form before the Courts which are or shall be there appointed to hear and determine Causes civil and maritime.

IV.

You or one of your Chief Officers shall bring or send the Master and Pilot and one or more principal Person or Persons of the Company of every Ship or Vessel by you taken, as soon after the Capture as may be, to the Judge or Judges of such Court as aforesaid, to be examined upon Oath, and make Answer to the Interrogatories which may be propounded touching the Interest or Property of the Ship or Vessel and her Lading; and at the same Time you shall deliver or cause to be delivered to the Judge or Judges, all Passes, Sea-Briefs, Charter-Parties, Bills of Lading, Cockets, Letters, and other Documents and Writings found on Board, proving the said Papers by the Affidavit of yourself, or of some other Person present at the Capture, to be produced as they were received, without Fraud, Addition, Subduction, or Embezzlement.

V.

You shall keep and preserve every Ship or Vessel and Cargo by you taken, until they shall by Sentence of a Court properly authorised be adjudged lawful Prize, not selling, spoiling, wasting, or diminishing the same or breaking the Bulk thereof, nor suffering any such Thing to be done.

VI.

If you, or any of your Officers or Crew shall, in cold Blood, kill or maim, or, by Torture or otherwise, cruelly, inhumanly, and contrary to common Usage and the Practice of civilized Nations in War, treat any Person or Persons surprized in the Ship or Vessel you shall take, the Offender shall be severely punished.

VII.

You shall, by all convenient Opportunities, send to Congress written Accounts of the Captures you shall make, with the Number and Names of the Captives, Copies of your Journal from Time to Time, and Intelligence of what may occur or be discovered concerning the Designs of the Enemy, and the Destinations, Motions, and Operations of their Fleets and Armies.

VIII.

One Third, at the least, of your whole Company shall be Land-Men.

IX.

You shall not ransome any Prisoners or Captives, but shall dispose of them in such Manner as the Congress, or if that be not sitting in the Colony whither they shall be brought, as the General Assembly, Convention, or Council or Committee of Safety of such Colony shall direct.

X.

You shall observe all such further Instructions as Congress shall hereafter give in the Premises, when you shall have Notice thereof.

XI.

If you shall do any Thing contrary to these Instructions, or to others hereafter to be given, or willingly suffer such Thing to be done, you shall not only forfeit your Commission, and be liable to an Action for Breach of the Condition of your Bond, but be responsible to the Party grieved for Damages sustained by such Mal-versation.

By Order of Congress,

John Hancock PRESIDENT.

Instructions to privateers, 1776.

From an original.

The *General Stark*, also, was commissioned from Massachusetts.

These reverses were in some degree counterbalanced by the Massachusetts 26-gun ship *Protector*, Captain John Foster Williams, which, while cruising at sea January 9th, fell in with the British privateer *Admiral Duff*, Captain R. Strange, carrying thirty guns 'and about one hundred men. The *Protector* had a complement of nearly two hundred men and boys. The two ships quickly came to close quarters, and for an hour and a half maintained a fierce contest, when a shot from the *Protector* penetrated the Englishmen's magazine and blew them up, only fifty-five of their crew being saved. Edward Preble, afterward famous in the navy, was a young midshipman at this time, serving in the *Protector*. Soon after this the *Protector* had a running fight with the British frigate *Thames*, but after being within gunshot several hours Captain Williams effected his escape. Ultimately the *Protector* was lost at sea.

It was in 1779 that the armed sloops *Active*, Captain P. Day, of Pennsylvania, and *American Revenue*, Captain N. Shaw (afterward commanded by Captain Leeds), of Connecticut, got to sea and made important captures. The *Active* carried fourteen guns, with sixty men, and captured, after a slight resistance, the British privateer *Mercury*, of eight guns, commanded by Captain Campbell. The *American Revenue*, armed with twelve guns and manned by about one hundred men, took the 8-gun schooner *Sally*, besides another schooner laden with tobacco, and a sloop with a cargo of rum.

Three other armed vessels, the *Baltimore Hero*, the *Cat*, and the *Intrepid*, made prizes early this year. The *Baltimore Hero* had a drawn battle with a British vessel of equal force in the Chesapeake, and afterward made a prize. This privateer carried fourteen guns, eight swivels, and a crew of thirty men, under Captain J. Earle. The *Cat*, a 2-gun schooner with seventy men, under Captain E. Ledger, of Pennsylvania, made one capture, while the *Intrepid*, of New Hampshire, a ship of twenty guns and one hundred and sixty men, under Captain M. Brown, took four vessels from the enemy.

Early in 1779 the 14-gun brig *Hibernia*, Captain R. Collins, manned by only thirty-five men, fell in with a king's cruiser mounting an equal number of guns, but having a complement of eighty men. A severe action followed, and it was only after several had been killed on each side that the vessels mutually separated. Another private armed brig bearing this name, also from Pennsylvania, but commanded by Captain J. Angus, while on a voyage to Teneriffe, had an action with a snow mounting sixteen guns. The Americans managed to beat their adversary off. Shortly afterward this *Hibernia* was attacked by two armed schooners and a sloop, which she also beat off, with a loss of two killed and eight wounded. The loss of the British is unknown.

In April the 16-gun brig *Holker*, manned by one hundred men, under Captain M. Lawler, of Pennsylvania, while at sea captured a schooner of ten guns, with forty-eight men, besides two armed sloops. In the following July the *Holker* captured, after an action of an hour and a half, with a loss of six killed and sixteen wounded, among the latter being Captain Lawler and his first officer, a brig of sixteen guns. The enemy's loss was six killed and twenty wounded. There was another brig bearing the name *Holker*, commissioned from the same State, carrying ten guns and thirty-five men, under Captain George Geddes, which in June captured the British ship *Diana*, having on board, as a part of her cargo, eighty cannon, sixty swivels, ten coehorns, and other military supplies. In the following August this *Holker* captured three brigs laden with rum and sugar, one of which was wrecked off Cape

May. Before returning to port the *Holker* took a 6-gun sloop laden with drygoods.

One of the largest privateers commissioned from New Hampshire was the *Hampden*, mounting twenty-two guns and manned by one hundred and fifty men. While under the command of Captain Salter the *Hampden*, in latitude 48° north, longitude 28° west, fell in with a large Indiaman armed with twenty-six guns. The vessels began an action which lasted three hours, when they separated, both in a crippled condition, the Americans having twenty-one killed or injured. The *Hampden* was captured by the British in the Penobscot expedition. They found her to be such a fine craft that they took her into the king's service.

A privateer of the name *Franklin*, Captain J. Robinson, mounting eight guns, some time in 1779 captured the British schooner *True Blue*, of ten guns, and two other vessels.

In April the little 1-gun schooner *Two Brothers*, of twenty-five men, Captain W. Gray, from Massachusetts, took aboard a number of volunteers at Salem, and captured a privateer of eight guns and sixty men. In the same month the 12-gun private schooner *Hunter*, of Pennsylvania, with a complement of sixty men, under Captain J. Douglass, fell in with a well-armed British ship, which she engaged for one hour, when the Englishmen made sail in flight, leaving the Americans with four men wounded. Afterward the *Hunter* captured a schooner. A privateer bearing this name, commissioned in Massachusetts, a ship of twenty guns and one hundred and fifty men, under Captain Brown, was lost in the Penobscot expedition.

In April of the same year the 14-gun ship *Roebuck*, Captain G. Hemfield—afterward commanded by Captain Gray—of Massachusetts, while cruising off Salem, captured the British privateer *Castor*, of eight guns and sixty men.

In June, 1779, the 10-gun sloop *Hancock*, Captain

T. Chester, of Connecticut, captured the British armed schooner *Hawke*, and in the same month the little schooner *Terrible*, Captain J. Baker, of Pennsylvania, made a prize of a schooner. In August the 18-gun brig *Hancock*, Captain P. Richards, of Connecticut, captured three brigs laden with rum.

In the following month prizes were taken by the 8-gun brig *Impertinent*, Captain J. Young, of Pennsylvania, by the 6-gun brig *Macaroni*, and by the 12-gun brig *Wild Cat*. It was on July 6th that the *Impertinent* fell in with a suspicious-looking sail, and promptly gave chase. The American brig rapidly gained, and it was seen that the stranger was lightening herself by throwing overboard heavy articles, some of which afterward were known to have been her cannon. In spite of these extreme measures the fleeing Englishman—for such the stranger proved to be—steadily lost ground, and soon was under the *Impertinent's* guns. The stranger surrendered at the first summons, and on sending a boat aboard Captain Young learned that it was the king's cruiser *Harlem*, of fourteen guns, with a crew of eighty-five men. The commander of the *Harlem*, when he found that he must be overtaken, got into a boat with a few men and endeavored to escape, but before they had proceeded any great distance the boat upset, and all hands were lost.

A brig and two schooners were captured by the *Macaroni*, Captain D. Keybold, of Pennsylvania, in July, and on the 13th of the same month the 14-gun craft *Wild Cat*, with a complement of seventy-five men, after a severe action, took the king's schooner *Egmont*, commanded by a lieutenant in the Royal Navy. Before the *Wild Cat* could secure her prize, however, she was captured by the British frigate *Surprise*.

One of the first prizes made by an American privateer in August, 1779, was the brig *Pitt*, loaded with rum and sugar, which was taken by the 18-gun

schooner *Jay*, Captain Courter, with one hundred
men, from Pennsylvania. About the same time the
14-gun brig *Mars*, Captain Y. Taylor, of the same
State, captured the British sloop *Active*, mounting
twelve guns, under the command of Captain Irvine.
This vessel was taken by boarding, the English having their first officer and steward killed. The *Mars*
also captured the transport brig *Polly*, having on
board two hundred and fourteen Hessians, besides
a snow of fourteen guns and forty-five men. These
vessels were taken off Sandy Hook. The snow was
retaken by the British on the following day. It was
in August of this year that the 12-gun sloop *Polly*,
with one hundred men, under Captain Leech, of Massachusetts, took a brig laden with tobacco.

In September the 6-gun sloop *Happy Return*, Captain J. Leach, of New Jersey, took a brig, and two
sloops laden with fustic and rum, and in the following month Captain Craig, of the Continental army,
with a detachment of his company, captured the
British sloop *Neptune*, carrying ten guns, four swivels, and two coehorns, manned by twenty-one men,
near Elizabethtown. Before her cargo could be got
ashore, however, a British war ship appeared and
recaptured the *Neptune*.

Some of the other privateers making prizes this
year were the 18-gun ship *Oliver Cromwell*, Captain
Parker, of Massachusetts, which captured a tender
of ten guns belonging to the ship of the line *St.
George*—the *Oliver Cromwell* also took a ship and a
schooner, making sixty prisoners in all—the *Pallas*,
of Massachusetts, which took a ship loaded with provisions, and the 6-gun brig *Resolution*, Captain Z.
Seare, of Massachusetts, which made five prizes.
The private armed sloop *Sally*, Captain J. Smith, of
New York, had a severe battle with a British transport carrying eight guns. The vessels finally separated by mutual consent, the Americans having a
loss of five killed and twelve wounded.

12

CHAPTER XI.

JONATHAN HARADEN.

THE action between the *Kearsarge* and the *Alabama*, fought off Cherbourg, June 19, 1864, has justly been regarded as one of the most dramatic naval duels on record. Farragut, in a letter to his son, said of it: "I would sooner have fought that fight than any ever fought on the ocean. Only think! It was fought like a tournament, in full view of thousands of French and English, with a perfect confidence, on the part of all but the Union people, that we would be whipped." There was an action fought between an American and an English privateer off the Spanish coast nearly a hundred years before this, however, which may well be called the "*Kearsarge-Alabama* fight of the Revolution." Like the famous naval duel in the civil war, this action took place near land, where thousands of people watched the struggle in breathless eagerness or wildly speculated on the result. The battle referred to was fought off Bilbóa, June 4, 1780, between the American privateer *General Pickering*, commanded by Jonathan Haraden, and the British letter of marque *Achilles*, of London. The *General Pickering* was from Salem, where she had been fitted out and manned. She was a ship of one hundred and eighty tons, mounted fourteen 6-pounders—the ordinary caliber in ships of her class in that day—and carried a crew of forty-five men and boys.

Haraden was one of the most daring and skillful

138

navigators that ever sailed from Salem, and that is saying a great deal when we come to consider the long list of successful commanders who have hailed from that port. He belonged to that group of men who have made old Salem town famous the world over, such as John Carnes, Benjamin Crowninshield, Thomas Benson, John Felt, William Gray, Joseph Waters, Simon Forrester, Thomas Perkins, and John Derby. Haraden had the reputation of being one of the most intrepid commanders known even to Salem ship lore. It has been said of him, that " amid the din of battle he was calm and self-possessed. The more deadly the strife, the more imminent the peril, the more terrific the scene, the more perfect seemed his self-command and serene intrepidity. He was a hero among heroes, and his name should live in honored and affectionate remembrance." Rather lavish praise, but the man deserved it, as will soon appear.

Haraden certainly was a daring sailor and a seaman of extraordinary ability. His many successes in the struggle for independence fully bear out this statement, and entitle him to be placed with such naval heroes of the Revolution as Connyngham, Whipple, Hopkins, and John Paul Jones. He was born in Gloucester, Massachusetts, in 1745, and died in Salem in 1803, spending most of his active life on the sea. He came to Salem as a boy and entered the service of Richard Cabot, father of the president of the famous Hartford Convention. Soon after hostilities broke out between the American colonies and the mother country he hastened to draw his sword in defense of his native land, and early in 1776 was appointed a " lieutenant " in the *Tyrannicide*, commanded by Captain J. Fiske, of Salem. The name of this vessel is sufficiently suggestive of the spirit of her owners and crew, and she soon justified the appellation in a striking manner by capturing a royal cutter and carrying her in tri-

umph into Salem, the prize being bound from Halifax to New York with important papers aboard. In
the same cruise the *Tyrannicide*, June 13, 1776, had
a spirited action with the British packet schooner
Despatch, carrying eight guns, twelve swivels, and
thirty-one men. The privateer was a brig carrying
fourteen guns and one hundred men. After a lively
fight of about an hour the *Despatch* surrendered, having sustained a loss of seven men wounded, with her
commander, Mr. Gutteridge, and one killed. The
Americans had one man killed and two wounded. In
the following month the *Tyrannicide* captured the
armed ship *Glasgow* and made thirty prisoners. In
August she took the brig *St. John* and the schooner
Three Brothers. In the following year this vessel,
while in company with the privateer brig *Massachusetts*, of that State, attacked the British bark
Lawnsdale, and after a struggle lasting three hours
captured her. The enemy had three men killed. In
the same cruise the *Massachusetts* took a ship and
six other vessels, in one of which were sixty-three
Hessian chasseurs.

On the 29th of March, 1779, the *Tyrannicide*, while
cruising off Bermuda, fell in with the English brig
Revenge, Captain Kendall, carrying fourteen guns
and eighty-five men. The privateer at this time had
a complement of ninety men, but mounted the same
number of guns as formerly, so that the two vessels
were about evenly matched. The ships quickly came
to close quarters, and it was not long before the
Americans managed to make fast alongside. Then
began a tooth-and-nail fight. For over an hour the
two crews fought each other over their bulwarks,
when the English, having a large number of killed
or wounded and two of their cannon dismounted,
surrendered.   The Americans had eight men
wounded. This was the last important service performed by the *Tyrannicide*. She was one of the thirteen privateers that took part in the ill-fated Penob-

scot expedition, and was destroyed by her own people, August 14, 1779, to prevent her falling into the hands of the enemy.

Having received his baptism of fire in this well-named vessel, Haraden was not long in finding a suitable berth, and in the spring of 1780 he sailed from Salem as commander of the 180-ton privateer *General Pickering*, with a cargo of sugar for Bilboa. At that time this port was a famous rendezvous for privateers, not only of the United States, but for those of England and France. It was customary for our ships to sail for this place with a cargo of sugar, and capture a prize or two on the passage over if possible. After disposing of the sugar the privateers went on a general cruise after the enemy's merchantmen, filling their empty holds with such goods as they could readily move from a prize and returning to the United States, where the cargoes were sold to the best advantage.

On this passage over Haraden had an unusually exciting time. On May 29th he was attacked by a British cutter, but although his antagonist carried six guns more than he did Haraden, after a desperate fight of two hours, succeeded in beating the enemy off. As the *General Pickering* entered the Bay of Biscay she fell in with the English privateer schooner *Golden Eagle*, carrying twenty-two guns and sixty men, the American mounting only sixteen cannon. Having come upon the Englishman at night and unobserved, and having formed a fairly accurate idea of her force, Haraden boldly ran alongside and called on the stranger to surrender, declaring at the same time that his craft was an American frigate of the largest class, and that he would blow the British privateer out of water if she did not surrender.

This was no ill-considered threat on the part of the *General Pickering's* commander, for less than a year before Captain John Paul Jones, in the *Bon-*

homme Richard, had sunk one of the finest frigates
in the British navy, the *Scrapis,* within pistol-shot
of the English coast, and such was the effect of that
astounding achievement on the mind of the British
public that the most extravagant stories as to the
number and force of Yankee war ships, and as to
their whereabouts and daring, found ready credence. So when Haraden announced himself as having an " American frigate of the largest class " he
well knew, from what he had learned of the consternation produced in Great Britain by the unparalleled victories of the American navy, that his confused enemy would be more than likely to believe
it. Such proved to be the case, for the Englishmen
were taken so completely by surprise that they were
unable to make any defense, and promptly struck
their flag. When the British skipper came aboard
the *General Pickering* he expressed great humiliation
at having given in to such an inferior force. But
it was too late to repent, for Second Officer John
Carnes had been sent aboard the *Golden Eagle* with
a prize crew, and soon had the Stars and Stripes
waving at her gaff.

It was only a few days after this that the *General
Pickering* gave battle to the *Achilles.* Early in the
morning of June 3d, when the American privateer
was approaching Bilboa, a large sail was observed
working out of that port. Inquiring of his prisoner,
the master of the captured schooner, Haraden was
told that the stranger was the *Achilles,* a privateer
of London, mounting forty-two guns and carrying
one hundred and forty men. Thinking that this
might be merely a trick on the part of the commander of the *Golden Eagle* to induce the American
to run away from the sail, or to surrender if he once
found himself under the *Achilles's* guns, Haraden
coolly replied, " I shan't run from her," and boldly
held on his course. The light wind prevented the
vessels from coming together that day, but the

Americans saw enough of the stranger to realize that they were in the presence of a powerful foe. Before sunset the *Achilles*—for such she proved to be —had recaptured the *General Pickering's* prize, and placing a crew aboard slowly beat to a favorable position for attacking the Americans. Night coming on, the British deferred their attack until daylight so as make sure of the Yankee so nearly within their grasp. The presence of the powerful *Achilles* did not in the least disturb Haraden, for it is recorded that he took a "sound night's sleep and recruited a boatswain and eight sailors from his prisoners in the morning, when they went to work on shore."

By this time the news had spread that an American and British war ship, in full view of the land, were about to fight, and thousands of people flocked down to the water's edge and occupied all vantage points, eager to witness a naval battle. They were disappointed that day, but when day broke June 4th it found the ships ready for action, and the same multitude of Spaniards again assembled and impatiently waited to see the contest.

The British lost no time in beginning the attack, and shortly after daylight they bore down on the Yankees with confident hurrahs. But Haraden had made his preparations for defense with his usual skill. Availing himself of the conformation of the land and some shoals which he knew to be in the vicinity, he placed his ship in such a position that the Englishman, in approaching, would be exposed to a raking fire from the *General Pickering's* entire broadside. It so happened that the wind gradually died out, just as the British were getting into effective range, so that they were exposed to a murderous raking fire from the Americans much longer than they had counted upon. Still the English commander had a vastly superior force, and as it would never do for a British war ship to run away from an American of inferior strength, especially when thousands of Spaniards were watching every move, he bravely held on his course.

After enduring the destructive fire from the *General Pickering* about two hours, without being able to gain his desired position, the British commander brought the head of his ship about and opened with his broadside guns. Several efforts were made to bring the ships into closer quarters, but conscious of the advantage his position gave him, and knowing that he had a brave foe with superior force to contend with, Haraden tenaciously maintained his tactics, and finally, after a battle of three hours, he compelled the *Achilles* to make sail to escape. It is said that toward the close of the action Haraden, finding himself running short of ammunition, ordered his gunner to load with crowbars, which had been taken out of a prize. This "flight of crowbars" produced the utmost consternation in the English craft, and is believed to have precipitated her retreat. The *General Pickering* vainly endeavored to come up with her. Haraden offered a large reward to the gunner who carried away one of the Englishman's spars, but for once "the man behind the gun" was not equal to the emergency, and the *Achilles* escaped. The Americans did succeed, however, in retaking their prize, which was carried safely into Bilboa. Aboard the *Golden Eagle* were found a British prize crew and the second officer of the *Achilles*.

So interested had the people on shore become in the battle that they took to boats and drew nearer and nearer to the contestants, until finally, toward the close of the action, the *General Pickering* found herself literally surrounded by a wildly enthusiastic crowd. This impromptu escort of boats accompanied the privateer and her prize to their anchorage in the harbor, and soon after they dropped anchor it is stated that it was possible to have walked ashore over the craft of all kinds that swarmed

about. Captain Haraden had occasion to go ashore
shortly afterward, and so great was the enthusiasm
and admiration of the Spaniards over his heroic defense that they raised him bodily on their shoulders
and bore him in triumph through the city.

The venerable Robert Cowan, who witnessed this
battle, said, shortly before he died: " The *General
Pickering*, in comparison with her antagonist, looked
like a longboat by the side of a ship." Speaking of
Haraden's conduct in the battle, Cowan said: " He
fought with a determination that seemed super-
human, and that, although in the most exposed positions, where the shot flew around him, he was all
the while as calm and steady as amid a shower of
snowflakes."

Returning to the United States after this adventure Captain Haraden, in October, while off Sandy
Hook, fell in with three armed merchantmen—the
ship *Hope*, carrying fourteen guns; the brig *Pomone*,
of twelve guns; and the cutter *Royal George*, of fourteen guns. By skillful maneuvering Haraden managed to separate the enemy, and after an exciting
action of an hour and a half captured all of them.

During the Revolution Haraden captured vessels
from the enemy the guns of which aggregated over
one thousand. In one of his cruises, subsequent to
his heroic fight with the *Achilles*, Haraden, still in
command of his favorite ship, the *General Pickering*,
fell in with a homeward-bound king's packet from
one of the West India islands. This ship proved to
be unusually heavily armed and manned, so that
after an action of four hours Haraden found it
necessary to haul off to repair damages. He also
discovered that he had expended all but one round
of his ammunition. An ordinary commander of a
ship, under such circumstances as these, would have
thought himself fortunate in retiring from the contest with his colors flying. But Haraden was not
an ordinary commander. He, like John Paul Jones,

was one of those few seamen who are equal to any
emergency, and who have the faculty of turning their
misfortunes into the very instruments of success.

Having repaired the damages as well as his limited time and means would allow, he rammed home
his last round of powder and shot, and boldly running alongside his antagonist quietly informed the
Englishmen that he would give them exactly five
minutes in which to haul down their colors, and that
if they did not do so at the expiration of that time
he would send every man of them to the bottom of
the sea. Then running up the red flag, " no quarter,"
he coolly took out a timepiece, and standing where
he could be plainly seen by the enemy he called out
every few seconds the various lapses of time that
had expired.

This singular summons had a peculiar effect on
the minds of the Englishmen, which the shrewd
American commander doubtless had calculated
upon. The Englishman probably would have renewed the battle, and would have fought to the last
plank with his usual courage, had the Yankee gone
about it in the customary blood-and-thunder way.
But this sudden calm within short range (where the
two crews were actually staring into one another's
faces, and could almost shake hands across their bulwarks), this dreadful suspense before shotted guns,
with a man holding a lighted match in one hand
and a timepiece in the other, was too much for the
nerves of the Englishmen, and before the expiration
of the five minutes they hauled down their colors.

Haraden, in his five or six years fighting against
the English, evidently had come to the conclusion
reached by Napoleon some years later—namely,
" that an Englishman never knows when he is
whipped." In this case the American commander
thought it best to give them five minutes in which
to think it over. The wisdom of doing so is seen in
the result, for there seems to have been no question

about the packet's having been hopelessly beaten
before the *General Pickering* hauled off for repairs,
as, when the Americans went aboard to take possession, they found the decks of their prize covered
with dead and wounded men and the blood was oozing from the scuppers in a sluggish stream.

Just two years after his extraordinary action
with the *Achilles*, or on June 5, 1782, Haraden, then
in command of the 14-gun ship *Cæsar*, fell in with
an armed ship and brig. Of course there was
a fight right off, and for two hours neither side
could gain a decisive advantage, when, as Captain
Haraden quaintly remarked, "both parties separated, sufficiently amused."

CHAPTER XII.

AN ESCAPE FROM OLD MILL PRISON.

In the chapter on " Navy Officers in Privateers " mention was made of the capture of the armed brig *Pomona*, commanded by Captain Isaiah Robinson, of the navy, who had as his first officer Lieutenant Joshua Barney, also of the regular service. The experiences of the latter officer in British prisons were so extraordinary as to be deserving of special mention. On the capture of the *Pomona*, as related in the chapter referred to, Barney was placed in one of the prison ships at Wale Bogt. The arrival of Admiral Byron, who relieved Lord Howe as the commander in chief of the British naval forces on the American station, did much to improve the condition of these prisoners. A few days after taking command, Byron visited the prison ships and ordered several large, airy vessels to be fitted for the Americans, special accommodations and better food being reserved for the sick. Those officers who belonged to the regular navy were taken aboard the war ships, and some of them enjoyed the freedom of the flagship *Ardent*. Admiral Byron made it a point to personally inspect the prison ships regularly every week, accompanied by his fleet captain and secretary, and to inquire minutely into the conduct of the prisoners and listen to any complaints they had to make.

Among the American officers who had the good fortune to come under the ministrations of Admiral

148

Byron was Lieutenant Barney.   This officer was transferred to the *Ardent*, and one of his duties was to visit the prison ships and report on their condition to the admiral.   Barney had a boat placed under his command, and was permitted to go ashore whenever he pleased, being required only to sleep aboard the *Ardent*.   It was on one of his trips on shore that Barney found he was safer in the hands of his captors than among the townsfolk.   He had been invited to breakfast ashore with Sir William Tevisden, one of the admiral's aids, and had landed for that purpose, when he was roughly seized by a mob of men and boys.   It seems that a large fire had broken out in New York and was raging at the time the lieutenant landed.   Being dressed in the full American naval uniform, a crowd immediately set upon him, and, accusing him of having originated the fire, proceeded to throw him into the flames.   The threat undoubtedly would have been carried out had it not been for the intervention of a British officer.   Even then the mob declared that the lieutenant's explanation of having just landed for the purpose of breakfasting with Sir William Tevisden was a hoax, and it was not until, at the suggestion of the British officer, they had proceeded to the aid's house and heard the story from his lips that Lieutenant Barney was released.

Unfortunately for the American prisoners Admiral Byron was soon superseded by Admiral Rodney, who, in December, 1780, ordered the 64-gun ship of the line *Yarmouth*, Captain Lutwidge—the same that blew up the *Randolph* two years before [1]— to transport seventy-one officers to England, Barney being among them.   From the time these Americans stepped aboard the *Yarmouth* their captors gave it to be understood, by hints and innuendoes, that they were being taken to England to " be hanged as

---

[1] See Maclay's History of the United States Navy, vol. i, pp. 83-85.

rebels " ; and, indeed, the treatment they received aboard the *Yarmouth* on the passage over led them to believe that the British officers intended to cheat the gallows of their prey by causing the prisoners to die before reaching port. On coming aboard the ship of the line these officers were stowed away in the lower hold, next to the keel, under five decks, and many feet below the water line. Here in a twelve-by-twenty-foot room with upcurving floor, and only three feet high, the seventy-one men were stowed for fifty-three days like so much merchandise, without light or good air, unable to stand upright, with no means and with no attempt made to remove the accumulating filth! Their food was of the poorest quality, and was supplied in such insufficient quantities that whenever one of the prisoners died the survivors concealed the fact until the body began to putrify in order that the dead man's allowance might be added to theirs. The water served them for drink was so thick with repulsive matter that the prisoners were compelled to strain it between set teeth.

From the time the *Yarmouth* left New York till she reached Plymouth, in a most tempestuous winter's passage, these men were kept in this loathsome dungeon. Eleven died in delirium, their wild ravings and piercing shrieks appalling their comrades, and giving them a foretaste of what they themselves might soon expect. Not even a surgeon was permitted to visit them. Arriving at Plymouth the pale, emaciated, festering men were ordered to come on deck. Not one obeyed, for they were unable to stand upright. Consequently they were hoisted up, the ceremony being grimly suggestive of the manner in which they had been treated—like merchandise. And what were they to do, now that they had been placed on deck? The light of the sun, which they had scarcely seen for fifty-three days, fell upon their weak, dilated pupils with blinding force, their limbs unable to uphold them, their frames wasted by disease and want. Seeking for support they fell in a helpless mass, one upon the other, waiting and almost hoping for the blow that was to fall upon them next. Captain Silas Talbot was one of these prisoners.[1]

To send them ashore in this condition was "impracticable," so the British officers said, and we readily discover that this "impracticable" served the further purpose of diverting the just indignation of the landsfolk, which surely would be aroused if they saw such brutality practiced under St. George's cross. Waiting, then, until the captives could at least endure the light of day, and could walk without leaning on one another or clutching at every object for support, the officers had them moved to Old Mill Prison. Nor must it be forgotten that these weak captives were thus moved with a "strong military guard"—certainly not to prevent their escape; probably to guard against the curious gaze of the people. First they were taken before a certain tribunal—whether military or civic the prisoners did not know—where a number of questions were put to them, the words "revolt," "allegiance," "rebels," predominating, after which they were taken to the prison.

Mill Prison was a massive stone building in the center of an extensive court. The court was surrounded by a high wall, and twenty feet beyond that was another wall, parallel to the first, completely surrounding it. The only apertures in these walls were a gate in each, the inner one being formed with massive iron bars eight feet high. The outer gate during the day usually was left open so as to allow free communication between the keepers and their dwellings which were placed just outside the outer wall. Between eight o'clock in the morning and

[1] See page 111.

sunset the prisoners were allowed the privilege of
the inner court, but at night they were securely
locked in the prison house. Many sentinels were
stationed among the prisoners in the inner court
and in the prison itself, besides the regular patrols
on the two encircling walls and at the gates.

To the unfortunate Americans who had just arrived from the *Yarmouth* this place seemed a para-
dise, for at Mill Prison they could at least get light,
air, and exercise. Yet even here there were many
causes for complaint, for the American prisoners
seem to have been picked out for severe treatment.
It was shown that they were " treated with less humanity than the French and Spaniards, . . . they had
not a sufficient allowance of bread, and were very
scantily furnished with clothing." [1]   In 1781 the
Duke of Richmond presented a memorial to the
House of Peers.   " Several motions were grounded
on these petitions, but those proposed by the lords
and gentlemen in the Opposition were determined
in the negative; and others, to exculpate the Government in this business, were resolved in the
affirmative. It appeared upon inquiry that the
American prisoners were allowed half a pound of
bread less per day than the French and Spanish
prisoners. But the petition of the Americans produced no alterations in their favor, and the conduct of the administration was equally impolitic and
illiberal." [2]

Many attempts to escape were made by the
Americans during the period of their confinement in
Mill Prison, and some of them were successful. On
one occasion a number of them volunteered to attempt escape through the common sewer that emptied into the river. Several days and nights were
spent in sawing the iron bars that guarded the entrance to the sewer, and when an opening was made

[1] British Annual Register for 1781, p. 152.   [2] Ibid.

it was agreed that a few of the prisoners should endeavor to escape through it, and if they did not return in a given time it was to be understood that they had been successful and that others might follow. The pioneers in this attempt were lowered into the foul hole, and had waded several hundred feet in the dark passage, when they found a double iron grating, which they in vain endeavored to remove. They returned to their companions more dead than alive, and that method of escape was abandoned.

Barney soon came to be suspected as a bold and dangerous prisoner, and at one time was placed in heavy double irons and confined thirty days in a dark dungeon for a " suspected " attempt to escape. This solitary confinement determined him to effect his escape at the earliest moment possible. Realizing that he was watched more than any of the other prisoners, Barney resorted to a *ruse* to deceive his keepers.

When the common liberty of the yard was allowed the prisoners, it was their custom to while away their time with athletic games. Indulging in a game of leapfrog with his companions one day Barney pretended to have sprained his ankle, and for some time after that walked about with crutches. This seems to have thrown the jailers entirely off their guard, and, indeed, so well was the deception kept up that only a few of Barney's most intimate companions knew of the trick.

Among the soldiers who had been detailed to guard Mill Prison at this time was a man who had served in the British army in the United States. It seems that he had received some kindness from the Americans, and he now delighted in showing civility to the prisoners from that country. Barney soon discovered this, and managed to hold several conversations with the soldier, which resulted in a warm friendship springing up between them. On May 18, 1781, it was this soldier's turn to mount guard between the two gates of the inner and outer walls

13

of the prison, already described, his hours being
from noon till two o'clock. Some kind of an understanding had been reached between them, and on
the day mentioned Barney, hobbling about on his
crutches, gradually drew near the gate, and, observing that no one was near, he whispered inter-
rogatively through the bars, "To-day?" to which
the soldier replied, in a low tone, "Dinner." From
this answer Barney knew that one o'clock was
meant, for at that hour all the jailers took dinner,
leaving only the sentinels on guard.

Hastening to his cell Barney put on the undress
uniform of a British officer, which he had secured
from the friendly sentinel, and threw over it his
greatcoat. This coat he had been wearing about
the prison since the "spraining" of his ankle, so
that he would not "catch cold." As a matter of fact,
Barney had worn the coat so as to accustom the
jailers at seeing him in it, for it reached quite down
to his heels and entirely concealed any dress or
uniform that he might choose to wear. Having made
this change, Barney stepped out of his cell, though
still using his crutches, and sought the confidential
friends who were to assist him in his escape. At
a given signal these friends repaired to different
parts of the yard and engaged the various sentinels
in conversation so that they would not see what was
going on at the gates.

Observing that everything was ready, Barney
cast aside his crutches, entered the court, and boldly
walked toward the gate. Here he exchanged a
wink with the English sentinel, from which he knew
that all was right. Beside the gate stood a tall, mus-
cular man, a prisoner, an accomplice of Barney's.
With the agility of a cat, Barney sprang upon this
man's shoulders and then over the wall. It took
him but an instant to whip off his greatcoat and
throw it over his arm, and thrusting four guineas
into the hand of the friendly sentinel he started

Barney's escape from Mill Prison.

toward the outer gate, which, as usual, was standing
open. The back of the guardian of the outer gate was
turned, so that Barney passed through unchallenged.
Walking leisurely down the road he, in a few minutes, arrived at the house of a well-known friend to
the American cause.

The sudden appearance of a man dressed in the
uniform of a British officer at the door of this
house startled the inmates, which was not lessened
when Barney explained who he was, for to harbor
an escaped prisoner was high treason, especially
when the American sentiments of that family were
so well known to the officials. Notwithstanding this,
the good people consented to hide the prisoner for
the day. Contrary to their fears, no inquiry was
made for Barney that day, for his absence had not yet
been discovered. With a view of having his escape
unknown to the prison officials as long as possible,
Barney had arranged with a slender youth (who was
able to creep through the window bars at pleasure) to crawl through the aperture so as to answer to Barney's name in his cell every day at
roll call. In the evening Barney was taken to the
house of his host's father, a venerable clergyman
of Plymouth, where it was customary for Americans, whether free or in bondage, to resort. Here
he found two friends from his native State, New
Jersey, Colonel William Richardson and Dr. Hindman, who, with their servant, had been taken as
passengers in a merchantman, and were awaiting
an opportunity to return to America.

Arrangements were soon made to purchase a fishing smack, in which they were to make their way to
France, where they had a much better chance to
secure passage to the United States. A suitable
craft was secured, and the two gentlemen, with their
servant, slept in it that night. Among the effects
of the servant Barney found a suit of rough clothes,
which he put on over his uniform, as being bet-

ter adapted for carrying out the rôle of fisherman he was about to assume.   Then with an old
overcoat tied around the waist, a tarpaulin hat,
and a "knowing tie," made with a handkerchief
around his neck, he looked fairly like a fisherman,
and at daybreak he joined his countrymen in the
smack.

No time was lost in getting under way, for at
any moment Barney's escape might be discovered,
and as the alarm would immediately be given to Admiral Digby's fleet, which was anchored in the
mouth of the river, the closest inspection would
be made of every craft passing out.   As not one of
Barney's companions knew how to handle a rope,
all the work of navigating the craft devolved upon
him, but as he was a thorough seaman he soon had
the smack standing down the river.   With a fine
breeze and ebbing tide the adventurers were soon
in the midst of the formidable fleet of war vessels,
the frowning batteries of which yawned at them in
sullen silence, while the sentinels paced to and fro,
casting unsuspicious glances at the innocent-looking craft.   With the fleet safely behind him, Barney
boldly stood out to sea and made for the French
coast.   His companions were more helpless now
even than before, as they were prostrated by sea-
sickness, so that the entire safety of the party was in
the hands of the lieutenant.

Just as the shores of England began to fade,
and the adventurers were congratulating themselves on their escape, a sail loomed up on the horizon, and was soon made out to be a swift-sailing
vessel evidently in pursuit of the smack.   In a few
minutes she had come alongside, and, after ordering
the craft to heave to, sent a boat aboard with an
officer.   The sail proved to be a privateer, out from
Guernsey, and to her officer's demand of what was
on board the smack, and where she was bound, Lieutenant Barney replied:

"I have nothing on board, and am bound to the coast of France."

"Your business there?" asked the officer.

"I can not disclose to you my business;" and untying the rope that bound his greatcoat around him Barney showed his British uniform. The sight of the uniform had its desired effect. The privateersman instantly changed his commanding tone to one of respect and touched his hat. Following up his advantage Barney said, in a severe tone:

"Sir, I must not be detained; my business is urgent, and you must suffer me to proceed or you will, perhaps, find cause to regret it." To this the boarding officer politely replied that he would immediately go aboard and report to his commander. This he did, but in a few minutes the captain of the privateer himself came aboard, and, though very polite, he desired to know what business could carry a British officer to the enemy's coast:

"I should be very sorry to stop you, sir," he said, "if you are on public business; and if this be the fact it must surely be in your power to give me some proof of it without disclosing the secrets of Government, which I have no desire to know."

Barney replied that to show him such proofs would be to hazard the success of his mission, which depended entirely on its being kept absolutely secret from all save those intrusted in its execution.

"Then, sir," replied the privateersman, "I shall be under the necessity of carrying you to England."

"Do as you please," said Barney calmly, "but, remember, it is at your peril. All I have to say further, sir, is that if you persist in interrupting my voyage I must demand of you to carry me directly on board Admiral Digby's flagship, at Plymouth."

The American officer well knew that this was an unpleasant request for the privateersman, for if he ventured in the fleet he might expect to be relieved of some of his crew by the admiral's press gangs, who were constantly on the lookout for men. Barney hoped this would induce the privateersman to let him go, and in fact the Englishman did hesitate for a few minutes. Barney followed up the stroke by commenting on the fine, manly appearance of the privateer's crew. But all to no purpose, the Englishman deciding to take them to Plymouth.

All that night the two vessels were beating their way back to the English coast, and on the following morning entered a small port about six miles from Plymouth. Here the English commander, leaving Barney aboard the privateer, went ashore to make his report to Admiral Digby, and under pretense of keeping out of the way of press gangs nearly all the crew went ashore also. The few that remained aboard treated Barney with the respect due to his assumed character and he was allowed every liberty save that of going ashore. Seizing a favorable opportunity, when those aboard were at dinner, Barney slid down a rope over the stern and got into a boat. In doing this he badly injured his leg, but unmindful of the pain he rapidly sculled ashore unseen by any of the privateersmen.

As he approached the beach many of the idlers came to the landing to watch him, but made no attempt to interfere. Boldly jumping ashore he called for aid to haul his boat up. Several responded, when Barney was startled by a loud voice calling out:

"Hollo there! Where did you catch her? What has she got aboard?"

Looking around Barney saw that he was addressed by the customhouse officer. He soon satisfied that important person that he had nothing of a contraband nature, and complaining of the hurt on his leg—the blood now plainly oozing out from his stocking—he made that an excuse for hurrying away to get "something onto it." Before leaving, however, he dispelled whatever suspicions might have been lingering in the customhouse officer's mind by asking:

"Pray, sir, can you tell me where our people are?"

"I think, sir, you'll find them all at the Red Lion, the very last house in the village."

"Thank you, sir. I wish you a very good morning;" and with that the American walked off in the direction indicated.

It was the least of Barney's desires to meet any of "our people," but he found that there was only one street in the village, so that he was compelled to pass the Red Lion. He passed the tavern unperceived, as he thought, but just as he had turned the corner he heard a gruff voice calling after him:

"Hollo, lieutenant! I'm glad you're come ashore. We was jist some on us to off arter you."

"And what for, pray?" asked Barney with considerable uneasiness.

"Why, may be as how some on us might ship if we knowed a thing or two."

Barney saw at once that his assumed disguise had gained full credence among the sailors in the privateers, and that some of them believed, through his interest, they could get better berths in Admiral Digby's fleet. Engaging the man in conversation, and at the same time walking rapidly away from the Red Lion so as to get away from the rest of the men, Barney gave encouragement to the seaman's idea of shipping in the fleet, when the latter suddenly asked:

"Where are you going?"

"To Plymouth. Come, you might as well go along with me."

The tar hesitated a moment, seemed to think better of his plan of entering a navy noted for its cruelty to seamen, and finally said he'd go back to his old shipmates.

As soon as the tar was out of sight, Barney

quickened his pace into a run lest he be overtaken
by others of the crew. Realizing, also, that as soon
as the captain of the privateer had explained his
capture to Admiral Digby his escape from the
prison would in all probability be discovered, and
a guard be sent to secure him, he deemed it advis-
able to jump over a hedge and seclude himself in a
private garden. This precaution was doubly necessary, as the highway on which he was traveling was
the direct route from Plymouth, and the one a guard
would take in coming for him.

On leaping over the hedge he found himself in
the superb private grounds of Lord Edgecombe.
Wandering about in search of the servants' house,
he was discovered by the gardener, who was much
incensed by the intrusion. Barney pacified him by
explaining that he had injured his leg and was seeking the shortest way to Plymouth. Giving the gardener a tip, Barney was conducted to a private gate
opening on the river, and hailing a butcher who
was going by in a small wherry with two sheep to
market our adventurer got aboard. By this means
Barney avoided the necessity of crossing the river
by the public ferry, and also that of passing by Mill
Prison and of a chance of meeting the guard.

Immediately on receiving the report of the privateer's commander, Admiral Digby caused an inquiry
to be made in all the prisons and places of confinement in or near Plymouth, and at the time Barney
was sliding down the rope over the privateer's stern
to get into a boat his escape from Mill Prison was
discovered; and at the moment he passed through
Lord Edgecombe's private gate to the riverside the
tramp of the soldiers—all of whom were familiar
with Barney—was heard passing the very hedge he
had just vaulted over on their way to take him back
to prison.

That night Barney gained the house of the venerable clergyman that he had left only the morn-

ing before. The same evening Colonel Richardson
and Dr. Hindman arrived at this house also, having
been released from the privateer after the guard
from Mill Prison had inspected them. While these
fugitives were seated at supper laughing and jok-
ing over their hapless adventures, the bell of the
town-crier was heard under the windows, and the
reward of five guineas for the apprehension of
Joshua Barney, a rebel deserter from Mill Prison,
was proclaimed. For a moment it was thought that
the proclamation was addressed to this particular
house, and that a military guard would follow to
search the premises; but in a few minutes the bell
and voice began to die away in the distance, and
finally could be heard no more.

Three days longer the fugitive remained in his
place of concealment, by which time a fashionable
suit of clothes was procured for him and a post
chaise was engaged to take him to Exeter. At midnight Barney, accompanied by one of the clergyman's sons, repaired to the secluded spot where the
vehicle was in waiting, and bidding farewell to his
friends stepped in and was rapidly driven away.
Reaching the gate of the town they were brought
to by a stern "Halt!" from the sentry. The driver
obeyed, and in a moment an officer thrust a lantern
into the carriage and began reading aloud the exact
description of the person and dress Barney had
worn in his escape from the prison. Of course the
dress had been changed, and Barney succeeded so
well in distorting his features that the facial description did not fit, so with an apology the officer
allowed the post chaise to proceed. At Exeter our
adventurer took the stage to Bristol, and from there
made his way to London, France, and Holland.

In Holland Barney secured passage in the armed
ship *South Carolina*, Captain Gillon. We get an interesting side light on Barney's ability as a seaman
from the diary of John Trumbull, the famous

painter. " The want of funds or credit," says Trumbull, " and the dread of those who had advanced money on her [the *South Carolina's*] outfit occasioned her officers—after she had been permitted to drop down to the Texel—to run her out of the Roads, and to anchor outside, beyond the jurisdiction of the port, at a distance of more than a league from land. Here several of us passengers went on board, and on the 12th of August [1781], soon after sunrise, the wind began to blow from the northwest, directly on shore, with every appearance of a heavy gale. The proper thing to have done was to have run back into the Texel Roads, but that we dared not do lest the ship should be seized. We dared not run for the English Channel lest we should fall in with British cruisers of superior force. The gale soon increased to such a degree that it would have been madness to remain at anchor on such a lee shore. The only thing which could be done, therefore, was to lay the ship's head to the northeast and carry sail. A fog soon came on, so thick that we could hardly see from stem to stern; the gale increased to a very hurricane, and soon brought us to close-reefed topsails; the coast of Holland was under our lee, and we knew that we were running upon the very edge of the sands, which extended so far from the shore that if the ship should touch she must go to pieces before we could even see the land and all hands must perish. We passed the morning in the deepest anxiety; in the afternoon we discovered that we had started several of the bolts of the weather main chain plates. This forced us to take in our close-reefed topsails, as the masts would no longer bear the strain of any sail aloft, and we were obliged to rely upon a reefed foresail. By this time we knew that we must be not far from Heligoland, at the mouth of the Elbe, where the coast begins to trend northward, which increased the danger. At ten o'clock at night a squall struck

us, heavier than the gale, and threw our only sail
aback; the ship became unmanageable, the officers
lost their self-possession, and the crew all confidence in them, while for a few minutes all was confusion and dismay.   Happily for us, Commodore
Barney was among the passengers—he had just
escaped from Mill Prison, in England. Hearing the
increased tumult aloft, and feeling the ungoverned
motion of the ship, he flew upon deck, saw the danger, assumed command, the men obeyed, and he
soon had her again under control.   It was found
that with the squall the wind had shifted several
points, so that on the other tack we could lay a safe
course to the westward, and thus relieve our mainmast.   That our danger was imminent no one will
doubt when informed that on the following morning the shore of the Texel Island was covered with
the wreck of ships which were afterward ascertained to have been Swedish; among them was a
ship of seventy-four guns, convoying twelve merchantmen—all were wrecked and every soul on
board perished.   The figurehead of the ship of war,
a yellow lion, the same as ours, was found upon the
shore, and gave sad cause to our friends for believing, for some time, that the *South Carolina* had perished."

When the gale subsided the *South Carolina* made
the Orkneys, and when off Faroe encountered another terrific gale, which, together with a deficiency
of provisions, induced Gillon to run into Coruña,
Spain. "There," continues Trumbull, "we found
the *Cicero* [Captain Hill], a fine letter-of-marque
ship of twenty guns and one hundred and twenty
men, belonging to the house of Cabot, in Beverly,
Massachusetts. [On her outward passage this privateer had made several valuable prizes, which were
disposed of in Spain.] She was to sail immediately
for Bilboa, there to take a cargo on board which
was lying ready for her, and to sail to America. Sev-

eral of us—among whom were Major Jackson, who
had been secretary to Colonel John Laurens' in his
late mission to France, Captain Barney, Mr. Brom-
field, and Charles Adams—tired of the management
of the *South Carolina*, endeavored to get a passage to
Bilboa on board of this ship, and were permitted
to go on board their [the *Cicero's*] prize, a fine British Lisbon packet. The usual time required to run
from Coruña to Bilboa was two to three days. We
were again unfortunate; the wind being east, dead
ahead, we were twenty-one days in making the passage. . . . At the end of eighteen days we fell in
with a little fleet of Spanish coasters and fishermen,
running to the westward before the wind, who told
us that when off the bar of Bilboa they had seen
a ship and two brigs, which they believed to be British cruisers, and cautioned us to keep a good lookout. Captain Hill immediately hailed his prize, a
ship of sixteen guns, and a fine brig of sixteen guns,
which was also in company, and directed them to
keep close to him and prepare to meet an enemy.
At sunset we saw what appeared to be the force
described, and about midnight found we were within
hail. The *Cicero* ran close alongside of the ship and
hailed her in English—no answer; in French—no
answer. The men who were at their guns, impatient of delay, did not wait for orders, but poured
in her a broadside; the hostile squadron—as we supposed them—separated and made all sail in different directions, when a boat from the large ship came
alongside with her captain, a Spaniard, who informed us that they were Spanish vessels from St.
Sebastian, bound for the West Indies; that his ship
was very much cut in her rigging, but happily no
lives lost. He had mistaken us for British vessels
and was delighted to find his mistake. We apolo-
gized for ours, offered assistance, etc., and we parted
most amicably. Soon after we entered the river of
Bilboa and ran up to Porto Galette. The disabled

[Spanish] ship, with her comrades, put into Coruña, where it was found that one of our 9-pound shot had wounded the mainmast of our antagonist so severely that it was necessary to take it—the mast—out and put in a new one. This was not the work of a day, and her consorts were detained until their flagship was ready. Meantime we had almost completed taking in our cargo at Bilboa, when a messenger from Madrid arrived with orders to unhang the rudders of all American ships in the port until the bill for repairs of the wounded ship, demurrage of her consorts, etc., were paid."

When the *Cicero* finally got away she made directly for America, and, after narrowly escaping shipwreck on Cape Ann, gained the port of Beverly, "where we found," continues Trumbull, "eleven other ships, all larger and finer than the *Cicero*—all belonging to the same owners, the brothers Cabot— laid up for the winter. Yet such are the vicissitudes of war and the elements that before the close of the year they were all lost by capture or wreck, and the house of Cabot had not a single ship afloat upon the ocean." At Beverly Lieutenant Barney received an offer from the Messrs. Cabot to command a fine privateer ship of twenty guns, but he declined. At Boston he met several of his fellow-prisoners who also had effected their escape from Mill Prison. After this Barney proceeded to Philadelphia and assumed command of the *Hyder Ally*, in which he fought one of the most remarkable battles of the war.[1]

Two years after the miraculous escape of Lieutenant Barney from Mill Prison he again visited Plymouth, then as captain of the United States frigate *General Washington*. He took occasion to give a dinner aboard his ship, at which his friends who aided in his escape, besides all the British offi-

---

[1] See chapter xiv, Career of the *General Washington*.

cers in the town and on the station, attended. Barney learned that the manner of his escape still remained a mystery to the prison officials, and no suspicion had attached to those who aided him. He also visited the gardener who unconsciously had been instrumental in saving the fugitive from recapture, and gave him a purse of gold.

CHAPTER XIII.

CRUISE OF DR. SOLOMON DROWNE.

THAT all classes of society in the North American colonies were influenced by the " craze for privateering " has been amply demonstrated in the foregoing pages. In the chapter on A Boy Privateersman we followed the adventures of a farmer's lad, in the career of Silas Talbot we have seen how an army officer and a company of soldiers could conduct themselves aboard a private armed craft, and in the extracts bearing on Joshua Davis we have discovered creditable fighting capacities in a barber's apprentice. In the private journal of Dr. Solomon Drowne we have perhaps one of the most satisfactory accounts of a privateering cruise during the Revolution, and, being written by a man of education, having a keen eye to matters of human interest, the record is given *verbatim*. Dr. Drowne was born in Providence, Rhode Island, March 11, 1753, was graduated from Brown University in 1773, and completed his medical studies in the University of Pennsylvania. He served in the Continental army as surgeon throughout the war—excepting the seventeen days he imprudently ventured on the high seas—and afterward became professor of botany in Brown University.

This journal has been preserved through the efforts of two youthful " amateurs in the black art," Henry Russell Drowne and Charles L. Moreau, who printed the manuscript on private presses in 1872.

In a letter to the Hon. John Russell Bartlett, of Providence, Rhode Island, young Drowne says: "As you are interested in the black art, I beg your acceptance of a copy of Dr. Drowne's journal, in 1780, on the *Hope*, from the undersigned, his great grandson. It was printed by two boys, Master Moreau and myself, both novices in the art." The original manuscript of Dr. Drowne's journal was prepared for these young Franklins by Henry Thayer Drowne, brother of Dr. Solomon Drowne, together with a few explanatory notes; and the result is one of the most complete records of a privateering cruise during the war for independence.

"An emergency at home," says Mr. H. T. Drowne, "caused him [Dr. Solomon Drowne] to embark as surgeon in the *Hope*." This privateer was a sloop, mounting seven guns, with a complement of twenty men, under the command of Captain J. Munroe, and was fitted out for a cruise at Providence, Rhode Island, in the fall of 1780. "Tuesday, October 3d," writes Dr. Drowne in his journal, " [we] sailed from Providence on board the sloop *Hope*. Wind at northeast, drizzly, dirty weather. Outsailed Mr. John Brown [one of the leading shipowners in Rhode Island] in his famous boat. Put about for Captain Munroe and take Mr. Brown and Captain S—— Smith on board, who dine with us. Some time after noon Captain Munroe comes on board and a few glasses of good wishes, founded on the *Hope*, having circled, Colonel Nightingale, etc., depart and we proceed on our course. Toward evening come to anchor between Dutch Island and Conanicut [opposite Newport] to get in readiness for the sea. [I] officiate as clerk, copying articles, etc.

"October 4th.—This morning sail from Dutch Island harbor. At 7 A. M. pass the lighthouse walls on Beaver Tail. Wind northeast, hazy weather. A heavy sea from the southward. I begin to be excessively seasick, but do not take my station upon the lee quarter till that side is pretty well manned. [Evidently a large portion of the *Hope's* crew were rendered helpless by this evil of the sea, and we can not but admire the doughty doctor in holding out so long as he did.—E. S. M.] This is a sickness that is indeed enough to depress the spirits even of the brave.

"October 5th.—Fresh breezes and cloudy. Treble reef mainsail. Excessive sickness. Hove to. A heavy sea, with squalls of rain.

" October 6th.—[I] keep the cabin. Strong gales and squally; still lying by. Saw a ship and made sail from her, then brought to again.

" October 7th.—Get the topmast down; balance the mainsail and lie to. Put our guns in the hold, etc. [In the] afternoon the gale becomes violent. Only one long-practiced seaman on board who says he ever knew it more tempestuous. Nail down our hatches and secure everything in the best manner possible. [We] have a hole cut through the store-room to open a communication fore and aft below the deck. The storm increases. Ship a sea, which carries away some of our crane irons [davits]. Get our axes into the cabin, ready to cut away the mast should there be occasion. A becoming fortitude in general predominates on board, though horror stalks around. They who go down to the sea in ships do indeed see the wonders of the Lord in the deep. The description of a tempest, translated by Boileau from Longinus, occurs to my mind with peculiar energy:

> ' Comme l'on voit les flots, soulevés par l'Orage,
> Fondre sur un Vaisseau qui s'oppose à leur Rage,
> Le vent avec Fureur dans les Voiles frémit ;
> La Mer blanchit d'écume, et l'air au loin gémit
> Le Matelot troublé, que son Art abondonne,
> Croit voir dans chaque Flot qui l'environne.'

" I like this description, because there are no trifling incidents thrown in. 'Tis short and energetic—

14

grand and forcive, like the storm itself. One now
can scarce refrain from envying the husbandman
who, folded on his bed of placid quiet, hears the wild
whistle round his steady mansion, whilst our ears
are assailed by its rude howling through the cordage, our vessel tossed upon the foaming surges.
Thrice happy rural life, and too happy countrymen, did they but know their happiness! [The foregoing outburst from Dr. Drowne leads us to believe
that he must have been very ill indeed at that time.
—E. S. M.] The gale moderates, the wind shifts,
and the sea begins to be appeased. God of Nature!
Who that sees thy greatness on the wide, extended
ocean but must be filled with adoration, and feel a
submission of heart to thy eternal orders.

"October 8th.—Moderate weather after the
storm. Get our clothes, etc., out to dry. Cloudy still.
Our mariners wonder we came off so well as we did;
and indeed we escaped to admiration, owing, in some
measure, to the goodness of our vessel and the taking every precaution previous to the severity of the
gale. Toward evening a sail is seen from the masthead; [we] set sail and stand for her.

"October 9th.—*Post nubila, Phœbus!* A beautiful
morning. How cheering are the beams of the sun!
I view him almost with the sentiments of a Persian.
Those surly billows that erewhile buffeted us to and
fro, and would suffer us no peace, are composed as
the infant that has bawled itself to rest. A large
number of whale of the spermaceti kind [are] playing round us this morning, and let them sport. The
Father of the universe has given them the expanded
ocean for the wide scene of their happiness. Nothing of said sail to be seen. Have an observation for
the first time. Latitude 38° 37'. My variation chart
of no use for want of an azimuth compass. [In]
afternoon discover a ship standing to the eastward.

"October 10th.—No remarkable occurrence.
Latitude 54'.

"October 11th.—Whilst at dinner a sail is cried. Immediately give chase and discover another. One a sloop, which bears down upon us, the other a brig. Make every preparation for an engagement, but on approaching and hailing the sloop she proves to be the *Randolph*, Captain Fosdick, from New London, mounting eighteen 4-pounders. The brig, with only two guns, her prize from England, taken at eight o'clock this morning. Captain Fosdick says her cargo amounted to twenty thousand pounds sterling."

The learned doctor now apparently begins to think better (or worse) of his privateering, for he continues: "What good and ill fortune were consequent on that capture! Hard for those poor fellows, their tedious voyage being just accomplished, thus to have their brightening prospect clouded in a moment. If virtue is the doing good to others, privateering can not be justified upon the principles of virtue, although I know it is not repugnant to the 'laws of nations,' but rather deemed policy among warring powers thus to distress each other regardless of the suffering individual. But however agreeable to and supportable by the rights of war, yet when individuals come to thus despoil individuals of their property 'tis hard; the cruelty then appears, however political." [Had Dr. Drowne been a delegate to the Peace Conference at The Hague in 1899 he could not have summed up the arguments of the American commissioners in favor of protection of private property on the high seas better than by using these words.—E. S. M.]

"October 12th.—Early this morning two sail in sight, a ship and a brig. Chase them chief of the day to no purpose. We conclude they sail well and may be bound to Philadelphia. Latitude 39° 6'. Soundings nineteen fathoms. Lost sight of the *Randolph* by the chase.

"October 13th.—A foggy morning and Scotch

mist. Clears away pleasant. Latitude 39° 31'. This afternoon a sloop is discovered under the lee bow standing before the wind. All hands [are] upon deck preparing for the chase. [There is] but little wind, so the oars are to be plied. I must go and see how we come on. Night obliges us to give over the pursuit.

"October 14th.—A sail [is] seen from the masthead; proves a ship. We chase. Catch a herring hog, which makes us a fine breakfast and dinner for the whole crew. Another sail heaves in sight. Upon a nearer approach the ship appears to be of the line [the heaviest class of war ships]. Several in sight. Toward evening signal guns heard. We take them to be men-of-war standing in, northwest by west. Longitude, by reckoning, 73° 30"; latitude 39° 34'; twenty-six fathoms. A pleasant moonlight evening. Spend it in walking the quarter-deck.

"October 15th.—A pleasant day. See a sail to windward. As she rather approaches us we lie a-hull for her. I think it is more agreeable waiting for them than rowing after them. Get a fishing line under way. Catch a hake and a few dogfish. It being Sunday, try the efficacy of a clean shirt, in order to be something like folks ashore. Give chase, as the vessel comes down rather slow. On approaching discover her to be a snow.[1] She hauls her wind and stands from us. Sails very heavy, and Captain Munroe is sanguine in the belief we shall make a prize of her. Get everything in readiness to board her.

"There seems something awful in the preparation for an attack and the immediate prospect of an action. She hauls up her courses and hoists English colors. I take my station in the cabin, where [I] remain not long before I hear the huzza on deck in

---

[1] A vessel equipped with two masts, resembling the main and fore masts of a ship, and a third, small mast, just abaft the mainmast, carrying a trysail.

consequence of her striking. Send our boat for the
captain and his papers. She sailed from Kingston,
Jamaica, upwards of forty days since, in a fleet, and
was bound to New York, Captain William Small,
commander. She has ten men on board and four excellent 4-pounders. Her cargo consists of one hundred and forty-nine puncheons, twenty-three hogsheads, three quarter casks and nine barrels of rum,
and twenty hogsheads of muscovado sugar. [We]
send two prize masters and ten men on board, get
the prisoners on board our vessel and taking the
prize in tow. Stand towards Egg Harbor. We hardly know what to do with the prize. The wind shift-
ing a little we stand to the eastward.

"October 16.—Keep on eastern course to try to
get her into our harbor, if possible. Now we are
terribly apprehensive of seeing a sail. About sunset
a sail is seen from the masthead which excites no
small anxiety. Cast off the snow's hawser, etc.
However, night coming on, and seeing no more of
the sail, pursue our course. Sound forty-two fathoms of water.

"October 17th.—Strong gales at north—northwest and very cold. Latitude 40° 30'. Afternoon,
moderates somewhat. [We] take the old snow in
tow again. We expect to bring up somewhere in the
neighborhood of Martha's Vineyard. A squall with
hail and snow comes up which splits the snow's
jib to pieces. A little bird came on board, rendered
quite tame by its long, hazardous flight. Amuse
myself with looking over a quarter waggoner taken
out of the snow. Take a drink of grog, made of
snow water. Very heavy squalls indeed this night,
with a rough, bad sea. Obliged to cast off the dull
snow and let her go her pace. About forty-two
fathoms water. Sleep little.

"October 18th.—Boisterous weather still, a tumbling sea going. Feel qualmish. Latitude 40° 40'.
The wind so contrary that we make but slow ad-

vances towards our desired haven. Just as I was
pleasing myself with the idea of a speedy conclusion
to this disagreeable cruise a sail is cried, which perhaps will protract it, if not show us [New] York in
our way home. The sail appears to be a brig and
not standing for us, as we at first apprehended. We
chase till night prevents. Lose sight of the snow.
Fire signal guns, show flash fires and a lantern, but
see no answer.

"October 19th.—The snow is in sight again this
morning. Run alongside and take her in tow again.
They say they answered our signals, though unseen
by us. A pretty bird caught on board, the Carolina
redbird. More moderate weather. Latitude 40° 30".
At this rate, the West Indies will bring us up sooner
than Martha's Vineyard or Nantucket. Forty-nine
fathoms. Have our pistols hung up in the cabin,
to be in readiness for the prisoners should they take
in it into their heads to rise upon the watch in the
night.

"October 20th.—Thick weather and the wind
contrary. Depth of water seventeen fathoms. Surely we must be nigh some land, and, were it not for
such weather, perhaps [we] might see it. Latitude
39° 59". A good southwardly breeze last evening
shoved us up to this latitude. Here we are, becalmed and fairly lost; for, whether we are to the
eastward of Nantucket, or between Martha's Vineyard or Block Island, or the last and Montauk Point [1]
[a little to the southward of them all], is a matter
in question amongst our seamen. About sunset I
go on board the snow at Captain Small's request to
do something for his rheumatic knee and see a very
sick boy. After prescribing for him, examining the
medicine box, giving directions, etc., return to the
sloop.

"October 21st.—Very calm. Not a breath to

---

[1] For map, see page 104.

ruffle the ocean. How uneasy every one on board
is, fearing to lose the prize! But if we can't stir
hence others can't come here to molest us. Fourteen fathoms of water with yellowish, small gravel
stones—according to some the sign of No Man's
Land, to others Montauk. I hope we shall know
where we are soon. The horizon too hazy yet to
see far. Half past ten o'clock. At length the agreeable prospect presents itself. Martha's Vineyard,
etc., full in view. What an excellent landfall! To
one who was never out of sight of land a whole day
before the seeing it again is very pleasing, though
after only seventeen days' deprivation. It is very
disagreeable tossing about in so small a vessel at
this season of the year. Latitude 41° 17'. A pilot
comes on board, and soon another, but too late. We
go in between No Man's Land and Gay Head, so
called from its exhibiting a variety of colors when
the sun shines bright upon it—especially just after
a rain. Elizabeth Islands in sight on the starboard
side, Cuddy Hunk the westmost. Ten o'clock P. M.
We now have Sakonnet Point astern [see map on
page 96], therefore are safe. Pass up the east side
of Rhode Island. Our men are in uncommon spirits.
Anchor about a league up the passage.

"October 22d. — Sunday. Very foggy. What
wind there is [is] ahead. Weigh anchor and [get]
out oars. A fair, gentle breeze springs from the
south. Pass through Bristol Ferry way with hard
tugging about the middle of the afternoon. Come
to anchor in the Bay, but where rendered uncertain
by the fog having come up again. About six o'clock
Captain Munroe and I, with four of the hands, set
off for Providence in the boat. Being enveloped in
an uncommon thick fog, take a compass and a lantern on board. But proceed not far, the smallness
of the boat and the inexpertness of the rowers occasioning a motion agitating our compass beyond use.
Therefore we are glad to find the way back to the

Hope, which is effected by their fixing lanterns in the shrouds, in consequence of our raising ours and hailing.

" October 23d.—Early after breakfast we set off again in the boat with the compass, being still surrounded with an excessive fog. Run ashore to the eastward of Nayatt Point and mistake it for Conimicut. However, arrive at Providence about eleven o'clock, it having cleared off very pleasant. Thus ends our short but tedious cruise. At sunset the sloop and snow arrive, firing thirteen cannon each."

CHAPTER XIV.

CAREER OF THE GENERAL WASHINGTON.

FEW privateers in the war for independence had such a remarkable career as the *General Washington*. She was a swift-sailing craft pierced for twenty guns, and ordinarily carried a complement of one hundred and twenty men. In 1780 this privateer, then commanded by Captain Walker, had an action with a ship of eighteen guns and a brig of six guns that lasted six hours, when the enemy, being satisfied that they could not take her without too much sacrifice, hauled off, leaving the *General Washington* with her mainmast gone by the board, and having four guns dismounted, three men killed and three wounded. In the same cruise the *General Washington* came across a fleet of British war vessels, and escaped only by superior seamanship and her fine running qualities. The *General Washington* soon afterward was captured by Admiral Arbuthnot's squadron. Her name was changed to *General Monk*, and, being refitted, was taken into the British navy and placed under the command of Captain Rodgers.

Captain Rodgers was an officer of unusual ability and courage. He was born at Lynington in 1755, and at an early age shipped as a midshipman in the frigate *Arethusa*, Captain Hammond. The first active service of young Rodgers was on the North American station, where he followed his commander to the 44-gun frigate *Roebuck*. In March, 1776, Rodgers was detailed, with the second lieutenant of

177

the *Roebuck*, to man an armed tender of the frigate, with orders to surprise the town of Lewes, within the Capes of the Delaware. The tender succeeded in capturing a sloop, and Rodgers was placed aboard with several of his men.

The British prize crew, however, proved untrue to their colors, and, conspiring with the American prisoners, ran the sloop ashore while Mr. Rodgers was asleep and made a prisoner of him. He was taken into the interior and sent to Williamsburg, Virginia, and then through Richmond to Charlottesville, " where he pleasantly spent eight months with other prisoners. Their chief enjoyment was to ramble among the woods and mountains and to gather wild fruits and salads, with which they would regale themselves during the noontide heats on the banks of some sheltered rivulet." In April, 1777, the prisoners were marched to Alexandria, from which place Rodgers and several others contrived to escape, and after an exhausting tramp of four hundred miles reached the Delaware, where they were fortunate enough to find the *Roebuck* and get aboard.

From this time on Rodgers was entirely engaged in predatory expeditions on the shores of Virginia and Maryland, and succeeded in cutting out several armed vessels. He was in the *Roebuck* when she, with other British war ships, came up the Delaware in August, 1778, to bombard Fort Mifflin. Afterward he distinguished himself at the siege of Charleston. On the fall of that place Admiral Arbuthnot gave Rodgers the command of the *General Washington*, then called *General Monk*. During the two years Rodgers commanded this vessel he took and assisted in taking more than sixty vessels, his services in connection with the capture of the *Trumbull*, Captain Nicholson, having been noted.[1]

On the evening of April 7, 1782, while the *General*

---

[1] See Maclay's History of the Navy, vol. i, pp. 142, 143.

Monk was cruising off Cape Henlopen in company with the frigate *Quebec*, Captain Mason, the sails of eight vessels were discovered lying at anchor in Cape May Roads. Believing them to be Americans waiting for an opportunity to get to sea, Captain Mason anchored his ships so as to prevent the strange sails from getting to sea under cover of night. These vessels were merchantmen under the convoy of the Pennsylvania merchant ship *Hyder Ally*. At this period of the war it was the custom of the British to fit out privateers in New York and send them to cruise in the Chesapeake and off the Delaware, to capture merchantmen passing in and out. Many vessels were taken in this way. Another source of danger in these waters was the swarm of refugee boats. Usually these were light-draught vessels manned by Tories and other disaffected Americans. They concealed their craft in the small bays and creeks, and under cover of night attacked unsuspecting merchantmen.

The damage inflicted by these boats became so great that on April 9, 1782, the Pennsylvania Legislature determined to equip a war vessel at the expense of the State—as Congress, at that time, was unable to give adequate protection—for the purpose of cruising in these waters. Twenty-five thousand pounds were appropriated, and authority was granted to borrow twenty-five thousand pounds more if necessary, and Messrs. Francis Gurney, John Patton, and William Allibone were appointed commissioners to secure the necessary vessels. The merchants of Philadelphia, however, had anticipated this measure, and on their own responsibility, in March, 1782, purchased of John Willcocks the trading vessel *Hyder Ally*. At the time the merchants concluded to take this step, the *Hyder Ally* dropped down the river, outward bound, with a cargo of flour. As she was the only vessel in any way suited for the service, she was recalled, her flour landed, and she was pierced for sixteen 6-pounders. A complement of one hundred and ten men was shipped and the command given to Lieutenant Joshua Barney, of the navy. Barney, as we have just noticed, had returned to the United States after his extraordinary escape from Mill Prison. She sailed as convoy to the merchantmen alluded to early in April, strict orders being given to Barney to confine his cruising ground within the Capes, as the merchants had no intention of protecting their commerce beyond that limit. The convoy had got as far as Cape May Roads, where it was discovered by Captain Mason's blockading force.

Not knowing the exact force of the vessels he had seen within the Roads, Captain Mason on the following morning ordered Rodgers to enter the roads and reconnoiter, and, in case the vessels were not too strong for him, to attack, while the *Quebec* would proceed higher up, so as to prevent them from entering the Delaware. Before Captain Rodgers could carry out his instructions, he saw three sails standing toward him, which were soon made out to be British privateers fitted out at New York, one of them being the *Fair American*, a ship of fourteen guns, which had been taken from the colonists. This privateer had been one of the squadron under the orders of Captain Biddle, of the *Randolph*, when that unfortunate vessel was blown up by the *Yarmouth*.

Captain Rodgers communicated his design to the commanders of the privateers, and asked for their support. The captain of the *Fair American* promised to co-operate, but the other two held aloof, preferring to take their chances in independent action. The *General Monk* stood into the Roads with the *Fair American*, and about noon rounded Cape May Point. This discovered them to the convoy, and signaling the merchantmen to make sail up the bay Lieutenant Barney maneuvered so as to cover their

retreat.   Both the English vessels made straight
for the convoy.   The *Fair American* in passing the
Hyder Ally gave her a broadside, to which the Americans made no reply, and then hastened on in chase of
the fleeing traders.   One of these, a ship, surrendered at the first summons; another, the only armed
vessel, aside from the *Hyder Ally*, in the convoy, ran
ashore and was deserted by her crew, who escaped
over the jib boom, while a brig and two ships endeavored to enter Morris River, and in the effort to
cut them off the *Fair American* ran aground.

This left the *Hyder Ally* and the *General Monk*
alone to dispute the supremacy of the Roads.   Captain Rodgers made for the *Hyder Ally* with the intention of discharging his broadside at close quarters,
and then boarding in the smoke.   When within pistol
shot the Americans poured in their broadside, and
perceiving that it was the enemy's programme to
board Barney instructed his men at the wheel to
execute the next order " by the rule of contrary."
Just as the ships were about to foul, Barney called
out to the helmsmen in a loud voice, which was intended to be heard aboard the enemy's ship: " Hard
aport your helm!   Do you want him to run aboard
us? "   The helmsmen understood their cue, and clapping the wheel hard to starboard brought the Englishman's jib boom afoul of the *Hyder Ally's* fore rigging, which exposed the *General Monk* to a raking
fire from the entire American broadside.   It took
but a minute for the Americans to lash the ships
together, and then they began delivering a destructive, raking fire, to which the enemy was unable to
make reply except with small arms.

The Englishmen endeavored to board, but Lieutenant Barney had made such admirable defense
against this that they were frustrated.   The enemy
then endeavored to pick off the Americans with their
small arms, and a lively, rattling fire of musketry
was the consequence.   Many of the marines in the

Hyder Ally were thoroughbred " backwoodsmen," to whom the use of firearms was as natural as walking. One of these men, a Buck County rifleman, particularly attracted the attention of Captain Barney. In the hottest of the fight, when both sides were making every exertion to gain the victory, this man several times asked his commander, " Who made this gun I'm using?" Such a seemingly useless question in the heat of battle, as might be expected, drew a rough answer from the captain. But Barney knew the man had never been on a ship before, and that fact prevented severer treatment for his breach of marine etiquette. The man, however, was not idle. The coolness and deliberation with which he fired showed that he was not in the least excited, and seemed as much pleased as if he were engaging in some harmless pastime. Asking the question for the third time, Captain Barney sharply inquired why he wanted to know. " W-a-a-l," replied the man, with the drawl peculiar to the mountaineers, " this 'ere bit o' iron is jes' the best smoothbore I ever fired in my life."

A few minutes after this another Buck County " marine," who was equally ignorant of nautical etiquette, with the familiarity of a backwoodsman called out to Barney: " Say, Cap, do you see that fellow with the white hat?" and firing as he spoke Captain Barney looked in the direction indicated, and saw a man with a white hat on the enemy's deck jump at least three feet and fall to rise no more. " Cap," again called out the marksman, " that's the third fellow I've made hop." After the battle was over the Americans found that every one of the Englishmen who had been killed or wounded by small arms had been struck either in the head or breast.

During the heat of the action Captain Barney, in order that he might get a better view of the battle, stood on the binnacle on the quarter-deck, where he presented an excellent target for the enemy's sharpshooters—as he soon found out. One ball from the enemy's tops passed through his hat, just grazing the crown of his head, while another tore off a part of the skirt of his coat. Objecting to this treatment, he called out to his marine officer, Mr. Scull, to direct the fire of his men at the enemy's tops and it was obeyed, and with such effect that every shot brought down its man, so that in a few minutes the tops were cleared.

At the opening of the battle, just as Captain Barney had taken his station on the binnacle, he observed one of his officers with the cook's axe uplifted in his hand, about to strike one of his own men who had deserted his gun and was skulking behind the mainmast. At this moment a round shot hit the binnacle on which Barney was standing and threw him to the deck. Supposing that his commander was hurt, the officer threw down the axe and ran to Barney's assistance, but the commander quickly regained his feet, uninjured, whereupon the officer deliberately picked up the axe and again sought the skulker. By this time, however, the fellow had got over his " first scare," and was found at his gun, where he fought courageously to the close of the battle.

A brother-in-law of Captain Barney, Joseph Bedford, was serving in the *Hyder Ally* at this time as a volunteer and behaved with marked gallantry. He was stationed in the maintop, and was wounded by a musket ball in the groin, but so interested was he in the strife that he did not discover his hurt until after the action, when he descended to the deck and fell exhausted from loss of blood.

Captain Rodgers made heroic attempts to extricate his ship from her unlucky position, but the Americans seemed to anticipate every move. They cut his shrouds and running rigging so that he could not handle the sails. After the battle had lasted

twenty minutes nearly half the British had been
slain or injured. Their decks were covered with the
killed or wounded, the first lieutenant, purser, surgeon, boatswain, gunner—in fact, every officer in the
ship (excepting one midshipman) was either killed or
injured. Captain Rodgers himself had received a
painful wound in the foot. Finding that the *Quebec*
was too far away to render him immediate assistance, Captain Rodgers, thirty minutes from the time
the action opened, surrendered, having had twenty
men killed and· thirty-three wounded. The *Hyder
Ally* had four killed and eleven wounded.

When the American first officer came aboard to
take possession Captain Rodgers ordered one of his
men to go into his cabin and bring up his fowling
piece—a beautiful silver-mounted gun—and in the
presence of the boarding officer threw it overboard,
remarking: " This shall never become the property
of any d——d rebel! " Captain Rodgers, however,
forgot to destroy his book of signals, which fell into
the hands of the Americans, and materially assisted
them in eluding the frigate, as will be seen.

Throwing a prize crew of thirty-five men aboard
the *General Monk*, Barney, without waiting even to
learn the name of his prize, ordered her British
ensign to be rehoisted, and showing English colors
on the *Hyder Ally* he put up the bay as if in chase
of the merchantmen, while the *Hyder Ally* prepared
to cover the rear. The *Fair American* was found to
be in too shallow water to warrant an .attack on
her, so Barney contented himself with making sure
of his present conquest. Deceived by the flag on
the *General Monk* and *Hyder Ally*, Captain Mason
made no great effort to hasten to the scene of conflict, as by the aid of the signal book Captain Barney
was able to answer his signals, so that the merchantmen and two war ships were able to reach a place
of safety before dark.

A gentleman who visited the *Hyder Ally* and her

prize on their arrival describes the scene: "I was then in Philadelphia, quite a lad, when the action took place. Both ships arrived at the lower part of the city with a leading wind, immediately after the action, bringing with them all their killed and wounded. Attracted to the wharf by the salute which the *Hyder Ally* fired, of thirteen guns, which was then the custom, one for each State, I saw the two ships lying in the stream, anchored near each other. In a short time, however, they warped into the wharf to land their killed and wounded, and curiosity induced me, as well as many others, to go on board each vessel. . . . The *General Monk's* decks were in every direction besmeared with blood, covered with the dead and wounded, and resembled a charnel house. Several of her bow ports were knocked into one, a plain evidence of the well-directed fire of the *Hyder Ally*. The killed and wounded were carried ashore in hammocks.

"I was present at a conversation which took place on the quarter-deck of the *General Monk* between Captain Barney and several merchants in Philadelphia. I remember one of them observing: 'Why, Captain Barney, you have been truly fortunate in capturing this vessel, considering she is so far superior to you in point of size, guns, men, and metal.' 'Yes, sir,' Barney replied. 'I do consider myself fortunate. When we were about to engage, it was the opinion of myself, as well as my crew, that she would blow us to atoms, but we were determined she should gain her victory dearly.' One of the wounded British sailors observed: 'Yes, sir. Captain Rodgers said to our crew, a little before the action commenced, "Now, my boys, we shall have the Yankee ship in five minutes," and so we all thought, but here we are.'" For a long time after the battle the mizzen staysail of the *General Monk* was exhibited in a sail loft in Philadelphia, in which were counted three hundred and sixty-five shot holes.

15

Every attention was shown to the wounded prisoners, which was in marked contrast to the barbarous treatment Captain Barney had received aboard the *Yarmouth* and in Mill Prison. Captain Barney personally attended to the removal of the wounded, and secured for Captain Rodgers comfortable quarters in the home of a Quaker lady, who nursed him carefully until fully recovered from his injuries. For two or three years afterward, however, he was obliged to use crutches, and it was seven years before he could walk any considerable distance. On the close of the war Captain Rodgers again served in the Royal Navy. He assisted in the siege of Dunkirk, and was active during the whole war with France. In 1794 he was attached to the British fleet in the West Indies, and won distinction at the storming of the forts of St. Lucia, Martinique, Guadeloupe, and Cabrit. In the following year he died from yellow fever, April 24th, at Grenada. It is of interest to note in this connection that the commanding British officer on this station to whom Captain Rodgers made report of his capture was Admiral Digby, whom we remember as having commanded the British fleet off Plymouth, England, when Barney made his escape from Mill Prison.

For this truly brilliant action Captain Barney received a sword from the State of Pennsylvania, and his prize, which was purchased by the United States under her original name, *General Washington*, was refitted and placed under his command. While this was being effected Captain Barney again went down the bay in the *Hyder Ally* to see what chance there was of getting his convoy to sea. In this trip he captured the refugee schooner *Hook 'em Snivey*, and brought her back to Philadelphia.

We have now followed the career of the *General Washington* as an American privateer, as an English cruiser, as the prize to the merchants of Philadelphia, and now we find her as a United States cruiser,

and, as will be seen, for several years the only vessel
retained in the service. On May 18, 1782, Captain
Barney sailed from Philadelphia in the *General
Washington* as escort to a fleet of fifteen or sixteen
merchantmen. On reaching the Capes it was found
that a powerful British blockading squadron made
it hazardous to attempt getting to sea, upon which
the traders returned.

A sealed packet had been given to Barney which
he was not to open until "you get about forty
leagues to sea, keeping as much to the eastward as
circumstances will admit, always keeping the packet
slung with weights sufficient to sink it in case of
your falling in with an enemy of superior force. To
this matter we request *you will pay particular attention*, as the dispatches *are of the utmost consequence.*"
When the *General Washington* had reached the desired distance from land Barney opened the packet,
which he found to be from Robert Morris, Superintendent of Finance of the United States. The
instructions, in part, were: "You are to proceed
directly to Cape François, in Hispaniola, and if the
French and Spanish fleets should not be there you
must proceed to the place where they may be, and
when you shall have found them you are to deliver
to the French and Spanish admirals the inclosed
letters. I expect that, in consequence of these letters, a frigate will be ordered to convoy you to
Havana, and thence to America. You will go to
Havana, where you will deliver the inclosed letter
to Robert Smith, Esq., agent for the United States
at that place. You will also inform all persons concerned in the American trade that you are bound for
such port of the United States as you may be able
to make, and you will take on board your ship, as
freight, any moneys which they think proper to
ship, but no goods or merchandise of any kind.
For the moneys you are to charge a freight of two
per cent., one half of which you shall have; the

other is to be applied toward the expense of your voyage.

"If a frigate is granted by the French admiral to convoy you, the captain of her will be instructed by the admiral to receive any moneys which it may be thought proper to put on board of him. I should suppose that by dividing the risk, or shipping a part on board of each, there will be greater safety than by putting all in one bottom. You are to stay as short a time as possible at Havana, and then, in company with the frigate, make the best of your way to some port in the United States. This port of Baltimore would be the best, but you must be guided by your own discretion on the occasion, together with such information as you may be able to procure. It is not improbable that a stronger escort than one frigate may be granted, in which case you will find a greater security, and a division of the money among many will multiply the chances for receiving it." Captain Barney also had an order for the commander of the American frigate *Deane*, Captain Samuel Nicholson, which was thought to be cruising somewhere in his course, to accompany the *General Washington* as an escort. Nothing, however, was seen of this frigate and Captain Barney shaped his course for Cape François.

While off Turk's Island the *General Washington* at nighttime overhauled a heavily armed vessel which acted in a very suspicious manner. When within hailing distance the usual questions were passed, but they were so unsatisfactory that Captain Barney determined to inquire more closely into the stranger's character. With this idea in mind he ordered a gun to be fired over her; but the American crew, standing at their guns with lighted matches, expecting the order to fire at any moment, mistook the command and poured in a broadside. This was ineffectual, as the stranger, evidently disliking the appearance of the cruiser, had dropped astern and was preparing to make off. The Englishman now came round and managed to get in a raking fire, which caused some confusion in the cruiser and hampered her maneuvers for the rest of the action.

Captain Barney was soon alongside the stranger, and a running fight followed. The enemy, however, availed herself of the tangled condition of the *General Washington's* rigging and got in several raking fires. It was soon found that she was very ably manned, and was armed with 9-pounders, so that the situation began to get serious for the Americans. The *General Washington*, it is true, had 9-pounders also, but they were made so by having bored 6-pounders to this larger caliber—a dangerous experiment—and on this occasion six of the guns were upset in the first broadside, being unable to stand the 9-pounder charges of powder. It required much precious time to remount these guns.

As the ships were about to open fire Captain Barney turned to one of his passengers, James H. McCulloch, and told him he had better go below, where he would be out of danger. Mr. McCulloch begged to stay on deck. Coolly walking over to the arms chest, he examined several muskets, looked at their flints, tried them to his shoulder, and finally selected one that suited him. He then slung a cartridge box over his shoulder, and adjusting a handkerchief to his head fired the first musket shot at the enemy. Throughout the whole of the action he was conspicuous for his cool intrepidity. At one time his gun missed fire, upon which he calmly sat on the arms chest, took out a knife or key, and after bringing the flint to the proper edge resumed his " target practice," as he expressed it. He fired more times than any other man in the ship. Thirty-two years afterward Mr. McCulloch was wounded and taken prisoner by the English in the action at North Point. After peace was declared he held the position of collector of the port of Baltimore. Two of

Captain Barney's brothers were serving in the *General Washington* at this time and commanded in the tops.

Captain Barney realized that his best place was at close quarters, and he ran his ship close alongside, until the yards nearly interlocked with those of the enemy. Orders were then given to bring the ship aboard the enemy; but the Englishman, having the full use of his sails, kept away and soon drew ahead. But still it was known that the enemy were seriously injured, and there was every hope that they would soon surrender, when a 9-pound shot passed through the *General Washington's* mainmast, and about the same time another shot struck the head of her mizzenmast, splitting it halfway down to the deck. This compelled the Americans to sheer off if they would save their masts, and the privateer, as she was then known to be, made her escape in the night. On the same day the *General Washington* had captured a brig laden with rum, which was sent to Cape François, where Captain Barney arrived in safety.

It was here learned that the magnificent French fleet had been defeated by the British, and that only a remnant was left at Cape François. One of these, the 64-gun ship of the line *Éveillié*, was detailed to escort the *General Washington* to Havana, where six hundred thousand dollars in specie were taken aboard, and both vessels sailed for the United States. Arriving off the Delaware they were chased by a British line of battle ship and two frigates, but the Frenchmen used their stern chasers with such good effect that the leading frigate had her fore-topmast cut away, and as her consorts could not come within gunshot of the Frenchmen and the Americans they gained the Delaware in safety. Here the French frigate took leave, and, seizing the first opportunity, made sail for France.

During that night the *General Washington* passed rapidly up the bay, and about three o'clock on the

following morning she suddenly came upon a fleet
of refugee boats.   Barney ran among them, anchored, and, pouring in a heavy fire, sank one of the
barges, with sixty men, captured several others,
recaptured five American vessels with thirty men
aboard, and dispersed the others.   Reaching Philadelphia Barney landed the money, and in the following October he sailed for Europe with important
dispatches to our ministers, who were conducting
negotiations for peace.   Early in January, 1783, he
received a passport from the king of England for
the "ship *General Washington*, belonging to the
United States of North America," and sailed again
for the United States.   As the *General Washington*
had a large amount of specie aboard, her commander was instructed to avoid all British cruisers,
in spite of the passport, lest the money might tempt
them to detain her.   She arrived safely at Philadelphia, March 12th.   In the following June the *General
Washington*, then the only United States war vessel
in commission, again sailed to England, still under
the command of Captain Barney.   Returning from
this cruise, she was sold in 1784.

CHAPTER XV.

CAPTAIN JOHN MANLY.

IF further evidence is needed to show the intimate relationship between the United States navy and our early privateer service, we have it in the fact that of our twenty-five torpedo boats bearing the names of officers commanding in the navy of the Revolution and in the War of 1812 fifteen were named after men who at one time commanded privateers. Torpedo boat No. 22 bears the name of one of our successful privateersmen, John Manly. Under a resolution of Congress, October 10, 1776, Manly was placed second on the list of the twenty-four captains in the navy, being ranked only by James Nicholson. His first command was the Massachusetts State cruiser *Lee*, in which vessel he made one of the first important captures of the war.[1] While in command of the Continental 32-gun frigate *Hancock*, Manly, in 1777, took the 28-gun British frigate *Fox* after a severe action.[2]

Owing to the scarcity of vessels in the regular navy, Manly, early in 1779, put to sea from Boston as commander of the 16-gun privateer *Cumberland*, but when only a short time out he was captured by the British frigate *Pomona*—by another account the *Thunderer*—and carried into Barbadoes, with his men, where he was imprisoned and treated with great severity. Determined to regain his liberty, Manly

---

[1] See Maclay's History of the Navy, vol. i, pp. 48, 49. [2] Ibid., pp. 88–90.

managed to bribe the jailer, and getting out of the
prison with his men at night he seized an English
Government tender and, placing her crew in irons,
reached the United States. Making his way to Boston, Manly was soon provided with another command, the fine 20-gun ship *Jason*, manned by one hundred men. That Manly should have found so little
difficulty in securing this splendid craft so soon
after his loss of the *Cumberland*, particularly at a
time when desirable ships were scarce, is a sufficient
commentary on his ability.

The *Jason* sailed from Boston about June 25, 1779,
for Portsmouth, New Hampshire, where her second
officer, Mr. Frost, had been engaged in securing additional men for her complement. Arriving at Portsmouth a day or so after leaving Boston, the *Jason*
took aboard Mr. Frost and the men, and then put
to sea for a general cruise against the enemy. On
the morning of the second day out the man at the
masthead reported two sails directly ahead, and
Captain Manly ascended to the foretop with his glass
to discover their force and character. On returning
to the deck he told First Officer Thayer that he believed the strangers to be an American privateer
with a prize in company. Mr. Thayer then went forward, and after a careful scrutiny through the glass
came to the conclusion that one of the vessels was
a frigate and the other a brig. Running closer to
them, so as to clear up all question as to their character, the Americans gradually became convinced that
the strangers were British vessels of war, and on
Mr. Thayer's advice the *Jason* was put about to see
if the sails would give chase. As soon as this maneuver was completed, the strangers promptly put
about in pursuit, the Americans making every effort
to recover the port they had so recently left. When
the privateer had reached the Isle of Shoals, off the
entrance to Portsmouth harbor, her pursuers had
gained upon her so as to be within two gunshots.

At this moment a heavy squall from the west struck the *Jason*, and in spite of their utmost efforts the Americans saw their ship taken aback, thrown on her beam ends, and their three masts carried away. Relieved of the weight of her masts, the privateer righted, by which time the squall had blown over, the vessels pursuing the privateer evidently having all they could attend to in standing under the squall, for they made way to sea and were not seen again. Captain Manly immediately went to work clearing away the wreckage and repairing damages. When the sails were got aboard it was found that one of the crew had been caught under the fore-topsail and drowned.

The circumstance of Captain Manly having lost his first private armed ship, the *Cumberland*, at the outset of her cruise, and having the misfortune to lose the masts of his second ship, the *Jason*, when only two days out, was argued by the superstitious seamen as a sign that he was an unlucky commander, which, taken in connection with the drowning of the seaman in the wreckage, led the crew of the *Jason* to mutiny. It is here that we have a good illustration of the qualities called for in the successful privateersman. The difficulties confronting Captain Manly certainly were enough to discourage the ordinary commander. The way he faced the situation is graphically described by one of the crew, Joshua Davis, a hairdresser's apprentice, of Boston, nineteen years old, who had left his father's shop to make his maiden voyage on the ocean.

Davis writes: "We got up jury masts and ran in between the Isle of Shoals and Portsmouth, where our captain was determined to take our masts in. In a few days Captain Manly went on shore to see to getting the masts on board. While he was gone Patrick Cruckshanks, our boatswain, Michael Wall, boatswain's mate, and John Graves, captain of the forecastle, went forward and sat down on the stump

of the bowsprit and said they would not step the
masts in such a wild roadstead to endanger their
lives, but if the ship was taken into the harbor they
would do it with pleasure.   [This meant that the
men would then have a good chance to desert, which
Captain Manly was most desirous they should not
do.—E. S. M.]   When Captain Manly came on
board he asked Mr. Thayer why the people were not
at work, and was told that they wished to get into
the harbor first.   The captain answered, ' I'll harbor
them!' and stepped up to the sentry at the cabin
door, took his cutlass out of his hand and ran forward, and said:

"'Boatswain, why do you not go to work?'

"He [the boatswain] began to tell him the im-
propriety of getting the masts in where the ship then
was, when Captain Manly struck him with the cutlass on the cheek with such force that his teeth were
to be seen from the upper part of his jaw to the
lower part of his chin.   He next spoke to John
Graves and interrogated, and was answered in a
similar manner, when the captain struck him with
the cutlass on the head, which cut him so badly that
he was obliged to be sent to the hospital with the
boatswain.   The captain then called the other to
come down and to go to work.   Michael Wall came
down to him.   The captain made a stroke at him,
which missed, and, while the captain was lifting up
the cutlass to strike him again, Wall gave him a
push against the stump of the foremast and ran aft.
The captain made after him.   Wall ran to the main
hatchway and jumped down between the decks and
hurt himself very much.   The captain then, with
severe threats, ordered the people to go to work.
They went to work and stepped the masts, got the
topmasts on end, lower yards athwart, the topsail
yards on the caps, topgallant masts on end, sails
bent, running rigging rove, boats on booms, etc., and
all done in thirty-six hours."

Having repaired his extensive damages through sheer force of will power Captain Manly prepared to sail without touching port. On the day he was ready the privateer *Hazard*, of Boston, hove in sight, and running down under the *Jason's* stern hailed, informed Captain Manly that she had orders from the General Court of Massachusetts to instruct every armed craft from that State to repair to the Penobscot " without fail." This order was given in connection with the ill-fated Penobscot expedition which Massachusetts was at that time undertaking against the enemy. Captain Manly indicated his readiness to obey the order; but as soon as the *Hazard* was out of sight he tripped anchor and stood to sea, shaping his course, not toward the Penobscot, but toward Sandy Hook. Evidently Manly did not relish the idea of adding another to his already formidable list of disasters.

When off the harbor of New York the *Jason* hove to, and under easy stretches waited for a sail to appear. On July 25th the sailing master went to the fore-topmast head to take his turn. About three o'clock in the afternoon he cried out, " A sail on the weather bow!" and shortly afterward he reported another sail. Both the strangers were soon made out to be brigs. The *Jason* was promptly put about in pursuit, but as soon as the brigs made her out they spread every sail in escape. The swift-sailing American in two hours had come within two gunshots of the brigs, when Captain Manly sent his men to quarters. At this time the strangers boarded their port tacks and, hoisting English colors, gave the privateer a broadside. Manly now ordered the sailing master to get his best bower anchor out so that the bill of it would hook into the foreshrouds of the leading enemy when the moment came to board. Having completed his preparations Manly ordered his helm hard aport, and running alongside caught his anchor in the enemy's fore rigging, as intended, and then opened from every gun that would bear. The first shots from the *Jason* caused great havoc aboard the stranger, killing many men and wounding more.

Observing that the British crew, with the exception of their commander, had run below, Manly ordered Second Officer Frost to board and send the English commander to the *Jason*. This was quickly done, when the Americans cut away the enemy's fore rigging so as to disengage the privateer, and the *Jason* was in swift pursuit of the other Englishman, who was doing his best to escape. Getting within gunshot Manly gave the chase a few shots from his bow guns, which induced her to heave to. Captain Manly ordered them to send their boat aboard, and on receiving, in reply, "Our boat won't swim," he called out, "Then sink in her. You shall come on board or I will fire into you!" This answer had the desired effect, for in a few minutes they sent a boat aboard. The prizes were the English privateers *Hazard*, of eighteen guns, from Liverpool, and the *Adventurer*, of the same force, from Glasgow. The only man of the Americans hurt was the sailing master of the *Jason*—the one who first discovered the brigs—who was struck in the head by a shot. He died a few days later. As soon as possible the prisoners were placed in irons, and after a few days' sail the three vessels arrived safely at Boston.

Captain Manly had been in Boston only a few days when he learned that a large fleet of British merchantmen homeward bound was skirting the New England coast. He hastened aboard the *Jason* and put to sea with all dispatch, in hopes of falling in with the traders. Early in August, when the privateer had been out only a few days, and by carrying a press of sail had reached the Nantucket Shoals, there being a heavy fog at the time, the man at the masthead cried out, "A sail ahead within one cable's length [seven hundred and twenty feet] of us!" The *Jason* ran under the stranger's stern, and, in response to First Officer Thayer's hail, was informed that they were from Liverpool, bound for New York. Captain Manly, who had been below, now came on deck and told Mr. Thayer that he would fire a shot at her so as to make the vessel heave to. A gun accordingly was trained on the stranger, but before it could be discharged a seaman called out, "A sail to windward!" and almost at the same instant the man in the foretop shouted, "There is a fleet bearing down upon us!" Feeling that it was imprudent to run into a large fleet, which undoubtedly would have a strong escort, Captain Manly stood northward until he judged himself clear. After sailing one hour on this course the fog lifted, revealing to the astonished Americans forty large sails, with a heavy ship astern of them. This last vessel, on making the privateer out, crowded all sail as if to escape. The *Jason* made after her under a press of canvas and gained very fast. Captain Manly, who with Mr. Thayer was closely watching the chase, suddenly discovered that the stranger had drags out, which, notwithstanding the large area of sail she was carrying, greatly retarded her progress through the water. Captain Manly instantly saw through the trick, and remarked to Mr. Thayer: "That ship has got drags alongside and means to trap us. We will go about and try them." Accordingly the privateer's course was changed, upon which the stranger immediately imitated the maneuver and made every effort to overtake her. The Englishman —for there could now be no doubt of her nationality —soon proved that she was a fast sailer and was rapidly overhauling the *Jason*, having come within two gunshots of her, when, fortunately for the Americans, the fog rolled over again, and by changing his course Captain Manly eluded his crafty foe.

Standing eastward a few days, after this narrow escape, a sail to leeward was reported and the *Jason*

crowded on all sail in pursuit.   In two hours the
stranger's hull was visible from the privateer's deck.
At this juncture the man at the main topmast head
reported: "Two sails bearing down on the ship we
are chasing."   As it was now dark, Captain Manly
deemed it prudent to give over the chase and to run
under easy sail until the following morning.   At
dawn he discovered two ships in chase of the *Jason*,
their hulls well above the horizon and apparently
gaining very fast.   All hands were sent to quarters,
and the guns on both sides were manned preparatory
to a desperate fight.   Soon one of the ships came
under the privateer's starboard quarter, when the
man in the maintop reported that he recognized the
ship as the American frigate *Deane*, and that he
could make out her commander as Captain James
Nicholson, the man having at one time served in that
ship under Nicholson.   After a careful scrutiny
through the glass Captain Manly was satisfied that it
was Nicholson and that the frigate was the *Deane*,
a ship that Manly was destined soon to command.
After exchanging hails Manly went aboard the *Deane*.
The other ship was the 24-gun frigate *Boston*, Captain Samuel Tucker.   These three vessels sailed in
company ten or twelve days, when the *Jason* parted
with them, giving and receiving a salute of thirteen
guns.

Running eastward, after his separation from the
American frigates, "the ship's company had pork
served out to them," records one of the *Jason's* men.
"Thirty-two pieces were hung over the ship's side to
soak overnight.   The next morning a man went to
his rope, and on pulling it up found the rope bit and
the pork gone.   Every man ran to his rope and found
them bitten in the same way.   They went aft and
looked over the taffrail and saw a shark under the
stern.   Our captain came on deck and ordered the
boatswain to bring him a shark hook.   He baited
it with three pounds of pork.   The shark took hold

of the bait and hooked himself. We made the chain
fast to the main brace, and when we got him half-
way up he slapped his tail and stove in four panes of
the cabin windows. We got a bit of a rope round his
tail and pulled him on board, and when he found
himself on deck he drove the man from the helm
and broke two spokes of the wheel. The carpenter
took an axe and struck him on the neck, which cut
his head nearly off, the boatswain tickling the shark
under the belly with a handspike to keep his eyes
off the carpenter. When he had nearly bled to death
the carpenter gave him another blow, which severed
his head from the body. Our captain then ordered
the steward to give the ship's company two casks
of butter and the cook to prepare the shark for the
people's dinner. He was eleven and a half feet
long."

About eight days after the adventure with the
shark, a sail ahead was reported. Captain Manly
gave chase, and in six hours came up with the
stranger, which proved to be a British privateer from
Bristol, England, for Barbadoes. Mr. Thayer was
put aboard to take possession, and sent back her
master with four men and two bags of dollars which
they had just taken from a Spanish vessel. A prize
master and crew were then placed aboard the ship
and carried her safely into Boston. The privateer
mounted sixteen 6-pounders, and had a valuable
cargo of beef, pork, cheese, hats, etc.

Continuing eastward for several days after this
capture without sighting a sail, Captain Manly
changed his course northwest, and in a few days was
on the Newfoundland Banks. While cruising in this
vicinity a sail was discovered bearing down on the
Jason. Manly waited for her to come up, and on hailing learned that she was a neutral from Martinique,
and so short of water that her master offered to give
a barrel of sugar or rum for every barrel of water
the privateer could spare. Manly sent over four bar-

rels of the indispensable liquid, and received in return two barrels of sugar and two of rum. The master of the merchantman came aboard the *Jason*.
"He dined and supped with us and went on board
his vessel about ten o'clock."

Early on the 30th of September a sail was discovered on the starboard beam. As it was calm at
the time Captain Manly could not chase, but about
eight o'clock in the morning a light breeze sprang
up, and the stranger, feeling it first, came toward
the privateer rapidly. Recognizing her to be a ship
of force Captain Manly made sail from her, but after
an all-day run the stranger, about eleven o'clock at
night, managed to get under the *Jason's* port quarter.
On hailing she was found to be the British frigate
Surprise,[1] at that time one of the swiftest vessels
in the British navy.

"What ship is that?" demanded the Englishman.

"The United States 32-gun frigate *Deane*," responded Captain Manly.

"Heave to or we will fire into you," came a voice
from the frigate.

"Fire away and be damned. We have got as
many guns as you," defiantly answered Manly. Upon
this the *Surprise* delivered her broadside. Manly
reserved his fire until fairly abreast of his enemy.
Before the Americans opened with their guns the
British delivered another broadside, which cut some
of the privateer's rigging and drove the men out
of her tops. When fairly alongside of the frigate
Captain Manly poured a broadside into his opponent
which silenced two of the enemy's forward guns.
The next broadside cut away the Englishman's main
topsail and drove her maintop men to the deck. Both
vessels now maintained a rapid fire until one o'clock
in the morning. By that time the *Jason's* studding

---

[1] By another account it was the *Perseus*.

16

sails and booms, her canvas, rigging, and yards, were
so injured as to be unmanageable. Battle lanterns
were hung on nails along the inside of the bulwarks
between the guns so as to enable the gunners to see
how to load and fire, but these were constantly
shaken down by the concussion resulting from the
recoil of the guns. It was so dark that the men could
not handle the cannon. At this moment the men
forward broke open the fore hatches and ran below,
refusing to fight against a frigate. Noticing that
the forward guns were silent, Captain Manly sent
the sailing master to ascertain the cause of it, but
that officer did not return. Manly then sent the master's mate on the same errand, but he also failed to
return.

Realizing the hopelessness of fighting a regular
man-of-war and his own mutinous men at the same
time, Captain Manly seized his trumpet and called
for quarter; then returning to the men who had remained faithful to him he ordered them into the
cabin to receive their shares of the prize money. The
two bags of dollars taken from the British privateer a few days before were emptied on a table and
shared out to the men according to their stations.
"Eight dollars were given to me," said the boy
Davis, "as my share. I went on deck and found the
ship reeling one way and the other. The helmsman was killed and no one to take the wheel. The
rigging, sails, yards, etc., were spread all over the
deck. The wounded men were carried to the cock-
pit, the dead men lying on the deck and no one to
throw them overboard. The well men were gone
below to get their clothes in order to go on board
the frigate. Soon after the frigate's longboat came,
with their first lieutenant and about twenty sailors
and marines, when every man that could be found
on deck was drove into the boat. I went down into
the steward's room in order to stay on board until
we got into port. The doctor bad me stay with him

and attend to the wounded. The next night, about
twelve o'clock, one of the marines went into the hold
to get some water. He overheard some of our men
talking and listened to them, and heard them say
that at two o'clock they intended rising on the men
on deck and carrying the ship into Boston. The
man went on deck and told his officer what he had
heard. The officer took all his men into the cabin
and armed them with pistols and cutlasses, and went
into the hold and ordered every man to come forward or he would destroy them. They all, to the
amount of thirty-two men, came forward and were
put in irons by the feet. I was taken from the doctor
and put in irons with the rest. In the course of ten
days we arrived at St. John's, Newfoundland, October
10th. We were all taken out of irons and ordered
on deck to be searched for the money we had shared
among us when we were taken. I took four dollars
out of my pocket and hid them in the linings of the
ship, in order to save them from the plunderers. I
went on deck, when they searched me and took the
other four dollars from me. I went below again to
get my money, but, alas! it was gone."

In this action the *Jason* had eighteen men killed
and twelve wounded, while the English had seven
killed and a number injured. Arriving at St. John's
Captain Manly was called before Rear-Admiral Edwards, of the 50-gun ship *Portland*, and asked his
name. Our privateersman replied, " John Manly."

" Are you not the same John Manly that commanded a privateer from Boston called the *Columbia?* " [*Cumberland*] asked the admiral.

" Yes," said Captain Manly.

" Were you not taken by his majesty's ship
Thunderer [*Pomona?*] and carried into Barbadoes? "
questioned Admiral Edwards.

" Yes," calmly replied the American commander.

" Did you not go to the jail keeper and bribe him,
make your escape out of jail, take a king's tender

by night, put the men in irons, and carry her into Philadelphia?" thundered the admiral.

To these questions Manly made no answer, as he did not wish to incriminate the jail keeper. Thereupon Admiral Edwards informed Manly that he was to be sent to England in irons and confined in Mill Prison to the end of the war. This threat was carried out to the letter, excepting that in 1782 Manly was exchanged. Making his way to France he reached Boston and was at once placed in command of the 32-gun frigate *Deane*, the same to which he had spoken while cruising in the privateer *Jason*. Getting to sea in this favorite ship Captain Manly made for the West Indies, and in the course of thirteen days took a valuable ship of twenty guns laden with provisions for the British army in New York. Soon afterward he was driven into Martinique by a 50-gun ship and a frigate, where he was blockaded until peace was declared.

CHAPTER XVI.

CLOSING YEARS OF THE WAR.

SPEAKING of the land operations of the Americans, Henry Cabot Lodge, in his Story of the Revolution, describes the last three years of the war as the most critical in our struggle for independence. He says: "When Washington retreated through the Jerseys in 1776 it looked as if the end had come, but at least there had been hard fighting, and the end was to be met, if at all, in the open field, with arms in hand and all the chances that war and action and courage could give. Now, four years later, the Revolution seemed to be going down in mere inaction through the utter helplessness of what passed for the central government. To those who looked beneath the surface the prospect was profoundly disheartening. It was a very dark hour, perhaps the darkest of the whole war. . . . In October, 1780, he [Washington] wrote: 'Our present distresses are so great and complicated that it is scarcely within the powers of description to give an adequate idea of them. . . . We are without money, without provisions and forage, except what is taken by impress; without clothing, and shortly shall be, in a manner, without men.' . . . To young Laurens, going abroad, Washington wrote that our only hope was in financial aid from Europe; without it the next campaign would flicker out and the Revolution die. Money and superiority of sea power, he cried, were what we must have. . . . It was Gouverneur Morris who wrote: 'Finance. Ah, my friend, all that is left of the American Revolution grounds there.'"[1] A careful study of the situation at this time will show that our privateers supplied a very considerable—if not a supremacy of—sea power for the struggling colonists toward the close of the Revolution, and were the means of transporting munitions of war and money across the Atlantic.

The last three years of the war for American independence were marked by an almost complete suspension of maritime activity on the part of Continental war ships, and a remarkable increase in the number and activity of our privateers. By the fall of Charleston, in May, 1780, the 28-gun frigate *Providence*, the 28-gun frigate *Queen of France*, the 24-gun frigate *Boston*, and the 18-gun ship sloop *Ranger*, of Captain John Paul Jones fame, were captured or destroyed. This left the United States with only six war craft: the 32-gun frigate *Alliance*, the 32-gun frigate *Confederacy*, the 32-gun frigate *Deane*, the 28-gun frigate *Trumbull*, the 20-gun ship *Duc de Lauzun*, and the 18-gun ship *Saratoga*. Of these vessels, the *Trumbull* was captured in 1781, and in 1780 the *Saratoga* put to sea and was never heard from, it being supposed that she had foundered. The *Confederacy* was captured by the enemy in 1781, so that only the *Alliance*, the *Deane*, the *Duc de Lauzun*, and the *General Washington*—the last captured from the British in 1782—were left to carry the flag of the newborn nation on the high seas.

It can readily be understood, therefore, that had it not been for our privateers the Stars and Stripes would have been, for all practical purposes, completely swept from the seas. It was the astonishing development of this form of maritime warfare that enabled the struggling colonists to hold their own on the ocean. In the year 1780 two hundred

---

[1] See Scribner's Magazine for November, 1898.

and twenty-eight American privateers were commissioned, carrying in all three thousand four hundred and twenty guns; in 1781 there were four hundred and forty-nine, with about six thousand seven hundred and thirty-five guns; and in 1782 three hundred and twenty-three, mounting four thousand eight hundred and forty-five guns. It is very much to be regretted that many of the cruises and actions of these craft have not been recorded. A number of battles were fought, daring raids on the enemy's coasts were undertaken, and many heroic incidents occurred that might well fill a volume of most valuable historical reading; but as these vessels sailed merely in a private capacity most of their logs were lost a few years after they returned to port, and what data have been preserved are, as a rule, meager and fragmentary. Enough, however, is known to show that these private ventures were fraught with thrilling incidents, and were most important in their bearing on the results of the war.

Among the first privateers to get to sea in 1780 was the 2-gun schooner *Chance*, Captain N. Palmer. This little vessel was manned by only fifteen men. She was commissioned in Pennsylvania and took one vessel, a sloop, as a prize.

The 10-gun schooner *Hope*, Captain N. Goodwin, got to sea in the same year and made several captures. Two years later, while off the coast of Labrador, she was taken by an English brig carrying sixteen guns. The Englishmen took their prize into one of the harbors near by, and while lying there the crew of the *Hope*, numbering only twenty-one men, rose on their captors, overpowered the brig's people, and carried her into Beverly, Massachusetts, the home port of the *Hope*.

Almost as successful was the 12-gun sloop *Retaliation*, Captain W. Havens — afterward commanded by Captain E. Hart. This vessel was commissioned from Connecticut in 1780, but it seems

that she had made a cruise in the preceding year,
and while off St. Kitts, May 14, 1779, she was attacked by a British armed cutter and a brig. The
enemy made several attempts to board, but each
time were repulsed with heavy loss. They finally
sheered off and left the *Retaliation* to make the best
of her way to an American port.

About a year after this, on June 12, 1780, the
10-gun sloop *Comet*, Captain C. Harris, of Pennsylvania, fell in with a convoy of British merchantmen
off Sandy Hook, and by adroit maneuvering captured eight of them, which were sent into Philadelphia. The *Comet* was commissioned in 1778
and carried a complement of fifty men. There
seems to be no record of her having made any other
prizes.

On the 22d of October, 1780, the 16-gun privateer *Viper*, Captain William Williams, sailed from
Boston, and early in November sighted a sail bearing down on her near Cape Hatteras. Captain Williams at once gave chase, whereupon the stranger
turned in flight. About noon the two vessels were
within pistol shot, when the Americans showed their
colors and delivered a broadside, to which the chase
replied after hoisting English colors. A spirited
cannonade followed for half an hour, when the
Englishman drew ahead. Captain Williams then
ported his helm and managed to deliver a raking
fire. At this time the American commander received
a musket ball in his breast, which caused his death
six hours later. Some confusion occurring in the
Viper at this moment, the Englishman made his
escape. Afterward it was learned that she was the
16-gun privateer *Hetty*, of New York. Captain Williams was the only man injured in the American
vessel. The first officer of the *Viper* now headed for
the Capes of the Delaware, intending to make Philadelphia. On the following day he captured the ship
Margaret, laden with beef, pork, butter, and porter,

from South Carolina for New York, which was carried safely into Philadelphia.

The year 1781 opened with a hard-fought action between the 18-gun ship *Pilgrim*, Captain J. Robinson, of Massachusetts, and the heavily armed British ship *Mary*, of twenty-two guns. In the year 1779 the *Pilgrim* had made three prizes with valuable cargoes. While at sea, January 5, 1781, she fell in with the *Mary*, which was manned by eighty-three men, under the command of Captain Stowards. One of the most desperate actions between privateers in this war resulted. The Englishmen finally were overcome, but not until their commander and a number of the crew had been killed. The American loss also was very serious and both vessels were badly shattered.

We get an interesting side light on this cruise of the *Pilgrim* in the account of a seaman named Joshua. He says: "On the 16th of May, 1781, I entered on board of the privateer *Essex*, of twenty guns, Captain John Cathcart, and sailed from Boston on the 22d of the same month to cruise off Cape Clear. On the 4th of June, about four o'clock in the afternoon, we discovered a sail directly ahead of us. We had to put away until they hoisted their colors, and when we hoisted we found them to be English. Our captain said he would not attack her, as she appeared to be a 20-gun coppered ship and full of men, for fear of spoiling our cruise. She chased us all that night, and in the morning we found that she had carried away her main topmast and gave over the chase. We ran on for two days, when the man at the masthead cried out, 'A sail!' which we stood for, when she made a signal which we knew and returned. She came alongside of us and proved to be the *Pilgrim*, Captain Robinson, who came on board of us and informed [us] that he had taken five prizes out of the Jamaica fleet. Captain Robinson being the oldest commander, ordered our captain to follow him while they cruised together off the coast of Ireland. The next day both gave chase to a ship to the leeward and came up with her. She proved to be the privateer *Defense*, of eighteen guns, out of Salem, and kept company with us. Next day we gave chase to a brig, which we found to be from Barbadoes for Cork, with invalids, very leaky, and all hands at the pumps; had been taken by the privateer *Rambler*, from Salem, who gave them a passport to go on. The *Pilgrim* boarded her first and let her proceed. We afterward boarded her and took two 6-pounders and a few sails from them. Next morning a sail was discovered ahead; the *Pilgrim* gave chase and we followed her, the *Defense* following us. About one o'clock another sail was seen on our larboard [port] beam, to which we gave chase, and in two-hours ran her hull down. We soon found that she was too heavy for us, when we hove about and stood from her. She gave chase and came up with us very fast, and gave us a shot which struck alongside, when our captain ordered the quartermaster to pull down the colors. They sent an officer on board, who told our lieutenant that their ship was the *Queen Charlotte*, of thirty-two 12- and 9-pounders, from London. We were all sent on board of her and put in irons. In the meantime the *Pilgrim* got up to the ship we first gave chase to, and by her signal we perceived her to be the *Rambler* privateer." Joshua, with his unfortunate shipmates, was carried to England and confined there to the close of the war.

Three other private armed American vessels bore the name *Pilgrim*: One a 16-gun brig with ninety men, under Captain H. Crary, from Connecticut, which in 1782 captured a vessel with a cargo of tobacco; another a brig of four guns and fourteen men, under Captain M. Strong, from Pennsylvania; and the third an 8-gun brig with eighteen men, under Captain J. Starr, from Virginia.

In February, 1781, the 16-gun brig *Holker*, Captain R. Kean, of Pennsylvania, fell in with the British cutter *Hypocrite*, of sixteen guns, and after an action of fifteen minutes captured her, with a loss of three killed and one wounded, the enemy having four killed and seven wounded. In the following year, while cruising in the West Indies, the *Holker* fought the 18-gun ship *Experiment*. These vessels were hotly engaged, and the result was still in doubt when another American privateer appeared on the scene, which induced the *Experiment* to sheer off.

One of the most creditable actions of this war in which an American privateer was engaged took place on September 6, 1781. It had been the habit of the smaller British cruisers stationed on the North American coast to send boat expeditions at night for the purpose of plundering estates along the shore. One of the most persistent English commanders in this questionable style of warfare was Captain Sterling, of the 16-gun sloop of war *Savage*. About the time mentioned Captain Sterling had been exploring Chesapeake Bay, and on one occasion sent a boat expedition to Mount Vernon and plundered Washington's estate. Soon after the *Savage* had put to sea from the Chesapeake, and was cruising off the coast of Georgia in search of other estates to plunder, she fell in with the American privateer *Congress*, of twenty-four guns and two hundred men, under the command of Captain George Geddes, of Philadelphia. Mr. Geddes, as we have noticed, had been a highly successful officer in the privateer service, having two years before commanded the 10-gun brig *Holker*, in which he made a most creditable record.

Upon making out the *Congress* to be an American war craft of superior force, Captain Sterling made all sail to escape, upon which the *Congress* gave chase. It was early in the morning when the two

vessels discovered each other, and by half past ten
o'clock the American had gained so much that she
was able to open with her bow chasers, and by
eleven o'clock Captain Geddes was close on the Englishman's quarter, when he opened a rapid fire of
small arms, to which the enemy answered with
energy. Observing that he had the swifter ship of
the two, Captain Geddes forged ahead until he got
fairly abreast of his antagonist, when a fierce broadside duel took place. Notwithstanding the American superiority in armament, this fire at close range
so injured the privateer's rigging that it became unmanageable, and Captain Geddes was compelled to
fall back to make repairs. As soon as he had completed this work, the *Congress* again closed on the
Savage and engaged in a heavy cannon fire. In the
course of an hour the Englishman was reduced to
a wreck, the vessels at times being so near each
other that the men frequently were scorched by the
flashes of the opposing cannon; and it is even asserted that shot were thrown with effect by hand.
Seeing that the Englishman was reduced to a de-
plorable condition, that his quarter-deck and forecastle were swept clear of men, and that his mizzenmast had gone by the board, while the mainmast
threatened to follow it, Captain Geddes prepared to
board and settle the sanguinary conflict on the
enemy's decks.

Just as the Americans were about to carry out
this programme the boatswain of the *Savage* appeared on the forecastle, and waving his cap announced that they had surrendered, upon which
Captain Geddes immediately took possession. The
Englishmen's losses, according to their own statements, were eight killed and twenty-four wounded,
while those of the Americans were thirty killed or
wounded. Among the enemy's killed was Captain
Sterling himself, who appears to have fought with
the most determined bravery. Unfortunately Cap-

tain Geddes was not able to secure his prize, as both vessels were captured by a British frigate and carried into Charleston.   The *Congress* was taken into the British service under the name of *Duchess of Cumberland*, Captain Samuel Marsh, and was wrecked off the coast of Newfoundland soon afterward while on her way to England with American prisoners.[1]

That our privateersmen in the Revolution were exposed to attacks other than those from their open enemies is seen in the following account of Thomas Wentworth Higginson.   In the winter of 1781 the 8-gun privateer brig *Ranger*, Captain T. Simmons, sailed from Salem with a cargo of salt for Richmond, Virginia.   The cargo being disposed of at that port, the *Ranger* loaded with flour at Alexandria for Havana.   "Part of the flour," says Mr. Higginson, "being from General Washington's plantation, was received at Havana at the marked weight; all was sold, and the

Joseph Peabody.

Ranger returned to Alexandria for another freight. Anchoring at the mouth of the Potomac, because of head winds, the officers turned in, but were aroused before midnight by the watch, with news that large boats were coming toward the ship from different directions.   Simmons and Second Officer Joseph Peabody rushed to the deck, the latter in his night clothes.   As they reached it a volley of musketry met them, and the captain fell wounded. Peabody ran forward, shouting to the crew to seize the boarding pikes, and he himself attacked some men who were climbing on board.   Meantime an-

[1] See page 125.

other strange boat opened fire from another quarter. All was confusion; they knew not who were their assailants or whence; the captain lay helpless, the first officer was serving out ammunition, and Peabody, still conspicuous in his white raiment, had command of the deck. Two boats were already grappled to the *Ranger*; he ordered cold shot to be dropped into them, and frightened one crew so that it cast off; then he ordered his men against the other boat, shouting, 'We have sunk one, boys; now let us sink the other!' His men cheered, and presently both boats dropped astern, leaving one of the *Ranger's* crew dead and three wounded. Peabody himself was hurt in three places, not counting the loss of his club of hair, worn in the fashion of those days, which had been shot clean off, and was found on deck the next morning. The enemy proved to be a guerrilla band of Tories, whose rendezvous was at St. George's Island, near where the *Ranger* lay at anchor. There had been sixty men in their boats, while the crew of the *Ranger* numbered twenty; and the same guerrillas had lately captured a brig of seven guns and thirty men by the same tactics, which the promptness of Peabody had foiled."

A month after the brilliant action between the *Congress* and the *Savage* the 14-gun brig *Fair America*, Captain S. Chaplin, of Connecticut, in company with the privateer *Holker*, captured four English merchantmen.

No better illustration of the extraordinary development of privateering during the Revolution can be had than the manner in which they made concerted attacks upon the English toward the latter part of the war. Not content with merely capturing the enemy's merchantmen—and even cruisers—our privateers arranged expeditions against the common foe in squadrons, and attacked towns.

Early in March, 1782, four American privateers united in an attack on a squadron of armed British

vessels at Tortola, in the West Indies. Among the
American craft were the *Holker* and the 20-gun ship
Junius Brutus, having a complement of one hundred
and twenty men, under Captain N. Broadhouse. Unfortunately the details of this ambitious expedition
have not been preserved, but enough is known to
show that a severe engagement resulted and two
of the enemy's vessels were captured.

In July, 1782, four American privateers united
in the attack on the town of Luenburg. They were
the 9-gun schooner *Hero*, Captain G. Babcock; the
6-gun brig *Hope*, Captain H. Woodbury; the 2-gun
cutter *Swallow*, Captain J. Tibbets, and one other.
The first two were from Massachusetts, and carried twenty-five and thirty-five men, respectively,
while the *Swallow* was from New Hampshire, and
had a complement of only twenty men. Landing a
force of men to attack the town from the shore, the
four privateers entered the harbor and soon had
the place in their possession. After holding it some
time they released the town on a payment of one
thousand pounds.

Another instance of concerted action among
American privateers was that in which the 10-gun
ship *Charming Sally*, Captain T. Dunn, of Massachusetts, took part. This privateer, in company with
other private armed craft, some time in 1782, attacked the formidable English ship *Blaze Castle*,
carrying twenty-six guns. An action of two hours'
duration followed, when the enemy surrendered, the
loss to the Americans being five killed or wounded.

In this year the British made a daring and successful attempt to cut out of Gloucester harbor the
ship *Harriet*, which they manned and sent to sea
with the intention of running her into Halifax. Before reaching that port, however, the *Harriet* fell in
with the American privateer *General Sullivan*, a brig
of fourteen guns and one hundred men, under Captain T. Dalling, of New Hampshire, and was recap-

tured. Four years before this the *General Sullivan*
had taken the British ship *Mary*, of eight guns.

It was in 1782 that Captain D. Adams, of the
10-gun sloop *Lively*, of Massachusetts, had the pleasure of rescuing the officers and men of the British frigate *Blonde* that had been wrecked on a
barren island, where the Englishmen must have
perished in a short time had they not been discovered.

In October the 16-gun schooner *Scammel*, Captain
N. Stoddard, of Massachusetts, was chased ashore
on the New Jersey coast by two British war ships.
The enemy endeavored to send their boats aboard
to make sure of the destruction of the privateer, but
they met with such a hot fire that they were compelled to retire. Shortly afterward the *Scammel* got
afloat, and having sustained no material injury
made her way to port.

In the same month Captain S. Thompson, of
Massachusetts, led a small party of men in a row-
boat in an attack on a British packet ship. After
skirmishing two hours the Americans were compelled to retire, having sustained a loss of three
killed and ten wounded. Soon after this Mr. Thompson captured a snow laden with oats, and in the
following November he took a ship with a cargo
of fish.

These captures were among the last made by
American privateers in the Revolution. The entire
number of vessels taken in this struggle from the
British by our maritime forces, including the Continental cruisers, was about eight hundred, of which
one hundred and ninety-eight were secured by craft
commissioned directly by Congress and the remaining six hundred were taken by private enterprise.
Perhaps the most remarkable feature of the audacity
of our privateers was the number of king's cruisers
taken by them. Not more than twelve regular war
ships were taken by the Continental cruisers, while

sixteen vessels of this class were captured by our privateers or by private enterprise.[1]

James, in his History of the British Navy, records an action between the French privateer *Atalante* and the British packet *Antelope*, Captain Curtis. The *Atalante*, very likely, was one of the old American privateers engaged in the war for American independence, and on the close of that struggle passed into French hands. She was manned largely by American and Irish seamen, and it is probable that she was owned by Americans, for we find that she was fitted out in Charleston, South Carolina.

James says: "On the 1st of December, 1793, the king's packet *Antelope*, being off Cumberland harbor, in Cuba, on her way to England from Port Royal, Jamaica, which port she had quitted three days previous, fell in with two French schooner privateers of formidable appearance. The packet immediately bore up for Jamaica, and was followed, under all sail, by the privateers. The *Atalante*, one of the two, outsailing her consort, continued the chase alone. During that and the following day until 4 P. M., the packet rather gained upon her pursuer; but the wind suddenly failing, the latter took to her sweeps, and soon swept up alongside of the *Antelope*. After the exchange of a few shots the schooner sheered off. On the 2d, at 5 A. M., it still being calm, the *Atalante* again swept up, and on reaching her opponent grappled her on the starboard side. The privateer then poured in a broadside, and attempted, under cover of the smoke, to carry the *Antelope* by boarding; but the crew of the latter drove back the assailants with great slaughter.

"Among the sufferers by the privateer's broadside was the packet's commander, Mr. Curtis, who fell to rise no more, as did also the steward and a

---

[1] For complete list see Maclay's History of the Navy, vol. i, pp. 150, 151.

17

French gentleman, a passenger. The first mate, too, was shot through the body, but survived. The second mate, having died of the fever soon after the packet had sailed from Port Royal, the command now devolved upon Mr. Pasco, the boatswain, who, with the few brave men left, assisted by the passengers, repulsed the repeated attempts to board, made at intervals during the long period that the vessels remained lashed together. At last, the privateersmen, finding they had caught a tartar, cut the grapplings and attempted to sheer off. The boatswain, observing this, ran aloft, and lashed the schooner's square-sail yard to the *Antelope's* fore shrouds. Immediately a well-directed volley of small arms was poured into the privateer and the crew called for quarter. This was granted, notwithstanding the *Atalante* had fought with the red or bloody flag at her masthead, to indicate that no quarter would be shown by her, and possession was forthwith taken of the prize.

" The *Antelope* mounted six 3-pounders, and had sailed with twenty-seven hands, but she had lost four by the fever and two were ill in their hammocks; consequently, the packet commenced the action with only twenty-one men exclusive of the passengers. Her total loss in the action was three killed and four wounded. The *Atalante* mounted eight 3-pounders, and her complement was sixty-five men, composed of French, Americans, and Irish. Of these the first and second captains and thirty men were killed and seventeen officers and men were wounded. The *Antelope* now carried her prize in triumph to Annotta Bay, Jamaica, where the two vessels arrived on the morning succeeding the action. The unparalleled bravery of one of the *Antelope's* passengers, a M. Nodin, formerly a midshipman in the French navy, deserves to be recorded. It is related of this young man that he stood by the helm and worked the ship, armed with a musket and a pike,

JOHN ADAMS, PRESIDENT *of the* UNITED STATES *of* AMERICA,

To all who shall see these presents, Greeting:

Know Ye, THAT in purfuance of an Act of Congrefs of the United States in this cafe provided, paffed on the ninth day of July, one thoufand feven hundred and ninety-eight, I have commiffioned, and by thefe prefents do commiffion the private armed *Ship* called the *Herald* of the burthen of *Three hundred twentyfive* tons, or thereabouts, owned by *Ebenezer Preble, & Samuel Parkman of Boston Merchants. & Nathaniel Silsbee of Salem Mariner, all in the State of Maffachusetts.*

mounting *Ten* carriage guns, and navigated by *Thirty* men; hereby licenfing and authorizing *Nathaniel Silsbee* captain, and *Nathaniel Hathorne 1st & Alexander Anderson 2d* lieutenants of the faid *Ship* and the other officers and crew thereof to fubdue, feize and take any armed French veffel which fhall be found within the jurifdictional limits of the United States, or elfewhere on the high feas ; and fuch captured veffel, with her apparel, guns and appurtenances, and the goods or effects which fhall be found on board the fame, together with all French perfons and others, who fhall be found acting on board, to bring within fome port of the United States ; and alfo to retake any veffels goods and effects of the people of the United States, which may have been captured by any French armed veffel ; in order that proceedings may be had concerning fuch capture or re-capture in due form of law, and as to right and juftice fhall appertain. This commiffion to continue in force during the pleafure of the Prefident of the United States for the time being.

GIVEN under my Hand and the Seal of the United States of America, at Philadelphia, the *twenty second* day of *January*, in the year of our Lord, one thoufand *feven* *eight* hundred *and ninety* and of the Independence of the faid States, the twenty *fourth*.

John Adams

By the President,

Timothy Pickering *Secretary of State.*

The President's letter of marque to the privateer Herald.

From the original.

which he alternately made use of; that when he perceived the *Atalante's* men climbing the quarters of the *Antelope* he quitted the helm, and with the pike dispatched such as came within his reach, returning at proper intervals to right the vessel; that with the pike and musket he killed or disabled several men, and continued his astonishing exertions for upward of an hour and a quarter." For this defense of the packet the Jamaica House of Assembly voted five hundred guineas for distribution among the men of the *Antelope*.

Little or nothing was accomplished by our privateers in the war with France, owing to the fact that the French had only a few merchantmen at that time, and these were confined in their ports by the rigor of the British blockade. There is an account of one action, however, in which the American privateer *Louisa*, of Philadelphia, defeated a number of French gunboats that came out to attack her off Algeciras. After a desultory action of some hours a lateen-rigged craft, filled with men, made several desperate attempts to carry the *Louisa* by boarding, but was steadily repelled. Toward the close of the fight the commander of the *Louisa* was shot through the shoulder, and while his first officer was taking him into his cabin, to have the injury attended to, the crew, with the exception of the man at the wheel, deserted their stations and ran below. Observing the confusion in the *Louisa*, the Frenchmen rallied for a final effort, and when the first officer came on deck again he found the enemy approaching to board. Taking in the situation at a glance the quick-witted officer ran to the hatchway and called on his men to come on deck and "take a last shot at the fleeing" Frenchmen. The *ruse* had the desired effect. The sailors hastened to the deck and were immediately sent to quarters, and a destructive fire was opened on the enemy, which swept away the men who had gathered on her bowsprit and forecastle in readiness to spring aboard. Believing that the apparent confusion in the American was a stratagem to induce them to come to close quarters again, the Frenchmen hastened to rejoin their discomfited consorts. The *Louisa* then continued her course to Gibraltar, where she was greeted by the throngs who had witnessed the affair from the Rock.

Another action which took place in the French war was that between the American privateer *Herald*, Captain Nathaniel Silsbee — afterward United States Senator from Massachusetts—and the French privateer *La Gloire*. The *Herald*, though bearing a letter of marque, had been engaged in a trading voyage to India. On November 1, 1800, Captain Silsbee left Calcutta, having in company the American merchantmen *Perseverance*, Captain Williamson; *Cleopatra*, Captain Naylor; *Grace*, Captain Davis—all of Philadelphia; and the *Sphinx*, Captain Brantz, of Baltimore. As it was know that several French privateers were cruising in those seas it was agreed between the commanders of these vessels to sail in company for mutual safety, the merchantmen being laden with cargoes invoiced at over a million dollars.

"On the morning of November 3d, at daylight," records Captain Silsbee, " two strange sails were discovered a few leagues to windward of us, one of which was soon recognized to be the East India Company's packet ship *Cornwallis*, of eighteen guns, which left the river at the same time with us. At about 8 A. M. the other ship stood toward the *Cornwallis*, soon after which the latter bore down upon us under full sail, commencing at the same time a running fight with the other ship, which then displayed French colors. We soon perceived that they were both plying their sweeps very briskly, that the Frenchman's grape was making great havoc on the *Cornwallis*, and that the crew of the latter ship had

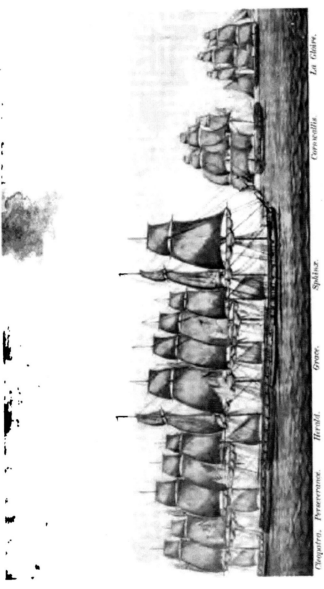

Cleopatra. Perseverance. Herald. Grace. Sphinx. Cornwallis. La Gloire.

Rescue of the British cruiser Cornwallis from the French privateer La Gloire by American merchantmen.

From the original painting by Captain Brantz, of the Sphinx.

cut away her boats and were throwing overboard
their ballast and other articles for the purpose of
lightening their ship. The sea was perfectly smooth
and the wind very light, so much so that it was quite
midday before either of the ships were within gunshot of us, by which time we (the five American
ships) were in close line,
our decks cleared of a large
stock of poultry—which,
with their coops, could be
seen for a considerable distance round us—and every
preparation made to defend
ourselves to the extent of
our ability. But this display of resistance on our
part seemed to be quite dis-
regarded by the pursuing
ship, and she continued
steering for my own ship,
which was in the center of
our fleet, until she was fully
and fairly within gunshot,
when my own guns were first opened upon her, which
were instantly followed by those of each and all of
the other four ships.

"When the matches were applied to our guns
the French ship was plying her sweeps, and, with
studding sails on both sides, coming directly upon
us. But when the smoke of our guns, caused by repeated broadsides from each of our ships, had so
passed off as to enable us to see her distinctly, she
was close upon the wind and going from us. The
captain of the *Cornwallis* (which was then within
hailing distance) expressed a desire to exchange signals with us and to keep company while the French
ship—which was known by him to be *La Gloire*, a
privateer of twenty-two 9-pounders and four hundred men—was in sight, which request was com-

plied with; and he having lost all his boats, I went on board his ship, where our signals were made known to him, and where the captain and officers of the *Cornwallis* acknowledged the protection which we had afforded them in the most grateful terms. The *Cornwallis* continued with us two days, in the course of which the privateer approached us several times in the night, but, finding that we were awake, hauled off, and after the second night we saw no more of her."

PART SECOND.

THE WAR OF 1812.

CHAPTER I.

FIRST VENTURES.

WHEN the United States declared war against
Great Britain, June 18, 1812, our navy consisted of
only seventeen vessels, carrying four hundred and
forty-two guns and five thousand men. Of these
only eight, in the first few months of the war, were
able to get to sea. At the time hostilities broke
out no American privateer was in existence; but
the rapidity with which a great fleet of this class of
war craft was created and sent to sea forms one
of the most important and significant episodes in
American history. At the first sound of war our
merchants hastened to repeat their marvelous
achievements on the ocean in the struggle for independence. Every available pilot boat, merchant
craft, coasting vessel, and fishing smack was quickly
overhauled, mounted with a few guns, and sent out
with a commission to " burn, sink, and destroy." A
newspaper under date of July 1, 1812, notes: " The
people in the Eastern States are laboring almost
night and day to fit out privateers. Two have
already sailed from Salem and ten others are getting ready for sea. This looks well, and does credit
to our Eastern friends." By the middle of October
New York had sent out twenty-six privateers, mounting some three hundred guns and manned by more
than two thousand men. A Baltimore paper, dated
July 4, 1812, says: " Several small, swift privateers
will sail from the United States in a few days. Some

already have been sent to sea, and many others of a larger class, better fitted and better equipped, will soon follow."

Niles, in his Register of July 15, 1812, says: "In sixty days, counting the day on which war was declared, there will be afloat from the United States not less than one hundred and fifty privateers, carrying, on an average, seventy-five men and six guns. If they succeed pretty well their number will be doubled in a short time. Sixty-five were at sea on the 15th inst. Many others are probably out that we have not heard of." And this, too, in spite of the fact that there were off the coasts of the United States at that time more than one hundred British vessels of war. When we remember that our national war ships, at the beginning of the struggle, numbered only seventeen vessels, carrying four hundred and forty-two guns, it will be readily seen that one hundred and fifty privateers, carrying about one thousand guns and more than ten thousand men, was no inconsiderable augmentation of our sea power.

It is interesting to note, however, that although the first English merchant vessel taken on the high seas by the Americans in the war—a ship from Jamaica bound for London—was captured by a United States revenue cutter, July 1st, off Cape Hatteras and sent into Norfolk, the first British Government vessel was taken by an American privateer. The English schooner *Whiting*, Lieutenant Maxcey, having on board dispatches from the British Government for Washington, was taken in Hampton Roads, July 10, 1812, by the privateer *Dash*, Captain Carroway, of Baltimore. The privateer was armed with one gun and carried a complement of forty men. The *Whiting* carried four guns. The former had come down from the Chesapeake prepared for a cruise against the enemy, when she found the *Whiting* lying at anchor in the Roads. At that moment Lieutenant Maxcey, being ignorant of the existence of hostilities, was in a boat pulling toward shore, intending to land at Hampton. Captain Carroway seized the boat and then made for the schooner. Running alongside he called on the officer in charge to surrender, which, after several papers had been thrown overboard, was done without opposition. These papers "were said to relate to Henry's affair." [1]

As the seizure of the *Whiting* was clearly unfair, the Government ordered her to be returned. " On Wednesday last [August 12, 1812] His Britannic Majesty's schooner *Whiting*, Lieutenant Maxcey—detained by the *Dash* privateer—was conducted to Hampton Roads by the revenue cutter *Gallatin*, Captain Edward Herbert. The crew of the *Whiting* was given in charge to Captain Herbert, with orders to deliver them up to their commander at the very place where they had been taken, which was done, and Lieutenant Maxcey was then ordered to quit the waters of the United States with all possible speed." [2]

About the time the *Whiting* was captured, Captain J. Gold, of the 8-gun privateer schooner *Cora*, of Baltimore, captured another English dispatch boat, the *Bloodhound*, and carried her into Annapolis. The *Bloodhound* also was released by our Government; "but she will find some difficulty," remarks a contemporary newspaper, "in working her passage home, the greater part of her crew having been carried on shore as prisoners, refusing their liberty, have claimed the protection of the soil, and preferred to reside among us. It is stated that the crew of the *Whiting* also have absolutely refused to go on board that vessel again, and that we have no law, if we had the will, to compel them." Among

---

[1] Norfolk Ledger, July 10, 1812.
[2] Norfolk Herald, August 14, 1812.

the crew of the *Bloodhound*, several gentlemen at Annapolis recognized an American who had been impressed three years before. He was restored to his country. We learn that several of the British sailors, panting for revenge, have already enlisted in the United States service, or entered on board our privateers." Aside from her capture of the *Bloodhound*, the career of the *Cora* was uneventful. She was captured in Chesapeake Bay by the British squadron in February, 1813, four of her men escaping in a boat to the shore. The *Dash's* usefulness also seems to have been limited to the capture of the *Whiting*, no other seizures being credited to her.

Many of the first privateers to get to sea were small pilot boats, mounting one long tom amidships, with several smaller guns, and carrying a crew of fifty to sixty men, whose chief dependence in battle was on muskets, sabers, and boarding pikes. These vessels, as a rule, were intended merely for short cruises in the Gulf of St. Lawrence, off Nova Scotia, Newfoundland, and among the West India Islands. At that time they were sufficiently formidable to capture the average British merchantman, but as the war progressed the great increase in armaments and complements of English trading vessels made our smaller privateers almost impotent. As soon as it was known that war had been declared a swift pilot boat hastened across the Atlantic to Gottenborg, and gave warning to all American merchantmen then in the ports of Sweden, Denmark, Prussia, and Russia. In this way a large number of our merchant craft were saved from capture, those that did venture out being fast-sailing vessels that could easily outsail the average British cruiser, or letter of marque.

Among the first pilot-boat privateers to get to sea were the *Black Joke*, Captain B. Brenow, and *Jack's Favorite*, Captain Johnson, both of New York.

The first, a sloop of five guns and sixty men, brought in two small prizes. *Jack's Favorite* was more successful, that vessel returning to New York early in July, 1812, having taken the schooner *Rebecca*, laden with sugar and molasses from Trinidad for Halifax, which was sent into New London; the brig *Betsey*, taken two hundred and fifty miles west of Rock of Lisbon, with a full cargo of wine and raisins from Malaga for St. Petersburg valued at seventy-five thousand dollars, which arrived at Plymouth, Massachusetts, safely; and three sloops that were destroyed at sea. The *Jack's Favorite*, like the *Black Joke*, carried five guns and a crew of eighty men.

At the time the *Jack's Favorite* and the *Black Joke* were operating against British commerce, the privateers *Rapid*, of Portland, the *Dolphin*, the *Jefferson*, the *Lion*, the *Snowbird*, and the *Fair Trader*, all of Salem, were cruising on the high seas. The first had, at different times, two commanders, the first being Captain W. Crabtree, and the second Captain J. Weeks. The *Rapid* took one ship and two brigs. The ship was the *Experience*, her cargo being valued at two hundred and fifty thousand dollars. One of the brigs was ransomed, and the other, the *St. Andrews*, of eight guns, for Bristol, England, in ballast, was sent into Portland. The *Rapid* also had an action with a British privateer, the schooner *Searcher*, mounting one gun and having a complement of twenty men. The *Rapid* was a brig carrying fourteen guns and eighty-four men. The *Searcher* was taken without difficulty and burned. Soon afterward the *Rapid's* career was cut short by the British frigates *Maidstone* and *Spartan*, which on October 17, 1812, captured her after a chase of eleven hours, during which the Americans had thrown overboard all their guns, boats, and every movable article in a vain endeavor to escape. The *Rapid*, however, had paid for herself many times over.

The privateers *Dolphin* and *Jefferson*, the latter

commanded by Captain J. Downer, and carrying two guns and forty men, also sent into Salem a brig, four schooners, and a shallop laden with dry goods. In all the *Jefferson* took one brig, four schooners, and one sloop. The *Jefferson* was a schooner carrying two guns and forty men, while the *Dolphin* is credited with one gun and twenty men.

In July, 1812, three Nova Scotia shallops arrived in Marblehead as prizes of the privateer *Lion*, Captain J. Hitch, of Salem. The *Lion* was a sloop carrying two guns and twenty men. With the assistance of the armed schooner *Snowbird*, Captain S. Stacy, the *Lion* also captured five English brigs from Liverpool bound for St. John's. One brig taken by the *Lion* and *Snowbird* carried six guns, but made no resistance. The *Lion* is credited in this war with having taken in all one brig, two schooners, and three sloops.

Although carrying only one gun and a crew of twenty-five men, the armed schooner *Fair Trader*, Captain J. Morgan, performed more valuable services than any of the foregoing privateers. Getting to sea at the outbreak of hostilities Captain Morgan, in one cruise, took three schooners: one having a cargo of beef, flour, fish, etc.; another being laden with gin and tobacco for St. Andrews; and the third with lumber on deck. After seizing these vessels the *Fair Trader* fell in with the British ship *Jarrett*, Captain Richard Jacobs, from Bristol, England, for St. Andrews, in ballast. She was a fine craft of four hundred tons burden, carrying two 6-pounders and eighteen men. At this time the privateer's complement had been reduced—through manning her previous prizes—to fifteen men. Notwithstanding his short-handed condition Captain Morgan boldly ran under the *Jarrett's* stern and demanded her surrender, at the same time discharging his single gun. It seems that of the *Jarrett's* eighteen men four were Americans, and on their making out the privateer

to be an American they left their stations and refused to fight. Captain Jacobs decided to surrender,
the four Americans enlisting in the *Fair Trader*.
This privateer took in all one ship, one brig, and five
schooners; but on July 16, 1812, while in the Bay of
Fundy, a few days after sending the *Jarrett* safely
into Salem, she was chased by the 18-gun brig of
war *Indian*, Captain Jane, and was captured. Later
in the war another privateer, pierced for eighteen
guns, was built under the same name, but that also
fell into the hands of the enemy and was destroyed
in Buzzards Bay.

But the loss of the first *Fair Trader* had been
avenged in advance, two days before her capture by
the *Indian*, when that cruiser attempted to capture
the privateer schooner *Polly*. That much advantage
was gained by privateers sailing in couples is shown
in the cruise of this vessel and the 2-gun schooner
Madison, of fifty men, Captain D. Elwell. The *Polly*
carried five guns and fifty-seven men, under the command of Captain T. Handy, both of Salem. They got
to sea early in the war. Their first success was the
seizure of a valuable transport by a clever stratagem. These two privateers were cruising in company on July 14, 1812, when they gave chase to two
vessels which they took to be merchantmen. It was
not until they were nearly within gunshot that one of
the strangers was discovered to be an 18-gun brig
of war carrying in all twenty-two guns. She was, in
fact, the *Indian*, which only two days after destroyed
the *Fair Trader*. Captain Jane promptly stood for
the privateers under a press of sail.

The American vessels separated, the cruiser
selecting the *Polly* and giving her a hard chase.
While the brig of war was almost within gunshot it
fell calm and the Englishmen got out their launch
and longboat, with forty men, and pulled toward the
Polly. When within musket shot the British crew
gave three cheers, and opening a brisk fire of small

arms, and from their 4-pounder, dashed toward the
privateer. This was the signal for the Americans to
open, and for a few minutes the water in the vicinity
of the launch was whipped into froth by musket balls
and langrage. In a short time the launch surrendered, while the other boat made a hasty retreat.
Captain Handy was unable to take possession of the
launch, however, for the cruiser was dangerously
near, so he seized this opportunity to man his sweeps
and thus made his escape. But the Americans had
the satisfaction of noting that when the launch advanced to the attack she showed sixteen sweeps,
while on her retreat only five were seen. About this
time the *Polly* captured the schooner *Eliza*, of Halifax, for Jamaica, and sent her into Salem. Before
returning to port Captain Handy took the sloop
Endeavor, Captain Newman, from Bermuda for Newfoundland, laden with sugar, and sent her into
Salem. Another prize credited to this privateer was
the brig *President*, laden with molasses, which was
sent into Savannah, October, 1813. On April 10,
1814, the *Polly* was captured by the 16-gun brig of
war *Barbadoes* off San Domingo after a chase of sixty
hours.

By the time the *Polly* had beaten off the *Indian's*
boats the *Madison* was not in sight, Captain Elwell
having made all speed for the brig that had been
in the cruiser's company. He had little trouble in
taking her. She was found to be the British Government transport No. 50, a fine brig of two hundred
and ninety tons, mounting two guns and manned by
twelve men. She was from Halifax for St. John's,
and had on board one hundred casks of gunpowder,
eight hundred and eighty suits of uniform for the
One Hundred and Fourth Light Infantry, some bales
of cloth for officers' uniforms, ten casks of wine, besides drums, trumpets, and other camp equipage,
the entire cargo being computed to be worth some
fifty thousand dollars.

Before reaching port the *Madison* captured, after a sharp engagement, the brig *Eliza*, carrying six guns to the privateer's two. The Americans had two men wounded, while the master of the prize was badly injured. Putting into Eastport, Maine, with a prize, a schooner, and another privateer, the *Madison*, on August 3, 1812, fell in with the 38-gun frigate *Spartan*, Captain Brenton, and the 32-gun frigate *Maidstone*. Anticipating trouble, Captain Elwell had moved to a point about six miles below Eastport, and running close inshore landed his men and guns and erected a battery. Scarcely had this been done when six boats, full of men from the cruisers, were discovered approaching. When within range the privateersmen opened a heavy fire, which was returned. After sustaining a loss of twenty or thirty killed or wounded the enemy retreated. On the following day they renewed the attack with overpowering forces, and this time succeeded in taking the privateer and her prize, the privateersmen escaping into the woods. Not one of the Americans was injured in the first attack, but several casualties were reported in the second day's fight. The *Madison* had taken in all four ships, three brigs, and a schooner.

Four days after the action between the *Polly* and the *Indian's* boats the American privateer *Falcon*, Captain George Wilson, had a running fight with the British cutter *Hero*. The *Falcon* was making the voyage from Boston to Bordeaux, and on July 18, 1812, while off the coast of France, she fell in with the *Hero*, carrying five guns and fifty men. The American mounted four guns and had a complement of only sixteen men. After a fight lasting two hours and a half Captain Wilson compelled the cutter to haul off, the enemy having made three unsuccessful attempts to board. On the following day Captain Wilson, while engaged in repairing his considerable injuries, was attacked by a British privateer

18

carrying six guns and forty men. The Americans
made another gallant fight, and for an hour and a
half kept the privateer off, but after Captain Wilson
and several of his men had been wounded the *Falcon*
was carried by boarding, though with her colors
flying. She was taken into Guernsey, where the
wounded were sent ashore.

About the same time the privateer *Gypsey*, of
New York, also making for Bordeaux, was seized
by a British cruiser. The Englishmen placed a prize
crew aboard the *Gypsey*, and ordered her to a British
port. Scarcely had the cruiser separated from her
prize, however, when the Americans hit upon a plan
for recapturing the schooner. Seizing a favorable
opportunity they rose on their captors and carried
the vessel into a French port.

The *Wile Renard*—at first commissioned as the
"*Wiley Reynard*, of one gun "—was a Boston schooner
hastily prepared for private enterprise on the high
seas. She made a short but successful cruise early
in the war, taking in all three ships, two brigs, and
four schooners, all of which reached port in safety.
Among her prizes was the schooner *Sally*, from Syd-
ney, Nova Scotia, which got safely into Boston, August 5, 1812. In her second venture the *Wile Renard*
was captured, October 4, 1812, by the 38-gun frigate
Shannon, Captain Philip Bowes Vere Broke.

Less successful than the *Wile Renard* was the 6-
gun sloop *Gleaner*—sometimes called the "Gleaner
packet"—Captain N. Lord. She was from Kennebunk, Maine, with a complement of forty men, and
was captured on her maiden cruise, July 23, 1812,
when off Cape Sable, by the 18-gun brig of war
Colibri, Captain Thompson. Three days later the
Colibri took the privateer *Catherine*, of fourteen guns
and eighty-eight men, Captain F. Burham, of Boston.
The *Catherine* was cruising off Cape Sable and had
captured one bark, when she fell into the clutches
of the cruiser. Captain Burham resisted for an hour

and a half, and did not surrender until his boatswain
had been killed and his first officer and several men
had been wounded. The British had six men killed
and a number wounded.

About this time the 5-gun schooner *Nancy*, Captain R. Smart, of Portsmouth, New Hampshire, carrying forty men, made a prize of the British ship
Resolution, laden with flour. She was sent into Portsmouth.

The fortunes of war were well illustrated in the
cases of the American privateers *Gossamer* and *Curlew* and the British brig of war *Emulous*, Captain
Mulcaster. The *Gossamer* was a 14-gun privateer of
Salem, commanded by Captain C. Goodrich, and was
one of the largest privateers sent out of Boston in
1812, she having a complement of one hundred men.
Her first and only prize was the ship *Ann Green*, from
Jamaica for Quebec, which was taken into Boston.
The prize was armed with eight 12-pounders and two
long 6-pounders, a very formidable armament for a
merchantman at that time. Part of her cargo consisted of one hundred hogsheads of rum, and the
entire " catch " netted her captors forty thousand
dollars.

A few days later, July 30th, the *Gossamer's* career
was cut short by the British 18-gun brig of war
Emulous, which made easy capture of the privateer
off Cape Sable. The *Emulous* had not long been in
possession of her prize, however, when the cruiser
was lost on Ragged Island, near the scene of the
Gossamer's capture. Though the officers and crew
of the cruiser were now without a ship, fortune soon
placed at their disposal another craft, to which they
transferred their quarters. It seems that six days
before the *Emulous* took the *Gossamer* the British
frigate *Acasta*, Captain Kerr, while in a dense fog,
had drifted alongside of the fine American privateer brig *Curlew*, of Boston. It was not until the
fog had lifted that Captain William Wyer, of the

privateer, discovered the undesirable proximity of the frigate, and being politely requested to surrender did so with all the grace possible under the circumstances. The *Curlew* carried sixteen guns and a complement of one hundred and seventy-two men, and being in every way as good a vessel, and almost of the same size as the *Emulous*, the officers and crew of the unlucky war brig were transferred to her, and they continued to cruise after the mischievous Yankees. On May 2d of the following year the *Curlew*, then under the command of Captain Michael Head, had a narrow escape from Captain John Rodgers, then cruising in the 44-gun frigate *President*. As it was the *Curlew* showed a "clean pair of heels," and kept up the reputation of American shipbuilders by outsailing the frigate.

Two days after the inhabitants of Gloucester, Massachusetts, had celebrated the "Glorious Fourth" of 1812 there appeared in the harbor of that town a brig which had slowly worked her way into the Roads with two flags flying at half-mast, one American and the other English. This singular apparition attracted the attention of the townsfolk, who gathered at the wharf awaiting an explanation. Soon a boat came ashore announcing that the brig was the American merchantman *Pickering*, Captain Davis, from Gibraltar, which had been taken only a few days before by the British 36-gun frigate *Belvidera*, Captain Richard Byron. That frigate had just made her escape from Captain Rodgers' squadron, and falling in with the *Pickering* took her. Captain Byron, after placing a prize master and eight men aboard the *Pickering*, with orders to make for Halifax, continued his cruise.

When the merchantman had come within six miles of her port, the Americans, with the assistance of four passengers, overpowered the prize crew and carried the *Pickering* into Gloucester. The British prisoners "spoke very unfavorably of Captain Rodgers. The *Belvidera* was much shattered in her stern and lost one topmast. She had one man killed and one wounded, who died."[1] The singular circumstance of the *Pickering* coming into port with American and English flags at half-mast is explained in another account, which says: " When the prisoners were landed the flags of the two vessels, belonging to a wretch born in the United States, but nevertheless not an American, were hoisted half-mast high to show his regret that certain citizens had recovered their property from the subjects of his king." It is claimed that the *Pickering* had sixty thousand dollars on board, which the officers of the *Belvidera* did not discover.

Another instance of an American ship being recaptured by her own people was that of the brig *Nerina*, Captain Stewart, which arrived in New London, August 4, 1812. This recapture was the result of a stratagem practiced by the long-headed Yankee commander. The *Nerina* had sailed from Newry, Ireland, before it was known that war existed between the United States and Great Britain. When off the American coast the *Nerina* was seized by a British cruiser, and all her men, with the exception of Captain Stewart, were taken aboard the man-of-war. A prize crew was then placed in the merchantman and ordered to make for Halifax. Believing that Captain Stewart was the only prisoner aboard, the English prize master relaxed his vigilance. It seems, however, that there were some fifty American passengers in the brig, and when it was seen that they must be captured Captain Stewart induced the passengers to conceal themselves in the hold, promising their release as soon as the cruiser was out of sight. Scarcely had the man-of-war disappeared below the horizon when the Yankee skipper innocently suggested to the British prize master the propriety of

[1] Private letter, dated Salem, July 6, 1812.

opening the hatches, "as the hold needed airing." The suggestion was promptly adopted, and much to the surprise of the captors fifty men sprang on deck, overpowered the unsuspecting prize crew, and brought the ship into New London.

The armed schooner *Paul Jones*, of sixteen guns and one hundred and twenty men, Captain J. Hazard (afterward commanded by Captain A. Taylor), of New York, captured the English brig *Ulysses*, from the West Indies bound for Halifax, and sent her into Norfolk. Later in the war (May 23, 1813) the *Paul Jones* took the *Leonidas* after a hard chase, in which five of the eighty-five Americans were wounded. In all, this vessel captured six ships, seven brigs, and two sloops. The *Paul Jones* sailed on her second cruise early in January, 1813. On January 7th she captured the ship *Seaton*, of twelve 6-pounders, laden with flour, from San Salvador for Lisbon. On the 25th she recaptured the American brig *Little James*, besides the following valuable prizes: *St. Martin's Planter*, of twelve guns, from Malta for London; the transport *Canada*, of ten guns, and having on board one hundred soldiers and forty-two horses;[1] the *Quebec*, from London for Gibraltar, of twelve guns, and laden with seven hundred and fifty packages of drygoods. The *Canada* was ransomed for three thousand pounds, after the troops had been disarmed. On February 27th the *Paul Jones* captured the sloop *Pearl*, of London, for St. Michael's, laden with fruit; the brig *Return*, of London; the brig *John and Isabella*, of Berwick-on-Tweed; and the brig *London Packet*, of six guns. The *John and Isabella* was given up as a cartel for the prisoners.

On the evening of July 9, 1812, the armed schooner *Fame*, Captain William Webb, of Salem, entered that port after having captured an English ship of about three hundred tons burden, laden with

---

[1] Log book of the *Paul Jones*.

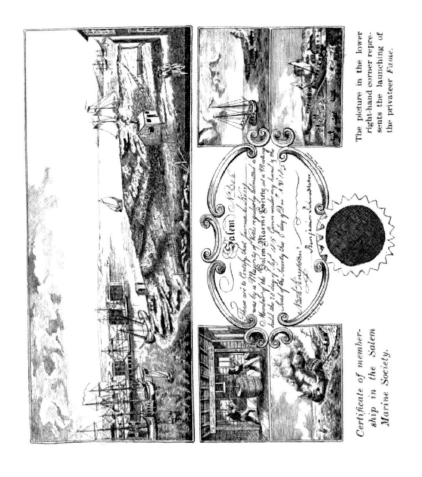

The picture in the lower right-hand corner represents the launching of the privateer *Fame*.

Certificate of membership in the Salem Marine Society.

lumber, and a brig of two hundred tons, laden with tar. The ship was armed with two 4-pounders, but was unable to make use of them, as the Americans boarded her unexpectedly. The *Fame* was a small vessel of only thirty tons, carrying one gun and a crew of twenty men. She was an old craft, having been used as a privateer in the Revolution. Perhaps this vessel won her greatest distinction in her next voyage, in which she took several vessels having a singular series of names. Under the command of Captain Green she returned to Boston, October 11, 1812, from a highly successful cruise of only fifteen days, in which time she had captured five vessels, all schooners, one of them bearing the name *Four Sons*, from the Bay of Chaleur, laden with fish and furs; another, called the *Four Brothers*, from the West Indies for Newfoundland; and a third, named the *Three Sisters*. The other two prizes were the *Betsey Ann*, laden with sugar, from the West Indies, taken in sight of Halifax harbor, and the *Delight*, from Bermuda for Halifax, laden with wine and silks, which was sent into Machias. All these prizes reached port.

The privateer sloop *Science*, carrying five guns and fifty-two men, under the command of Captain W. Fernald, sailed from Portsmouth, New Hampshire, August 12, 1812, in company with the armed schooner *Thomas*, Captain T. Shaw, of twelve guns and eighty men. The *Science* was captured when thirteen days out by the omnipresent *Emulous*. The *Thomas* took three ships, one brig, and one schooner, with a total valuation of six hundred thousand dollars. One of these ships, the *Dromo*, mounted twelve guns, and two of them carried fourteen each, but had for complements only twenty-five and thirty men respectively. The *Dromo* was from Liverpool for Halifax, and had a cargo invoiced at seventy thousand pounds sterling. She was sent into Wiscasset. Sailing again, September 23, 1813, the *Thomas*, when six days out, was captured off Cape North by the 32-gun frigate *Nymph*, after a chase of thirty-four hours, in which eight of the privateer's guns were thrown overboard.

The ship (or schooner, by some accounts) *Orlando*, of two hundred and eighteen tons, eight guns, and seventy-five men, Captain J. Babson, returned to Gloucester, August 28, 1812, after a successful cruise, in which she had taken two brigs, one schooner, and one sloop.

On July 23, 1812, the schooner *Dolphin*, Captain Endicott, of Salem, returned to port after a venture of twenty days on the sea. She had been chased several times by British cruisers, but always escaped. Captain Endicott took six prizes, and treated his prisoners with such kindness that when, on one occasion, he was for twenty-four hours hard pressed by an English frigate, the prisoners gave a willing hand in manning the boats and assisted in towing the privateer out of gunshot. They declared that they would much rather go to America than enter a British man-of-war. Some of the *Dolphin's* prizes were the ship *Wabisch*, laden with timber, the brig *Antelope*, and the ship *Empress*, which were sent into port; a schooner (name not given), which was released for one hundred thousand dollars in specie and a quantity of beaver skins; a brig of twelve guns, with an assorted cargo from St. Michael, which was sent into New London; the schooner *Ann Kelly*, of Halifax, with a miscellaneous cargo; the brig *St. Andrews*, bound for England; the ship *Mary*, from Bristol, England, for St. John's, carrying fourteen guns and having a considerable quantity of arms and ammunition on board; the ship *Venus*, an American vessel, with English property on board valued at sixty thousand dollars; and the schooner *Jane*, from the West Indies for Halifax, sent into Marblehead. After this highly successful cruise the *Dolphin* got to sea again, but on August

12, 1812, she was captured by the enemy. Another *Dolphin*, according to British accounts, was captured by the *Columbia*, December 4, 1812.

In the first eight weeks of the war the British captured one of our Government vessels, the *Nautilus*, thirteen privateers, fifteen ships, fourteen brigs, ten schooners, and one sloop. In the same time our Government cruisers took eight merchantmen, while our privateers seized one British Government craft, besides nearly one hundred vessels. The Essex Register records thirty-seven prizes of privateers which sailed from Salem, Gloucester, and Marblehead.

CHAPTER II.

ONE of the first services required of our sea forces
in the War of 1812 was the suppression of the illicit
trade that sprang up between the United States and
the British armies in Spain. At the time war was
declared Great Britain was operating extensively
against the French on the Iberian Peninsula, and
depended largely on America for provisions. High
prices for such supplies tempted many of our merchants not only to run the risk of capture and confiscation of their cargoes, but to brave the odium
of their fellow-countrymen. Many cargoes were
sent from the ports of the United States to Halifax
and thence to Spain, and though some of them got
safely to their destination, yet the vigilance of our
cruisers and privateersmen caused the seizure of a
large number. In September, 1813, seventeen thousand barrels of flour arrived from our ports in Halifax. In November of the same year a sloop arrived
in Boston ostensibly from Kennebunk, but on investigation it was shown that she came from Halifax. The sloop was seized by the customhouse officers and two men were placed aboard as a guard.
On the night of November 17th a number of men
suddenly took possession of the craft, and, securing
the guard with ropes, removed the cargo.

This illicit trade was early brought to the attention of the public by a capture made by the little
2-gun American schooner *Teazer*, manned by fifty

men. This vessel recaptured the fine, newly coppered American ship *Margaret*, which had been taken
by the British war schooner *Plumper*, Captain Bray.
The *Margaret* had sailed from Liverpool before it was
known that war between the United States and England had broken out. She was laden with a valuable cargo of earthenware and ironmongery, besides
having on board thirteen thousand bushels of salt,
the ship and cargo being worth fifty thousand dollars. On falling in with the *Plumper*, a British prize
master and twelve men were placed in charge of
the *Margaret*, with orders to make for Halifax.

Captain Bray seems to have followed a practice
which was largely indulged in early in the war by
British commanders on the North American station.
In order to evade the embargo a number of American vessels hastened to Lisbon with cargoes of provisions for the allied British and Spanish armies,
which were sold at great profit. As these provisions, at that time, were very difficult to get in Europe, the British encouraged American merchants
by issuing "British licenses" to all American vessels engaged in this trade whose masters were
"well inclined toward British interests," by which
such craft were exempt from seizure by British
cruisers or privateers; notwithstanding the fact
that the two countries were at war. A considerable
fee was charged for the protection. It was deemed
unpatriotic for Americans to avail themselves of
such licenses, but nevertheless a number of our merchants made the venture, while others sent cargoes
without the protection of licenses. British cruisers
were especially watchful for the latter class, and in
some instances did not scruple to seize the cash in
vessels returning from the Peninsula with a British
license. An American paper of 1813 notes that " fifteen or twenty *semi-American* vessels with British
licenses have been condemned at Bermuda. A grand
double speculation of the enemy; in first selling the

licenses, and then making good prizes of those that had them!"

The commander of the *Plumper* was particularly successful in this line of work. He took from eight to ten of our merchantmen. From one of them he helped himself to two thousand one hundred dollars in specie, from another two thousand three hundred dollars, and from a third five thousand three hundred dollars. In almost every case vessels despoiled in this way were allowed to proceed after being relieved of their cash, possibly in the hope that their owners might renew the venture. Even larger amounts of specie are recorded as having been taken from such American traders. The *Maria*, of New York, for instance, was stopped by the *Vixen* and relieved of thirty thousand dollars; the *Nautilus*, from Oporto, was fleeced of twelve thousand dollars by the frigate *Spartan*, which also took the same amount out of the *Hiram*, from Lisbon; seven thousand dollars from the brig *Jew*, and twelve thousand dollars from the brig *Mary*. The frigate *Melampus* took thirty-two thousand dollars out of one ship, and twenty-two thousand dollars were taken in the *Cordelia* by the *Emulous*. Notwithstanding these seizures, some five million dollars arrived in American ports from Lisbon during the first six weeks of the war. How much the British naval commander respected these licenses is shown in the following extract from a contemporary newspaper: "May 22, 1813.—The ship *Action*, of and for Boston from Cadiz, though protected by a 'real genuine Prince Regent's license,' was captured off our coast by the 74-gun ship of the line *La Hague*. Her captain, the 'honorable' Thomas Blanden Capel, plundered the brig *Charles*, also with a license, and would have burnt her, but thought it best to give her up to get rid of his prisoners, and she has arrived at Boston. He said he was determined to destroy every vessel that had a license, and if his Govern-

ment would not put a stop to the use of them, the
navy should do it."

Judge Story, of the United States Circuit Court,
sitting at Boston, June, 1813, in an elaborate opinion, decreed the condemnation of an American vessel sailing under a British license on the general
principle of being denaturalized by the acceptance
of the license. About the same time Judge Croke,
of Halifax, adjudged, in the case of the brig *Orion*,
Captain Jubin, from New York bound for Lisbon,
with a license and captured by the British blockading vessels and sent into Halifax, that the vessel
and cargo be restored to her owner; "that the
license having been granted previous to the blockade, it protected her and all vessels from condemnation with such a license, although they should be
captured departing from such blockaded ports in
the United States."

This peculiar weakness of British naval commanders on the North American station—namely,
that of taking all the cash out of a prize and allowing the vessel itself, with her cargo, to depart in
peace—has an explanation from one of the commanders himself which is almost as singular as the
practice. When the *Margaret* was recaptured by the
Teazer, as just narrated, two letters were found
aboard her written by Captain Bray. The free-and-
easy commander of the *Plumper*, in one of these letters, refreshingly explains his penchant for ready
cash as follows: "Finding some few dollars in the
brig [one of his quasi prizes] which I have taken,
I thought it more wise to take them out, as there is
no difficulty in sharing them, and our people are
very poor, some of them having had no money for
these nine years past." In the light of Captain
Bray's statement, that "some of them [the English
sailors] having had no money for these nine years,"
we can readily believe the statement published in
a Baltimore paper under date of April 10, 1813: "A

number of British seamen, from thirty to fifty, have lately escaped from the [British blockading] squadron. One poor fellow had not been on shore for thirteen years, during which time he had never received one cent of pay or prize money." Some of the other prizes made by the *Teazer* were the brig *Ann*, which was sent in, and the brig *Peter*, from Newcastle for Halifax, with a full cargo of British merchandise, which arrived safely in Portland in the latter part of August, 1812. In all the *Teazer* captured two ships, six brigs, and six schooners, all but one reaching port.[1]

On July 29, 1813, the President ordered all our navy officers to exercise the greatest vigilance in capturing American vessels engaged, or suspected of being engaged, in carrying provisions to the enemy. On August 5, 1813, the Secretary of War directed that " all officers of the army of the United States commanding districts, forts, or fortresses are commanded to turn back, and, in case of any attempt to evade this order, to detain all vessels, or river or bay craft, which may be suspected of proceeding to or communicating with, any station, vessel, squadron, or fleet of the enemy within the waters of the United States." [2] In September, 1813, the Americans fitted out the three-masted vessel *Timothy Pickering* at Gloucester to cruise after " licensed vessels."

Another instance of the respect with which English officers treated American vessels protected by British licenses is had in the following account published in a Boston paper August 4, 1813: " The ship *Fair American*, Captain Weathers, which arrived here Monday from Lisbon, was boarded on the 26th of July in latitude 42°, longitude 64° from his Britannic Majesty's frigate *Maidstone*, Captain Burdett,

---

[1] For the subsequent remarkable career of the *Teazer*, see preface.

[2] C. K. Gardner, assistant adjutant-general.

after a chase of seventeen hours, and the following particulars respecting the infamous treatment received from Captain Burdett were noted by the passengers, and are published at their request: 'At nine o'clock in the morning we were brought to and hailed by Captain Burdett, who stood in the main rigging, as follows: " Where are you from?" Answer, " From Lisbon." " Why did you not heave to and not run me so far out of my way?" Answer, "I understood there was a French squadron out, and I thought you might have been one of them." To which Burdett replied, "You have heard no such thing, sir. You are a liar—you are a damned liar, sir—and your country are a damned set of liars— you are a nation of liars!" and repeated the same several times over. He then continued, "I will cut your cabin to pieces. Lower your topsail down, sir! Get a bag of dollars ready to pay for the shot I have hove at you—they were the king's shot, sir. You are an enemy, sir" (twice repeated), "for you have no license from my Government, sir, or you would not have run away from me." He then repeated over several of the above blackguard expressions, and ordered Captain Weathers to come on board with his papers, which he complied with, and while there was grossly insulted with the foulest language.' "

"The brig *Despatch*," records a contemporary periodical, "a licensed vessel belonging to Boston, was captured on the coast by the privateer *Castigator*, regularly commissioned, of Salem. News of the incident having reached the owners of the *Despatch*, they fitted out two boats and filled them with about fifty armed men for the avowed purpose of retaking the brig, then in the bay. Anticipating this attack, the people in the privateer sent aboard the *Despatch* a quantity of arms and ammunition to the prize master and his crew, with instructions to resist to the last. The boats approached. They were warned to keep off, but, persisting in closing, a hot fire was opened on both sides. By making a dash the men in the boats succeeded in recapturing the *Despatch*, and, confining the prize master and his men in the hold, made sail for Boston. On entering the harbor the brig was stopped by a shot from the fort, taken possession of by the garrison and turned over to the customhouse officers. She was then libelled by the owners of the privateers. The leaders in the recapture were arrested and examined before Judge Davis, of the United States District Court." "Their counsel," says the Boston Chronicle, "first endeavored to soften the affair into a riot, and secondly to show that, as the alleged offense was committed within the county of Suffolk, that the United States district courts had no jurisdiction over the case. Without attending much to the first, as being of little consequence at the time, the judge of course repelled the latter plea and held the parties to bail. After the defendants had been recognized, inquiry being made for the witnesses who had testified on behalf of the United States, that they might be recognized, as usual, information was given that some of them had during the trial been arrested by the State authorities to answer for their conduct before the State courts. The honorable judge expressed a strong disapprobation of such a hasty procedure, and observed that it was by no means the mode of ascertaining and deciding the rights of the parties in that stage. The privateersmen were held under recognizance by the State courts." One of these men proved to be an "alien enemy," and was seized by a marshal and lodged in the guard ship to the end of the war. The *Castigator* also took the *Liverpool Packet*, Captain Richards, from Lisbon for Boston, but the prize was released.

In the first few weeks of the war several prizes were made by our revenue cutters. The *Madison*, Captain George Brooks, returned to Savannah, July 24, 1812, with a British snow mounting six guns, 6-

and 9-pounders, and manned by fourteen men. She was from Liverpool, making for Amelia Island, and had a quantity of small arms and ammunition aboard. The *Madison* also took the 300-ton brig *Shamrock*, carrying six guns and sixteen men, which was sent into Savannah. The revenue cutter *Gallatin*, Captain Edward Herbert, took the brig *General Blake*, August 10, 1812, while sailing under Spanish colors, and sent her into Charleston.[1] A few months later, or on April 1, 1813, the *Gallatin*, then commanded by Captain John H. Silliman, was destroyed by an explosion of her magazine while lying in Charleston harbor, South Carolina. The cutter had arrived only the day before from a short cruise down the coast and had anchored off the town. Soon afterward Captain Silliman went ashore, leaving orders for all the muskets and pistols which were kept in the cabin to be thoroughly cleaned. Of the thirty-five men on board when the explosion occurred ten of them were in the cabin or on the quarter-deck engaged in carrying out their commander's orders. " Thus situated the dreadful explosion took place, and in an instant the whole quarter-deck of the vessel, with all those upon it, were hurled into the air. Some of the bodies were thrown nearly as high as the masthead of the vessel; others were driven through the cabin and lodged upon the main deck. The whole stern of the vessel was torn down to a level with the water; the mainsail, which had been hoisted to dry, was torn to rags, and the fragments of broken spars were scattered in all directions. As soon as the accident had happened, boats put off from the wharves and from the vessels near by to the relief of the crew.

" An attempt was made to slip the cables and run her into one of the docks to prevent her from sink-

---

[1] For the capture of the revenue cutter *Surveyor*, see Maclay's History of the Navy, vol. i, pp. 586, 587.

ing, but before this could be fully accomplished the fire in the cabin had communicated with the mainsail and main rigging, at the same time the vessel was found to be filling very fast. In this extremity the wounded men were hastened into the boats alongside, and by the time the persons on board could leave her she went down sternforemost, a few yards from the head of Blake's Wharf. The bodies of three of the unfortunate sufferers were never seen; and happier would it have been for some of those who were brought on shore if they had shared their fate, as they can not survive the dreadful wounds and bruises which they have received. It has been found impossible, after the most diligent inquiries, to ascertain the manner in which fire was communicated to the magazine; the persons immediately adjoining the cabin steps where the door opened from the cabin to the magazine were destroyed." [1] First Lieutenant Philips, of the *Gallatin*, had left the cutter only a few minutes before the explosion took place, the magazine being locked and the key being in a drawer in the cabin. The only other person of the vessel's complement who had any business with this key, besides the captain and Lieutenant Philips, was the gunner, and he was known to have been on deck at the time of the disaster. No satisfactory explanation of the accident has ever been made.

---

[1] Charleston Courier.

CHAPTER III.

CAPTAINS MAFFITT AND SHALER.

Two distinguished American privateersmen who got to sea early in this war were David Maffitt and Nathaniel Shaler. The former, at the beginning of hostilities, commanded the *Atlas*, carrying twelve short 9-pounders and one long 9-pounder, with a complement of one hundred and four men. The *Atlas*, early in July, 1812, cleared the Capes of the Delaware, and when two days out she overhauled the brig *Tulip*, Captain Monk, just out from New York. The *Tulip* carried one of the British licenses referred to in the preceding chapter, and had on board one thousand four hundred barrels of flour and a quantity of salt beef. Suspecting that this cargo might be for the enemy, Maffitt pretended to be sailing under English colors, and kept up the delusion so well that the commander of the *Tulip* was satisfied that the *Atlas* was an English and not an American privateer. Acting on this belief, Captain Monk said that he ought not to be detained, as he had dispatches from "Mr. Foster," and then the commander of the *Tulip* showed his "British license."

"These papers," said Captain Maffitt, "are quite satisfactory; and now, instead of sending you into a British port, I will send you into the port of Philadelphia." He then placed five men and a prize master aboard the *Tulip*, who carried the brig safely into that port. "We heard of a contract," said a Philadelphia newspaper of that day, "made at New

York by Mr. Foster, and also one at Philadelphia, to supply the British armies [in Spain] with flour, etc., under British licenses, and we were in hopes that the ingenuity, enterprise, and management of our privateersmen would discover the traitors who were thus adhering to our enemies, giving them aid and comfort. Captain Maffitt deserves and will have the thanks of his fellow-citizens for the adroitness and judgment with which he captured the *Tulip*."

Continuing his cruise after his interception of the *Tulip*, Captain Maffitt, at half past eight o'clock on the morning of August 5th—or two weeks before the first frigate action of the war—discovered two sails to the west standing northeast, and he immediately tacked southward to reconnoiter. The *Atlas* at that time was in latitude 37° 50' north and longitude 46° west. An hour later she tacked northward, and when satisfied he had merchantmen to deal with Captain Maffitt beat to quarters and cleared for action. At half past ten o'clock the *Atlas* bore away for both ships, and, showing American colors, prepared to close with them.

Quarter of an hour later the smaller ship opened fire on the privateer and hoisted English colors, her example being followed a few minutes later by her consort. Captain Maffitt, however, reserved his fire, as he was anxious to come to close quarters immediately. At eleven o'clock, having placed his vessel between the two English ships, he opened with a broadside from each battery, which was followed up with volleys of musketry. The effect of the privateer's cannon fire at such close quarters was terrific, and in an hour the smaller ship hauled her colors down. This enabled Captain Maffitt to devote his entire attention to the larger ship, which had been making a gallant fight and was keeping up a destructive fire. Scarcely had the *Atlas* turned from the smaller ship, however, when, to the surprise of the Americans, the latter opened fire again, notwithstanding the fact that she had surrendered and her colors were down. Captain Maffitt reopened on this vessel, and in a few minutes drove every man below decks.

All this time a heavy fire had been kept up by the Americans from their opposite battery on the larger ship, and it was seen that she was suffering heavily. At twenty minutes past twelve her flag came down, upon which a prize crew was placed aboard her and her people disarmed. She was the *Pursuit*, a vessel of four hundred and fifty tons, carrying sixteen guns and a crew of thirty-five men. A prize crew also was sent aboard the second ship, the *Planter*. She was of two hundred and eighty tons burden, and carried twelve 12-pounders and a crew of fifteen men. Both ships were thirty days out from Surinam for London, laden with a cargo of coffee, cotton, cocoa, and six hundred hogsheads of sugar.

In this action the *Atlas* was badly cut up in her rigging and spars. Every one of her shrouds on the port side was carried away, which, with the loss of other standing rigging and the foreyard, placed her masts in a critical condition. Two of her crew had been killed and five were wounded. In view of the shattered condition of his vessel, Captain Maffitt determined to make for the first port in the United States and refit. Taking the crews of both the *Pursuit* and the *Planter* aboard the *Atlas* for safer keeping, he headed southward, with his prizes in company.

For nearly a month the three vessels continued on their voyage westward without molestation, but at half past four o'clock on the morning of September 2d a large ship was discovered to the east standing southward. An hour later it was seen that she was a frigate, and shortly afterward she tacked and gave chase to the three vessels. Believing her to be an Englishman, Captain Maffitt promptly bore down and directed the prize master of the *Pursuit* to tack southward and make the first port he could. The *Atlas* then ran close to the *Planter* and told her prize master that in all probability the frigate was an enemy, and ordered him to sail northward, Captain Maffitt deciding to take his chances with the frigate alone.

By ten o'clock the *Pursuit* was out of sight to the south; but instead of singling out the *Atlas*, as was expected, the frigate made for the *Planter*, and by eleven o'clock it was seen that she was fast coming up with her. Captain Maffitt now backed his main topsail and awaited developments. At half past one o'clock the frigate opened on the *Planter* with her bow chasers, and at the fifth shot obliged her to heave to. Observing that the frigate was flying English colors, and realizing that he could be of no possible assistance to his late prize, Captain Maffitt made sail westward. At half past three the ships were still in sight, the *Planter* flying American colors at the mizzen peak. As this display of the United States ensign on the *Planter* could easily have been resorted to by an English frigate as a *ruse* for decoying the privateer under her guns, Captain Maffitt kept on his course and gained port. Subsequently, he learned that the man-of-war was, in truth, an American, the 32-gun frigate *Essex*, Captain David Porter. Both of the *Atlas'* prizes arrived safely in port.

Refitting after her first successful cruise, the *Atlas* got to sea again; but Captain Maffitt, early in the summer of 1813, was compelled to run into Ocracoke Inlet, North Carolina, where he found the 18-gun privateer *Anaconda*, Captain Nathaniel Shaler, of New York. Captain Shaler, like Captain Maffitt, was one of the successful privateersmen of this struggle. His first command was the 14-gun schooner *Governor Tompkins*, of New York, but owned principally by people living in Baltimore. This vessel had left port about the time the *Atlas* made her first venture and had met with some success. In order to relieve himself of a number of prisoners, Captain Shaler placed them aboard a whaler from London, bound for the South Sea. The whaler had been intercepted by the *Governor Tompkins* and ordered to Falmouth.

In chasing the whaler Captain Shaler had been drawn some distance from his cruising ground, and, owing to calms, did not regain it until December 25, 1812. At sunrise on that day Captain Shaler discovered three ships ahead and made sail in chase. As the wind was light the privateer came up to them slowly, but it was not long before they were made out to be two ships and a brig. There was something about the appearance of one of the ships that caused Captain Shaler anxiety,. and he prepared to act with more caution. He noticed that she seemed to be industriously engaged in communicating with her consorts. Boats were observed to be hurriedly pulling between her and the other vessels. Besides this, she had boarding nettings almost up to her tops, with her topmast studding sail booms out and sails at their ends ready for spreading. Her ports were painted, and she carried something on her deck that resembled a merchantman's boat.

Believing her to be a large transport, Captain Shaler was approaching cautiously under English colors, when suddenly, at three o'clock in the afternoon, a squall from the north struck the privateer, and as the supposed transport had not yet felt the wind the Americans in a few minutes found themselves carried within a quarter of a mile of the stranger. Captain Shaler had done his best to get his light sails in, but such was the force of the wind that he found his vessel carried toward the stranger almost before he could turn round. Just before

the squall struck him he had told First Officer Farnum that he thought the stranger too heavy to be a
privateer, and he ordered the first officer to go forward and take another look through his glass.   It
was then that the stranger showed herself to be, not
a transport, but a first-class frigate, and, tricing up
their ports, her people delivered a broadside that
killed two and wounded six of the Americans, one
of the latter mortally.   Among the wounded was
Mr. Farnum.   Seeing that further concealment was
unnecessary, the American commander hauled down
the English colors and sent up three American en-
signs, and, trimming his sails by the wind, began
an animated fire from his puny battery.

At this moment the privateer was a little abaft
the frigate's beam, and for Captain Shaler to have
attempted to tack in a hard squall would have exposed him to a raking fire.   To have attempted to
tack and failing to do so would have placed his
schooner hopelessly within the power of her huge
antagonist.   Captain Shaler, therefore, determined
to receive the enemy's fire on the tack on which he
had been standing, hoping to outsail the frigate and
pass beyond her bow, where he would not be exposed
to her dreaded broadside.

The Englishman also kept on the same tack, and
the two vessels ran along side by side, giving and
receiving a spirited fire.   Unfortunately for Captain
Shaler's calculations, the English frigate proved to
be a remarkably fast sailer—almost as fast as the
privateer—so that she managed to keep her broadside guns playing with full effect on the chase much
longer than the American had anticipated.   "Such
a tune as was played round my ears," wrote Captain
Shaler, "I assure you I never wish to hear again in
the same key."

But in spite of the terrific fire they were exposed to, the Americans held their course, with their
triple colors defiantly flying in the gale.   Almost at

her first fire, a shot from the frigate blew up one
of the *Governor Tompkins'* shot boxes, in which were
two 9-pounder cartridges. Their explosion set fire
to a number of pistols and three tube boxes, which
were lying in the companion way, all of which ex-
ploded. Some of the tubes passed through a crevice
under the companion leaf and fell to the cabin floor,
near the entrance to the magazine. For an instant
it was feared that the ship would be blown up, but
fortunately the precaution of wetting the cabin
floor and drenching the screen, or woolen blanket
over the hatch leading to the powder room, prevented any further explosion.

Soon after this a heavy shot hit a colored seaman named John Thompson on the hip, taking off
both legs and horribly mutilating the lower part of
his body. Notwithstanding his agony he lay on the
deck, and before he died he exclaimed several times
to those around him, " Fire away, boys! Nebber haul
de colors down." Another black sailor, named John
Davis, was mortally hurt in much the same way. He
fell to the deck near where Captain Shaler was
standing, and requested that he might be thrown
overboard, so that his body would not encumber the
working of the guns.

For half an hour the *Governor Tompkins* was subjected to this destructive fire. At the end of that
time she began to draw ahead of the frigate and the
enemy's shot gradually fell short. At half past
four, however, the wind died away, but the English
ship still holding a good breeze, her shot again
began to fly unpleasantly round the ears of the
Americans. Captain Shaler now relieved his
schooner of all the lumber on her deck and threw
overboard some two thousand pounds of shot from
the after hold. He then got out his sweeps, and, setting all hands to work, gradually drew away from
" one of the most quarrelsome companions that I
ever met," as he grimly expressed it.

Finding that he was steadily losing ground, the English ship, at 5.25 P. M., hove about and returned to her consorts. From information subsequently gained, Captain Shaler believed that his "quarrelsome foe" was the British frigate *Laurel*, one of the ships manned and fitted expressly to cope with the heavy American 44-gun frigates. The *Laurel* was reputed to be one of the fastest sailers in the long list of British frigates.

Returning from this cruise Captain Shaler assumed the command of the 13-gun brig *Anaconda*, of New York. The subsequent career of the *Governor Tompkins* was one fraught with riches for her men and owners. Among her commanders was Captain J. Skinner, and among the prizes was the *Nereid*, which was sold in New York, the gross receipts, exclusive of jewelry, amounting to two hundred and seventy thousand dollars. Other prizes taken by this favorite ship were the brig *Ajax*, mounting two guns, from which a quantity of valuable drygoods was taken; the 2-gun brig *Hartley*, from Gibraltar for San Salvador, which was burned; and the brig *Young Husband*, laden with drygoods, hardware, etc., from Bristol for Madeira, which was sent into Newport. Of these prizes the *Nereid* was the most valuable. She was of two hundred and eighty tons burden and carried ten guns. She was taken off Madeira, from London for Buenos Ayres, and had on board two hundred and fifty bales of drygoods, two hundred and sixty-three packages and trunks of the same, one hundred and fifty casks, hogsheads, and tierces of hardware and jewelry, eight hundred and sixty-nine bundles of iron hoops, eighty bars of iron, and a quantity of coal, the entire cargo being valued at seventy-five thousand pounds. In February, 1814, the *Governor Tompkins* captured a whaler bound to the South Sea, which was divested and turned into a cartel. In March of the same year she took the brig *Henry*, of six guns, which was sent into New

York and sold for two hundred thousand dollars. In a brief cruise in the English Channel the *Governor Tompkins* made ten prizes. In her entire career she made twenty prizes, three of which were valued at half a million dollars.

Captain Shaler's career in the *Anaconda* was marked at the outset by an occurrence which well illustrates the disadvantages of having our commerce destroyers under private management. While off Cape Cod, January 16, 1813, the *Anaconda*, through lack of a good system of signaling between our Government war ships and the privateers, mistook the United States war schooner *Commodore Hull* for an enemy, and fired a broadside into her before the mistake was discovered. By this fire the commander of the *Commodore Hull*, Lieutenant H. S. Newcomb, was seriously wounded. First Officer Burbank, of the *Anaconda*, was blamed for the mistake, but on court-martial the privateer's people were relieved from responsibility in the matter.

Making for European waters, the *Anaconda*, on May 14, 1813, while in the latitude of the Cape de Verde Islands, fell in with the British packet ship *Express*, a brig carrying eleven 12-pounders and a crew of thirty-eight men. She was from Rio de Janeiro bound for England, having on board eighty thousand dollars in specie and two hundred and thirty stands of muskets. In the sharp action of thirty-five minutes that followed the Englishmen made a brave resistance, but finally were overcome, having their spars and rigging much cut and five feet of water in their hold. The prize, after the specie and valuables were taken out of her, was ransomed for eight thousand dollars. Soon afterward the *Anaconda* seized the 8-gun brig *Mary*, from Gibraltar for Brazil, having on board wine and silks valued at thirty-five thousand dollars. This prize was sent into New Haven. In the same month, June, Captain Shaler captured the brig *Harriet*, from

Buenos Ayres for London, laden with hides and tallow, invoiced at one hundred thousand dollars. This
vessel was carried into New Bedford. The estimated

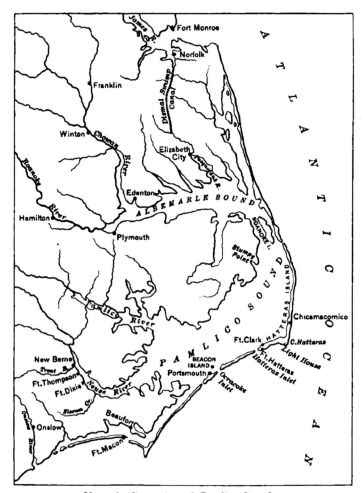

Map of Albemarle and Pamlico Sounds.

value of all the *Anaconda's* prizes was two hundred
and fifteen thousand dollars. Early in July Captain
Shaler ran into Ocracoke Inlet, where he found the
Atlas, as we have seen.

On the night of July 12, 1813, Rear-Admiral Cockburn appeared off this inlet with the 74-gun ship
of the line *Sceptre*, the frigates *Romulus*, *Fox*, and
Nemesis, the war brig *Conflict*, and the tenders *Highflyer* and *Cockchafer*, having on board about five hundred men of the One Hundred and Third Regiment
and a detachment of artillery, for the purpose of
destroying these two privateers, which Cockburn
had learned had taken refuge there. As this powerful squadron approached the inlet the masts of the
Atlas and *Anaconda* were plainly seen, and the enemy
at once made preparations for an attack. At 2 A. M.
on the 13th the troops embarked in boats, and, under
the escort of the light-draft tenders and the *Conflict*,
made toward the shore in three divisions. Owing
to the heavy ocean swell and the great distance at
which the heavier vessels were obliged to anchor
from the beach, the division under Lieutenant West-
phal, of the *Sceptre*, did not land until daylight,
which deprived the enemy of the advantages of a
night attack.

Having arranged their plan of attack, the British
boats, under cover of a rapid discharge of rockets,
doubled the point of land behind which the privateers were anchored, and dashed toward them in
gallant style. Realizing that it would be madness
to oppose the overwhelming force that was advancing upon him, Captain Shaler cut his cables and got
ashore with his men, the British taking possession
of the *Anaconda* without opposition. The guns of
that vessel were now turned upon the *Atlas*, and
Captain Maffitt, seeing the uselessness of resistance,
surrendered. Elated with their easy capture of
these two formidable privateers, the enemy advanced
against the village of Portsmouth, seizing that place,
and were preparing to attack New Berne, when they
learned that vigorous measures were being taken
by the inhabitants to repel an assault. The project
against New Berne was abandoned, and, after hold-

ing Portsmouth two days, the enemy retired to their
ships and sailed away.   Both the *Atlas* and the *Anaconda* were taken into the British navy, the latter
retaining her name and the former rechristened
St. Laurence.   The *St. Laurence*, as will be shown
in another chapter,[1] was recaptured, after one of the
most brilliant actions of the war, by the Americans.
The *Highflyer*, also one of the vessels engaged in this
affair, was captured on the 23d of the following September by the American 44-gun frigate *President*,
Captain John Rodgers.   The *Highflyer* at that time
was commanded by Lieutenant George Hutchinson.

Captain Shaler did not get to sea again as a commander of an American privateer; but Captain Maffitt, notwithstanding the loss of his ship, soon secured the command of the splendid 16-gun brig *Rattlesnake*, and in company with the privateer *Scourge*,
Captain Samuel Nicoll, a native of Stratford, Connecticut, made one of the most successful ventures of
the war; the *Rattlesnake* alone sending into Norway
one million dollars' worth of prizes.   The *Scourge* had
sailed from New York in April, 1813, for a cruise on
the north coast of England.   After taking a number
of prizes Captain Nicoll, on July 19th, while off Cape
North, fell in with the United States 44-gun frigate
President, Captain John Rodgers, and cruised in her
company some time.   A number of British vessels
sailing to and from Archangel were secured, most
of them being sent into Norwegian ports.

Soon after parting from the *President* the *Scourge*
met the *Rattlesnake*, and, having a number of prisoners aboard, both privateers ran into Drontheim,
where Captain Nicoll went ashore to attend to the
sale of his prizes, while the *Scourge* was refitted and
went to sea, in the following spring, under the command of her first officer, J. R. Perry.   This was on
March 10, 1814, and on April 1st, while off Cape

[1] See pages 295-300.

Wrath, the privateer took the *Symmetry*, a fine vessel from Liverpool, coppered, and laden with salt, crates, hardware, etc. This vessel was in company with the ship *Winchester* and the brig *Union*, both of which were soon taken by the nimble *Scourge*. These vessels were bound for Long Hope, where they were to get a convoy. Having taken out the most valuable goods, Captain Perry burned the vessels and placed the prisoners aboard a Swedish ship.

The *Scourge* hovered on the English coast some time. On April 7th she chased a Greenland whaler and fired ten broadsides into her, and undoubtedly would have captured her had not a sloop of war close inshore given chase. For six hours it was a hard run, but the privateer finally escaped, although she strained her fore-topmast. A week later, while in a moderate breeze, both her topmasts were carried away, the wreckage killing one man and wounding three. This mishap, however, did not prevent the *Scourge* from refitting at sea and continuing her cruise. On May 9th she boarded the American privateer *Fox*, Captain Brown, of Portsmouth, New Hampshire, forty days out. The *Fox*, it seems, had made four prizes, two of which had been destroyed, the other two being ordered into port. Captain Brown at one time had been hotly pursued by a British frigate, and, though effecting his escape, he had been obliged to throw overboard ten of his guns. Subsequently he chased a vessel which he took to be a merchantman, and did not discover she was a sloop of war until he was close aboard, when she triced up her ports and let go two broadsides at the *Fox*. The privateer, although hit several times— one shot going through an arms chest—managed to escape. The *Scourge* sailed for the United States, arriving at Chatham, Cape Cod, in May, having been absent more than a year, in which time she had taken twenty-seven vessels and four hundred and twenty prisoners.

Meantime the *Rattlesnake* had been giving a good account of herself. Between August 10 and August 22, 1813, Captain Maffitt took the brigs *Betsey, Pax, Thetis, Diligent,* and *Friends Adventure,* besides the sloops *Perseverance* and *Fame.* In all, the *Rattlesnake* took eighteen vessels. Captain Maffitt spent the winter of 1813–'14 in Europe, and early in the latter year we find him at La Rochelle, where, after witnessing the marvelous escape of the *Ida,* as narrated in another chapter,[1] he was blockaded by a British squadron. Escaping from that port, after the *Ida* got to sea, the *Rattlesnake* was captured, June 3, 1814, by the British frigate *Hyperion.*

---

[1] See chapter xv, Escape of the Ida.

CHAPTER IV.

PRIVATEERS OF RHODE ISLAND.

ALTHOUGH one of the smallest States in the Union, Rhode Island sent out several privateers in this war which made up for deficiency in number by the vast amount of damage they inflicted upon the enemy's commerce. A peculiarity of Rhode Island's privateers was the fact that they monopolized the name " Yankee." They had the *Yankee*, the *True Blooded Yankee*, the *Yankee Lass*, the *Yankee American*, and the *Yankee Porter*. The last two, though hailing from Salem and New York respectively, were largely manned by Rhode Island seamen. The first to get to sea was the *Yankee*. She was a brig of one hundred and sixty-eight tons, armed with the usual long tom amidships, a 12-pounder, and fourteen short guns, 9- and 6-pounders, in her broadsides. Her owners were James De Wolf and John Smith, of Bristol, the former having three fourths and the latter one fourth interest in her. She sailed on her first cruise the middle of July, 1812, under the command of Captain Oliver Wilson, and made for the coast of Nova Scotia. About noon, August 1st, when off the harbor of Halifax, a sail was reported to Captain Wilson bearing off the lee bow some four miles away, the thick weather having prevented her discovery before this. The stranger was seen to be a large ship, apparently well armed. Captain Wilson boldly ran down, and by 1 P. M. he was near enough to observe that she was preparing for battle. The Americans were then sent to quarters, and being to windward they approached the stranger on her weather quarter. When within close range the ship showed English colors, whereupon Captain Wilson fired his first division of guns. As the *Yankee* began to double on the Englishman's quarter the Americans poured in a full broadside, to which the stranger promptly replied, and the firing became rapid and well sustained on both sides. As the two vessels were at close quarters, the American marksmen in the tops opened an effective fire with their small arms.

It was not long before the enemy's sails and rigging were cut to pieces and their helmsman was shot at the wheel. This caused some confusion in their ship, which rapidly increased under the destructive fire maintained by the Americans. About this time the *Yankee* ran off a short distance and then luffed across the stranger's bow, where a terrific raking broadside was delivered, which, followed up with a shower of musket balls, compelled the Englishman to surrender. The prize proved to be the British privateer *Royal Bounty*, Captain Henry Gambles, a splendid vessel of six hundred and fifty-eight tons—about four times as large as the *Yankee*—mounting ten guns, but manned by only twenty-five men. It was probably owing to the circumstance of her being short-handed that she yielded so soon as she did. Captain Wilson displayed true mettle in attacking such a formidable-looking ship when he was necessarily ignorant of her condition. The *Yankee's* complement consisted of one hundred and twenty officers and men. The *Royal Bounty* was seven weeks out from Hull in ballast, bound for Prince Edward Island.

In this action the Americans had three men wounded, while their sails and rigging were somewhat damaged. The English craft had two men killed and seven wounded, among the latter being their commander and one or two of his officers. The hull, sails, and rigging of the *Royal Bounty* were cut to pieces and all her boats were shattered, more than one hundred and fifty heavy shot having struck her. With characteristic kindness the American commander, on hearing of the casualties in his prize, sent his surgeon aboard to attend to the enemy's wounded. Transferring the prisoners to his own ship, Captain Wilson placed a prize crew in the *Royal Bounty* and ordered her to an American port. Continuing her cruise the *Yankee* captured several other British vessels—the most valuable being the *Eliza Ann*, from Liverpool, with a full cargo of British goods, which was sent into Boston, August 26th—and then returned to port.

About the middle of October, 1812, the *Yankee* sailed on her second cruise, still under the command of Captain Wilson. This time the privateer steered for the west coast of Africa, and was not long in making known her arrival. Her first " appropriation " was the British sloop *Mary Ann*, Captain Sutherland, a coppered vessel from London, carrying four guns and eleven men. The Englishmen did not have an opportunity to resist, and were taken aboard the privateer as prisoners. The *Mary Ann* was found to have on board gold dust, ivory, and camwood to the value of twenty-eight thousand dollars, which were taken aboard the *Yankee* and then the sloop was burned. The next prize was another coppered vessel, the schooner *Alder*, Captain Crowley, from Liverpool, carrying six 9-pounders and twenty-one men. These people made a stubborn defense, but on the blowing up of their quarter-deck, by which their commander and six of his crew were killed, they surrendered. The *Alder* had in her hold four hundred casks of musket flints, a quantity of bar lead, iron, and drygoods, the entire cargo and vessels being valued at twenty-four thousand dollars.

Skirting along the coast of Africa, Captain Wilson looked into every port, river, and factory town in search of the enemy. At one place there was a fort called Appollonia, mounting fifty guns, though it is probable that most of them were not serviceable. Discovering a brig snugly anchored under the guns of this formidable-looking fort, Captain Wilson organized an expedition for the purpose of cutting the brig out. The plan was put through in a most audacious manner. The brig, which proved to be the *Fly*, was taken from her anchorage near the fort and brought out in safety. Her commander was Captain Tydeman. The *Fly* carried six guns and had fourteen men aboard. Her cargo consisted of gold dust, ivory, gunpowder, iron, drygoods, and various other articles, the vessel and cargo being valued at thirty-six thousand dollars. Captain Wilson placed a prize crew aboard the *Fly* and ordered her to the United States.

Another vessel taken by the *Yankee* on this cruise was the brig *Thames*, Captain Toole, of Liverpool, carrying eight guns and fourteen men, with a cargo of drygoods, camwood, and redwood worth forty thousand dollars. This vessel also was manned and arrived safely in Boston. Not long after he had seen the *Thames* fairly off, Captain Wilson fell in with the brig *Harriet and Matilda*, Captain Inman, from Cork for Pernambuco, carrying eight guns and fourteen men. This vessel at one time had been a Portuguese war brig, captured by the English in 1808. At the time of her falling into the clutches of the *Yankee* she had on board a cargo of fine cloths, linens, iron, salt, and porter to the value of forty-one thousand dollars, which were duly appropriated by the captors. The fifth prize made by Captain Wilson was the brig *Shannon*—by one account the *Andalusia*—Captain Kendall, from Maranham for Liverpool, having on board ten guns and one hundred men, of whom eighty-one were free blacks. This vessel and cargo, worth thirty-four thousand dollars, arrived safely at Savannah.

While looking into Tradetown Captain Wilson observed a schooner lying there at anchor. He made a bold dash into the port and came out with the schooner *George*, having on board a cargo of rice. Taking out two thousand five hundred dollars' worth of this commodity, Captain Wilson placed all his prisoners in the *George* and gave them permission to make for whatever port they pleased, while he turned the prow of the *Yankee* westward. Before reaching the American side of the Atlantic Captain Wilson made his eighth prize, the schooner *Alfred*. The *Yankee*, after touching at several Portuguese islands for water and "information," arrived in Newport—by another account Bristol—in March, 1813, having taken, in a cruise of one hundred and fifty days, eight vessels, one hundred and ninety-six men, four hundred and six muskets, and property to the value of two hundred and ninety-six thousand dollars. Soon after gaining port the owners of the *Yankee* had the satisfaction of learning that the cargo of the *Shannon*, which had been appraised by Captain Wilson at only thirty-four thousand dollars, had realized sixty-seven thousand five hundred and twenty-one dollars.

But the thrifty *Yankee* could not long remain in port, and soon after settling her accounts, and after giving herself a little brushing up, she put to sea again at seven o'clock on the evening of May 20, 1813, this time under the command of Captain Elisha Snow. It was known to Captain Snow that an English frigate and a 14-gun brig of war were waiting for him in the neighborhood of Block Island, but under cover of night he succeeded in giving the cruisers the slip, and was again in blue water. Two days after leaving port the *Yankee* captured the British brig *William* and ordered her in, but unfortunately the latter fell into the clutches of the frigate which the *Yankee* had eluded. On the day he took the *William* Captain Snow fell in with a Portuguese schooner, and after paroling the men he had taken out of his prize he placed them aboard the Portuguese and resumed his cruise.

On May 30th the *Yankee* came across the English brig *Thames*, the second vessel bearing that name which she had met during her career in this war. The *Thames* carried fourteen guns, but was manned by only twenty men. Nevertheless the Britons made a gallant fight, and it was not until after an action of more than an hour that they could be induced to surrender. She was sent into Portland, where the brig and cargo of more than two thousand bales of cotton were sold for one hundred and ten thousand dollars. On June 3d the privateer overhauled a Portuguese brig from New York, and Captain Snow placed in her the officers and men of the *Thames*, after they had given their promise not to serve against the United States again in this war.

By the middle of June Captain Snow was nearing the coast of Ireland, and on the 22d, when in sight of land, he captured the sloop *Earl Camden*, of one hundred and ten tons, valued at ten thousand dollars, which was ordered to France. Eight days later, while still in sight of the Irish coast, he took the English brig *Elizabeth*, of one hundred and fifty-six tons, laden with cotton estimated to be worth eighty thousand dollars, which also was ordered to France. On the same day Captain Snow took the brig *Watson*, carrying three guns and fifteen men. She had on board bale cotton valued at sixty thousand dollars.

Still clinging to the Irish coast, Captain Snow on July 1st stood close in to land, and after paroling his prisoners placed them in two boats and " directed " them to make for the shore. Scarcely had these boats put off when the lookouts reported a strange sail. Chase was promptly given, and in a short time the *Yankee* overhauled the schooner *Ceres*, of Londonderry, laden with produce. As this vessel was of little value she was released after some articles of value to her captors had been taken out. Continuing within sight of the coast, the *Yankee* on the following day seized the brig *Mariner*, laden with rum and sugar to the value of seventy thousand dollars, which was ordered to France. The officers and crew of this prize, after being paroled, were placed in a boat and permitted to land.

The whereabouts of the mischievous *Yankee* were now so well known to the enemy, through the reports brought by these paroled prisoners, that Captain Snow deemed it prudent to stand out to sea, and on July 23d he gave chase to a promising sail. When within gunshot the *Yankee* discharged her bow chaser, but as no attention was paid to this summons to heave to a second gun was fired. This shot also was unheeded, whereupon Captain Snow hoisted American colors with a pennant and sent a shot into the stranger. The latter then displayed Spanish colors and discharged her stern gun. Meantime the *Yankee* was rapidly gaining, and on coming within pistol shot the Americans fired a lee gun as an indication of friendship, but the chase luffed up and opened with grape from her stern guns. Satisfied that he was dealing with an Englishman in disguise, Captain Snow began firing in earnest, and after five or six broadsides he brought the Spanish colors down. On sending a boat aboard it was found that the stranger was, in truth, a Spaniard, being the privateer *Nueva Constitucion*, a ship of three hundred tons, mounting six 24-pounders and two 12-pounders and carrying a crew of twenty-five men. Assured of his mistake, Captain Snow hastened to apologize and released the Spaniard.

Three days later the *Yankee* gave chase to a brig, which, when the vessels were within three miles of each other, was seen to be a war craft. Upon discovering this, Captain Snow hauled close upon the wind, and notwithstanding the fact that the stranger showed American colors he declined taking chances and continued on his course, so that in a few hours he left her far behind. On August 20th the *Yankee* returned to port, having captured twenty-two English vessels in her first three cruises, without the loss of a man on her part.

Her fourth venture also was very successful. She sailed September 13, 1813, having Thomas Jones as her commander. Her first prizes were the brigs *Ann*, laden with rum, salt, and drygoods, for Newfoundland, valued at forty thousand dollars, and the *Mary*, having a cargo of salt, coal, and crockery, valued at twenty thousand dollars, which were sent into Chatham. Captain Jones also took the brigs *Dispatch* and *Telemachus*, the former having a cargo of drygoods and cutlery invoiced at forty thousand dollars, and the latter—which was recaptured—with a cargo of rigging, coal, and provisions. The most valuable part of the *Telemachus'* cargo had been transferred to the privateer before she was ordered to port.

After taking the brig *Favorite*, which was transformed into a cartel, and the schooner *Katy*, which was sent into New Bedford, Captain Jones met the bark *Paris*, armed with ten guns and manned with a strong crew. The *Yankee's* complement had by this time been much reduced by drafts for manning her prizes, so that it required a hot fight of thirty-five minutes before she could prevail upon the *Paris* to surrender. The prize had a valuable cargo, which was transferred to the privateer. The *Paris* was then manned and ordered to an American port, but soon afterward she was recaptured. All of these vessels had formed a part of a great fleet of merchantmen which had sailed from Cork under the protection of a strong force of war ships. They had become separated by a storm, and the *Yankee* com-

ing along just then made easy capture of the stray
ones.   After taking two more vessels of this fleet,
the brigs *John and Mary* and the *Howe*, Captain Jones
made for home, arriving forty-nine days after sailing.   The *John and Mary* was found to be laden with
shot and provisions worth forty-nine thousand dollars, while the *Howe*, being comparatively of little
value, was released and the prisoners placed in
her and allowed to go.   In this short cruise the
Yankee made one hundred and eighty prisoners.

Owing to the rigorous blockade maintained by
the British fleet off Rhode Island the *Yankee* did not
get to sea again until May or June, 1814, when she
again was under the command of Captain Elisha
Snow.   In this cruise of only a few weeks the *Yankee*
took four vessels—the ship *Sir Hugh Jones*, from Belfast for Guadeloupe, which was divested of her valuable cargo and ordered in; the ship *Berry Castle*, of
six guns, which was released after Captain Snow
had divested the vessel of her cargo of barilla and
wine; the brig *Maria Wirman*, from Havana for Scotland; and the ship *San José Indiano*, from Liverpool
for Rio Janeiro.   The last vessel was of enormous
value, and on being taken into Portland the gross
receipts from the sale of the ship and cargo was
nearly six hundred thousand dollars.   The owners
of the *Yankee* received as their share of the profits
nearly a quarter of a million dollars, while not a
boy in the *Yankee* got less than seven hundred dollars.   Captain Snow received for his portion fifteen
thousand seven hundred and eighty-nine dollars,
while the negro waiters in the cabin, Cuffee Cock-
roach and Jack Jibsheet, received one thousand one
hundred and twenty-one dollars and eighty-eight
cents and seven hundred and thirty-eight dollars and
nineteen cents, respectively.

In her sixth and last cruise the *Yankee* was commanded by William C. Jenkes, until he was succeeded
by B. K. Churchill, Jenkes losing one of his legs be-

fore the end of the cruise. She sailed October 1, 1814, and on January 21, 1815, put into Beaufort, North Carolina, after a successful cruise, having taken six vessels—the brigs *Lady Prevost, Courtney,* and *Speculator;* the ships *St. Andrews* and *General Wellesley,* and a schooner from Bermuda laden with flour. The *Speculator,* which had a cargo of jerked beef, was given up to the prisoners. The *Courtney* was taken into New Bedford, and on sale realized seventy thousand dollars. The *General Wellesley* was a splendid vessel of six hundred tons, built in the strongest possible manner of teak wood, newly coppered, and fitted with all the improvements then known. She carried an armament of sixteen guns and a crew of thirty-six Englishmen and fifty Lascars, and it was only after a running fight of several hours that the *Yankee* finally captured her. The prize was from London for Calcutta, and consequently was well stocked with miscellaneous articles, a part of her cargo consisting of eighteen thousand bars of iron. As this prize was worth at least two hundred and fifty thousand dollars, an unusually strong prize crew was placed aboard her under the orders of James M. Blum, with instructions to make for Charleston, South Carolina. Unfortunately, while endeavoring to enter the harbor, the *General Wellesley* struck on the bar and became a total wreck—all of her original crew, besides two of the Americans, perishing.

From these six cruises of the *Yankee* it will be seen that her record was an unusual one. She had taken altogether nine ships, twenty-five brigs, five schooners, and one sloop, making in all forty vessels captured from the British. She had seized or destroyed property to the value of five million dollars, and had sent into Bristol alone one million dollars' worth of goods.

Equally successful and even more remarkable than the career of the *Yankee* was that of the *True*

Blooded Yankee. This vessel, although fitted out in France, is entitled to a place among " those ' Yankees ' of Rhode Island," inasmuch as she was fitted out by a Mr. Preble, a Rhode Islander, then living in Paris. She was a French brig, carrying sixteen guns, and had been captured by the English and taken into their navy shortly before the war with the United States broke out. Afterward she was recaptured by the French, from whom Mr. Preble purchased her and fitted her out as an American privateer. Captain W. F. Wise, of the British frigate *Granicus,* said of her, in a conversation with one of his prisoners, the captain of an American privateer: " She outsailed everything, and not one of our cruisers could touch her."

The *True Blooded Yankee* sailed from Brest, March 1, 1813, under the command of Captain Hailey, and made directly for the Irish Channel. Her first prize was the little coasting craft *Margaret,* in which Captain Hailey placed a prize master and six men, with orders to make for Morlaix. The peculiar dangers of privateering were well illustrated in the fate of this prize. It seems that Mr. Preble had some difficulty in getting together a sufficient number of men to fill out the complement of the *True Blooded Yankee*; as, being in a French port, American seamen were scarce, and recourse had to be taken to unusual means. By the connivance of the French authorities the Americans were permitted to search through the prisons in the hope of inducing sailors to serve in the privateer. A number of men were thus secured, as they were glad to exchange their dreary confinement for a life full of adventure and promise of large financial rewards. Among these prisoners was an Englishman named John Wiltshire, who had been in a French dungeon three years. Hearing that an American privateer was being fitted out, he declared himself to be an American citizen, and accordingly was released and allowed to enlist in the

True Blooded Yankee. He was one of the men detailed
to act as a part of the prize crew of the *Margaret.*
The *Margaret* had scarcely lost sight of the privateer when she was recaptured by the British cutter
Nimrod, and her prize crew made prisoners. Wiltshire was recognized as an English subject and was
promptly hanged.

Continuing his cruise along the coast of Ireland,
Captain Hailey took prizes daily, and on one occasion he seized an island near the enemy's mainland
and held it for six days, until he had made necessary
repairs, when he resumed his cruise. He returned to
Brest in thirty-seven days, having in that time made
two hundred and seventy prisoners and secured
enormously valuable cargoes. Among the goods
stowed in the hold of the *True Blooded Yankee* were
eighteen bales of Turkish carpets, forty-three bales
of raw silk, twenty boxes of gum, twenty-four packs
of beaver skins, etc., showing that every quarter of
the globe had contributed to the wealth of the privateersmen. Sailing from France again, Captain
Hailey made a rapid circuit of Ireland and Scotland.
He landed several times and held small towns for
a ransom, and on one occasion he burned seven vessels in an Irish port. In May he had the audacity
to run into the harbor of Dublin, where he sank
a schooner that had eluded him the day before.
Again returning to France, the *True Blooded Yankee*
disposed of her prizes and their cargoes at great
profit.

On September 30, 1813, the following notice,
copied from a Paris newspaper, dated September
25th, was posted in Lloyd's Coffee House, London:
" The *True Blooded Yankee*, American privateer, has
been completely refitted for sea, manned with a crew
of two hundred men, and sailed from Brest the 21st
inst. supposed for the purpose of cruising in the
British Channel. Her orders are to sink, burn, and
destroy, and not to capture with the intention of

carrying into port." These orders were faithfully carried out, an immense amount of damage being inflicted on British commerce at the hands of this "Yankee" scourge. It was on this cruise that the *True Blooded Yankee* was finally captured, she having at the time only thirty-two men out of her original complement of two hundred, the rest having been drawn off to form prize crews for vessels captured from the enemy. The privateer and her people were taken to Gibraltar, where they were confined until the close of the war. In all the *True Blooded Yankee* took six ships and twenty-one smaller craft, one of her prizes being worth four hundred thousand dollars.

Of the other " Yankees of Rhode Island," of which mention has been made, there remains little to record. The *Yankee Lass*, a schooner of nine guns and eighty-five men, was commanded by Captain B. K. Churchill, who had served with distinction in the *Yankee* under Captain Jenkes. The *Yankee Lass* was captured at sea on her maiden cruise when only twenty days out, May 1, 1814, by the British frigate *Severn*. The *Yankee American* made a short cruise on the outbreak of hostilities under Captain Stanwood. She was a schooner of seven guns and carried forty-four men. In her second venture, under Captain T. Pillsbury, she was captured October 24, 1812, when one month out, while off Sombrero lighthouse, by the sloop of war *Peruvian*. Of the *Yankee Porter* little is known except that she was a sloop of two guns with thirty-five men, under the command of Captain J. Welden. Not one prize is credited to her.

There were five other privateers sent out from Rhode Island in this war, but they were small vessels carrying from one to three guns, and accomplished nothing, save the *Waterwitch*, Captain T. Milton, which seized an American vessel laden with seven hundred barrels of flour intended for the enemy. The names of the others are *Hiram, Huntress, Juno,* and *Swift.* The *Governor Gerry,* a fine brig of eighteen guns, was launched in forty-eight days after the laying of her keel, but did not get to sea in time to make a single prize.

CHAPTER V.

CAPTAIN THOMAS BOYLE.

FOR a privateersman to match his ship successfully against a regular war vessel is sufficient distinction in itself to mark her commander as a man
of extraordinary daring. To be twice successful in
such an encounter is remarkable even for the commander of an American private armed craft. A
number of our privateersmen have won this distinction; but few have equaled, in this particular, the
success of Captain Thomas Boyle. He had the en-
viable honor of twice worsting a cruiser and of several times putting up a good defense against government war craft. Even in the light of the proverbial
daring of American privateersmen, Captain Boyle's
career in the War of 1812 was extraordinary and
well worthy of extended notice. He has been described, by one who knew him well, as being a quiet,
unassuming man, who said little but did much;
" always annoying the enemy wherever he chanced
to steer, sometimes on the coasts of Spain and Portugal, and, anon, in the British and Irish Channels,
carrying dismay and terror to British trade and commerce, in defiance of their fleetest frigates and sloops
of war, which strove again and again to capture
him, but never were able. He appeared frequently
to tantalize and vex them as if for mere sport, and at
the same time convince them that he could out-
maneuver and outsail them in any trial of seamanship."

When this commander put to sea, early in the war, he knew that he might be called upon to defend his ship against the attacks of British cruisers, but he did not count upon the interference of other foreign naval powers. Our regular cruisers sometimes experienced the covert sympathy of Spanish and Portuguese officials at the several ports in which they were compelled to enter, and, as will be seen, our privateers, on one occasion at least, felt the full force of their broadsides. Captain Boyle began his extraordinary career in this war in the privateer *Comet*, of Baltimore. Several of our privateers had borne this name in the struggle for independence, and had met with considerable success, so it is not surprising that we find one of the most successful private armed craft in the second war with Great Britain bearing this lucky name. Before hostilities broke out this vessel, a stanch schooner, had been engaged in the merchant service, and, like all merchantmen of her class in those troublous times, she had been constructed quite as much with a view to speed and fighting as stowing away cargo. The *Comet* had been selected for the privateer service because of her splendid sailing qualities and her ability to carry a heavy armament.

In her first cruise, which began in July, 1812, she had a desperate engagement with the British merchantman *Hopewell*, a ship of four hundred tons, carrying fourteen guns and a crew of twenty-five men. She was from Surinam bound for London, laden with seven hundred and ten hogsheads of sugar, fifty-four hogsheads of molasses, one hundred and eleven bales of cotton, and two hundred and sixty bags and casks of coffee and cocoa—a prize well worth fighting for. The vessels quickly came to close quarters, and the English surrendered only after one of their number had been killed and six wounded—nearly a third of the crew. The *Hopewell*, with her cargo, was valued at one hundred and fifty thousand dollars. She had been one of a squadron of five vessels that had left Surinam, the *Hopewell* having become separated from her consorts two days before her capture.   Another of the *Comet's* valuable prizes was the ship *Henry*, of four hundred tons, coppered to the bends and mounting four 12-pounders and six 6-pounders.   She was from St. Croix bound for London, and had on board seven hundred hogsheads of sugar and thirteen pipes of old Madeira wine, the vessel and cargo netting her captors more than one hundred thousand dollars. The *Comet* also took the ship *John*, of four hundred tons, carrying fourteen guns and a crew of thirty-five men, from Demerara for Liverpool. She was laden with cotton, sugar, rum, and coffee, besides a large quantity of old copper and dyewood, the entire cargo and vessel being worth at least one hundred and fifty thousand dollars—fifty thousand dollars of which went into the Treasury of the United States in the form of bounty.

In one of his prizes Captain Boyle found a copy of " Recommendations by their Lordships of the Admiralty," which shows what extraordinary measures were resorted to by the English to check the dreadful ravages wrought by American cruisers and privateers on British commerce: " The Lords Commissioners of the Admiralty recommend that all masters of merchant vessels do supply themselves with a quantity of false fires, to give the alarm on the approach of an enemy's cruiser in the night, or in the day to make the usual signals for an enemy being chased by or discovering a suspicious vessel; and, in the event of their capture being inevitable, either by night or by day, the masters do cause their gears, trusses, and halyards to be cut and unrove, and their vessel to be otherwise so disabled as to prevent their being immediately capable of making sail."

The *Comet* returned from her first cruise in No-
21

vember, 1812, and hasty preparations were made to refit and get her to sea again. A strong force of British war ships blocked Chesapeake Bay so completely that it was some weeks before Captain Boyle ventured to run the gantlet. The night of December 23, 1812, coming on dark and boisterous, Captain Boyle quietly passed the word round that the attempt would be made that evening. Accordingly, soon after dark, the schooner slipped her moorings and sped rapidly down the bay. For several hours it seemed as if the venture would be entirely successful, for no trace of a British war craft was to be found, but shortly before daylight the *Comet* received a broadside from a frigate which the thick weather had concealed from view. Little or no attention was paid to this, and the privateer slipped out to sea with only a little rigging damaged and one spar hurt. The last was soon fished, and with repaired rigging the *Comet* headed south, and in two weeks was off Cape St. Roque, and on January 9, 1813, appeared off Pernambuco.

On that day Captain Boyle spoke a trading vessel just out of the port, and learned that in a few days some English vessels were about to sail, with valuable cargoes. This determined him to hover in that vicinity and make a dash for prizes. On the 11th he spoke the Portuguese brig *Wasa*, from St. Michael for Pernambuco, and then stood on and off shore, maintaining a careful watch for any indication of the vessels leaving the harbor. At one o'clock on the afternoon of January 14th his vigilance was rewarded by the discovery of four sails standing out of the harbor. They proved to be a ship and three brigs. Instead of making directly for them, the privateer stood away so as to give them an opportunity to get an offing where it would be easier to cut them out.

By three o'clock the vessels were upon the wind, standing southeast about thirty-six miles from land.

This was the time for the privateer to strike, and, bearing up, she made all sail in chase. By five o'clock the splendid sailing qualities of the American schooner had enabled her to draw up on the enemy very fast, and by six o'clock their lead had so decreased that Captain Boyle was able to make them out clearly. But just about this time the fourth sail was discovered to be a large man-of-war brig. This was an unexpected result of the chase; for Captain Boyle had been informed, through reliable sources, that no English war craft was in port, so that when he saw four instead of three sails coming out he supposed that another merchant vessel had joined the squadron, which would only make his capture the more valuable. The announcement that the fourth vessel was a heavy war brig somewhat disconcerted his plan of action, which was to close on the merchantmen under cover of night and take them one after another. Captain Boyle, however, was not a man to be frightened off by a few cannon, and although he was aware that the merchantmen were well armed, and were capable of giving the war brig material assistance, he called all hands, cleared the decks for action, and, loading his cannon with round and grape shot, boldly stood for the cruiser.

By seven o'clock the *Comet* had gained a position close abeam the brig when the American colors were hoisted. The brig responded with Portuguese colors, and her commander hailed and said that he would send a boat aboard. Anxious to discover if the stranger really were a Portuguese, and, if such, what her object could be in sailing as an escort to English merchantmen, Captain Boyle hove to. Soon a boat put off from the side of the brig and came alongside the *Comet*, and an officer, dressed in Portuguese uniform, stepped aboard. He reported that the brig was a regular war ship of the Portuguese Government, carrying a crew of one hundred and sixty-five men and mounting twenty 32-pounders—doubtless

an exaggeration made to intimidate the privateersmen. The *Comet* carried fourteen guns, and had a
crew of about one hundred and twenty men. The
officer furthermore said that the three vessels in the
brig's company were English, and, being under the
protection of the brig, must not be molested by the
privateer. Captain Boyle replied that his ship was
an American cruiser, and as such he had a right to attack the English vessels, and that if the Portuguese
attempted to interfere the *Comet* would open with
her guns. In order that there should be no misunder-
standing in the case, Captain Boyle insisted upon the
officer seeing his papers from the American Government authorizing the *Comet* to capture English vessels. Captain Boyle then informed the officer that
the privateer would capture the merchantmen if she
could; that they were upon the high seas, the common highway of all nations; that the Portuguese
brig had no right to interfere, and that the ocean,
of right, belonged to America as much as any other
power in the world. To this the Portuguese replied
that he would be sorry if anything disagreeable took
place; that his brig had received orders to protect
the merchant vessels, and would do so at any hazard.
Captain Boyle said that he also would keenly regret
if "anything disagreeable" took place between his
vessel and the brig, but that if the latter became
the aggressor he would promptly fire into her before
leaving. The officer remarked that the merchant
vessels were well armed and strongly manned, and
would support the brig in case of battle, to which
the American commander replied that he valued
their strength very little, but would soon give them
all the opportunity they wanted to test it.

The Portuguese then returned to his brig so as
to give the result of his interview with Captain
Boyle to his commander. Before he left the *Comet*
he promised to return shortly. After waiting in
vain some time for the boat to report, Captain Boyle

spoke the Portuguese, asking if they intended sending their boat back, to which they replied that they
would speak the convoy first, and that, in the meantime, the Portuguese commander would be much
obliged if Captain Boyle would send his boat aboard.
Entertaining some doubt as to the sincerity of this
request, Captain Boyle replied that he did not make
a practice of sending his boat away at night, and
would not do so in this case. He then avowed his
determination of attacking the English vessels at
once. He said this with such distinctness as to leave
no chance for him to be misunderstood. The *Comet*
accordingly began to forge ahead, and in a short
time came up with the ship and ordered her people
to back their main topsail. Having too much headway Captain Boyle drew ahead of the ship, but finding that little or no attention was paid to his order
he shouted that he would be alongside again in a
few minutes, and if by that time his order were not
obeyed he would pour a broadside into them.

True to his word, Captain Boyle a few minutes
later, or at about half past eight, tacked, with the
Portuguese man-of-war close after him, and ran
alongside the ship. By that time one of the merchant brigs also was close to the ship, and the *Comet*
opened fire on both of them. All the vessels at the
time were carrying a press of sail, but the privateer,
from her superior sailing qualities, was obliged to
tack frequently in order to keep her place at close
quarters. About this time the Portuguese man-of-
war opened fire with round and grape shot, to which
the *Comet* replied with her long tom and broadside
guns. The bright moonlight enabled the gunners
to take good aim; but in a short time such volumes
of smoke collected around the vessels that it was
difficult to distinguish one vessel from another.
This was a circumstance that operated greatly in
favor of the Americans, for they were sure of hitting
an enemy no matter which vessel their shot struck,

while the English and Portuguese soon became confused by the smoke, and were unable to distinguish
between friend and foe.

Caring nothing about the Portuguese except to
keep him at a distance, Captain Boyle tenaciously
held a position close to the British merchantmen
and kept up a heavy fire on them. The English vessels occasionally separated, so as to give the man-
of-war a chance at the Americans, but the gunnery
of the Portuguese was so bad that little damage was
occasioned by it. In this way the battle was maintained until a little after midnight, when a voice
from the ship was heard announcing that they had
surrendered, as their vessel was cut to pieces and
unmanageable. Shortly afterward the merchant brig
also surrendered, being much cut up. But as Captain Boyle was about to take possession of the latter
the Portuguese man-of-war fired a broadside which
came near sinking the boat in which the boarding
party was proceeding to the prize and compelled it
to return to the *Comet*. Captain Boyle then devoted
all his attention to the man-of-war, and after some
heavy firing induced her to sheer off, the privateer
following and capturing the third English vessel,
which, like its consorts, was badly cut up.

But the victory of the Americans was still far
from being assured; for the Portuguese, although
driven away, persisted in remaining within gunshot,
and threatened to come to close action at the first
opportunity. Fully aware of his danger, Captain
Boyle hastened to take possession of his second
prize, the merchant brig, but in doing so passed the
ship and ordered her commander to follow. The
Englishmen then called out that their ship was in
a sinking condition, having many shot holes between
wind and water and with nearly all their rigging
cut away. They intimated, however, that they
would carry out the order with all possible dispatch.
At half past one in the morning the Americans took

possession of the merchant brig and placed a prize crew aboard. The Portuguese, however, followed the *Comet* closely, endeavoring to prevent her from securing the other vessels. This compelled Captain Boyle to fire an occasional broadside at the cruiser, so as to keep them at a more respectful distance. At one time they fired into the brig held by the Americans, but could not induce the prize crew to surrender.

By two o'clock the moon was down, and, as the weather blew up squally, Captain Boyle became separated from his prizes. The Portuguese man-of-war at that time was standing southward in the direction of the prize brig and ship and was soon lost to view. Captain Boyle now deemed it prudent to remain until daylight by his prize, which proved to be the brig *Bowes*. From the master of this vessel it was learned that the other vessels of the convoy were laden with wheat.

For the remainder of the night the *Comet* kept near her prize, and as day began to dawn the Portuguese man-of-war was discovered bearing down on her. The privateer promptly hove about and stood for her, when the war brig tacked and made signals for the convoy to make for the first port. Observing that the English ship and second brig seemed to be in a very distressed condition, Captain Boyle determined not to take possession of them, but to watch their maneuvers. Both of them bore up before the wind, making for land in company with the man-of-war, the last appearing to be much damaged. The Americans followed the three crippled ships, and could see that extraordinary exertions were being made to keep the ship and the brig afloat. With great difficulty the three vessels gained the harbor of Pernambuco; the ship, which proved to be the *George*, Captain Wilson, of Liverpool, with her masts tottering and her cargo destroyed so that she had to be dismantled; and the brig, the *Gambia*,

Captain Smith, of Hull, in much the same plight. The man-of-war was seriously damaged, besides having her first lieutenant and five men killed and a number wounded. Among the latter was her commander, who had his thigh shattered by a cannon ball and died shortly after reaching Pernambuco. Several American gentlemen, a few months after this action, happened to be in Lisbon when this man-of-war brig was there. They visited her, and reported that she was " a very large vessel, with high bulwarks and a very formidable battery."

Scarcely had the Portuguese gained the harbor of Pernambuco with her crippled convoy when Captain Boyle, with his rich prize, was again scouring the high seas in search of British merchantmen. He soon had the good fortune to seize the Scotch ship *Adelphi*, of Aberdeen, of thirty-six tons, from Liverpool bound for Bahia. She was laden with salt and drygoods, and, although well manned and armed with eight long 12-pounders, her commander made no serious resistance. The prize was manned and ordered to the United States. Subsequently the *Comet* was chased by the British frigate *Surprise*, which was justly regarded as being one of the swiftest vessels on the station. By superior seamanship Captain Boyle effected his escape and continued his successful cruise in the West Indies.

At daylight February 6, 1813, while some twelve miles off the island of St. John's Captain Boyle discovered two brigs to leeward and made all sail in chase of them. The nearest craft was soon made out to be armed, and Captain Boyle sent his men to quarters. By six o'clock this brig hoisted English colors, fired a gun, but, observing that she was in the presence of a vessel of superior force, promptly hauled down her flag. She was the *Alexis*, of Greenock, from Demerara, laden with sugar, rum, cotton, and coffee. Placing a Mr. Ball and six men aboard, and receiving most of the prisoners in the

Comet, Captain Boyle ordered her to the United States, and made sail for the second brig. By eight o'clock a third brig, apparently a war ship, was discovered standing to the southeast. From his prisoners Captain Boyle learned that these vessels were a part of a convoy of nine sail that had left Demerara for St. Thomas some days before, and that most of them had got into port the preceding night, but that the man-of-war then in sight, and named the *Swaggerer*, with two brigs, had failed to make the harbor.

Learning this, Captain Boyle prepared to give the brig he had been chasing a broadside as he passed her, hoping to compel her to surrender before the man-of-war could aid her. At nine o'clock the *Comet* showed her colors, and being nearly up with the chase received the enemy's fire, which was promptly returned. The effect of this was to induce the Englishmen to surrender, but before the Americans could get aboard the British master, in pursuance with the " recommendations " of the Admiralty, already noted, caused his topsail and jib halyards and other rigging to be cut away, in addition to the damage done by the American shot—which was considerable—hoping thereby so to cripple his ship that it would be impossible for the Americans to get her under sufficient sail to escape the man-of-war.

Captain Boyle saw the trick, and promptly sent First Officer Cashell and several men aboard to take possession and repair damages as rapidly as possible. Meantime most of the prisoners were sent aboard the *Comet* and secured below. All this time the man-of-war was rapidly approaching, and, her rigging and decks full of men, could be made out distinctly. Seeing that he must either run or fight a vastly superior force, Captain Boyle sent Mr. Gilpin and seven men to aid Mr. Cashell, ordering them to get up what sail they could, and make their way through the passage between the islands of St.

John's and St. Thomas. Mr. Cashell followed out the order as well as he could, while the *Comet* advanced toward the *Swaggerer* as if to offer battle. Not that Captain Boyle intended to make his ship an easy prey for the cruiser, for he fully realized that he was in the presence of hopeless odds, but he hoped to divert the enemy's attention from his prize to himself, and then trust to his skill and seamanship to escape. The reason for thus exposing his own vessel to capture was because the prize had an unusually valuable cargo. She was the packet *Dominica*, of Liverpool, from Demerara bound for St. Thomas, and was laden with rum, sugar, cotton, and coffee.

Captain Boyle allowed the *Swaggerer* to come within long gunshot of the *Comet*, when he put his vessel through a series of maneuvers, with a view to test the relative speed of the two vessels. Finding that he could easily outpoint and outsail the Englishman, he began to tantalize the *Swaggerer* by sailing under her nose, "at long balls," and tempting her into the continuance of a hopeless chase, during which time the *Dominica* was making the best of her way through the passage. Captain Boyle kept up these tactics until about noon, when, seeing that his prize was at a safe distance, he headed the *Comet* northward so as to pass round to the windward of St. John's, the *Swaggerer* still in hot pursuit.

By two o'clock in the afternoon the *Comet* had so increased her lead that she was fully four miles to windward of the enemy, and no one aboard the privateer felt the least alarm for the safety of the schooner. At that moment a sail was reported on the weather bow, and an hour later it was seen to be a schooner running before the wind. Changing his course a little, Captain Boyle ran alongside, and, after firing several musket shots, induced the stranger to surrender. She was found to be the schooner *Jane*, from Demerara to St. Thomas, laden with rum, sugar, and coffee. Meantime, the *Swag-*

gerer had been tumbling along, far in the rear
of the swift *Comet*, in a hopeless effort to overtake her. Her lumbering efforts to reach the swift
privateer only afforded amusement for our officers,
and after coolly transferring the prisoners to his
own ship and placing Prize-Master Wild and six men
aboard the *Jane*, with instructions to go through
the passage between Tortola and St. John's, Captain Boyle leisurely resumed his course and soon
ran his enraged pursuer out of sight.

Finding that he was overburdened with prisoners Captain Boyle made for the United States, and
on March 17th, in spite of the vigilance of the British
blockading squadron, gained Chesapeake Bay and
arrived in Baltimore. Some of the other prizes
taken by the *Comet* were the schooner *Messenger*, from
the West Indies, laden with rum and molasses, which
was sent into Wilmington, North Carolina, and the
Vigilant, a tender to the British admiral of the Windward Island squadron, which also was sent into Wilmington. Nine of the vessels taken by the *Comet*
were divested of their most valuable articles and
sunk, as there was too much risk in attempting to
send them into port. The *Comet*, in 1814, had a fierce
action with the 22-gun ship *Hibernia*, of eight hundred tons, having on board a large complement of
officers and men. After a running fight lasting
eight hours the Englishman escaped, having sustained a loss of eight men killed and thirteen
wounded to three men killed and sixteen wounded
on the part of the Americans. The *Comet* put into
Porto Rico for repairs where she found one of her
prizes. Being short of provisions her prize master
asked for a supply. Instead of granting the request,
the local authorities seized her and gave her to the
British. In all, the *Comet* is credited with twenty-
seven prizes.

So great had been the success of Captain Boyle
in the *Comet* that soon after his return from his last

cruise he was placed in command of the formidable
privateer *Chasseur*, in which craft he achieved his
greatest renown. This vessel probably was one of
the best equipped and manned privateers that sailed
in this war. She was familiarly called the *Pride
of Baltimore*, mounting sixteen long 12-pounders and
usually carrying a complement of one hundred officers, seamen, and marines. Speaking of her sailing qualities a Baltimore paper said: "She is, perhaps, the most beautiful vessel that ever floated on
the ocean. Those who have not seen our schooners
have but little idea of her appearance. As you look
at her you may easily figure to yourself the idea that
she is almost about to rise out of the water and fly
into the air, seeming to sit so lightly. She has carried
terror and alarm throughout the West Indies, as appears by numerous extracts from the West Indian
papers received by her. She was frequently chased
by British vessels sent out on purpose to catch her.
She was once pretty hard run by the frigate *Barcosa*;
but sometimes, out of sheer wantonness, she affected
to chase the enemy's men-of-war of far superior
force."

In his first cruise in this formidable vessel Captain Boyle captured eighteen merchantmen, nearly
all of them of great value. Some of these were the
sloop *Christiana*, of Kilkade, Scotland; the brig *Reindeer*, of Aberdeen; schooner *Favorite*, laden with
wine; the brig *Marquis of Cornwallis*; the brigs *Alert*
and *Harmony*, from Newfoundland; the ship *Carl-
bury*, of London, from Jamaica, laden with cotton,
cocoa, hides, indigo, etc. (the goods taken from this
vessel were valued at fifty thousand dollars); the
brigs *Eclipse*, *Commerce*, and *Antelope*; the schooner
Fox; the ships *James* and *Theodore*; and the brigs
Atlantic and *Amicus*. The *Chasseur* brought into port
forty-three prisoners, having released on parole one
hundred and fifty.

Captain Boyle's favorite cruising ground was in

the British Channel and around the coasts of Great Britain. He seemed to act on the principle which led Farragut to immortal fame half a century later, namely: " The nearer you get to your enemy the harder you can strike." By thus " bearding the lion in his den " the *Chasseur* had some exceedingly narrow escapes, but always eluded the enemy by her fine sailing qualities and by the superb audacity of her commander. At one time the privateer was so near a British frigate as to exchange an effective broadside with her, and not long afterward she was completely surrounded by two frigates and two brigs of war. In making a dash to escape, the *Chasseur* received a shot from one of the frigates, which wounded three men, but in spite of the danger she finally eluded the enemy.

The " superb audacity " of Captain Boyle has already been mentioned, not that it was peculiar to him, for it was shared more or less by all our privateersmen, but because it was exhibited by him on this cruise in a unique and emphatic manner. It had been the custom of British admirals on the American stations to issue " paper blockades," declaring the entire coast of the United States to be blockaded. Several of these " paper blockades " had been recently issued by Admiral Sir John Borlaise Warren and by Admiral Sir Alexander Cochrane. On the strength of these foolish proclamations British cruisers were withdrawn, at will, from the ports blockaded and transferred to other points along the coast without—at least in the estimation of the English admirals—in the least invalidating the blockade. To show the absurdity of these proclamations, Captain Boyle, while cruising in the English Channel, sent by a cartel to London the following proclamation, which he " requested " to be posted in Lloyd's Coffee House:

" *By Thomas Boyle, Esquire, Commander of the Private Armed Brig Chasseur, etc.*

" PROCLAMATION:

" *Whereas*, It has become customary with the admirals of Great Britain, commanding small forces on the coast of the United States, particularly with Sir John Borlaise Warren and Sir Alexander Cochrane, to declare all the coast of the said United States in a state of strict and rigorous blockade without possessing the power to justify such a declaration or stationing an adequate force to maintain said blockade;

" I do therefore, by virtue of the power and authority in me vested (possessing sufficient force), declare all the ports, harbors, bays, creeks, rivers, inlets, outlets, islands, and seacoast of the United Kingdom of Great Britain and Ireland in a state of strict and rigorous blockade.

" And I do further declare that I consider the force under my command adequate to maintain strictly, rigorously, and effectually the said blockade.

" And I do hereby require the respective officers, whether captains, commanders, or commanding officers, under my command, employed or to be employed, on the coasts of England, Ireland, and Scotland, to pay strict attention to the execution of this my proclamation.

" And I do hereby caution and forbid the ships and vessels of all and every nation in amity and peace with the United States from entering or attempting to enter, or from coming or attempting to come out of, any of the said ports, harbors, bays, creeks, rivers, inlets, outlets, islands, or seacoast under any pretense whatsoever. And that no person may plead ignorance of this, my proclamation,

I have ordered the same to be made public in Eng-
land.   Given under my hand on board the *Chasseur*.
"THOMAS BOYLE.
" By command of the commanding officer.
"J. J. STANBURY, *Secretary*."

Quite in keeping with Captain Boyle's audacity
is the memorial presented by the merchants of St.
Vincent to Admiral Durham, in which it is stated
that the *Chasseur* had blockaded them for five days,
doing much damage, and requesting that the admiral
would sent them at least "a heavy sloop of war."
The frigate *Bareosa* was sent.   The memorial gave
a pitiful account of how the *Chasseur* was frequently
chased "in vain," at one time by three cruisers together.   It then quotes a letter from Martinique
stating that this vessel was permitted to supply herself with a new boom, that the captain was treated
very politely, that on Sunday he dined with M. Du
Buc, the French intendant at the island, "a fine companion, truly, for the governor of such a colony as
Martinique."   The memorial further complained that
the *Chasseur* ventured within gunshot of the forts
of St. Lucia to cut out the transport *Lord Eldon*, and
probably would have done it but for the sloop of war
Wolverine, which hove in sight; that the *Chasseur*
burned two sloops "in the face of the island "—
possibly a West Indian form of the expression
"under their noses "; that she hoisted the Yankee
stripes over the British ensign "and played many
curious pranks "; and other complaints in the same
tenor.   The *Chasseur* arrived in New York from her
European cruise in October, 1814.

It was in his last cruise in this war that Captain
Boyle gained his greatest reputation for daring and
success on the high seas.   On February 26, 1815,
when the *Chasseur* was about thirty-six miles to
windward of Havana and some twelve miles from
land, a schooner was discovered, about eleven

o'clock in the morning, to the northeast, apparently running before the wind.   This was the English war schooner *St. Lawrence*, Lieutenant Henry Cranmer Gordon, which, as we remember, was the American privateer *Atlas*, Captain David Maffitt, captured by boats from Rear-Admiral Cockburn's squadron in Ocracoke Inlet, July 12, 1813,[1] the *Atlas* having been taken into the British service under the new name. The *St. Lawrence* proved to be a valuable addition to the enemy's fleet, taking an active part in their many expeditions along the coast and acting as a dispatch boat, in which service her fine sailing qualities gave her every advantage.   Here we have an admirable opportunity to compare the relative merits of American and British man-of-warsmen; for the *St. Lawrence*, being built and equipped by Americans, deprives our friends, the English, of their oft-repeated cry that our vessels were better built, etc. The *Chasseur* carried fourteen guns and one hundred and two men, as opposed to the *St. Lawrence's* thirteen guns and seventy-six men.   Both vessels were schooners.   When sighted by Captain Boyle, the *St. Lawrence* was bearing important dispatches and troops from Rear-Admiral Cockburn relative to the New Orleans expedition.

Captain Boyle promptly made sail in chase, and soon discovered the stranger to be a war craft having a convoy in company, the latter being just discernible from the masthead.   By noon the *Chasseur* had perceptibly gained on the chase, which to the Americans appeared to be a long, narrow pilot-boat schooner with yellow sides.   When she made out the *Chasseur* she hauled up more to the north, evidently anxious to escape.   At half past twelve Captain Boyle fired a gun and showed his colors, hoping to ascertain to what nation the chase belonged, but the latter paid no attention to the summons, and in

---

[1] See pp. 260–262.

her efforts to carry a greater press of sail her fore-topmast was carried away.

At the time this happened she was about three miles ahead. Her people promptly cleared the wreck away and trimmed her sails sharp by the wind. Owing to this accident the *Chasseur* drew up on the chase very fast, and at one o'clock the latter fired a stern gun and hoisted English colors. As the stranger showed only three ports on the side nearest to the *Chasseur*, Captain Boyle got the impression that she was a "running vessel" bound for Havana which in all probability was poorly armed and manned. Acting on this impression he increased his efforts to get alongside, confident of making short work of her. This mistake of the Americans was encouraged by the fact that very few men were seen on the deck of the stranger.

As neither Captain Boyle nor his officers anticipated serious fighting, the regular preparations for battle were not made. At 1.26 P. M. the *Chasseur* was within pistol shot of the enemy, when the latter suddenly triced up ten port covers, showing that number of guns and her decks swarming with men wearing the uniform of a regular British man-of-war. Evidently they had been carefully concealed during the chase. It took the enemy scarcely five seconds to give three cheers, run out their guns, and pour in a whole broadside of round shot, grape, and musket balls into the *Chasseur*. For once, at least, the crafty Yankee skipper had been caught napping. He was fairly and squarely under the guns of an English man-of-war, so that either prompt surrender or fight were the only alternatives. It did not take Captain Boyle an instant to decide on the latter course, and, although taken somewhat by surprise, he made the best of the situation and returned the enemy's fire with both cannon and musketry.

Believing that his best chance for victory was at close quarters, Captain Boyle endeavored to board

23

in the smoke of his broadside; but the *Chasseur*, having the greater speed at that moment, shot ahead under the stranger's lee. The latter put up his helm for the purpose of wearing across the privateer's stern, with a view of pouring in a raking fire. Perceiving the enemy's object, Captain Boyle frustrated the maneuver by putting his helm up also. The Englishman now forged ahead and came within ten yards of the privateer, the fire of both vessels at that time being exceedingly destructive. At 1.40 P. M. Captain Boyle, seizing a favorable moment, put his helm to starboard and called on his men to follow him aboard the enemy. Just as the two vessels came together W. N. Christie, prize master, jumped aboard the stranger's deck, followed by a number of other Americans, but before they could strike a blow the English surrendered.

The *St. Lawrence*, according to British accounts, mounted twelve short 12-pounders and one long 9-pounder and had a complement of seventy-five men, besides a number of officers, soldiers, and civilians as passengers, who were bound for the British squadron off New Orleans. According to the report of her commander she had six men killed and seventeen wounded, several of them mortally. According to American accounts the English had fifteen killed and twenty-five wounded. The *St. Lawrence* was found to be seriously injured in the hull, while scarcely a rope was left intact, such had been the accuracy and rapidity of the *Chasseur's* fire. The privateer also suffered considerably in her sails and rigging, while five of her crew were killed and eight wounded, among the latter being Captain Boyle himself. In view of the fact that the action lasted only fifteen minutes these casualties reveal, better than words, the desperate nature of the encounter. The *Chasseur* mounted six 12-pounders and eight short 9-pounders—ten of her original sixteen 12-pounders having been thrown overboard when the privateer

Capture of the British cruiser St. Lawrence by the United States privateer Chasseur.

was chased by the British frigate *Barcosa*.   They
were replaced by the 9-pounders which had been
taken from a prize.

"From the number of hammocks, bedding, etc.,
found on board the enemy," said Captain Boyle, in
his official report to one of the owners of the *Chasseur*, George P. Stephenson, of Baltimore, "it led us
to believe that many more were killed than were
reported.   The *St. Lawrence* fired double the weight
of shot that we did.   From her 12-pounders at close
quarters she fired a stand of grape and two bags
containing two hundred and twenty musket balls
each, when from the *Chasseur's* 9-pounders were fired
6- and 4-pound shot, we having no other except
some few grape."   In closing his report, Captain
Boyle speaks in the highest terms of the gallantry
of his first officer, John Dieter, and of the second and third officers, Moran and Hammond N.
Stansbury.

That night the masts of the *St. Lawrence* went by
the board, and having no object in bringing home so
many prisoners Captain Boyle made a cartel of his
prize and sent the prisoners by her into Havana.
After this gallant affair the *Chasseur* returned to
the United States with her hold filled with valuable
goods.   She arrived in Baltimore, April 15, 1815,
where it was learned that a treaty of peace had been
signed.   So well pleased were the British officers at
the treatment they received from the Americans
that Lieutenant Gordon issued the following memorial or certificate dated: "At Sea, February 27,
1815, on board the United States Privateer *Chasseur*: In the event of Captain Boyle's becoming a
prisoner of war to any British cruiser I consider it a
tribute justly due to his humane and generous treatment of myself, the surviving officers and crew of
His Majesty's late schooner *St. Lawrence*, to state
that his obliging attention and watchful solicitude
to preserve our effects and render us comfortable

during the short time we were in his possession were such as justly entitle him to the indulgence and respect of every British subject. I also certify that his endeavors to render us comfortable and to secure our property were carefully seconded by all his officers, who did their utmost to that effect."

CHAPTER VI.

A DISTINGUISHED PRIVATEERSMAN.

ONE of the most distinguished American privateersmen in the War of 1812 was Captain Joshua
Barney, whose career both in the United States navy
and in the privateer service during the Revolution
has been already noted in this work. At the close of
the struggle for independence Barney, like all his
brother officers in the navy, retired to private life.
While trading in the West Indies, as commander
of the fine coppered ship *Sampson*, Barney, on July
12, 1793, fell in with three English privateers, two
from Jamaica and one from New Providence, and
was boarded. On looking over his papers the officers
from the Jamaica privateers permitted him to go
free, but the commander of the New Providence
craft declared that the iron chest, containing eighteen thousand dollars in specie, was suspicious, and
that "no American master ever had iron chests or
dollars on board his vessel," and that he was willing
to let the vessel go free if the money were given up.
As Barney refused to submit to the robbery, his crew
was taken aboard the privateer, with the exception
of the carpenter, boatswain, and cook, and a guard
of eleven men was placed in charge, with orders to
follow the privateer into New Providence; notwithstanding the two nations were at peace.

In the course of the afternoon Barney managed
to communicate with his carpenter, boatswain, and
cook, and found them ready to act with him in any

301

effort to recapture their ship.   The British prize
crew behaved in the most offensive manner toward
their victims, calling them " rebel rascals," " Yankee traitors," and threatening to " blow their brains
out " and " to throw them overboard," at the same
time searching the ship and helping themselves to
articles of value after the most approved piratical
fashion.   On the evening of July 19th, five days after
their capture, Barney learned that each of his men
had possessed himself of a gun and bayonet, which
they concealed in their berths, while Barney himself
managed to secrete a brass blunderbuss and a broadsword.   It was not long before the Americans had
arranged a plan of attack.   The following day being
rainy and squally, the prize crew was kept busy
navigating the ship.   At noon hour the three prize
officers dined together on a hencoop near the mainmast, while their men, except the one at the helm,
messed on the forecastle.

This was the moment chosen by Barney to recapture his ship.   Stepping to the roundhouse he
picked up his naked sword, put it under his arm,
seized the blunderbuss, cocked it, and, joined by his
carpenter and boatswain, who also had armed themselves, advanced upon the three officers seated upon
the quarter-deck.   One of these officers immediately
sprang upon Barney, closing with him, and endeavored to wrest the blunderbuss from his hand, but
in the scuffle the weapon went off and lodged its
charge of buckshot in the Englishman's right arm,
who then yielded.   Barney then knocked down the
second officer with a blow on the head with his
broadsword, while the third man ran below.   The
seven seamen who were on the forecastle, on hearing
the discharge of the blunderbuss, ran into the forecastle to get their arms, but before they could regain the deck the carpenter and boatswain had
fastened the scuttle and made prisoners of them.

The Americans were now in full possession of

their ship, and on the prize crew promising to serve their new masters they were allowed to come on deck, one at a time, where their arms were taken from them and thrown overboard. The course of the ship was then changed to Baltimore. For many days the Americans maintained a most anxious watch over their prisoners. Barney kept the deck night and day, sleeping only at daytime, in an armchair, with his sword between his legs and pistols in his belt, while either the cook or boatswain stood guard beside him, armed with a musket, sword, and pistols. No one, unless specially called, was allowed to come abaft the mainmast under penalty of instant death. In this manner Barney made for the United States, arriving in Baltimore early in August.

In the following December Barney was again trading among the West Indies, again in command of the *Sampson*. On January 2, 1794, he was seized by the British frigate *Penelope*, Captain Rowley. Barney was brought aboard the frigate and treated with great severity, and carried, with his men and ship, into Port Royal, Jamaica, where he was indicted for " piracy " and for " shooting with intent to kill." After a trial he was adjudged " not guilty." Meantime he had been seriously delayed in his mercantile pursuits. Barney was convinced that the commander of the *Penelope* was actuated by malignant feelings against him, and the circumstances in the case seem to justify that belief. When Barney was first taken aboard the frigate, as we have seen, Captain Rowley treated him in a most brutal manner, using vulgar and unofficer-like language. Barney resented this, and very properly told the English commander that he was a coward to take advantage of his position " to insult a man whom he would not dare to meet upon equal terms, at sea or on shore; that the opportunity might come for retaliation, when he should remember the poltroon who commanded the English frigate *Penelope*."

Captain Rowley interrupted this speech by ordering the marines to place the American between two guns with a sentinel over him, who had orders, given in a loud voice, "to blow the rascal's brains out" if he spoke again or attempted to leave the space allotted to him.

After the vessels had reached Port Royal Captain Rowley showed himself in the streets every day; but after the trial, when Barney was again free, the commander of the *Penelope* kept himself aboard ship. Barney believed that this was done to avoid a personal meeting. One evening, about dusk, shortly after the trial, Barney was walking through one of the streets unattended, when he suddenly heard a voice from the opposite side calling out:

"Barney, take care of yourself! Look behind!"

The American officer whirled round, and at the same time drew a pistol from his pocket. He was none too quick, for close behind him was a ruffian in sailor's dress with uplifted club in his hand, with which, but for the timely warning, he would have felled Barney to the ground. On the sight of the pistol the ruffian dropped his club and took to his heels. On inquiry Barney was convinced that this man was one of the *Penelope's* crew, and had been employed by Rowley to murder him.

This belief was strengthened a few days later, when Barney, being in a coffeehouse, heard his name mentioned in an insulting manner, coupled with the expressed wish of the speaker to "meet the rascal." Barney walked up to the group where the speaker was and announced himself as the man sought. The speaker proved to be an officer of the *Penelope*, but seemed disinclined to gratify his desire of "meeting the rascal." Thereupon Barney tweaked his nose and kicked the cowardly braggart out of the coffeehouse, as much to the amusement of the many Americans present as to a number of British army and navy officers who had become disgusted with their countryman's insufferable bearing.

In 1796 Barney entered the French navy, where he remained several years, attaining the rank of commodore. He returned to the United States in 1801 and again became a private citizen. Hearing of the *Chesapeake-Leopard* affair, in 1807, he at once tendered his services to the Government, but as that incident was amicably adjusted his services were not needed. It was not surprising, therefore, that an officer who had served with such distinction in both the American and French navies, and also in the privateer service, should be eagerly sought at the beginning of hostilities with Great Britain in 1812.

As soon as it was known that war had been declared a number of Baltimore merchants fitted out the fine schooner *Rossie* and tendered the command of her to Captain Barney. The *Rossie* was armed with ten short 12-pounders and three long guns, and carried a crew of one hundred and twenty men. Captain Barney, like the thoroughbred seaman he was, had got into the habit of being very careless in money matters. Probably few seamen of his period had earned so much money as he during a career on the ocean. Many thousand dollars had been credited to his account, but they were quickly scattered in a thoroughly careless manner almost as rapidly as received. He was not the kind of a jack tar to bother his head about ledgers and balance sheets, and when on land, or elsewhere, he ran up bills with appalling recklessness.

It seems on this occasion that Captain Barney had incurred an indebtedness amounting to something like one thousand dollars. Such an insignificant affair as this gave the redoubtable sailor, who was accustomed to make his thousands in one cruise, no more concern than a mosquito bite, and he was so absorbed in his preparations of again getting on blue water that he had forgotten this trifling obligation.

Not so, however, with his creditor. Just as the distinguished seaman, surrounded by crowds of well-wishers, got to the wharf, and was about to step into his boat to put off to the *Rossie*, a deputy sheriff gently tapped him on the shoulder, and, expressing regret at being obliged to detain him, said duty compelled him to report that there was a " suspicion of debt " against him to the amount of one thousand dollars, which it would be necessary for him to clear up before going away. Remembering that the " suspicion " was well founded, and being a man of honor, Barney quietly gave himself up to the officer, who contented himself very civilly with the captain's word that he would make his appearance when called for.

This, of course, postponed the contemplated cruise—which, though short, amounted to one million and a half dollars in captures—as Barney had no means of meeting the obligation. It would have been very easy for him to have quietly slipped aboard the *Rossie* and sailed away in spite of the sheriff, and to have paid the indebtedness out of the profits of the cruise, or to have put back into some other port where the sheriff could not have interfered with him. But this was not suited to the taste or manliness of Barney. He sauntered aimlessly about the town, not knowing what to do. Finally, as he was passing through South Street, he reached the house of his friend, Isaac McKim. Mr. McKim expressed much surprise at seeing Captain Barney, supposing that by that time the privateersman was at least half-way to the Capes. Barney explained the cause of the delay, upon which Mr. McKim promptly made good the amount, and on July 12, 1812, only twenty-four days after the declaration of war, the *Rossie* began a cruise of extraordinary success.

After taking several merchantmen of great value, the *Rossie*, on August 9th, fell in with the British privateer ship *Jeannie*, of twelve guns, 6- and 9-

pounders. After a sharp action the *Jeannie* surrendered. On the night of September 16th Captain
Barney fell in with the British Government packet
Princess Amelia, Captain Moorsom. The Americans,
being armed principally with short guns, quickly
came to close quarters, and as there was moonlight
they were able to fight it out. The enemy availed
themselves of this by concealing their sharpshooters
in the shadows of the mast, rigging, and bulwarks,
and firing with comparative impunity, while the
Americans in the *Rossie* (that ship having no bulwarks) were greatly exposed. After a severe struggle, lasting about an hour, the enemy called for
quarter, their commander, sailing master, and one
man being killed and seven wounded (ten according
to another account). On the part of the Americans,
First Officer Long was mortally injured and six men
were wounded.

After a cruise of ninety days the *Rossie* returned
to port, having captured four ships, eight brigs,
three schooners, and three sloops, valued at over one
million five hundred thousand dollars, including the
cargoes. Seven of these vessels were burned at sea
and two hundred and seventeen prisoners were
taken, many of whom were sent to Newfoundland
in one of the brigs. This was the first and only
cruise of Captain Barney in this war as a privateersman. Soon afterward he was again taken into the
regular navy and performed valuable services.[1]

---

[1] See Maclay's History of the Navy, vol. i, pp. 583–585.

CHAPTER VII.

DECATUR–DOMINICA FIGHT.

IF anything can excuse privateering it is the fact that so many of our private armed craft attacked and captured British war ships. It can not be denied that the mainspring of privateering in all countries pretending to maritime power was the chance of plunder. This was the object for which traders were fitted, armed, and sent out at private expense, and it was the booty the owners of the vessel expected to get from the enemy's commerce that was to reimburse them for this expenditure and risk. This license to "seize, burn, or destroy" ships and goods belonging to the enemy too frequently degenerated to a degree where it was hard to distinguish between privateering and piracy, and in this way the former was brought into general disrepute.

Privateering at the hands of American seamen, however, can not be said to have been thus degraded. On the contrary, the rules of war and the laws of humanity were quite as strictly observed by our privateersmen as by their brethren in the navy. Frequently the sordid love of gain was gallantly thrust aside by these amateur man-of-warsmen, and the enemy's war ships were attacked when it was only too well known that nothing but hard blows and empty holds would be found; or, worse yet, in case of capture, brutal impressment or speedy death at the yardarm if the British commander should take it into his head that some of the captured Americans were

308

deserters from the Royal Navy. Notwithstanding all these inducements to steer clear of the regular war ships of the enemy, there were several instances in which Yankee privateersmen gave battle to such craft, and by that act alone raised the American privateer to a high and respectable position in the maritime forces of the world. One of the most notable actions of this kind in the War of 1812 was that between the American privateer *Decatur*, Captain Dominique Diron, of Charleston, and the English cruiser *Dominica*, Lieutenant George Wilmot Barretté.

Three of the American privateers in this war bore the name Decatur. One was a schooner of four guns and twenty-three men, under Captain S. N. Lane, from Maine. This craft was pierced for sixteen guns, and the fact that she mounted only four indicates that her owners were unable to secure a larger number, and sent her to sea in the hope of filling out her armament from prizes, as so many of our private armed craft had done. This *Decatur* was not very successful, and on September 3, 1814, while under the command of Captain E. Brown, she was captured by an English squadron, but subsequently was lost at sea.

Another *Decatur*, a fine brig carrying fourteen guns and one hundred and sixty men, under Captain Nichols, of Newburyport, was one of the most successful privateers from the Eastern ports. She got to sea at the beginning of hostilities and captured four ships, six brigs, two barks, and two schooners. One of these prizes was destroyed at sea and three were converted into cartels. This was the privateer that on the night of August 18, 1812, was chased two hours by the United States 44-gun frigate *Constitution*, Captain Isaac Hull. Mistaking the frigate for the enemy, Captain Nichols threw overboard twelve of his fourteen guns; but even this extreme measure did not avail, for the *Constitution* succeeded

in getting alongside, and on sending a boat aboard
discovered the privateer's true character. Only the
day before the *Decatur* had been chased by the British frigate *Guerrière*, for which Captain Hull was
searching, but had easily outsailed her. Here we
have an excellent illustration of the superior qualities of the American craft over that of the English,
for the *Decatur* had eluded the *Guerrière*, but had
been unable to get away from the *Constitution*, even
by the sacrifice of most of her guns.

It was in reference to this incident that Rowan
Stevens, son of the late Rear-Admiral Thomas
Holdup Stevens, wrote:

> " And on through the summer seas we bore,
> . Until off stern Cape Clear
> Our ship fell in with a sloop-o'-war,
> A Yankee privateer.
> We hailed for news, and the sloop hove to,
> And off her skipper came,
> And boarded us in a leaky yawl
> With his wrathful cheek aflame;
> For 'Down to the south'ard he'd been chased
> By a powerful English ship
> That was just too slow for his flying heels,
> And just too big to whip.'
> We sent him back with a cheerful heart,
> And down to the south we swept,
> And a sharp lookout o'er the vacant sea
> Alow and aloft we kept."

The *Constitution* fell in with the *Guerrière* on the
following day, and the result is well known. The
Decatur returned to port, and, after renewing her
armament, she made a cruise in the West Indies.
On January 16, 1813, while off Barbadoes, she was
captured by the British frigate *Surprise*. Before the
war this *Decatur* had been the merchantman *Alert*.
Soon after hostilities broke out the *Alert* was captured by the British frigate *Vestal*, but Nichols, who
commanded the *Alert*, succeeded in recapturing his

ship and got her into port. When seized by the *Surprise*, Nichols was taken to Barbadoes, where he was recognized by the commander of the *Vestal*, who took this opportunity to "get even" with the privateersman who had the "presumption to recapture a prize of His Britannic Majesty's frigate" by confining Nichols in a room not larger than five by seven feet, where he was cruelly treated and then sent to England.

The third and last *Decatur* in this war hailed from Charleston, South Carolina. She was a schooner carrying six 12-pounders and one long 18-pounder on a pivot amidships, and on this, her most eventful cruise, she carried a complement of one hundred and three men and boys. Captain Diron, her commander, was one of the most celebrated privateersmen in his day. In September, 1806, while in command of the French privateer *Superbe*, he made a heroic defense against the British cruisers *Drake*, Captain Robert Nicolas, and the *Pitt*, Lieutenant Michael Fitton. For three nights and two days Diron maintained a plucky fight against these vessels, and finally succeeded in running his ship ashore and escaping with his men. At the outbreak of the War of 1812 he was placed in command of the privateer *Decatur*. Among his first prizes was the ship *Nelson*, which was described as "a monstrous three-decked vessel of six hundred tons, with an immensely valuable cargo." She was bound for Jamaica, and was sent into New Orleans, March, 1813. The *Decatur* also took the brig *Thomas*, of two guns, which was released and sent into Halifax with the prisoners.

The *Dominica* was a three-masted schooner carrying twelve short 12-pounders, two long 6-pounders, one brass 4-pounder, and a short 32-pounder on a pivot. She was manned by eighty-eight men and boys. On September 4, 1812, this cruiser captured the 8-gun armed schooner *Providence*, Captain N. Hopkins, of Providence. The *Providence* is not credited with any prizes, being taken shortly after leaving port.   In the chase of ten hours, Captain Hopkins had thrown overboard all his guns on the leeward side.   At the time the *Dominica* fell in with the *Decatur* she had under her convoy the Government packet ship *Princess Charlotte*, from St. Thomas for England, and the merchantman *London Trader*, from Surinam homeward bound.   The *Princess Charlotte* carried a formidable armament, and the *London Trader* also was well armed.

The *Decatur* left port in the summer of 1813 on a general cruise against British commerce, and early in August she was in the track of British West India traders homeward bound.   Early on the morning of August 5th, when in latitude 23° 4' north, longitude 67° 0' west, or a little to the south of the Bermudas, the *Decatur* was heading northward under easy sail, hoping for some prize to appear.   About 10.30 A. M. the man at the masthead reported a sail bearing away to the south, and shortly afterward another, steering in the same direction, was sighted. Captain Diron promptly tacked southward, with a view of getting the weather gauge of the strangers, so that, should they prove to be British cruisers, he would have the advantage in a chase.   This precaution was rendered doubly necessary, as the fact of two vessels cruising in company rendered it probable that they were the enemy's sloops of war, for so astonishing had been the victories of the little American navy, and so appalled had the British public become at the results of the war as far as it pertained to their navy, that their Lordships of the Admiralty had directed British 38-gun frigates to avoid the dreaded American 44-gun ships, while their sloops of war were to sail in pairs.

For this reason Captain Diron approached the strangers with caution, knowing that there was a strong probability of their being a couple of British sloops of war.   The danger of approaching a stronger force, however, did not prevent the Americans from coming to closer range, and at 11 A. M. it was seen that the sails were a ship and a schooner, which, on making out the sails of the *Decatur*, had changed their course to the north so as to meet her. The three vessels slowly reduced the distance between them, and at 12.30 P. M. the *Decatur*, having secured a position a little to windward, and being almost within gunshot, wore round and ran a little to leeward, upon which the schooner showed English colors. Captain Diron was now satisfied that he had an English war schooner to deal with and that the ship was under its protection. Half an hour later he wore again, still keeping the weather gauge, and about 1.30 P. M. the stranger fired a shot, which fell short.

Knowing that the British commander had a heavier armament than the privateer, but believing that he had the greater number of men to man his ship, Captain Diron determined to have the fight at the closest quarters, and to carry the Englishman by boarding. Accordingly he cleared for action, sent his men to quarters, loaded all his guns, and hoisted American colors. To make sure that no man could leave his post and run below, Captain Diron, after having got all his ammunition, water, sand, etc., on deck, ready for instant use, ordered all the hatches closed. It was the plan of the Americans to get as close to the enemy as possible before firing a shot, deliver their entire broadside and a volley from their small arms, and then to board in the smoke. In order to secure the British ship alongside grappling irons were in readiness to be thrown aboard.

Having made all his arrangements for the battle, Captain Diron about 2 P. M. wore ship, with a view of passing under the stern of the enemy and giving a raking fire, but as the schooners neared each other the Englishman luffed and gave his broadside, most of the shot passing over the American. This is only

23

another indication of the overconfidence of the British naval officer in this war. So confident was Lieutenant Barretté of taking the American that he ordered his gunners to aim at the Yankee's rigging so as to prevent her from running. But if this was the Englishman's motive in firing so high he soon had cause to repent it, for at 2.15 P. M. the Americans began the fire of their long tom, and as it was aimed with coolness and deliberation, within half-gunshot distance, the effect in so small a vessel was serious, disabling several of the Englishman's guns, besides injuring many men. At all events, it speedily changed the English commander's tactics, and the few guns that remained mounted on that side were now trained on the privateer's hull.

The destructive work done by the American's long tom, however, had given Captain Diron the advantage, and, so far from evincing a disposition to run away, he soon discovered that that was the purpose of his opponent, and in order to prevent it he filled away so as to bring his bowsprit over the enemy's stern. The English endeavored to frustrate this by directing a whole broadside at the advancing Yankee, but they were too excited, or their gunnery was so poor that the shot did little or no execution. Had they taken good aim the effect of those guns at such a short distance would have been terrific. The *Decatur* could respond to this fire only with her long tom, but as that was discharged with the usual skill and coolness of American gunners it effected far greater damage than the Englishman's broadside. It was now 3 P. M., and the vessels were so near to each other that the voices of the officers aboard the British ship, urging their men to renewed energy, could be distinctly heard. Captain Diron then order his boarders to leave their guns and assemble forward, arm themselves with muskets and cutlasses, and be in readiness to spring upon the enemy's decks.

The British at this stage of the battle evidently realized the seriousness of the fight, for their officers could be heard warning their gunners to take better aim, and to fire into the Yankee's hull instead of his rigging, as heretofore. The result of this admonition was seen in the effect of the next broadside which the enemy delivered. The shots hulled the *Decatur*, killed two of her crew, and materially injured her sails and rigging. This broadside did more damage than all the others. It also prevented Captain Diron from carrying out his plan of boarding; for, some of his ropes being severed, his sails became temporarily unmanageable. Repairs were quickly made, and, though foiled in their attempt to board, the Americans renewed the action with their long tom and 12-pounder, believing that an opportunity would yet be offered them to settle the fight on the Englishman's deck.

After delivering their first effective fire, the Englishmen filled away so as to prevent the Americans from boarding, while Captain Diron doggedly followed close under their stern, determined to board at any cost. In this way, bow to stern, the two craft ran several minutes, neither side being able to maintain a very effective fire. The Americans now made another attempt to board, but it was frustrated in the same manner as the first.

But the last move made by the British schooner, in her endeavor to avoid boarding, gave the *Decatur* the advantage in sailing, and, persisting in following close in the wake of his enemy, Captain Diron finally had the satisfaction of seeing his craft gradually overhaul the Englishman. Again he called for his boarders, and at 3.30 P. M. the *Decatur* ran her bowsprit over the enemy's stern, her jib boom piercing the Englishman's mainsail. This was the signal for the Americans to board, and while some of them poured in a heavy fire of musketry others, led by Vincent Safitt, the prize master, and Thomas Was-

born, the quartermaster, clambered along the bowsprit and sprang to the Englishman's deck.   Then
began a terrible scene of slaughter and bloodshed.
The two crews were soon intermingled in an inex-
tricable mass, which the narrow decks of the
schooner kept compact as long as the struggle
lasted.   Nearly two hundred men and boys armed
with pistols, cutlasses, and muskets were now shouting, yelling, and cheering, and slashing at each other
in a space not more than twenty feet wide and eighty
feet long.

One of the first to fall on the side of the enemy
was their gallant commander, Lieutenant Barretté,
a young man not more than twenty-five years old,
who had conducted himself from the beginning of
the fight with conspicuous gallantry, notwithstanding his contempt for the Yankee sailor.   He had received a bad wound early in the action, two musket
balls having passed through the left arm.   But this
did not prevent him from remaining at his post.   He
was urged several times by his surviving officers to
surrender, but refused to do so, avowing his determination not to survive the loss of his vessel.   A
few moments before he received his fatal wound he
severely injured one of the American officers with a
saber cut.   The sailing master, Isaac Sacker, and
the purser, David Brown, of the *Dominica*, also were
killed, while Midshipmen William Archer and William Parry were wounded.   In fact, the only English
officers not killed or wounded were the surgeon and
one midshipman.   It was not until eighteen of the
Dominica's crew were killed and forty-two wounded
that the few survivors were induced to surrender.
A total of sixty killed or wounded in a crew of
eighty-eight fully attests the desperate nature of
the struggle and the gallantry of the men against
whom the Americans fought.   Even with this appalling percentage of killed and wounded the Englishmen can not be reported as having surrendered,

for the Americans hauled down the colors with their own hands. On the part of the privateer five men were killed and fifteen wounded, which disparity of casualties is to be ascribed solely to the superior seamanship of Captain Diron and the better marksmanship of the Americans, both with the cannon and small arms.

That this was in truth a battle royal will be seen by comparing it with the regular naval actions between sloops of war in the conflict:

Comparative Casualties.

NAME OF ACTION.	Guns.	Crew.	Killed.	Wounded.	Total.
Decatur	7	103	5	15	20
Dominica	16	88	18	42	60
Hornet..	20	142	1	4	5
Peacock	20	130	5	33	38
Wasp	18	138	5	5	10
Frolic	22	110	15	47	62
Argus	20	125	6	17	23
Pelican	21	116	2	5	7
Enterprise	16	102	2	10	12
Boxer	14	100	4	17	21
Peacock	22	160	0	2	2
Épervier	18	128	8	15	23
Wasp	22	173	11	15	26
Reindeer	19	118	25	42	67
Wasp	22	168	2	1	3
Avon	18	117	10	32	42
Hornet	20	132	1	11	12
Penguin	19	128	10	28	38

While the battle between the American privateer and the British cruiser was raging the commander of the *Princess Charlotte* did not deem it his place to take part in the fight, and for over an hour remained a passive spectator. But as soon as it was seen that the American was the victor the *Princess Charlotte* tacked to the south, and by sunset had disappeared. She had left St. Thomas for England, and was to be under the escort of the *Dominica* until well clear of the American coast, when she had intended to proceed on her voyage alone. Arriving in England, the commander of the packet reported that he had left "the *Dominica* in hot pursuit of a Yankee privateer."

As soon as victory was assured Captain Diron employed all the men he could in repairing damages; for capturing a ship and taking her safely into port when the coasts of the United States were swarming with British cruisers were two very distinct achievements. Having given the dead a sailor's burial, and having attended the wounded (the English receiving quite as much attention as the Americans), Captain Diron headed for Charleston. The *Decatur* and the *Dominica* made land near Georgetown, and running down the coast crossed Charleston bar safely August 20th, the *Dominica* appearing under the colors she had taken from the *Providence*. For several days before two English brigs of war had been hovering off the port; but, fortunately, on the day Captain Diron approached they had been drawn off in chase to the south.

Arriving in port, Captain Diron heard that the British merchant ship *London Trader* had arrived safely at Savannah. This ship had been sailing in company with the *Dominica* and the *Princess Charlotte* when they fell in with the bold *Decatur*. The *London Trader* made her escape while the American privateer was engaged in fighting the *Dominica*, but on the following day Captain Diron fell in with and captured her. She had on board a cargo consisting of two hundred and nine hogsheads of sugar, one hundred and forty tierces of molasses, fifty-five hogsheads of rum, seven hundred bags of coffee, and sixty bales of cotton.

Captain George Coggeshall, who commanded several privateers in this war, happened to be in

Charleston about the time the *Decatur* entered that port with her prize, and, in conversation with the captors and prisoners, learned many details of this action.   He said: "The surviving officers of the *Dominica* attributed the loss of their vessel to the superior skill of the *Decatur's* crew in the use of musketry and to Captain Diron's adroit manner in maneuvering his schooner during the action, which rendered the Englishman's carriage guns in a manner almost useless.   It was acknowledged by the English prisoners that during their captivity they were treated with great kindness and humanity by Captain Diron, his officers and crew, and that the utmost care and attention were paid to the sick and wounded.   The crew of the captured vessel were all fine-looking young men.   There were among them eight or ten boys.   To see this youthful crew on their arrival at Charleston in their mangled condition was enough to freeze the blood with horror of any person not accustomed to such sanguinary scenes. Among the crew was a small boy, not eleven years old, who was twice wounded while contending for victory on the deck of the *Dominica*.   I saw daily one of the wounded English midshipmen with his arm in a sling, who had the privilege of walking about the city on his parole of honor."

The *Dominica* subsequently was fitted out as a privateer, carrying four guns and thirty-six men, but on May 23, 1814, she was captured by the British ship of the line *Majestic*.   In November, 1813, the *Decatur* got to sea again, but after a cruise of eighty days she returned to Charleston without having taken one vessel.   She made another venture in this war, but was captured June 5, 1814, by the British frigate *Phin* off Mona Passage, after a chase of eleven hours.

CHAPTER VIII.

SOUTHERN PRIVATEERS.

IN the War of 1812 the Southern ports, not including Baltimore, sent out thirty-six privateers, several of which were eminently successful. The brilliant achievement of the *Decatur*, in capturing a British cruiser, has been narrated in the preceding chapter. These commerce destroyers of the South sailed principally from Norfolk, Wilmington (North Carolina), Charleston, Savannah, and New Orleans. Of the six hailing from Norfolk the 1-gun schooner *Chance*, Captain W. Derick, a vessel of eighty-four tons; the 1-gun schooner *Four Friends*, Captain T. Rooke, of forty-six tons; the 2-gun schooner *Franklin*, Captain J. Glenn, of twenty-three tons; and the 3-gun schooner *George Washington*, Captain S. Sisson, seem to have accomplished little or nothing. The *Dash*, as we have seen,[1] distinguished herself by taking the first prize of the war, the British Government schooner *Whiting*, Lieutenant Maxcey.

The *Roger*, a fine schooner of ten guns, commanded by Captain R. Quarles, sailed from Norfolk late in 1813 or early in 1814 with a complement of one hundred and twenty men. She made her first prize in January, the schooner *Henry*, laden with fish, which was sent into Charleston. About the same time the *Roger* captured the schooner *Maria*, and as she was of little value she was burned. In

---

[1] See p. 226.

May, 1814, the *Roger* took the valuable ship *Fortuna*, sailing under the Russian flag with English property aboard. She was from Havana for Riga with an assorted cargo, which was sent into Beaufort, South Carolina. In this cruise the *Roger* made a prize of a brig laden with rum and sugar from Jamaica for England, which was sent into port. In the following August this privateer seized the schooner *Contract*, with a cargo of salt, which was sent into North Carolina, and in December of the same year she captured the ship *L'Aimable*, from Havana for England, under Spanish colors but with British property aboard. The seventh and last prize of this vessel was the packet *Windsor Castle*, from Falmouth for Halifax. She was armed with two long 9-pounders and eight short guns, and had on board nine passengers and a crew of thirty-two men. She was sent into Norfolk.[1]

Wilmington, in the course of the war, sent out three privateers. The 5-gun schooner *Hawk*, Captain W. H. Trippe, got to sea in March, 1814, with a complement of sixty-eight men. She made only one prize, the schooner *Phœbe*, laden with rum and molasses, which was sent into the privateer's home port. On April 26, 1814, the *Hawk* was captured by the British frigate *Pique* while off Silver Keys. Another 5-gun schooner from Wilmington, the *Lovely Lass*, Captain J. Smith, of the United States navy, got to sea in 1813 with a complement of sixty men, and in March sent into New Orleans a schooner valued at ten thousand dollars. On the following May 4th this privateer fell in with the British cruiser *Circée*, and after a hard chase of nineteen hours, in which the privateer threw overboard four of her guns, she was taken. On this cruise the *Lovely Lass* had been out forty days.

The 6-gun schooner *Snap Dragon*, Captain E. Pasteur (also commanded by Captains O. Burns and N.

[1] For action between the *Roger* and the *Highflyer* see p. 453.

Graham), was far more successful than either of the above, taking two barks, five brigs, and three schooners. In August and September, 1813, she captured the brigs *Good Intent*, *Venus*, and *Happy*, the bark *Reprisal*, and the schooner *Elizabeth*. All of these vessels were destroyed at sea after the more valuable portions of their cargoes had been taken out, except one which was given up to the prisoners. The *Snap Dragon* also took the brig *Ann*, with a cargo of drygoods worth half a million dollars. These goods had been purchased by American merchants with the expectation of smuggling them into the United States. In the following September the *Snap Dragon* captured the brig *Jane*, which, being in ballast, was given up to the prisoners. In April, 1814, this privateer seized two vessels—the *Linnet*, laden with fish and oil, and another, a schooner with a cargo of mahogany, which was sent into Beaufort.

New Orleans sent out six privateers, of which the lugger *Cora*, of four guns and thirty men, under Captain J. George; the 3-gun schooner *Hornet*, Captain F. Thomas; the boat *John*, Captain J. Coates; and the 1-gun schooner *Victory*, Captain J. Degres, accomplished little or nothing. The 4-gun schooner *Spy*, Captain R. Beluche, having one hundred men aboard, took the valuable ship *Jane*, laden with mahogany, which was sent into New Orleans. The 3-gun schooner *Two Friends*, Captain H. Ferlat, seized the sloop *Venus*, of Jamaica, and destroyed her at sea.

Five armed craft were sent out from Savannah, of which the 3-gun schooner *Atas*, Captain T. M. Newell; the 1-gun felucca *Bee*, Captain P. Masabeau; the 3-gun schooner *Elizabeth*, Captain R. Cleary; and the 4-gun schooner *Maria*, Captain J. Beecher, made no captures of importance. The 1-gun schooner *Nonpareil*, Captain H. Martin, seized a schooner, but the *Nonpareil* herself was captured by the *Découverte* on July 12, 1812.

Charleston put into commission thirteen armed

craft, besides those already mentioned. Several of them met with little if any success, among that class being the 1-gun schooner *Advocate*, Captain A. Dougle; the 2-gun sloop *Blockade*, Captain J. Graves; the schooner *Firefly*, Captain W. Clewley; the 1-gun sloop *Minerva*, Captain J. Peters; and the 4-gun schooner *Revenge*. The *Eagle*, a schooner carrying one gun and forty-five men, under Captain P. Lafete, captured four schooners, one of which was armed with three guns and was manned by twenty-four men.

The 3-gun schooner *Hazard*, Captain P. Le Chartrier, on February 22, 1813, had an action with the British privateer *Caledonia*, the result of which was peculiarly gratifying to the Americans. It seems that two days before this the *Hazard* captured the valuable British ship *Albion*, of twelve guns and twenty-five men. This merchantman was from Demerara for London, and had on board four hundred hogsheads of sugar, sixty-nine puncheons of rum, ten bales of cotton, and three hundred bags and thirty-six casks of coffee. Placing a prize crew aboard, with orders to make for port, Captain Le Chartrier resumed his cruise, supposing that his prize was making good headway toward the United States. On February 22d he fell in with the *Caledonia*, having the recaptured *Albion* in her company. The two privateers immediately began an action which resulted in the Englishman making sail in flight and the second capture of the *Albion* by the *Hazard*. "If we had had half an hour more of daylight," wrote Le Chartrier, "I should have brought in this privateer." In this affair the *Hazard* had seven men killed and the same number wounded. The *Caledonia* is credited with six guns and fifty men to the *Hazard's* three guns and twenty-eight men. This was the only capture made by the *Hazard* in this war. The *Lady Madison*, a schooner of one gun and forty-five men, under Captain A. Garrison, took two prizes in the course of the war, one of which was given up to prisoners.

The *Lovely Cornelia*, Captain P. Sicard, in October, 1813, took sixteen prizes off Jamaica, all of which were destroyed at sea, except one, which was sent to the United States, but was wrecked on the coast of Florida. The 1-gun schooner *Mary Ann*, also commanded by Captain Sicard and afterward by Captain J. P. Chazel, took one ship, two brigs, and two schooners. All of these prizes were armed, one with twelve and another with ten guns, each of which carried seventeen men. On May 5, 1813, the *Mary Ann* was captured by the 18-gun sloop of war *Sapphire*, one of the Americans being killed in the chase. The 1-gun *Poor Sailor*, Captain P. Lachlin, and the 1-gun schooner *Rapid*, Captains J. Princhett, W. Saunderson, etc., had moderate success. The former, though of only forty-four tons, captured a ship laden with rum. The *Poor Sailor* was lost at sea in 1813. The *Rapid* seized a ship, a brig, and two schooners. The ship was the *Experience*, with a cargo worth a quarter of a million dollars. One of the schooners was the *Searcher*, of one gun and twenty men, which was burned. One of the brigs was ransomed.

By far the most successful of the privateers that sailed for Charleston in this war was the 6-gun schooner *Saucy Jack*, Captain J. P. Chazel. This vessel was painted black, with a white streak along her side to distinguish her. While lying in Charleston harbor, August, 1812, preparatory to getting to sea, some person or persons spiked her guns. A reward of three hundred dollars was offered for the apprehension of the perpetrators of the act, but without avail. This craft took in all six ships, six brigs, nine schooners, and two sloops. In September she arrived in the St. Mary's from her third cruise, in which she had captured the *Three Sisters* and the ship *Eliza*, of ten guns, laden with flour and beef.

On August 17th she took the ship *Laura*, laden with coffee, and the *Three Brothers*, each mounting ten guns. Shortly after the *Laura* had been taken possession of by the American prize crew she was chased by the British sloop of war *Peruvian*. To prevent their prize from falling into the hands of the enemy the American fired the *Laura* and took to their boats, ultimately arriving in the United States. The *Peruvian* subsequently was wrecked on Silver Keys. In December, 1813, the *Saucy Jack* made a short cruise, in which she captured the brig *Agnes* and the sloop *John*, the privateer arriving at Charleston December 20th of the same year.

Early in 1814 this boat got to sea on her fourth venture, in which she made her most valuable prize, the *Pelham*, the following account of which was forwarded to the Secretary of the Navy: "Charleston, May 21, 1814.—Arrived at this port yesterday the large and elegant ship *Pelham* (late Captain Boyd), Alexander Taylor, prize master, prize to the privateer *Saucy Jack*, Captain Chazel, of this port.[1] The *Pelham* was captured on the 30th of April off Cape Nocola Mole after a well-contested action of upward of two hours. She was finally carried by boarding, after her crew had made a stout and gallant resistance of from ten to fifteen minutes on her own decks. We learnt on board that the officers and crew of the *Pelham* behaved throughout the action in the most heroic manner, and did not yield until actually overpowered by numbers. The *Saucy Jack*

---

[1] Her cargo consisted of drygoods, hardware, etc., as follows: One hundred and ninety-four packages drygoods, consisting of India checks and stripes, gurrahs, romals, seersuckers, bedticks, ginghams, calicoes, shawls, Madras and Malabar handkerchiefs. Irish linens, lawn, shirtings, brown linen, duck, sheetings, osnaburgs, bagging, shoes, boots, saddlery, etc., three hundred packages sundries, consisting of hardware, glassware, mustard pickles, sauces, preserves, porter, ale, Madeira and sherry wines. white lead, paints, gunpowder, linseed oil, glue, ochre, twines, seines, hats, etc. ; one organ and one pianoforte.

had her first officer and one man killed and the second officer, captain of arms, and seven men wounded. On board the *Pelham* were four killed and eleven wounded; among the latter was Captain Boyd, dangerously, in the breast. He, with the passengers, was landed at Port-au-Prince. The *Pelham* was from London bound to Port-au-Prince, and sailed from Portsmouth on the 9th of March with the same convoy, of which we have already had accounts from as having arrived at Halifax and bringing London dates to the 7th of March. Of course she brings nothing new. The day previous to her capture she had an engagement with two Carthaginian privateers, which she succeeded in beating off, but the courage and perseverance of the officers and crew of the *Saucy Jack* were not so easily overcome. This is another honorable specimen of the bravery and good conduct of American seamen. We hardly recollect to have seen a finer ship than the *Pelham*. She is five hundred and forty tons, coppered to the bends, mounts ten 12-pounders and 6-pounders and had a complement of from thirty-five to forty men, exclusive of several passengers. She is almost new, this being her second voyage, and is in every way fitted the most complete of any merchant ship that has entered our port for a long time. Her cabin is hung round with a great variety of large and elegant colored naval prints in rich gilt frames, among which was a representation of the engagement between the *Chesapeake* and the *Shannon* in two views. During her skirmish with the *SaucyJack*, an 18-pound shot from the long tom found its way through the ship's side and demolished one of its views, with several others." On the 31st of October, 1814, the British bomb ship *Volcano*, Lieutenant Price, and the transports *Golden Fleece* and *Balahoo*, with some two hundred and fifty English soldiers on board, fell in with this doughty privateer of Charleston. At that time the vessels were off the west end of San Do-

mingo. Captain Chazel had been cruising in this
vicinity with a little tender called the *Packet* when
he discovered the English vessels. He gave chase,
and, under the impression that they were merchantmen, he fired, about one o'clock on the following
morning, three shots from his long tom, which fire
the *Volcano* returned, at the same time shortening
sail with her consorts so as to allow the audacious
American to come up. The wind was light and the
darkness rendered it difficult to make out the exact
force of the strangers. At six o'clock in the morning the vessels were within half gunshot. It was
then that Captain Chazel discovered that one of the
ships mounted sixteen guns and the other eighteen;
but, as they did not appear to be well manned, he
determined upon an attack. At seven o'clock he
showed his colors and began an action with the *Volcano*, that craft being nearest to him. Following the
favorite tactics of American privateersmen, Captain
Chazel lost no time in getting alongside the enemy,
and prepared to board on her port beam.

Just as the Americans were about to spring to
the enemy's decks Captain Chazel suddenly discovered that the stranger was full of soldiers. The
order recalling boarders was promptly given, and
the *Saucy Jack* sheered off and made all sail to
escape. Two of the English ships, the *Volcano* and
the *Golden Fleece*, gave chase, and maintained a
spirited fire for nearly an hour, when, finding that
they were losing ground, they desisted. When the
Saucy Jack was close to them the British soldiers
poured in a destructive fire of musketry, killing eight
and wounding fifteen of the Americans. The privateer also was somewhat cut up in her hull, spars,
and rigging. The enemy had three men killed, including Lieutenant W. P. Futzen, and two men
wounded.

CHAPTER IX.

CAREER OF THE AMERICA.

OF the forty privateers sent out from Salem in the War of 1812, the *America*, with the possible exception of the *Grand Turk*, was the most successful. She is reputed to have been the fastest sailing craft afloat during that struggle, and her numerous escapes from British cruisers seem to bear out this reputation. She was a 350-ton craft, built in 1804, and usually carried twenty guns and a complement of one hundred and fifty men. In this war she made twenty-six prizes, and the property taken from them and brought safely into port realized one million one hundred thousand dollars, while the amount of property she destroyed at sea would be represented by a much larger figure. She thus proved to be a veritable "gold mine" for her owners, the Messrs. George Crowninshield & Sons.

This vessel frequently has been confused with the privateer *America*, which was commissioned by John Adams in 1802, and made one cruise before hostilities with France ceased. The Crowninshields took a prominent part in the struggle for American independence, Captain Benjamin Crowninshield having fought in the battle of Bunker Hill.

It was always the good fortune of the *America* to be commanded by the ablest captain that could be had, to which circumstance, doubtless, is largely due her uniform success. Joseph Ropes, one of the best-known "sea dogs" in his day, had charge of

328

this privateer on her maiden cruise, in 1812, while on her third and fourth ventures she was commanded by James Chever, Jr., who also was said to have been " as slick a skipper as ever gave slip to a British frigate." The *America* returned from her third cruise with twelve prizes and fifty prisoners.

In her essays against British commerce the *America* demonstrated what a terrible scourge a well equipped and manned commerce destroyer could be in the hands of a bold, skillful, and adroit commander. " She started on her first cruise from Salem Monday morning, September 7, 1812, at half past eleven o'clock," so her log reads. By noon she reached Baker's Island, and shortly afterward she was bowling along the ocean swells in quest of prey. The inauspicious omen of an accident at the beginning of the cruise—so potent with most sailors—did not seem to have seriously affected the gallant tars in this well-named craft, notwithstanding the additional significance of the accident occurring on Friday.

On Friday, September 11th, when the ship's company had scarcely begun to get well broken into their new surroundings, the main topmast was carried away, and the five men who were on it at the time were thrown into the sea. The accident happened in a heavy gale, these men having been sent up to make snug. The ship was promptly sent round, a boat lowered, and, after much risk and danger from the swamping of the boat, the sailors were rescued. All hands were called and set to work repairing the damage and in a few hours the wreck was cleared, a new spar sent up and rigged, and the good ship again was bounding along the ocean. About 5 20 A. M. Wednesday, September 23d, the *America* s a sail, and after a short chase captured the brig *James and Charlotte*, commanded by a from Liverpool bound for St. John's. was found to be well stocked with hat

24

coal, etc., and as the Americans stood in need of these articles they decided to take them. Mr. Tibbetts, with six men, was placed aboard the brig as a prize master, with orders to make for the nearest American port. He brought the brig safely into Salem.

Captain Ropes was one of those commanders who believed that fighting was not a happy-go-lucky operation, but a science, which by constant exercise could be reduced to the nicest perfection. He therefore employed much of his spare time between chases in exercising his men at the great guns and in rapid drills with small arms. The result was that, although his seamen were not uniformed and had served together only a short time, they soon became as dexterous in these matters as the most exacting man-of-warsman could desire.

Passing the island of St. Michael October 5th, Captain Ropes did not see a sail of note until a month afterward. At 4 P. M. Friday, November 6th, a stranger was reported to the south, and the *America* promptly wore round and gave chase. After a hard sail the stranger was brought to and boarded. She was found to be the British brig *Benjamin*, bound for England from Newfoundland, under the command of James Collins. Taking the mate, with seven men, aboard the *America*, and leaving Collins, one man, and a boy aboard the *Benjamin*, Captain Ropes resumed his cruise, after placing Joseph Dixon, and eight men, aboard the brig as a prize master, with instructions to make the most available port in America north of Nantucket.

The second week after this the *America* had an exciting chase lasting nearly two days. Early on It morning of November 18th a sail was reported be com northwest, and Captain Ropes promptly let had, to reefs from the topsails, in spite of the stiff due her umg at the time, and, setting his main top-best-known gave chase. All that night the stranger led the Yankee a hard stern chase, and at times disappeared from view altogether, but by keeping a sharp lookout, and with the aid of night glasses, the Americans managed to keep track of her. It was not until the afternoon of the following day that the chase was overtaken and brought to. She had proved to be a remarkably fast-sailing craft, and had given the *America* all she wanted to do in coming up with her. Captain Ropes found his prize to be the *Ralph Nickerson*, of and for London from Quebec, laden with lumber and having an armament of eight guns. John Procter and eleven men were placed aboard, and succeeded in running her into Marblehead.

Early on the morning of the following Tuesday, November 24th, the *America* made another sail, and by nine o'clock found her to be the British 12-gun ship *Hope*, from St. Thomas for Glasgow, laden with sugar, rum, and cotton. This proved to be the most valuable prize thus far the privateer had taken, and Captain Ropes placed twelve men, under Joseph Valpey, in charge of her, with orders to make for the United States. From the master of the *Hope* the Americans learned that she had left a fleet of forty-five merchantmen only three days before, which were under the convoy of the sloops of war *Ringdove* and *Scorpion*. As the *America* herself was a pretty good match for a sloop of war singly, Captain Ropes was not averse to meeting one of these cruisers, although, of course, he preferred capturing the merchantmen under their escort. At all events, he made sail in the direction of the fleet, hoping to meet the enemy.

Late in the afternoon of the following day a sail was discovered to the south standing easterly. Chase was promptly given, and with such success that within an hour a shot from one of the *America's* guns induced the stranger to heave to. She was the British brig *Dart*, carrying eight guns, also one of

the great fleet of merchantmen. Her cargo, like
the *Hope's*, consisted principally of rum and cotton.
The *America's* boat, in returning from the brig with
Mr. Sparhawk and Thomas Fuller and five prisoners,
unfortunately got under the privateer's counter and
foundered. The two American officers and three of
the prisoners were saved, but the other prisoners
were drowned. Captain Ropes kept in sight of this
prize all that and the following day, but as there
were no further signs of the great fleet he, at 3.30
P. M., November 27th, signaled the brig to bear down
under his lee. This being done, Anthony D. Caulfield,
with eight men, was placed aboard the *Dart* as the
prize master and sailed for the United States, after
all of the brig's people, excepting the captain, a passenger, and one man, had been transferred to the
privateer. The *Dart* safely arrived at Salem.

Finding that several of his officers and a number
of the crew were attacked with a very troublesome
inflammation of the eyes, which could not be accounted for and which seemed to be contagious, Captain Ropes determined to return to the United
States. His supply of water also was getting so low
that he was compelled to curtail the allowance to
three and a half pints every twenty-four hours for
a man. Even on her homeward passage the *America*
was attended with good fortune. Early on the
morning of December 16th, when near the Western
Isles, a sail was descried to the southeast, and the
privateer made all sail in chase. By eight o'clock
the stranger was seen to be a brig steering eastward, apparently anxious to avoid the *America*.
This only whetted the desire of the Yankees to get
alongside, and by eleven o'clock they had the chase
under their guns. She was the English brig *Euphemia*, of Glasgow, bound for Gibraltar from La
Guayra, with four hundred thousand pounds of coffee
aboard. She carried ten guns and was manned by
twenty-five men, under the command of John Gray.

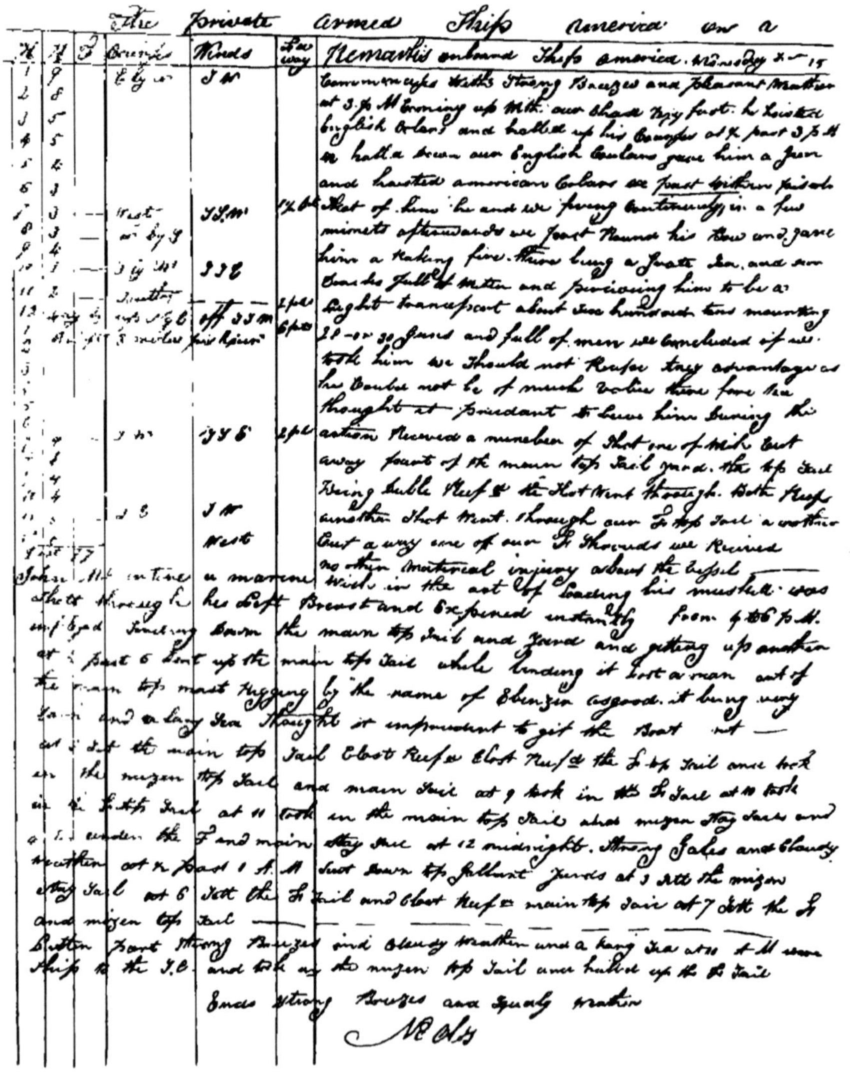

The Private armed Ship America on a

Remarks onboard Ship America. Wednesday 15

Commences with Strong Breezes and pleasant weather at 3 P M Coming up with our Chase very fast. he hoisted English Colors and hauled up his Courses at ½ past 3 P M we hauled down our English Colors gave him a gun and hoisted American Colors we past within pistol Shot of him he and we firing Continually in a few minutes afterwards we past Round his Bow and gave him a raking fire. there being a great Sea. and our Decks full of water and perceiving him to be a Light transport about two hundred tons mounting 20 or 30 guns and full of men we concluded if we took him we should not Reap any advantage as he would not be of much value therefore we thought it prudent to leave him during the action Received a number of shot one of which cut away part of the main top sail yard. the top sail being double Reef'd the shot went through. Both Reefs another shot went through our fore top sail a nother cut away one of our fore shrouds we Received no other material injury about the vessel —

John McIntire a marine which in the act of loading his musket was shott through the left Breast and expired instantly from 4 to 6 P. M. employed sending down the main top sail and yard and getting up another at ½ past 6 sent up the main top sail while bending it lost a man out of the main top mast rigging by the name of Ebenezer Osgood. it being very dark and a large sea thought it imprudent to get the Boat out — at 8 set the main top sail close reefed close reef'd the fore top sail and took in the mizen top sail and main sail at 9 took in the fore sail at 10 took in the fore top sail at 11 took in the main top sail also mizen stay sail and lay to under the F and main stay sail at 12 midnight. Strong Gales and cloudy weather at ½ past 1 A. M sent down top gallant yards at 3 set the mizen stay sail at 6 set the fore sail and close reef'd main top sail at 7 set the fore and mizen top sail — — — —

Latter part strong Breezes and cloudy weather and a large sea at 10 A M wore Ship to the S.E and took in the mizen top sail and hauled up the fore sail

Ends strong Breezes and squally weather

McClay

Facsimile (reduced) of a page in the America's log kept during her third cruise.

The next day Captain Ropes took the first and second officers, twenty-one men, and eight guns from his prize, and placing on board of her Archibald S. Dennis, with eleven men, as a prize master, resumed his course for the United States. The *Euphemia* in due time reached Portland, Maine. The *America* arrived in Salem harbor on the afternoon of January 7, 1813, having completed a highly successful cruise of one hundred and twenty-two days. Her six prizes were valued at one hundred and fifty-eight thousand dollars.

This privateer got to sea again for her second cruise in January, 1813, and returned to Bath, Maine, in July of the same year, having made ten prizes. Of these two were ordered to France, three arrived in American ports, two were recaptured, and three were converted into cartels so as to get rid of the prisoners, of whom one hundred and thirty were paroled and thirty were brought into port. One of these prizes was the American ship *St. Lawrence*, of New York, which had on board a full cargo of British goods from Liverpool, and on her arrival in Portsmouth, New Hampshire, both ship and goods were condemned.

We get some idea of the peculiar excitement attending the ventures of privateers on the high seas by looking over the cargoes captured by the *America* in her second and third cruises, in the latter venture the privateer being credited with twelve prizes. We have first the 220-ton brig *Margaret*, of ten guns, having one thousand hogsheads of salt aboard, from Cadiz bound for Newfoundland, which was carried into Salem; the 300-ton brig *Sovereign*, of and for Liverpool, with an assorted cargo, which was sold in Portsmouth, New Hampshire; the brig *Brothers*, which was sent into Fuenterrabia, Spain, and sold there by the consent of the officials; the 250-ton brig *Apollo*, of Poole, with one thousand hogsheads of salt, which shared the fate of the *Margaret*; the schooner *Hope*, from St. Andrews for Barbadoes, laden with lumber, beef, and oil; and the schooner *Sylph*, of Liverpool, Nova Scotia, with fish, oil, etc. Several prizes were destroyed at sea, and a number were released so as to get rid of prisoners. In this cruise the *America*, commanded by James Chever, Jr., left Bath December 3, 1813, and returned to Portsmouth April, 1814.

In her last cruise in this war the *America* had a battle with an English privateer. The Yankees sailed from port early in November, 1814, and made directly for European waters. On January 22, 1815, she took the schooner *Arrow*, from Catalonia for London, having on board one hundred casks of almonds and one thousand six hundred and fifty casks of hazelnuts, the prize being sent into Salem. About the same time the *America* took the valuable brig *Adcona*, with four hundred and fifty bales of broadcloth, which also was sent into Salem. One of the *America's* prizes, the schooner *Thistle*, was recaptured March 19, 1815, while off Cape Sable, by the British sloop of war *Cossack*; but on being sent into Halifax the *Thistle* was restored to the Americans, as her recapture had taken place after the time limit set by the treaty.

It was in March that the *America* came across the English privateer *Elizabeth*, a ship carrying eight guns and thirty-one men. The advantages in weight of metal and number of guns and men were so much in favor of the Americans that in twenty minutes the Englishmen surrendered, but not without making a gallant defense, in which two of their men were killed and thirteen wounded. So rapid and effective was the *America's* gunnery that, in the brief time the actual fighting lasted, the *Elizabeth* had seven hundred shot holes—including grape, canister, and musket shots—in her hull, spars, and sails. After depriving her of her armament the Americans returned the prize to her surviving

people, as, being in ballast, she was of little value
to her captors.

Some of the other prizes taken by the *America*
in this cruise were the schooner *Swift* and the brig
Enterprise. The *Enterprise*, on her passage to America, was overtaken by a severe storm, and was com-

The *America*, owned by George Crowninshield & Sons, the
most noted Salem privateer.

From an old painting owned by W. S. Chever, son of Captain James W. Chever,
who commanded the *America*.

pelled to put into Fayal in distress, where she was
condemned. The following vessels were destroyed
at sea by the *America:* the schooner *Robert*, the sloop
Jubilee, the cutter *Busy*, and the schooner *Black Joke*.

The *America* arrived at Salem from her last venture, April 10, 1815, after a cruise of one hundred and
thirty-four days. In the course of the war she
netted her owners six hundred thousand dollars.
On the close of hostilities she was tied up at Crowninshield's wharf, where she remained a number of
years. In June, 1831, she was sold at auction and
broken up.

CHAPTER X.

A TYPICAL PRIVATEERSMAN.

ON October 20, 1813, the American privateer *David Porter* was lying at Providence, Rhode Island, taking in an assorted cargo for Charleston, South Carolina. As her name implies, she was not one of the first privateers to get to sea, for Captain Porter did not make his great name in naval history until he went on his celebrated cruise around Cape Horn and devastated British commerce in the Pacific, and that was in 1813–'14. The privateer which bore his name had been one of our famous, swift-sailing pilot boats, and on being converted into a war craft carried a long 18-pounder amidships and four 6-pounders—a somewhat light armament, but, notwithstanding, a serviceable one, as will be seen. Her commander, George Coggeshall, was one of the ablest captains in the privateer service. He came from good New England stock, and had no superior in the art of " handling men." It was the good fortune of this craft to be officered largely by men who had served in the regular navy, for at that time the United States 44-gun frigate *President*, Captain John Rodgers, had come to this port after a long cruise, and some thirty of her petty officers and seamen enlisted in the *David Porter*.

Having finished loading, Captain Coggeshall dropped down the river to Newport, where he waited for a favorable opportunity to get to sea. So great had been the terror inspired by American frigates

in this war that whenever one of them was known
to be in port the British promptly stationed several
ships of the line and frigates for the express purpose of keeping her there. Such was the case with
the *President*, and when Captain Coggeshall reached
Newport he found that it would be extremely hazardous to run the blockade.

Determined, however, to get to sea at any risk,
Captain Coggeshall waited for a dark, boisterous
night, when he could trust to his superior knowledge
of the coast and the cover of the night to elude the
enemy. Such an opportunity was afforded November 14th, when toward evening a genuine New England snowstorm, from the northeast, caused the
British officers to linger over their porter and cheese
longer than usual, and discouraged all attempts to
keep the deck. The shrewd Yankee skipper undoubtedly was aware of this weakness of his British
cousins, and rightly judging that most of them would
be shivering in their bunks or hammocks, and that
the watch on deck would be more anxiously seeking
the lee side of a mast or cabin than watching for
American frigates, he boldly stood out to sea and
passed the hostile ships unchallenged.

On the run to Charleston the *David Porter* was
chased several times by British cruisers, for our
coast was swarming with craft of that ilk, but in
each instance she managed to escape. On November
26th, however, the privateer had a chase that was
too close to be pleasant. At daybreak, being in ten
fathoms of water off Cape Romain, Captain Coggeshall discovered a British brig of war just out of gunshot off his weather bow which promptly gave chase.
The wind at the time was off the land, and the British kept to windward, hoping to force the privateer
leeward. Just out of sight of Charleston bar were
stationed two more of the enemy's brigs of war, and
it was the purpose of the commander of the brig
first discovered to drive the chase into the open

arms of his consorts. Aware of the trap that was
being so nicely arranged for him, Captain Coggeshall resolved to hug the wind, push boldly for the
channel at the bar, and defend himself from attack
the best he could. Knowing that this was his only
chance of escape, the American skipper held steadily
on his course, the enemy making strenuous efforts
to get within striking distance.

For four hours the vessels bowed under a press
of canvas, the advantage being slightly with the
privateer, when the latter gained the bar and waited
for the leading brig to come within gunshot. In a
few minutes the *David Porter* let go her long tom,
and with such good aim that it struck the water
near the Briton and threw spray over his port
quarter. The brig, being armed with short guns,
could not return the compliment without coming to
much closer quarters, and this her commander hastily decided to do; for about that time the famous
American privateers *Decatur*, Captain Diron, and
Adeline, Captain R. Craycroft, came down Charleston
harbor in gallant style, ready to join the *David Porter* in a general fight with the brigs. The enemy,
probably overestimating the force of the Americans,
promptly squared their yards and ran to leeward.
The *Decatur* had recently arrived in Charleston after
her brilliant victory over the British war ship *Dominica*.[1] Proceeding up the harbor while the *Decatur*
and the *Adeline* stood to sea on another cruise, Captain Coggeshall unloaded, and obtaining a full cargo
sailed, December 20, 1813, for Bordeaux, France.

As showing the profits and risks of privateering
at that time, it will be noted that the *David Porter*
had on board three hundred and thirty-one bales of
cotton at twenty-six cents a pound, with five per
cent. " primage." The gross freight and primage
on this cotton was twenty-three thousand dollars,

---

[1] See pp. 311–319.

which, considering that she was a vessel of only two hundred tons, seems like an enormous freight on sea island cotton, which article at that time could be purchased for twelve or thirteen cents a pound. But this charge for freight, when the enormous expense of running a privateer, with her large crew, is considered, was not exorbitant. Marine insurance had risen to fifteen and even twenty per cent., and seamen's wages were thirty dollars a month.

One of the risks incurred by privateers was well illustrated when the *David Porter* was ready to sail. This was on December 18th, but adverse winds detained her. Meantime Captain Coggeshall learned that Congress was expected at any moment to declare an embargo. Should the privateer be caught in port when this new move of the Government was made it would result in the bankruptcy of the owners of the vessel and her officers. Determined to avoid detention in port, Captain Coggeshall kept his crew confined to the ship and dropped down the harbor as far as possible so as to watch for the first favorable opportunity to get to sea. This occurred December 20th, and aided by a fine breeze the *David Porter* made a good run off the coast.

Nothing worth noting occurred until about 4 P. M. December 27th, when, in a strong northwest gale, the privateer fell in with a small English vessel from Jamaica bound for Nova Scotia. As the seas were too violent to permit boarding, Captain Coggeshall ordered the prize to follow him on his course, intending to examine her more closely when favored with better weather. The Englishmen reluctantly obeyed, and as night came on showed a disposition to edge away. Thereupon the Americans hailed, and in pretty sharp language told the British master that if he continued to lag behind, or did not carry all the sail his brig could bear, he would feel the effects of the *David Porter's* stern guns. This admonition had the desired effect, but at midnight it suddenly came on very dark and squally, so that Captain Coggeshall lost all trace of his first prize, nor did he see her again.

From this time the *David Porter* scarcely descried a sail until she entered the Bay of Biscay. Knowing that several English war ships were stationed off the Bordeaux Light, Captain Coggeshall decided not to enter the Garonne, but to run for La Teste. About a week before reaching that port she was overtaken by a terrific gale, which began early on the morning of January 19, 1814, and continued through the following day. By eight o'clock in the morning of the first day it blew with the force of a hurricane, which raised a dangerous cross sea.

Captain Coggeshall hove to under double-reefed foresail, lowered his foreyard near the deck, and made everything as tight as possible. About noon a tremendous wave struck the *David Porter* just abaft the starboard fore shrouds, crushing in one of the stanchions, and split open the plank-sheer so that it was possible to see into the hold. The vessel was thrown nearly on her beam ends, where for some time it was uncertain whether she would right herself or continue to go over. Fortunately her foresail split and the lee bulwark was torn away by the water. Being relieved of this pressure the vessel gradually righted, but her people had become so alarmed for her safety that two of her lee guns were thrown overboard, together with some water casks.

After nailing tarred canvas and leather over the broken plank-sheer Captain Coggeshall got ready to veer ship, fearing that the injury the schooner had received might affect the foremast. A small piece of the mainsail accordingly was got in readiness for hoisting, and then, keeping her before the wind for a few minutes, they watched for a favorable opportunity to bring her to the wind on the other tack.

During the time she was running before the wind, so her officers declare, she appeared to leap from one wave to another. Captain Coggeshall brought his craft up to the wind on the other tack without accident, and under a small piece of canvas she lay to, waiting for the wind to subside. Fearing that he might ship another sea, Captain Coggeshall prepared a novel device for "anchoring" the head of his ship to the wind. Taking a square sail boom, spanned at each end with a four-inch rope, and with the small bower cable made fast to the bight of the span, the other end being made fast to the foremast, the boom was thrown overboard and was run out some sixty fathoms. The effect was miraculous. The boom broke the force of the waves and kept the schooner's head to the sea, so that she rode like a gull until the storm abated. It was not until afternoon of the following day that the *David Porter* again made sail, and six days later she made La Teste, thirty-six days from Charleston.

Arriving at this port Captain Coggeshall learned that a large number of vessels had foundered in the gale which so nearly ended his career, and that the coasts for miles were strewn with wrecks. Five English transports had been thrown ashore near La Teste, most of their people perishing.

La Teste proved to be a miserable village with little or no facilities for supplying ships. Besides this the people were greatly excited by the approach of the allied forces to Paris and the advance of Lord Wellington's army toward Bordeaux, only thirty. miles from La Teste. Such being the unsettled state of affairs, Captain Coggeshall found great difficulty in disposing of his cargo or in securing supplies for another cruise. Furthermore, it was expected that the English would seize Bordeaux and La Teste, in which case the career of the *David Porter* would probably be cut short. Proceeding to Bordeaux on horseback Captain Coggeshall finally induced his consignees to purchase for him one·hundred casks of wine and fifty pipes of brandy, which they were to send in a small coasting vessel to La Rochelle, there to be taken aboard the *David Porter*. This port was selected as it was strongly fortified and probably would hold out longer than Bordeaux. All the American vessels had left the latter place, and were at the mouth of the Garonne waiting for an opportunity to sail for the United States or La Rochelle.

Returning to La Teste Captain Coggeshall made strenuous though futile efforts to secure enough supplies for his vessel, the solitary baker in the place being able to furnish only two bags of bread for a ship having a complement of thirty-five healthy men. It was here that Captain Coggeshall learned of the capture of Bordeaux by the English, and he had reason to congratulate himself on his forethought in making La Teste rather than Bordeaux. But even his efforts to get away from La Teste before that place should be seized by the English were stubbornly combated by the weather and an obstinate pilot. Winds and tides frustrated all endeavors to make an offing until March 13th, when the pilot declared that five o'clock in the afternoon would be the time to cross the bar. Every minute the Americans expected to see British colors hoisted over the town and their ship made a prize, and as the hours dragged along to the time mentioned by the pilot they anxiously scanned the approaches to the village and harbor. At four o'clock Captain Coggeshall requested the pilot to get under way, but it was then learned that the pilot was unwilling to go out at all, fearing that he might be carried to America, so that his wife and family would be left unprovided for.

"Captain," he said, "if we should succeed in getting out it would be impossible to land me."

In vain did Captain Coggeshall assure him that

he would cruise in the vicinity a week if necessary
in order to land the pilot if he would only take the
ship over the bar.   In vain did he show how the
David Porter might become a prize of the British at
any moment, and equally futile were his offers to
double and treble the pilot's fees.   Finally, seeing
that persuasion was of no avail, the American commander resolved upon strategy.   To his proposition: " If you will not go to sea, just get the schooner
under way and go down below the fort and anchor
there within the bar," the pilot assented.   But when
below the fort Captain Coggeshall seized a loaded
pistol, held it to the pilot's head, and declared that
he would shoot if the latter did not take the ship
over the bar.   The American commander also declared that if the *David Porter* took the ground the
pilot would be held equally accountable.   Thoroughly frightened the pilot got the ship over in less than
fifteen minutes, and a few days later he was landed
on his native shore, while the *David Porter* stood off
to the northwest.

Scarcely had the privateer turned her head on
her new course when she had a narrow escape from
capture.   At daylight March 15, 1814, during a
heavy mist, the lookout reported a large ship on
the weather quarter, and as the haze lifted it was
seen to be a large frigate, without doubt an enemy.
Captain Coggeshall realized the danger of his position, and maneuvered some ten or fifteen minutes
in the hope of drawing the stranger down to leeward so he would be able to weather the frigate
on one tack or the other.   This was the favorite trick
of Yankee privateersmen in this war, for if the swift-
sailing boats once succeeded in getting an
enemy under their lee they could laugh at all efforts
to come to close quarters.   But the commander of
the frigate evidently was aware of this maneuver,
and instead of coming down he only kept off four
or six points and steadily gained on the privateer,

then only two gunshots to leeward. Realizing the
seriousness of the situation, Captain Coggeshall held
a consultation of his officers, at which it was urged
that their only chance was to run past the frigate,
receive her fire, and take their chances in a race to
windward. Captain Coggeshall, however, had good
reason to believe that the *David Porter* would be
crippled by the frigate's broadside, so he gave orders
to get the square sail and studding sails ready to
run up at the same moment.

When all was ready the helm was put up, the
square sail hoisted, and in an incredibly short time
the privateer had become a square-rigged craft and
was scudding before the wind like a cloud. The frigate's people apparently did not for a moment suppose that the privateer would attempt a run before
the wind, and were taken somewhat by surprise in
the schooner's sudden display of square sail, and
thereby allowed her to gain a mile at the beginning
of the chase. As the British skipper realized the
nature of the maneuver he bent on his studding
sails, and in five minutes had settled down to a determined chase. With a view of increasing the
speed of his vessel, Captain Coggeshall ordered holes
to be bored in all the water casks except four, and
the water pumped into buckets and thrown against
the sails so that the canvas would hold the wind better. Besides this the sand ballast was thrown overboard, and, thus lightened, the *David Porter* began to
draw away from the enemy, so that by noon she was
eight or ten miles in the lead, and by four in the
afternoon the frigate was a mere speck on the
horizon.

That evening, when the enemy had been left
safely out of sight, Captain Coggeshall examined
the condition of his ship and found that he was in
a critical situation. Instead of leaving four casks
filled with water the carpenter, in the confusion of
the moment, had left only two, and as the wind

began to freshen Captain Coggeshall found that it was unsafe—his schooner being relieved of her ballast—to haul upon the wind. The position of the privateer was indeed precarious. Wide off to sea in the Bay of Biscay, with scarcely ballast enough to stand upon her bottom, and having aboard only two casks of water and a few loaves of soft bread with which to feed thirty-five men, Captain Coggeshall found himself confronted by grave dangers.

Undecided as to what immediate steps to take, and hoping for some favorable turn in the wheel of fortune, he spent that night in restless anxiety. The wind continued light, and toward morning, March 16th, it was almost calm. As day began to dawn the lookout reported a sail, and shortly afterward another, and another. And by the time the sun had cleared the mists away Captain Coggeshall found himself in the presence of a small fleet of merchantmen. Had these vessels come to the privateer in answer to an appeal to Heaven they could not have surprised the sorely distressed Americans more nor have carried greater joy to their hearts. So quietly had the fleet approached, under cover of night, that the Americans could scarcely believe their eyes when day broke. In an instant all was bustle, haste, and exhilaration aboard the privateer, and she lost no time in running alongside a merchant brig and capturing her. Captain Coggeshall then learned that the vessels were a part of a fleet bound for St. Sebastian, laden with provisions for the British army, and that they had become separated from their convoy, a frigate and a sloop of war, only a few days before.

After taking possession of the brig, which was laden principally with provisions, Captain Coggeshall entered into an agreement with her master by which the latter was to assist, with his boats and men, in transporting his cargo to the schooner, after which he was to go free with his brig. The English-

25

man reluctantly consented, and in two hours the united crews had placed enough provisions aboard the *David Porter* to keep her at sea three months. Speaking with the fervor of a starving man beholding the good things of life, Captain Coggeshall quaintly describes the occurrence as follows: " His cabin was filled with bags of hard biscuit, the staff of life, which we took first, and then got a fine supply of butter, hams, cheese, potatoes, porter, etc., and last, though not least, six casks of fresh water. After this was done the captain asked me if I would make him a present of the brig and the residue of the cargo for his own private account, to which I willingly agreed, in consideration of the assistance I had received from him and his men. I showed him my commission from the Government of the United States authorizing me to take, burn, sink, or destroy our common enemy, and satisfied him that he was a lawful prize to my vessel. I then gave him a certificate stating that though his brig was a lawful prize, I voluntarily gave her to him as a present. This, of course, was only a piece of tomfoolery, but it pleased the captain, and we parted good friends."

With as little delay as possible Captain Coggeshall then hastened after other vessels in the fleet, which were making off in many directions. The light wind prevailing at the time did not enable them to get very far, and in a short time the *David Porter* had seized a ship and two brigs which had been a mile or two off her lee beam. The same arrangements relative to transferring cargo to the privateer as had been made with the first brig were made with the masters of these vessels, and in a short time the *David Porter* was nearly filled with a valuable assortment of goods, consisting principally of provisions, officers' and soldiers' uniforms, cocked hats, epaulets, small arms, instruments of music, cloths, and general merchandise.

While engaged in this agreeable occupation a

fresh breeze sprang up from the southwest, and
shortly afterward it came on dark and rainy,
which made it difficult to continue the work of transporting goods to the privateer. At five o'clock a sail
was reported to windward, and going aloft with a
glass Captain Coggeshall soon recognized her, from
her carrying a white bleached jib, while all her other
sails were of a dark color, as being the same frigate that had chased him only a few days before.
This time, however, circumstances were more favorable to the privateer. The schooner was in good
trim, the men well fed, and with a prospect of large
dividends they worked with a will. Furthermore, on-
coming night gave the schooner every chance for escape. Coming rapidly down the frigate approached
within five or six miles, when Captain Coggeshall ran near his prizes and ordered them all to
hoist lanterns. Strange to say not one of the British
masters had discovered the frigate, and they obeyed
the order, little thinking that they were inviting a
broadside from English guns into their own sides,
or were materially assisting in the escape of the
Yankee skipper. But this was just what they did.

Quickly extinguishing all his lights, Captain
Coggeshall quietly drew away in the night, and was
soon speeding off in another direction, while the lumbering frigate, observing the group of lights, made
directly for them. "Very soon after this," remarked
Captain Coggeshall, "I heard the frigate firing at
her unfortunate countrymen, while we were partak-
ing of an excellent supper at their expense." Two
days later the *David Porter* was chased by a frigate
and a brig of war, but had little difficulty in making
her escape. It may here be remarked that the captain of the *David Porter's* long tom was a colored
man. This was the only gun on which Captain Coggeshall placed the slightest dependence. "My only
dependence," he wrote, "was on my 18-pounder,
mounted amidships on a pivot." For this gun he

selected ten of the largest and strongest men of his crew. Philip, the colored captain of this gun, was a huge man, over six feet high, and a general favorite.

After running the frigate and the brig of war out of sight, Captain Coggeshall decided to land at l'Ile d'Yeu, a small island about thirty miles from St. Gilles, on the west coast of France, and send his ship home in charge of his first officer, Samuel Nichols, assisted by the second officer, Charles Coggeshall. This was done on March 24, 1814, and leaving her commander at this place the *David Porter* turned her head westward. Capturing several British merchantmen on the passage over, this schooner arrived safely at Gloucester, where her ten prisoners were landed, the owners of the privateer receiving one thousand dollars from the Government as bounty for them. This voyage of the *David Porter* brought her owners some twenty thousand dollars, and shortly after her arrival in Boston she was sold for ten thousand dollars.

Her new owners sent her to sea, under the command of Captain J. Fish, in the summer of 1814, when she took several valuable merchantmen. Among them were the brig *Mars*, from Mogador, which was divested of the most valuable part of her cargo and ordered to America; the brig *Cornwallis*, divested and converted into a cartel; the 6-gun ship *Vester*, from Rio Janeiro for England, divested and ordered in; and the brig *Horatio*, from and for the same places, laden with hides and tallow, which was ransomed for a bill of exchange on England amounting to twenty thousand dollars. In this cruise the *David Porter* was chased nine hundred and forty miles by a British frigate and two sloops of war, but she finally eluded them and arrived safely in New York, September, 1814.

On the following December 1st the *David Porter* again got to sea, and in a cruise of fifteen days took the brig *Hiram*, of Liverpool, with a cargo valued at one hundred thousand dollars, the *Ann Dorothy*, an American vessel in the possession of the enemy, and two other valuable brigs.   In January, 1815, this privateer sailed on her last cruise, in which she appeared off the Western Isles, Portugal, the Madeiras, the Canaries, Brazil, Cayenne, Surinam, and through the West Indies, returning to port in eighty days from the time of sailing.   In this protracted search for British merchantmen the privateer made only three prizes: the 3-masted schooner *George*, which, being of little value, was released, the coppered brig *Flying Fish*, with a cargo worth two hundred thousand dollars, which was sent into New Bedford; and the brig *Legal Tender*, the last being recaptured March 7, 1815, by the 74-gun ship of the line *Spencer*.

In her entire career during this war the *David Porter* made fifteen prizes.

CHAPTER XI.

AFTER the departure of the *David Porter* for
America, Captain Coggeshall remained several
months in France attending to the interests of his
employers. At this time, April, 1814, owing to the
unsettled political condition of the empire and the
near approach of the English army, there was
scarcely an American vessel in French waters. The
privateer schooner *Kemp*, Captain Jacobs, of Baltimore, was at Nantes, and the schooners *Lion* and
Spencer were at l' Orient, which about completes the
list. The *Lion*, sometimes known as *Lyon*, was a
fast vessel out of Salem, mounting twenty-two guns
and commanded by Captain T. Cloutman, and others
at different times. In her last cruise she had taken
fifteen prizes, many of which were destroyed at sea,
and the cargoes, which realized four hundred thousand dollars, had been sent into l'Orient. The
Spencer carried only nine guns and was commanded
by Captain G. Moore, of Philadelphia. She had
taken two of the enemy's schooners laden with wine.

There were a number of American gentlemen,
commanders of privateers, supercargoes, etc., in
France at this time, who had become well acquainted with each other, and when it was known
that such an able commander as Coggeshall was
there without a command they soon arranged to secure a fast-sailing vessel for him for the purpose of
operating against British commerce. The *Leo*, a fine

350

vessel of three hundred and twenty tons, built in Baltimore, then lying at l'Orient, was selected. She was owned by Thomas Lewis, an American residing in Bordeaux. This privateer, earlier in the war, while under the command of Captain J. Hewes, had taken fifteen prizes, ten of which had been destroyed, three were ransomed for sixty thousand dollars, and one, the brig *Alexander*, was cast away near Ferrol while the privateer was entering that port in a gale. One of her prizes was an East Indiaman valued at two million dollars. Sixty thousand dollars in specie were taken out of the Indiaman and she was sent to America in charge of a prize crew, but was recaptured by an English sloop of war before gaining port. On her first passage to France the *Leo* captured the brig *Pomona*, from Lisbon for Newfoundland, carrying eight 12-pounders. She was sent into Belfast, Maine. In the earlier part of the war Captain Hewes commanded the privateer *Bunker Hill*, a schooner of six guns, which made six prizes. She was captured while off our coast, August 21, 1812, by the British frigate *Belridera*. As this occurred shortly after the narrow escape of this frigate from Captain Rodgers' squadron, the commander of the *Belridera*, Captain Richard Byron, undoubtedly congratulated himself on his lucky capture. A second *Bunker Hill* was launched toward the close of the war.

On November 2, 1814, the *Leo* was purchased by an association of Americans abroad and under the sanction of William H. Crawford, the American minister to France, was commissioned as a privateer. It was proposed that the *Leo* should first make a short cruise in search of prizes and then proceed to Charleston, South Carolina, for a cargo of cotton. At this time there were a large number of American officers and seamen in several of the western ports of France supported by our Government. They were, as a rule, exchanged prisoners who had been detained in port by the failure of their ships to get to sea, and as their terms of enlistment had not expired they continued to draw pay from the Government. From these Captain Coggeshall was able to select a most desirable complement of officers and men. His first and second officers were Pierre G. Depeyster and Henry Allen. Azor O. Lewis, a brother of the former owner of the *Leo*, was taken as one of the prize masters. These, together with eighty-six petty officers and seamen, constituted the privateer's complement.

So much influence was exerted over the Government of Louis XVIII by England that the Americans were fearful of being detained in port on some technicality, and for this reason every exertion was made to hasten the *Leo's* departure. Captain Coggeshall found that her hull was in fairly good condition, but that her sails and rigging were much out of repair. By working night and day, however, he was ready for sea with provisions enough for fifty days by November 6th, and dropped down near the mouth of the outer harbor. How well founded were the fears of the Americans of detention in port will be seen by the orders Captain Coggeshall now received from the local authorities, which were to return to his anchorage and disarm his vessel. Waiting on the commanding officer of the port the American was told that he must take out all of his firearms and guns except one, but the commandant jokingly added that this gun would be sufficient to take a dozen English vessels before reaching Charleston. Every gun aboard, accordingly, was removed excepting the long brass 12-pounder amidships. In the night, however, Captain Coggeshall managed to smuggle aboard some twenty or thirty muskets, and with this armament he sailed on November 8th and steered for the chops of the British Channel.

It was soon found that the 12-pounder was nearly useless in action, so that the Americans were obliged to depend almost entirely upon boarding. This in rough weather was a dangerous operation, as the delicately built Baltimore craft in all probability would have her sides crushed in should she come in contact with a heavy English merchant ship. It was this circumstance that compelled Captain Coggeshall, when only a few days out, to allow a large merchantman to escape him. At six o'clock on the morning of November 13th, while near the Scilly Islands, the *Leo* discovered a brig to leeward, and after giving her a shot induced her to surrender. She was from Leghorn bound up the Channel. Taking her people into the *Leo* Captain Coggeshall placed a prize crew aboard, and ordered the brig to make for America.

Down to this time the *Leo* had been experiencing very heavy weather, which, together with the peculiar condition of her armament, induced her commander to change his cruising ground, and heading southward he appeared off the coast of Spain. On November 18th the *Leo* was chased by a brig of war. At eight o'clock in the evening she passed a merchant brig, but Captain Coggeshall did not deem it prudent to stop, as the cruiser was still in hot pursuit of him. By dawn of the following day all trace of the war brig had been lost. At 7 A. M. chase was given to a sail off the weather bow. Three hours later she was captured, and was found to be an English cutter, from Teneriffe for London, laden with wine. Taking out twenty quarter casks of wine, together with her crew and some rigging, Captain Coggeshall caused her to be scuttled.

On the morning of the following day the *Leo* made a sail to windward, and after four hours of maneuvering to get a favorable position he discovered her to be an English brig of war, armed with carronades, or guns having a short range. Being to windward, and having the superiority of sailing, Captain Coggeshall kept just within long range of the enemy and then indulged in some target practice with his long tom. This was kept up for about an hour, when the *Leo* hauled off, and in time the stranger disappeared below the horizon. The Englishmen fired some thirty or forty shots at the audacious privateer, most of them falling short, a few going over, and only one hitting the *Leo*. That shot passed through the bends amidships and lodged in the hold. The next day the *Leo* fell in with an English frigate, which endeavored to decoy the American under her guns by showing Portuguese colors; but the Yankees were not so easily deceived, and, showing the Stars and Stripes, Captain Coggeshall hauled close to the wind and soon ran the frigate out of sight.

During the night the weather was squally. Early in the morning an English schooner, from Malaga bound for Dublin, with a cargo of grapes, was captured and sent to the United States in charge of a prize crew. In the next two days the *Leo* spoke several neutral vessels, and on the afternoon of the 24th was chased by two frigates, but easily outsailed them. At three o'clock on the afternoon of the 25th the *Leo* chased a sail, but in half an hour Captain Coggeshall discovered her to be a frigate, when he hauled upon the wind. The frigate fired a gun and showed American colors, to which the privateer responded with the United States ensign, but after a few minutes this was replaced by the English colors. Upon seeing this the frigate fired three or four shots, but finding that they fell short desisted. In the night Captain Coggeshall lost sight of the frigate.

On November 26th the *Leo* captured an English ship, from Palermo for London, laden with brimstone, rags, mats, etc., which was ordered to the United States after her crew of twenty men had been taken out. At one o'clock on the afternoon of December 1st, while the *Leo* was off the Rock of

Lisbon, a large frigate was discovered making for her under a press of sail. The wind at this juncture was blowing strong from the north-northwest, and at times came on in squalls. Captain Coggeshall steered westward so as to weather the frigate, but unfortunately at 2 P. M. the *Leo* gave a sudden lurch, which carried away her foremast about a third below its head, and a few minutes later it broke again, close by the board. While in this unfortunate condition Captain Coggeshall had the mortification of seeing an English packet—probably with a large amount of specie aboard—pass within pistol shot of him. As night was fast coming on, and the frigate still was some miles distant, Captain Coggeshall entertained great hopes of being able to make Lisbon before morning. Accordingly he rigged a jury foremast and made good progress until near daylight, when it became almost calm, at which time the *Leo* was in sight of the Rock of Lisbon. The Americans then resorted to towing until 1 P. M., when a light breeze carried them to the mouth of the Tagus and a Lisbon pilot was taken aboard. But unfortunately the ebb tide began to run, and with it a British frigate came out of the Tagus and in a few minutes had the privateer under her guns, compelling the American to surrender. She was the 38-gun frigate *Granicus*, Captain W. F. Wise.

Captain Coggeshall, his officers, and men were taken aboard the frigate and carried to Gibraltar. The Americans were received by the British with great kindness. Captain Coggeshall said: "Captain Wise was a fine, gentlemanly man, and always treated me and my officers with respect and kindness. We messed in the wardroom. I had a stateroom to myself, and was as comfortable and happy as I could be under the circumstances. I used to dine with Captain Wise almost daily. He frequently said to me: 'Don't feel depressed by captivity, but strive to forget that you are a prisoner, and imagine

that you are only a passenger.' In the course of conversation he said to me: 'Coggeshall, you Americans
are a singular people as respects seamanship and
enterprise. In England we can not build such vessels as your Baltimore clippers. We have no such
models, and even if we had them they would be of
no service to us, for we never could sail them as you
do. We have now and then taken some of your
schooners with our fast-sailing frigates. They have
sometimes caught one of them under their lee in a
heavy gale of wind by outcarrying them. Then,
again, we have taken a few with our boats in calm
weather. We are afraid of their long masts and
heavy spars, and soon cut down and reduce them to
our standard. We strengthen them, put up bulk-
heads, etc., after which they lose their sailing qualities and are of no further service as cruising vessels.'
He also remarked that the famous privateer *True
Blooded Yankee*, which had done them so much mischief, once belonged to their navy; that they captured her from the French; that she afterward was
retaken, and finally got into the hands of the Americans; that she then outsailed everything and that
none of their cruisers could touch her, and concluded
by adding that we were a most ingenious people."

Captain Wise, in friendly conversation with Captain Coggeshall, revealed a little inside history of
American privateers as seen from the enemy's stand-
point, which is as amusing as it is gratifying. He
told how the 74-gun ship of the line *Superb* was
cruising off the mouth of the Garonne one morning,
when the fog lifted and revealed one of the American privateer schooners as snug as a bug in a rug
under her guns. No one aboard the huge war ship
for a moment anticipated that the little craft, so
completely at their mercy, would attempt to escape,
and so no preparations were made to clear the guns.
The quick eye of the Yankee skipper, however, noted
the overconfidence of the English, and suddenly mak-

ing sail, he was soon beyond the range of the war ship's broadside. The English, of course, made sail in chase, but their ship got into the wind and made stern board—so that, before they could get sufficient steerageway to tack after the schooner, the little craft had made three or four tacks right in the wind's eye, and was soon out of gunshot and escaped. It is a singular circumstance that Captain Coggeshall's father was a first cousin of Captain Isaac Hull, the famous commander of the *Constitution* when she fought the *Guerrière*, while the captain of the defeated frigate, Richard Dacres, was a cousin of Captain Wise.

Arriving at Gibraltar, Captain Coggeshall, with his first and second officers, Pierre G. Depeyster and Henry Allen, was taken to the Admiralty office to undergo an examination preparatory to the condemnation of the *Leo* by the authorities. On the first day, the American officers were landed without a guard, as they gave their promise not to attempt to escape. On the second day, however, the Americans refused to give the promise, so that a lieutenant, a sergeant, and four marines were detailed to guard them. It is needless to say that the privateersmen had made up their minds to escape at the first opportunity, and they secreted money about their persons to aid them in the attempt.

Arriving at the Admiralty office, Captain Coggeshall took a seat in the court room, waiting for the examination to recommence. His attention was soon attracted by Mr. Allen, who was standing in the doorway beckoning to him. Going to the door, it was found that the British lieutenant had left his post. Asking the sergeant to take a glass of wine in a neighboring shop, Captain Coggeshall led the way into the dingy place, followed by the sergeant and two American prisoners. While the sergeant was looking in another direction, Captain Coggeshall slipped out, passed quickly over a little park, turned a corner, and made his way to the Land Port Gate in the northwest extremity of the town. Although he had given the sergeant the slip, our privateersman was still far from being safe. He was within the walls of Gibraltar, each gate of which was strongly guarded. His dress consisted of a blue coat, black stock, and black cockade, with an eagle in the center. By removing the eagle he presented the appearance of an English naval officer; and relying on this semblance, he gave the sentinel a severe glance, who saluted respectfully, and in another moment the Yankee was without the walls.

At the mole he engaged a boatman, who took him aboard a Norwegian galiot. To the master of this vessel the privateersman made known his escape and begged for concealment. This was generously granted, and a few minutes later the American appeared on deck dressed in Norwegian costume and with a large pipe in his mouth. From this vessel Captain Coggeshall went aboard a smuggling craft, under cover of night, and in it made his way to Algeciras, on the west side of Gibraltar Bay, where for three days he remained concealed in the home of the leader of the smugglers. From this place Captain Coggeshall gradually made his way to Lisbon, and thence in the Portuguese brig *Tres Hermanos* to New York, arriving there May 9, 1815. Mr. Depeyster and Mr. Allen were not as fortunate in escaping. They gave the sergeant the slip as Captain Coggeshall had done, but on reaching the mole they were recaptured.

CHAPTER XII.

As nearly all the Americans taken prisoners on the high seas by the British in this war were privateersmen, an extended notice of their treatment will be necessary. Only a few of our man-of-warsmen were captured, and in most cases they were speedily exchanged. At Melville Island, near Halifax, there were, in 1813, some twelve hundred American sailors, the majority of them taken in privateers. This island is described as being "a little above the surface of the water, and from its low situation is generally very unhealthy. Its circumference is about one thousand six hundred feet. On this nauseous spot is situated a building of two stories, one hundred and thirty feet in length by forty broad, and of the upper room thirty feet is set apart for the sick. The remainder of this apartment now contains one hundred and eighty American prisoners. In the lower room are seven hundred and seventy more, cooped up to breathe the same air and generate diseases by this narrow confine. Three hundred and fifty more are near this island in a prison ship. In this situation, under the most rigorous treatment, our brethren remain. . . . To heighten the poignancy of their reflections, they are told by the British agent, Miller, 'to die and be damned, the king has one hundred and fifty acres of land to bury them in.'"

Many instances of the petty tyranny of the officials at this place are given. On one occasion some

British officers were endeavoring to persuade an
American lad to enter their navy. An officer of the
American privateer *Yorktown*, also a prisoner, happened to be standing by and overheard the conversation. He said, in an undertone, "Joe, don't go."
The boy didn't go, but for his "impertinence" in the
matter the officer of the *Yorktown* was placed in the
"black hole" on short allowance for ten days.

No less unfeeling were the British prison officials
at Jamaica and Barbadoes. At the former place an
American prisoner records, under date of December
13, 1812: "I wrote you on the 8th inst. informing you
of my being captured by the sloop of war *Fawn*, Captain Fellows, about twenty miles to northeast of
Cape Tiberon, and carried to Jamaica, where we were
all immediately sent to prison, and we were treated
more like brutes than human beings. Our allowance is half a pound of horse meat, a pound and a
half of bread that had been condemned, being more
of worms than bread, and one gill of beans. That
is all our allowance for twenty-four hours! When
I was taken I had all my charts, quadrant, and
clothes taken from me, and was not allowed even
to ask for them. There are now in this prison ship
four hundred and fifty-two prisoners and more arriving daily. It is reported to-day that we are all to be
sent to England by the fleet which is to sail in six
days." Another correspondent writes that the Jamaica prison ships are "infested with rats, centi-
pedes, snakes, roaches, and lizards."

From the Norfolk Herald we have the following:
"A young man by the name of Thomas King, a
native of Charleston, South Carolina, and formerly
a seaman in the United States brig *Vixen*, having
been paroled at Jamaica, was returning home in the
cartel *Rebecca Sims*, when he was impressed on board
the 74-gun ship *Poictiers*, as she was entering the
Delaware, under the pretext of his being an Englishman. The *Poictiers* soon afterward was ordered

to Bermuda, where, having arrived, young King was transferred to the 64-gun ship *Ruby*. Having determined to attempt his escape at the first opportunity that offered, he purchased of one of his messmates a small pocket compass, which he always carried about him. King kept his eye on a fine, large sailing boat belonging to the ship, which commonly was kept alongside. On Sunday of July 25, 1813, some of the officers had taken this boat out sailing and returned alongside in the dusk of the evening, where she remained some time with her masts, sails, rudder, etc., all standing. This youthful adventurer, having secured two loaves of bread and some water, got into the boat, cast off the fast, and drifted along with the tide till he had got some distance off, when he hoisted sail and took a very unceremonious leave of the *Ruby* and Bermuda. Thus in an open boat, with scarce provisions enough to last him two days, he committed himself to the wind and waves to traverse an expanse of six or seven hundred miles. When inclined to sleep he tied the tiller to his arm, so that if the boat wore round it would cause a sudden jerk of the tiller, which would wake him again. He experienced no debility or sickness from the scantiness of his meals, and, with fine weather nearly the whole way, he made a landing about ten miles south of Cape Henry on Tuesday, the 3d of August, being a passage of nine days. The boat is seven tons burden, and if she could be got round here would probably sell for a hundred and fifty dollars."

In a letter addressed to James Turner, the British agent of prisoners of war at Port Royal, Jamaica, the agents for the American prisoners—William Wescott, John McFate, and James Stevens—under date of March 30, 1813, wrote:

"L'Améthyste Prison Ship.

"SIR: Being agents for prisoners of war at this place, we conceive you to be the proper person to address in stating the grievances under which we

26

labor, relying on your attention to discover and will-ingness to adopt those measures which may be best calculated to afford us relief. This morning Lieutenant Dance, of the Fifth West India Regiment, accompanied by a guard of seven soldiers with loaded muskets, came on board this ship and informed us we must go with him to Kingston to attend a court-martial. Upon our replying that we did not know in what manner we were to be concerned in that court, he exclaimed, ' You must go, and if force is necessary to compel you, I am directed to resort to it!' Our hesitation increasing, he went on deck, and brought down with him four soldiers with naked bayonets, himself and Lieutenant Geddes (the officer of the guard) accompanying them with drawn swords. . . . We then asked Lieutenant Dance whether, in the event of our consenting to go, his officers were to escort us through the streets. He pledged his honor they should not, but that ourselves should go on one side of the street and they on the other. We then consented to go. But imagine what must have been our chagrin and disappointment when, on arriving at Kingston, the lieutenant, disregarding his promise, careless of our feelings, and not respecting our character as officers—two of us having the honor to belong to the United States navy—wantonly and ignominiously marched us through the streets of the city like malefactors, himself going before and his soldiers following and walking on either side of us. In this disgraceful manner we were deposited in the guardhouse of the barracks.

"In the guardhouse we remained from 8.30 A. M. till 1 P. M. without knowing whether our presence was necessary at the court-martial, without knowing for what purpose we were sent to Kingston, without having any sustenance or refreshment of any kind, and without being permitted, during our confinement, to have any person visit us. Having confined us as long as they thought proper, they consigned us to the care of Lieutenant Grant, who marched us to the boat and brought us to the prison ship again. You will perceive, sir, that, having eaten nothing the night before, we were deprived of everything for the support of nature from three o'clock P. M., 29th inst., till after three o'clock on the 30th (the time we were sent on board). But this is the least part of our complaint, though we leave you to reflect whether such treatment is becoming in the officers of one civilized nation at war with another. We are here for no crime. The fortune of war has placed us in your power. We have not degraded ourselves by any indecorous conduct since we became your prisoners. We preserve the same routine of duty here as we did on board our own vessels. Why, then, this insult—this wanton abuse? Why take the advantage of defenseless prisoners for the purpose of venting your malignity and contempt for the American nation? Your Government can never approve such proceedings; the American most certainly will not. Your Government, we are induced to believe, are desirous of preserving those sacred rules of justice and honor with regard to prisoners of war which they require of ours. You will therefore confer a favor on us by submitting the circumstances of our case to Vice-Admiral Stirling, who, from the kind regard he has ever paid to the petitions and remonstrances of American prisoners, will, we trust, use his best endeavors toward ameliorating our present unhappy condition."

Such being the treatment of Americans in British prisons on this side of the Atlantic, we feel no surprise in discovering that they were subjected to even greater cruelty on the other side of the ocean. At the outbreak of hostilities between the United States and Great Britain, many of the American seamen who had been impressed into English war ships refused to serve, and for this display of patriotism they were severely handled. When the news of the war reached Toulon, where the British fleet had assembled, many of our seamen refused to continue in that service, upon which they were thrown into prison at Malta.

Captain Jeduthan Upton, Jr., of Salem, who was a prisoner of war in this conflict, said: " The method of ascertaining whether these men who refused to serve on the ground of being Americans was to conduct the man to prison. He was then severely flogged for several days successively, and if he bore it manfully he was given up as an American. If not, he was kept on duty."

On December 16, 1812, the American 12-gun privateer schooner *Swordfish*, Captain J. Evans, of Gloucester, got to sea with a complement of eighty-two men and boys. Twelve days out she was chased by the British frigate *Elephant*. After a hard run of eleven hours, during which the privateer had thrown overboard ten of her guns, she was captured and sent to England. When the surgeon of the *Swordfish* was returned to the United States in a cartel, he reported that when he was in Portsmouth the 74-gun ship of the line *Cornwall* arrived there from a foreign port, having on board " thirty impressed American seamen; that a part of them requested to be considered as prisoners of war, and refused to do duty; that in consequence they were put in irons and ordered to be fed on bread and water. The British officer, suspecting that they had been advised to this step by the surgeon of the *Swordfish*, ordered him between decks; nor was he again permitted his usual liberty till he embarked in the cartel. We are also furnished with the names of one hundred and thirteen Americans who had been impressed who have been sent on board the *St. Antonia* prison ship; two of them had been enslaved eighteen years in the British service, and the others

from a half to fifteen years. There were about eight
hundred prisoners in the ship. It had been considered sickly; about thirty had died. Provisions were
bad in quality and scant: half a pound of beef and
one and a half pounds of bread per day; two days in
the week they had one pound pickled herring or
other fish and one pound potatoes as their allowance. From 5 P. M to 6 A. M the prisoners were confined under hatches."

There was no distinction between officers and
men allowed in the prisons which they had the misfortune to enter. Officers and men of privateers
were not permitted a parole unless the vessel in
which they were captured carried fourteen guns at
the time of capture. Upton was captured in the
brig *Hunter*, December 23, 1812, by the British frigate *Phœbe*, Captain James Hillyar, who always had
a high estimation of the American seaman—especially after his bloody encounter with Captain Porter in the *Essex*. Upton had thrown overboard
twelve of his fourteen guns in the hope of escaping.
When taken prisoner he made every effort to get a
parole, and, although the commander of the *Phœbe*
most honorably abetted these endeavors, Upton remained a common prisoner.

An American prisoner at Gibraltar wrote from
that place: "Our fare is but scant, I can assure you.
We are put on an allowance of six ounces per man
a day, and that of condemned and rotten provisions
which no American would attempt to give to his
dogs. Every American master, mate, or seaman
that is brought here is stripped of all his bedding.
For my part I was deprived of my last blanket, and
even to the most trifling things that were on board
my ship. Captain Selby, of the brig *Margaret*, had
his shirt stripped off his back, and the last farthing
of money he had was also taken from him, amounting to three hundred and forty-six dollars, all of
which was done by order of the British commodore

residing in Gibraltar.[1]   Before I was confined on
board the floating dungeon, if it had not been for the
fresh fish that my mate and myself caught alongside (all my crew being taken out on their arrival
and put under close confinement) we must certainly
have perished."

In August, 1813, a number of exchanged prisoners arrived in Rhode Island in a cartel, and the Providence Phœnix has the following note concerning
them: "Many of these prisoners, we learn, had been
impressed, and some of them had been detained during eight long years. On being released on board
the prison ships, after having refused to do duty in
his Majesty's floating hells, their bodies were found
to be scarred with wounds and their backs lacerated
by stripes, inflicted upon them for their obstinacy in
refusing to fight against their native country."

An American prisoner in the prison ship *Samson*,
at Chatham, England, writing on June 8, 1813, says:
" I have been now six weeks a prisoner, during which
time I have been on board eleven of their floating
hells. In this ship, besides Americans, are five hundred Frenchmen, some of whom have been prison-

---

[1] In striking contrast to this piratical treatment we have the following
correspondence between Captain Bainbridge, of the *Constitution*, and
Lieutenant-General Hislop, who was captured in the *Java*, December,
1812. Bainbridge wrote from San Salvador, January, 1813: " It is painful for me to learn that you have lost the plate presented by the colony
of Demerara. It can not be found on board here, and I candidly believe
it is not here. If, however, it should be on board, it will be found, and
you may rely on my sending it to England for you. If it came from the
Java, I have no doubt it was taken among some other baggage." On the
same day Lieutenant-General Hislop wrote: "I am happy in being able
to inform you that in opening the large cases of my baggage one of them
has been found to contain two chests, one of which proves to be the one
which could not be accounted for, which mistake arose from the silver-
smith in numbering the packages. I am extremely sorry that this circumstance should have occasioned you any trouble, and beg to assure you
that I shall always remain, with esteem and respect, dear sir,

" Your very obedient servant,

" T. Hislop."

ers ten years. Lice, hunger, and nakedness are no
strangers here. There are one thousand two hundred Americans and five thousand French prisoners
in this harbor. Of the Americans about seven hundred have been heretofore impressed, and have been
sent here from on board English men-of-war. Would
to God I were at home again!"

But it was at Dartmoor Prison that the greatest
atrocities were perpetrated against American prisoners. Dartmoor Prison, or Depot, as it was called
by the English, was about fifteen miles northeast
of Plymouth, in the County of Devonshire. "Its appearance and situation," wrote an American who
was confined there many months, "is the most unpleasant and disagreeable imaginable. The country
around, as far as the eye extends, is uneven, barren,
and dreary; not a tree, shrub, or scarce a plant is
seen for many miles round. Here and there appears
a miserable thatched cottage whose outward appearance well bespeaks the misery and poverty that
dwells within. Here no cheering prospect greets
the prisoner's eye; bountiful Nature denies all her
sweets and seems to sympathize with the unhappy
prisoners. The climate is rather unhealthy; the
prisoners are almost continually cold during nine
months of the year, owing probably to its height,
it being upward of one thousand seven hundred feet
from the surface of the sea."

That the above description of the dreariness of
Dartmoor is not exaggerated will be seen by the
following account taken from a London periodical
published in 1880, and referring to the condition of
the moor in 1845: "Lost on the moor! . . . Scores
of men had so vanished and been never heard of
since. Natives, even, accustomed to the dangers of
bog, crag, and fell, of overwhelming, blinding mist,
of overtaking nightfall, of the sudden, deep, obscur-
ing snow, and of the lost track—natives alive to all
these perils have been lost on the moor, nor any

trace of them ever found. What wonder, then, that a Londoner, entirely unused to and unknowing of the treachery lurking in such a wild, should now and again share the same fate? The thing, indeed, was too common to create much more than a nine-days' astonishment."

Dartmoor Prison, where many American prisoners were confined.

A more scathing commentary on the brutality of selecting Dartmoor as a prison for American and French prisoners could not be had. These unfortunate men, being strangers in the country, of course were unaware of the dangers lurking in these bogs—dangers which even the natives, though " alive to all these perils," have not been able to pass through in safety. What was the object, then, in placing several thousands of Americans in this place? Certainly they would endeavor to escape, but in this case not to liberty, but to a horrible death in the bogs and crags.

Dartmoor Prison was divided into seven yards, with adjoining apartments for the accommodation of prisoners at night, each of which was expected to hold from one thousand one hundred to one thousand five hundred men, guarded by two thousand militia and two companies of artillery. The prisons were strongly built of stone and surrounded by two circular walls, the outer wall measuring one mile in circumference. On the inner wall were military walks for sentinels. Within this wall were iron palisades, distant about twenty feet and ten feet in height. Adjoining the outer wall were guardhouses, placed north, east, and south. There were separate yards which communicated with each other through a passage about one hundred and fifty feet long and twenty broad, guarded on each side by iron bars, over which, and fronting No. 4, was a military walk for sentinels. Opposite this passage was the market square. The first yard contained three prisons, viz.: Nos. 1, 2, and 3, of which Nos. 1 and 3 only were (in 1814) occupied, No. 2 standing vacant. The next yard, No. 4, was occupied solely by blacks, and was separated from the other yards by two stone walls about fifteen feet high. The next yard contained prisons Nos. 5, 6, and 7, of which only Nos. 5 and 7 were occupied, No. 6, like No. 2, standing vacant. North of No. 1, between the inner wall and the iron railings, was the place of punishment, four Americans having been sentenced to suffer imprisonment during the war for attempting to blow up prize ships. This prison was calculated to contain sixty men, who were allowed a blanket and straw bedding, their daily allowance of provisions being considerably reduced. Fronting No. 1 yard was a wall separating it from the hospital, and fronting No. 3 was another wall separating it from the inner barracks. The market square was nearly square, and accommodated five thousand persons. It was opened every day, Sundays excepted, at eleven o'clock and closed at two o'clock. At the upper part of the market were two stone houses—one for the prisoners and the other for stores. The other buildings attached to the depot were houses for the turnkeys, clerks, one for the agent, and another for the doctor.

To enter either of the prison yards from without, it was necessary to pass through five gates. Fronting the outer gate was a reservoir of water, which was brought the distance of six miles by means of a canal. The hospital was under the superintendence of a physician, who had two assistants. Dr. George M'Grath, the superintendent in 1812–'15, was a man of eminence and skill, and will ever be remembered by Americans with esteem and respect. The sick uniformly received from him every attention. In 1815 there were five thousand six hundred Americans in this depot, nearly one half of whom were seamen impressed before the war.

Great hardships were suffered by Americans in the winter of 1813–'14, which proved to be unusually cold. Through the knavery of some British officials many of the prisoners had been robbed of most of their clothing, and, though almost naked, they were not allowed to have any fires. It was not until April, 1814, that these sufferers received from Mr. Beasly, the agent of the American Government for our seamen held as prisoners in Great Britain, a suit of clothes and the allowance of two and a half pence a day.

On the capture of the privateer *Rattlesnake*, in 1814, her men were thrown into Dartmoor Prison. In keeping with his reputation for needless cruelty, Major Thomas George Shortland, who then commanded the prison, made no distinction between the officers and seamen of the privateer, but placed them all in one apartment. Among the prisoners was the second officer of the *Rattlesnake*, who has concealed his identity under the initials R. G. Immediately upon his incarceration R. G. determined to make his escape, and with this object in view he secretly bought up all the old rope-yarn he could in the prison, and made from it a rope eighty feet long, the distance from the top window of the prison in which he was confined to the ground. By some ingenious

manner he also succeeded in making a suit of uniform like that worn by the sentinels, which he put
on under a greatcoat of the same color and pattern
worn by the guards. He had noticed that at night
the sentinels were accustomed to carry their muskets with muzzles downward and under their great-
coats. Not being able to procure a musket, R. G.
secured an umbrella, which, being concealed under
his coat, with just the end exposed to view, made a
good representation of a musket.

Having secured the countersign for the night
from one of the sentinels for a consideration of six
guineas, R. G. lowered himself from his window one
night shortly before twelve o'clock, when the guards
were changed. As the gates were thrown open for
the relief guards R. G. boldly presented himself at
the place with the other sentinels. He received the
usual challenge:

" Who goes there? "

" A friend," was the answer, and on advancing
and giving the countersign he was told to pass. At
this moment, however, the sentinel who had betrayed
the countersign to the prisoner for six guineas
stepped forward and told the gateman that the pretended sentinel was one of the prisoners. The gateman at first refused to credit this, but, on the traitor
insisting, R. G. was arrested and the deception discovered. Infuriated by this treachery, R. G. sprang
upon the fellow and attempted to kill him with the
only weapon he possessed, a dagger. The guards
were too quick for him, however, and, being overpowered, R. G. was thrown into the " black hole "
and kept there ten days on bread and water.

Being brought before Shortland, R. G. was asked
how he succeeded in getting the countersign. He
said: " If the man who gave it to me had behaved
honorably, death could not have wrested the secret
from me. That is the character, sir, of the Americans
—always true to their engagements. But as the sol-

dier evidently took my money only to deceive me,
I will turn the scale on him and expose his conduct.
His name is ——. He gave me the countersign for
six guineas, and then basely betrayed me." Assured
of the sentinel's treachery, Shortland had three
hundred lashes applied to him. Again questioning
R. G., Shortland said: "Mr. G., I respect you. You
are a brave man, and if you will not attempt to
escape again I will give you my honor, as a British
officer, that you shall be exchanged and go home
in the first cartel." Mr. G. declined this offer, declaring that he would make his escape that very
night.

As the guards had not noticed the rope from the
window, it seemed as if the daring prisoner might
make good his threat, in spite of Shortland's declaration that the sentries would be doubled and a special
watch kept on him. The guards were doubled on
the following night, but that very circumstance
seemed to favor the prisoner's attempt, for such an
unusual number of sentinels caused some confusion
at the gates when the relief came. True to his word,
R. G. made his second attempt to escape that night.
Having ascertained the password from another sentinel for three guineas, he descended the rope just at
midnight, and passed through the gate with the other
sentinels, having given the countersign "Wells."
He was similarly challenged and examined several
times before getting clear of the yard. On clearing
the prison he made for the coast, where he arrived
almost famished. Finding an 18-foot boat on the
beach with only one oar in it, he put to sea with the
intention of gaining the coast of France, using his
single oar as a rudder and his umbrella and greatcoat as sails. When he had covered half the distance, a brig of war passed very close to him, but
by taking in all his "sails" and lying down in the
bottom of the boat he avoided detection. After a
dangerous passage of thirty-six hours he reached the

coast of France, where he was most hospitably received.

The brutalities with which American prisoners in Dartmoor were treated reached a climax on April 6, 1815, when, under the orders of the infamous Shortland, the entire guard of one thousand men was ordered out and deliberately fired volley after volley into the thousands of unarmed and helpless men penned in the yards. The butchery took place on the evening of April 6th. Shortland, about nine o'clock that night, discovered a small hole that had been dug in one of the inner walls of the prison, and immediately jumped to the conclusion that an attempt to escape was about to be made. The existence of the hole was known to not more than a quarter of the Americans confined in the place. Shortland had been to Plymouth that day, where he had been imbibing liquor until, by the time he returned to the prison, he was in a drunken fury. He had long nourished a spite against his prisoners, which unfortunately had been encouraged by the bold and perhaps imprudent demeanor of our men, who, knowing that peace had existed for several months, were angry at what, to them, seemed unnecessary delay. Most of the men, knowing Shortland's resentment, very naturally attributed this additional vexation to his personal spite for them, and lost no opportunity for showing him " what they thought of him." Shortland, in the few preceding months, had frequently expressed his intention of " fixing the damned rascals " before they got beyond his power, and the discovery of the hole referred to gave him the desired excuse for calling out the entire guard.

Immediately upon the rapid ringing of the alarm bell and the ordering out of the whole guard, the mass of the prisoners, who were peaceably walking about the yards, ignorant of the cause of these unusual demonstrations, moved toward the gate, where alone they were able to discover what was going on. Glad of some excitement that would break the monotony of their imprisonment, the crowd of several thousand prisoners surged toward the gate, pushing and swaying in eager expectation of something new. Under the heavy pressure the gate gave way, forcing those in front into the second yard, while those behind, not knowing what had occurred, continued to press on, pushing those nearest the gateway farther into the second yard. At this moment Shortland came into the inner square at the head of his men, while a large force of guards suddenly appeared on the walls, ready to fire into the mass of human beings. The prisoners, not knowing that they were the object of this martial demonstration, continued to press forward in their eagerness to witness what was about to happen. At this moment one of the friendly British guards seized an opportunity to warn one of the prisoners that they were about to be fired upon, whereupon there was a rush of the captives to regain their proper yard, and from thence to their cells or prison rooms.

Observing that Shortland was about to begin a butchery of the helpless prisoners, the officers of the garrison declined to give the orders to fire, and resigned their powers to Shortland. But the drunken brute was not thus to be thwarted of his bloodthirsty purpose, and he gave the word for the soldiers to fire. The command was obeyed, and several volleys were poured into the helpless mass of men as they struggled to pass through their own gate and regain their prisons. That the British soldiery abhorred the criminal orders of Shortland is evidenced by the fact that a comparatively small number of men were struck, most of the bullets being aimed too high and taking effect on the surrounding walls. After the bulk of the prisoners had gained the cover of their cells Shortland led a charge, sword in hand, and began a "valorous" (as it seemed to him in his

rum-crazed senses) assault on the few men who had
not as yet gained the shelter of the cells. One of the
prisoners afterward said, under oath: "Their murderous pursuers had now entered the yard of each
prison, making a general charge on man and boy,
sheathing their ruthless bayonets in the bodies of
the retreating prisoners, and completing the work of
destruction by the discharge of another volley of
musketry in the backs of the hindmost, who were
forcing their passage over the wounded into their
prison. Nor did they stop here, but patroled the yard
to find some solitary fugitive who had sought safety
in flight. 'One poor, affrighted wretch had fled close
to the wall of one of the prisons, fearing to move lest
he should meet his death. Those demons of hell discovered him, and the bloody Shortland gave the fatal
order to fire. In vain the trembling victim fell on his
knees, and in that imploring attitude besought their
compassion, begged them to spare a life almost exhausted by suffering and confinement. He pleaded
to brutes; he appealed to tigers. 'Fire!' cried
Shortland, and several balls were discharged into
his bosom.

"One circumstance that occurred during the
massacre ought not to be omitted. One of the British soldiers belonging to the same regiment that performed this work was lighting a lamp at the door of
prison No. 3 when the carnage commenced, and in
the hurry of retreat he was forced inside among the
wounded and exasperated prisoners. In the height
of their resentment the eye of vengeance was for a
moment directed to the only enemy that chance
had thus thrown in their power. It was but for a
moment. The dignity of the American character was
not thus to be sullied. To the astonishment of this
affrighted soldier, who was expecting every moment
to be immolated on the altar of revenge as some
atonement for the manes of our murdered countrymen, he received assurances of safety and protec-

tion. Accordingly, when the doors were opened to discharge the wounded, this man was delivered up to his astonished comrades in perfect safety."

Satisfied with having " fixed the damned rascals " to the extent of seven men killed and sixty wounded, Shortland withdrew his troops, and, as if to cover his guilt, sent a dispatch to Plymouth stating his " danger," and on the following day a strong reënforcement arrived. It is needless to say that every honorable British officer who witnessed the butchery and the scene of it afterward denounced, in private, Shortland as a cowardly cur, though in their official capacity they were compelled to give some color to his faint-hearted plea of " duty." The matter was thoroughly investigated on both sides, and it leaves no room for doubt that the entire disgraceful occurrence was the result of the long-pent spite of a drunken officer who could not allow the objects of his cowardly enmity to escape him without one chance at " satisfaction."

CHAPTER XIII.

THE PRINCE DE NEUCHÂTEL.

ONE of the most remarkable actions of this war in which an American privateer was engaged was that between the British 40-gun frigate *Endymion*, Captain Henry Hope, and the armed ship *Prince de Neuchâtel*, of New York. The extraordinary feature of this affair lies in the fact that a vessel fitted out at private expense actually frustrated the utmost endeavors of an English frigate, of vastly superior force in guns and men, to capture the privateer. As the commander of the *Endymion* said, he lost as many men in his efforts to seize the *Prince de Neuchâtel* as he would have done had his ship engaged a regular man-or-war of equal force, and he generously acknowledged that the people in the privateer conducted their defense in the most heroic and skillful manner.

That this declaration of Captain Hope was singularly prophetic will be seen in the fact that this same *Endymion*, only three months after her disastrous attack on the *Prince de Neuchâtel*, had a running fight of two and a half hours' duration with the United States 44-gun frigate *President*, a sister ship of the famous *Constitution*, and a vessel "of equal force" to the *Endymion*. In the latter affair the *Endymion* had eleven men killed and fourteen wounded, a total of twenty-five out of a complement of three hundred and fifty. In her attack on the privateer the *Endymion* had forty-nine killed, thirty-seven wounded, and thirty of her crew were made prisoners, a total of one hundred and sixteen as against the total of twenty-five in her encounter with the *President*—a ship "of equal force." From these statements it will be seen that the privateer had quite as severe a fight as the *President*, and on this occasion contributed fully as much to the glory of American maritime prowess.

This notable action occurred off Nantucket on the night of October 11, 1814. The *Prince de Neuchâtel*, commanded by Captain J. Ordronaux, was considered a "splendid vessel" in her day. She was a hermaphrodite-rigged craft of three hundred and ten tons—the *Endymion* measuring about one thousand four hundred tons—and mounted seventeen guns as against the Englishman's fifty guns, to say nothing of the latter's immensely larger calibers. Her complement when she left New York on her most eventful cruise was about eighty men and boys, which number had been reduced by drafts for prize crews to thirty-seven. The *Prince de Neuchâtel* belonged to the estate of Mrs Charrten, of New York, who had recently died. This privateer was one of the many "lucky vessels" of the war, and made several profitable cruises, in the course of which she was chased by seventeen different men-of-war, but always managed to escape through superior seamanship and her great speed. The goods captured by her from the enemy and brought safely into port sold for nearly three millions of dollars, besides which a large amount of specie was secured.

This vessel did not begin her career as a war craft until the spring of 1814, at which time she was in Cherbourg, France. Here she was armed and fitted out as a privateer, and early in March she plunged into the thickest of British commerce in the English Channel, and in one brief cruise made nine valuable prizes, most of which arrived safely in French ports, while those of little value were burned.

In June the *Prince de Neuchâtel* made another dash against the enemy's shipping, sending six prizes into Havre between the 4th and 10th of that month, which were sold. In August this commerce destroyer was in the Irish Channel, where she came across a brig that refused to surrender, whereupon a broadside was poured into the stubborn merchant craft and she sank. In September the *Prince de Neuchâtel* destroyed the brigs *Steady*, *James*, *Triton* (of two guns, laden with coffee and wine), *Apollo*, *Sibron*, *Albion*, *Charlotte*, and *Mary Ann*, besides the sloops *Jane* and *George*, and the cutter *General Doyle*. She also captured and destroyed the transport *Aaron*, of four guns, from Gibraltar for Lisbon, and converted the following prizes into cartels in order to get rid of her constantly accumulating prisoners—the brigs *Barewick Packet*, from Cork for Bristol, which had fifty passengers aboard, and *Nymph*. She also captured the ship *Harmony*, of four guns, and an English privateer; but the latter was allowed to escape, as, just at the moment of taking possession, a suspicious sail hove in sight which proved to be a large war vessel, and the *Prince de Neuchâtel* was compelled to make sail in flight. A prize crew had been placed in the *Harmony*, with orders to make for the United States, but a few days later that ship was recaptured. Instead of returning to a French port after her last cruise, as had been her custom, the *Prince de Neuchâtel* made directly for Boston, where she refitted and put to sea again early in October.

Captain Ordronaux, of the *Prince de Neuchâtel*, was a seaman of unusual ability. At the outbreak of hostilities between the United States and Great Britain he commanded the French privateer *Marengo*. It was this vessel that Captain Richard Byron, of the British 36-gun frigate *Belvidera*, was so earnestly watching, on June 23, 1812, off these same Nantucket Shoals, when Captain John Rodgers' squadron, having the *President* as a flagship,

came along and chased the Englishman away. At
that time the *Marengo* was in New London, quite as
earnestly watching for a chance to pounce upon the
English brig *Lady Sherlock*, expected daily from Halifax bound for Jamaica with an exceedingly valuable cargo. It proved to be very much like a cat
watching a mouse to prevent it from getting a
morsel of cheese when the bulldog Rodgers came
tumbling along, chased the cat, *Belvidera*, into Halifax, when the mouse, *Marengo*, pounced upon the
unsuspecting *Lady Sherlock* as she was passing by
and carried her safely into New York, August 10,
1812.

It was on the very scene of this cat-dog-mouse-
and-cheese comedy, enacted in 1812, that the *Prince
de Neuchâtel*, on the night of October 11, 1814, made
one of the most heroic defenses in maritime history.
At this time the British squadron blockading the
port of New York consisted of the 56-gun frigate
Majestic, Captain John Hayes; the 40-gun frigate
Endymion, Captain Henry Hope; and the 38-gun
frigate *Pomone*, Captain John Richard Lumley. The
Endymion had been sent to Halifax for repairs, and
it was while she was returning from that port to
her station off New York that she fell in with the
Prince de Neuchâtel.

At noon, October 11th—October 9th according to
English accounts—while the *Prince de Neuchâtel*,
then only a few days out of Boston, was about
half a mile to the south of Nantucket Shoals, Captain Ordronaux discovered a sail off Gay Head,
and as it promptly gave chase he was satisfied that
it was a ship of force, and made his preparations
accordingly. Knowing that few, if any, of the
American frigates were on the high seas at that
time, owing to the rigor of the British blockade,
Captain Ordronaux made every effort to escape,
being satisfied that the stranger was a British
frigate. Unfortunately for the privateer, she was

so situated as to be becalmed at the moment, while the stranger was holding a fresh breeze and coming up very fast. The *Prince de Neuchâtel* had in tow the prize she recently captured, the English merchant ship *Douglass*, which the Americans were anxious to get safely into port.

At three o'clock in the afternoon the privateer caught the breeze, and, as the Englishman was still some twelve miles distant, hopes were entertained of effecting a timely retreat. By seven o'clock in the evening it was calm, at which time the three vessels were in sight of one another. Finding that the current was sweeping him shoreward, Captain Ordronaux cast off his tow, and the two vessels came to anchor about a quarter of a mile apart.

An hour and a half later, when it was quite dark, the people in the prize signaled, as previously agreed upon, that several boats were approaching from the frigate, apparently with the intention of atacking the privateer under cover of night. Observing the signal, Captain Ordronaux called all hands, and made every preparation for giving the British a warm reception. As soon as the English boats, which were under the command of Lieutenant Abel Hawkins, the first lieutenant of the *Endymion*, could be distinguished in the night, the privateer began a rapid discharge of her great guns and small arms. Paying no attention whatever to this, the English gallantly dashed ahead, and in a few moments were alongside the *Prince de Neuchâtel* and endeavoring to clamber up her sides. The enemy had planned the attack with considerable skill, for almost at the same moment it was reported to Captain Ordronaux that an English boat was on each side, one on each bow and one under the stern—five craft in all, completely surrounding the privateer, and compelling her crew to face five different points of attack at once.

This was the beginning of a desperate and bloody

struggle, in which men fought like wild beasts and grappled with each other in deadly embrace. Knives, pistols, cutlasses, marline spikes, belaying pins—anything that could deal an effective blow—were in requisition, while even bare fists, finger nails, and teeth came into play. Captain Ordronaux himself fired some eighty shots at the enemy. Springing up the sides of the vessel the British would endeavor to gain her deck, but every attempt was met with deadly blows by the sturdy defenders of the craft. A few of the British succeeded in gaining the decks and took the Americans in the rear, but the latter promptly turned on the enemy and dispatched them. It was well understood by the crew of the privateer that Captain Ordronaux had avowed his determination of never being taken alive by the British, and that he would blow up his ship, with all hands, before striking his colors. At one period of the fight, when the British had gained the deck, and were gradually driving the Americans back, Ordronaux seized a lighted match, ran to the companion way, directly over the magazine, and called out to his men that he would blow the ship up if they retreated further. The threat had the desired effect, the Americans rallied for a final struggle, overpowered the enemy, and drove the few survivors into their boats.

Such a sanguinary fight could not be of long duration, and at the end of twenty minutes the English cried out for quarter, upon which the Americans ceased firing. It was found that of the five barges one had been sunk, three had drifted off from alongside apparently without a living person in them, and the fifth boat was taken possession of by the Americans. There were forty-three men in the barge that was sunk, of whom only two were rescued; the remainder, it is supposed, were caught by the swift current, carried beyond the reach of help, and drowned. The boat seized by the Americans contained thirty-six men at the beginning of the action, of whom eight were killed and twenty were wounded, leaving only eight unhurt. The entire number of men in the five barges was one hundred and twenty, including the officers, marines, and boys. The entire number of men in the privateer fit for duty at the beginning of the action was thirty-seven, of whom seven were killed and twenty-four wounded. Among the killed was Charles Hilburn, a Nantucket pilot, who had been taken out of a fishing vessel. Among the British killed were First Lieutenant Hawkins and a master's mate, while the second lieutenant, two master's mates, and two midshipmen were wounded.

"So determined and effective a resistance," says an English naval historian, "did great credit to the American captain and his crew. On the 31st the *Endymion* fell in with the 56-gun ship *Saturn*, Captain James Nash, bound for Halifax, and, sending on board, with her surgeon and his servant, twenty-eight wounded officers and men, received from the *Saturn*, to replace the severe loss she had sustained, one lieutenant, four midshipmen, and thirty-three seamen and marines."

Captain Ordronaux now found himself in possession of so many prisoners that they outnumbered his own able-bodied men, there remaining only eight seamen unhurt in the privateer, while there were thirty prisoners to take care of. As a matter of precaution, Captain Ordronaux allowed only the second lieutenant of the *Endymion*, three midshipmen—two of them desperately wounded—and one wounded master's mate to come aboard; while the other prisoners, after having all their arms, oars, etc., taken from them, were kept in the launch under the stern of the *Prince de Neuchâtel*, where there would be less danger of attempting to overpower the few surviving Americans, capture the ship, and release their officers.

Anxious to be rid of his dangerous prisoners

Captain Ordronaux, on the following morning, signed an agreement with the lieutenant, midshipmen, and master's mates, in behalf of themselves and the British seamen and marines, not to serve against the United States again in this war unless duly exchanged. Under this agreement the prisoners were placed on shore at Nantucket by the privateer's launch, and were taken charge of by the United States marshal. Most of the American and English wounded also were sent ashore, where they could secure better attention. The *Prince de Neuchâtel*, as soon as the wind served, got under way, and easily evading the *Endymion*, ran into Boston Harbor, October 15th.

On gaining port Captain Ordronaux retired from the command of this lucky privateer and became a part owner. Her first officer in the fight with the *Endymion* succeeded to the command after promising " never to surrender the craft." He is described by one of the crew as " a Jew by persuasion, a Frenchman by birth, an American for convenience, and so diminutive in stature as to make it appear ridiculous, in the eyes of others, even for him to enforce authority among a hardy, weather-beaten crew should they do aught against his will." Her first officer is described as " a man who never uttered an angry or harsh word, made no use of profane language, but was terrible, even in his mildness, when faults occurred through carelessness or neglect. He knew what each man's duty was and his capacity for fulfilling it, never putting more to the men's tasks than they were able to get through with; but every jot and tittle must be performed, and that to the very letter, without flinching, or the task would be doubled. While maneuvering the men he would go through with the various duties without oaths, bluster, or even loud words, and do more in less time than all the other officers on board, with their harsh threatenings, profane swearings, or loud bawlings through their speaking trumpets. The men honored and obeyed him, and would have fought with any odds at his bidding." The second officer was put down as a "mere nobody." The third officer had been a warrant officer in the *Constitution* during her engagements with the *Guerrière* and *Java*, but was discharged for "unofficer-like conduct," and had shipped in the *Prince de Neuchâtel*. He proved to be an indifferent officer, and his negligence was the cause of the capture of the privateer on her next cruise.

On the night of December 21st the *Prince de Neuchâtel*, in spite of the vigilance of the British blockading force off Boston, got to sea. On the fifth day out she encountered a terrific storm which lasted several days, and came near ending the career of this formidable craft. "The morning of December 28th," records one of the American crew, "broke with no prospect of the gale ceasing, and the brig looked more like a wreck than the stanch and proud craft of the week previous. She was stripped to her stumps, all her yards, except her fore and fore-topsail, were on deck, her rigging in disorder, and the decks lumbered and in confusion from the effects of the sea which had so often broken over them during the past night. Much of this confusion was attributable to the third officer, who had the watch from 4 A. M. to 8 A. M. When he was relieved by the first officer, at 8 A. M., the latter severely reprimanded the third officer, and, among other things, asked if a sharp lookout had been maintained, and replied that the last man sent to the masthead had left his post without being relieved, and without the third officer knowing that the brig had been without a lookout all that time. . . . I saw the fire—or, what was its equal, anger—flash from the first lieutenant's eyes at this remissness of duty, and he instantly gave an order for the best man on board to go to the masthead, there to remain till ordered down." This man had not been at his post ten minutes when he reported a large sail bearing down on the *Prince de Neuchâtel*, and shortly afterward two others, apparently heavy men-of-war, making every effort to close on the privateer. These strangers were, in fact, the British frigates *Leander, Newcastle,* and *Acasta*, composing Sir George Collier's squadron, which had been off Boston, but was now hastening across the Atlantic in search of the *Constitution,* which had eluded them off Boston and was now at sea.[1]

As soon as the strangers were discovered the *Prince de Neuchâtel* was put on her best point of sailing, but in spite of every effort—the massive frigates having a great advantage over her in the heavy seas and wind—she was soon surrounded and captured. Only a few minutes after the surrender one of the frigates lost her jib boom, fore and main topgallant masts and broke her mizzen topsail yard in the slings, while another frigate carried away her mizzen topsail, main topgallant yard, and strained her fore-topsail yard so as to endanger it by carrying sail. Had the approach of the enemy been discovered when they made out the privateer the *Prince de Neuchâtel* would have escaped.

" At the time of our capture," said one of the privateer's crew, " there were on board five or six French and Portuguese seamen who had belonged to the brig during her former cruisings, and who appeared to be on good terms with the captain but had no intercourse with the crew. They messed by themselves and had as little to say to the Americans as the Americans manifested disposition to associate with them. These men were overheard to say, more than once during the chase, that the brig never would be taken by the frigates, assigning no

---

[1] For an account of the remarkable escape of *Old Ironsides* from Boston and her chase by this squadron, see Maclay's History of the Navy, vol. i, pp. 622–639.

reason why only, 'She shall never be under a British flag.' One of the men had been a prisoner of war ten times, and declared he would sooner go to the bottom of the ocean than again to prison. To this no one objected, provided he went without company; for he was a Frenchman by birth, a Calmuc in appearance, a savage in disposition, a cutthroat at heart, and a devil incarnate. Our first lieutenant kept a strict eye upon this coterie during the whole day that the chase continued, the idea strengthening, as the captain held on his course long after any hope remained of the chance of getting clear of the frigates, that all was not right. In the hurry of the moment [the surrender] at our rounding to, José, one of the men above spoken of, seized a brand from the caboose, proceeded toward the magazine, and would have carried his diabolical intentions into effect only for the vigilance of our ever-watchful lieutenant, who checked him ere too late, brought him on deck, nor quit his hold till the brand was cast overboard and the dastard thrown thrice his length by an indignant thrust of the lieutenant's powerful arm."

With much difficulty a small boarding party from the *Leander* took possession of the privateer, but as the sea and wind remained heavy it was found to be impossible to send a second detachment aboard. Realizing their advantage, the American officers, about half an hour before midnight, rallied their men, with a view of recapturing the brig, but on gaining the deck they observed that the condition of her spars and sails was such as to render such a move hopeless and the attempt was given up. On the following day the prisoners were taken aboard the *Leander*, where the Americans noticed a large placard nailed to her mainmast, on which were written these words: "Reward of £100 to the man who shall first descry the American frigate *Constitution* provided she can be brought to, and a smaller reward should they not be enabled to come up with her." The *Leander* had been fitted out expressly to capture *Old Ironsides*, and had a picked crew of more than five hundred men. "Every one [in the *Leander*]," continues the record, "was eager in his inquiries about this far-famed frigate, and most of the men appeared anxious to fall in with her, she being a constant theme of conversation, speculation, and curiosity. There were, however, two seamen and a marine—one of whom had had his shin sadly shattered from one of her [the *Constitution's*] grapeshot—who were in the frigate *Java* when she was captured. These I have often heard say, in return to their shipmates' boastings: 'If you had seen as much of the *Constitution* as we have, you would give her a wide berth, for she throws her shot almighty careless, fires quick, aims low, and is altogether an ugly customer.'"

The thoroughly American spirit of the *Prince de Neuchâtel's* crew is well brought out in the account of one of her men. After being taken aboard the *Leander* the prisoners were stowed away in the cable tier—a miserable hole at the bottom of the ship, where the anchor cables were stored. Here the Americans were compelled to remain from 4 P. M. to 8 A. M. every twenty-four hours. To while away the time they resorted to singing. "One night," says one of the men, "it was understood that some of our naval-victory songs were not well relished by the officers on deck, which only brought out others with a louder chorus than before and an extra 'hurrah for the Yankee thunders.' At this half a dozen of the best English songsters were picked, with some dozen to join in their choruses. These assembled around the hatch above us for the purpose of silencing us, singing us down, or to rival us in noisy melody and patriotic verse. They were allowed to finish their songs unmolested by us, but the moment they were through we struck up with ours, each one striving to outdo his shipmate, especially in the choruses. Knowing that the character of our country was at stake, and that it depended much upon our zeal and good management whether it should be upheld in the face of our enemies, we strove accordingly to do our best as its representatives. . . . The contest was kept up for some time, evidently to our advantage, not only as to the quality of the singing—for in this our opponents could not hold their own a moment—but to the number and subject of the songs, they having run out with their victories over the Yankees before our party was fairly warm with the contest. That they should not flag at the game, they took up with the First of June, the Battle of the Nile, besides many others, and we told them, in plain English, that they were dodging the contest. This they cared far less for than they did for a home-thrust victory over them from the Yankees to each one of theirs over the French. At last our fire became so warm that they were compelled to back out, chopfallen, and they had the satisfaction of having their defeat announced to all on board by three-times-three cheers from the victors, accompanied with the clapping of hands and such other noises as each and all could invent in our zeal to outdo one another and uphold the honor of the country we hailed from, whose emblem is the Stars and Stripes.

"Word came from the deck that such noises could not be tolerated and that we must be quiet. This only aroused the prisoners to greater exertions. . . . In a few minutes the officer of the deck came down with blustering threats. If the most savage tribe of Indians had at once broken loose with a terrific war whoop it could not have been louder nor more grating to the ear than the screamings that followed the termination of the watch officer's speech, who, when he could get a hearing, tried to reason as to the absurdity of the prisoners persisting, saying, 'The order of the ship must and shall be maintained; if by no other means, I will order the marines to fire into the hold.' This threat also was responded to by jeers, and soon afterward a line of marines drew up at the hatchway and prepared to shoot. This menace was met with louder jeers than before.

"'Crack away, my Johnny! You can make killing no murder, but you can't easily mend the shot holes in your best bower cable!' 'Hurrah for *Old Ironsides!*' 'Three cheers for the gallant Perry!' 'Down here, you Johnny Bull, and learn manners from your betters!' were a few of the shouts that saluted the ears of the marines. The officer, not daring to fire on the prisoners, now withdrew his marines, and was followed by the derisive shouts of the prisoners. . . . The noises were kept up till morning broke, not allowing the wardroom officers a moment's rest, as they were situated on the deck immediately above us." The next night the prisoners began their pandemonium again, but the officers arranged a number of 42-pound shot on the deck, just over the prisoners' heads, and started them rolling. " As they passed from one side to the other, at each roll of the ship, with a low, harsh, thunder-like rumbling, as deafening as dreadful, and more horrible than the booming of ten thousand Chinese gongs, intermingling with as many bell clappers, set in motion by one who is sworn to drown all else by his own noisy clatter, they made a noise little less than a discharge of artillery." This proved to be too much for our gallant tars, and they gradually gave up the contest.

Arriving at Fayal, Sir George transferred his prisoners to the sloop of war *Pheasant*, in which they were taken to England, while he resumed his search for the *Constitution*.[1]

---

[1] See Maclay's History of the Navy, vol. i, pp. 622–639.

CHAPTER XIV.

CRUISES OF THE GRAND TURK.

THE escape of the United States 44-gun frigate *Constitution*, Captain Isaac Hull, from a powerful British squadron off Sandy Hook, early in the War of 1812, has justly been regarded as one of most extraordinary feats of seamanship on record. Captain Hull won for himself and the service lasting fame by his masterly handling of the *Constitution*, and it is interesting to record that probably the nearest approach to this famous chase was that of the American privateer *Grand Turk* by a British squadron, March, 1815, off Pernambuco, in which the privateer escaped only by the superb seamanship of her commander, Nathan Green.

The *Grand Turk*, a 310-ton ship, was built for a privateer in the shipyards of Salem by Elias Hasket Derby toward the close of the Revolution, and made a number of prizes. "The war being over," wrote Thomas Wentworth Higginson, "she was sent by her owner on the first American voyage to the Cape of Good Hope in 1781, the cargo consisting largely of rum. The voyage proved profitable, and Captain Jonathan Ingersoll, her commander, bought in the West Indies on his return enough of Grenada rum to load two vessels, sent home the *Grand Turk*, and came himself in the *Atlantic*. On the way he rescued the captain and mate of an English schooner, the *Amity*, whose crew had mutinied and set them adrift in a boat. By one of those singular coincidences of which maritime life then seemed to yield so many, this very schooner was afterward recaptured in Salem harbor in this way: After their arrival the captain of the *Amity* was sitting with Mr. Derby in his countingroom, and presently saw through the spyglass his own vessel in the offing. Mr. Derby promptly put two pieces of ordnance on board one of his brigs, and gave the English captain the un-looked-for pleasure of recapturing the *Amity*, whose mutineers had no reason to suppose that they should happen upon the precise port into which their victims had been carried. This was not the only pioneer expedition of the *Grand Turk*, which also made, in 1785–'86, the first voyage direct from New England to the Isle of France and China."

When the War of 1812 broke out the *Grand Turk* was refitted as a privateer, carrying eighteen guns and a complement of one hundred and fifty men. At first she had as her commander Holten J. Breed, but toward the close of the war she was commanded by Nathan Green. Her first venture was made early in 1813, when she ran down to the coast of Brazil, cruised some time in the West Indies, and late in May put into Portland, Maine. In this time the *Grand Turk* captured three large vessels carrying heavy armaments and a schooner, all of which were ordered to France.

In her second cruise, which was begun in July, 1813, the *Grand Turk* made directly for European waters. On her voyage across the Atlantic she captured the schooner *Rebecca*, from Halifax bound for Bermuda, laden with live stock and provisions, which was sent into Portsmouth. Reaching the other side of the ocean, the *Grand Turk* cruised for twenty days in the chops of the English Channel without meeting a British war craft of any description. She came across many of their merchantmen, however, and took, in rapid succession, the schooner *Agnes*, laden with fish, which was sent into a French port; the ship *William*, of ten guns, having a valuable cargo of drygoods, crates, wine, etc., from Cork for Buenos Ayres, which was sent into Salem; the brig *Indian Lass*, from Liverpool for St. Michael, with drygoods, which also was sent into Salem with thirty prisoners; the brig *Catharine*, from Lisbon for London; and the schooner *Britannia*, for the West Indies, which was sent into Portland. The *Catharine* shortly afterward was recaptured by the English brig of war *Bacchus*, but before the prize could gain port the *Grand Turk* again loomed up on her horizon and seized her for the second time. To make sure that she would not again fall into the hands of the enemy, the Americans, after taking out the most valuable portion of the cargo, burned her.

Continuing her cruise in English waters, the *Grand Turk* added to her list of valuable prizes the sloop *Caroline*, from London for St. Michael, laden with drygoods. The cargo was transferred to the privateer, but the sloop being of little value, and the prisoners in the privateer becoming so numerous as to be dangerous, the *Caroline* was released and ordered to the nearest port with the prisoners. Soon afterward the privateer captured the merchantman *Cossack*, laden with wine. This vessel was recaptured by the 74-gun ship of the line *Bulwark*, but, like the *Catharine*, was again captured by the Americans; this time by the privateer *Surprise*, of Baltimore, and was sent into Salem. After burning or sinking the schooner *Pink*; the brig *Brothers*, from St. John's for Liverpool, with lumber aboard; the brig *Robert Stewart*, also with lumber; the schooner *Commerce*, laden with fish; and releasing the brig *Belgrade*, from Malta for Falmouth—after taking some guns out of her—the *Grand Turk* returned to Salem in November, 1813, having made a cruise of one hundred and three days, and with only forty-four men of her original complement of one hundred and fifty left. One of her prizes had a cargo in-

28

voiced at thirty thousand pounds sterling. This privateer made one or two more short runs to sea with fairly good success, but it was on her last cruise, when under the command of Captain Nathan Green, that she made her greatest reputation.

Scene of the *Grand Turk's* operations.

Half an hour after noon on Sunday, January 1, 1815, Captain Green stowed his anchors away and cleared his deck preparatory for sailing from Salem, and at 2 P. M. he passed Baker's Island. Nothing more than an occasional glimpse of a British frigate or a ship of the line, to which the *Grand Turk* promptly showed a clean pair of heels, served to break the monotony of the cruise until 3.30 P. M., February 17th, when the privateer was in the vicinity of Pernambuco. At that time a small sail was sighted, which proved to be a catamaran, and for the purpose of gaining information as to the proposed movements of British merchant ships Captain Green boarded her. It happened that the craft had just left the port, and her master informed the Americans that there were eight English vessels in the harbor, some of them ready to sail.

This was the news Captain Green had been longing for, and he determined to hover off the port until some of the ships sailed. At six o'clock that evening he had approached sufficiently near Pernambuco to distinguish the shipping. Two days later, or at 5.30 P. M., Sunday, February 19th, his patience was rewarded by a sail appearing to the north. Gradually drawing up on her during the night, he, at nine o'clock on the following morning, boarded the brig *Joven Francisco*, sailing under Spanish colors from Pernambuco to London, but laden with a cargo of tea, coffee, sugar, and cinnamon consigned to British merchants. From her invoices and some letters found aboard, Captain Green was satisfied that the Spanish flag had been used merely as a cover, and that the craft and her cargo were in truth English property. Accordingly he seized her as a prize and placed Nathaniel Archer and some of his men aboard, with orders to make for the United States.

Scarcely had the last speck of the *Joven Francisco* faded from the horizon when the people in the privateer were cheered by the sight of another sail, this one to the south, standing northward. Observing that she was coming directly upon the privateer, Captain Green allowed her to approach, and at 6.30 P. M., February 21st, he boarded her. She was found to be the British ship *Active Jane*, of Liverpool, from Rio Janeiro bound for Maranham. She had on board seven bags of specie, containing fourteen thousand milled rees, which were valued at about seventeen thousand five hundred dollars. A prize crew was placed aboard, with orders to keep near the *Grand Turk* during the night. At daylight on the following morning Captain Green made a more thorough search of his prize, but finding nothing else of much value, he transferred the specie to his vessel and scuttled the merchantman.

From this time until March 10th the *Grand Turk* cruised in this vicinity, occasioning much damage to the enemy's commerce. She stayed so long, however, that the English had time to collect several war ships, which were promptly sent out to capture the bold privateersman. Captain Green was fully alive to the growing danger of his position, and when at daylight, Friday, March 10th, the man at the masthead reported a sail in the eastern quarter, he promptly called all hands and sent them to quarters.

Thinking that the stranger might be a merchantman, Captain Green cautiously ran down to her, but soon afterward he discovered another sail, this one being on the weather bow. This did not deter the *Grand Turk* from continuing her approach to the first stranger, and she was fast drawing near to her, when, at 6.30 A. M., she passed very near the second stranger. Captain Green stopped only long enough to be satisfied that she was a Portuguese schooner. At seven o'clock a third stranger was made out from the *Grand Turk's* masthead three points off the lee bow. By this time the chase was seen to be a full-rigged ship, a fact that made Captain Green more cautious in approaching, but did not prevent him from continuing the chase.

By 8 A. M. the third stranger was seen to be a large, full-rigged ship also, standing by the wind to the northwest. With increasing anxiety Captain Green continued the chase after the first stranger and gradually drew up on her, but at ten o'clock, when he had reached a position three quarters of a mile to windward, he became satisfied that the chase was a frigate endeavoring to decoy the privateer

under her guns. Captain Green was not to be
caught by such a simple trick as that, and in an
instant the *Grand Turk* tacked and made all sail to
escape. With equal celerity the British frigate—
for such she proved to be—tacked also and was
spreading every sail that would draw.

It did not take the privateer long to demonstrate
her superior sailing qualities, and in less than an
hour she had so increased her lead on the enemy
as to relieve Captain Green of all fear of capture;
thereupon he ran up the American flag and fired a
shot in defiance. But at this juncture the wind,
most unfortunately for the privateer, suddenly
hauled around to the west, which was very favorable for the frigate, and in a short time enabled her
to approach dangerously near. At 11.30 A. M., finding that the Englishman was within gunshot and
was slowly getting alongside, Captain Green got
out his sweeps. By urging his men to their utmost
exertion he made considerable progress, notwithstanding the fact that, though it was calm where
the *Grand Turk* was, there was a choppy head sea.

Observing that the American was slipping from
his grasp, the Englishman began firing with his
chase guns, and manning all his boats, sent them
ahead to tow. Four different times the frigate attempted to tack, but without success. In the hope
of damaging the enemy's rigging, Captain Green
opened on the frigate with his long guns and again
hoisted his colors. About this time a ship was discovered to leeward which also proved to be a British frigate, and joined in the pursuit of the privateer. At noon Captain Green swept his brig round
with her head northward, and having a more favorable sea, managed to increase his lead on the enemy.

In this manner the chase was kept up all that
night, and the following day, March 11th, the Americans were making every exertion at their sweeps,
while the British were equally diligent in endeav-

oring to tow their ships within gunshot. The weather all this time was extremely warm and sultry, which made it especially trying on the American crew. The British, having a larger complement of men, were enabled to form relief crews. At dusk, Saturday, March 11th, the enemy made a great effort to get within range, but the vigilant Americans were equal to the emergency, and by putting forth renewed efforts managed to hold their own.

When Sunday, March 12th, dawned, Captain Green was much relieved to find that the enemy was out of sight; but at 1.30 P. M. the two frigates, favored by a breeze that did not reach the *Grand Turk*, hove in sight again off the lee bow and gradually drew up on the chase. By five o'clock the wind had died out and the Americans again took to their sweeps. During the night, by ceaseless application of the sweeps, the privateer gained so much as to be out of sight of her pursuers when day broke. At two o'clock on Monday afternoon, not having seen anything of the enemy for some time, Captain Green employed all hands in getting down the fore-topmast, which had been strained in the chase, and replacing it with a new one. While busy at this task a sail was descried to the northwest, and at four o'clock another was observed standing for the privateer. By half past five Captain Green had his new fore-topmast and topgallant mast in place, rigged and yards aloft. He then made sail for the second stranger, and at seven o'clock boarded her. She proved to be a Portuguese brig from Bahia bound for La Grande, with a cargo of salt. Captain Green took this opportunity of placing five British prisoners, under parole, in this vessel, and, discharging ten Spaniards, he placed them aboard the brig with the necessary supply of provisions and resumed his course.

After this narrow escape the *Grand Turk* saw nothing more of the British frigates until five days

later, when her intrepid commander, unruffled by
the danger he had escaped, persisted in remaining
in these waters. At two o'clock on the afternoon of
Saturday, March 18th, Captain Green overhauled
and spoke a Portuguese brig from Africa bound for
Rio Janeiro with a cargo of slaves. At this moment
another sail to the northwest was reported from
the masthead, and away went the privateer in chase
of it. As the American gradually overhauled the
stranger it became more and more evident that she
was a ship of force, and at half past four o'clock she
hoisted English colors and began firing her stern
guns. No attention was paid to this by the Americans, who kept silently and persistently in the wake
of the chase, confident in their ability to overtake
her.

Forty minutes later the stranger took in her
steering sails, gave a broad yaw, and fired a broadside. Upon this invitation to a square yardarm fight
the *Grand Turk* promptly followed the maneuver
and opened with her port battery, and maintained
such a heavy fire that in ten minutes the Englishman struck. On taking possession, the Americans
found her to be the British brig *Acorn*, from Liverpool, bound for Rio Janeiro. The prize carried fourteen 12-pounders, and had a cargo of drygoods. No
time was lost in getting the cargo aboard the privateer, for Captain Green well knew that British
cruisers were swarming in this part of the ocean.
In twenty minutes the first boat load of goods was
brought aboard the *Grand Turk*. All night long the
crew was kept busy transferring the merchandise,
but at daylight Sunday morning the work was interrupted by the appearance of two frigates and a
war brig in full chase of the privateer, and on her
lee beam. These frigates proved to be the same
that had given the *Grand Turk* such a hard and persistent chase the week before. Taking a " very full
boat load of goods on board," Captain Green placed

Joseph Phippen and eleven men aboard the *Acorn*, with orders to make for the United States, and then gave attention to his own safety. As the wind was fair, he soon found that he was drawing away from the frigates, and by nightfall he had run them out of sight.

Having had a tolerably successful cruise of nearly three months, and believing that the treaty of peace, signed at Ghent, would be ratified, Captain Green decided to return home. Another reason for terminating his cruise was the fact that the *Grand Turk's* copper and rigging were very much out of repair and she was running short of water.

While homeward bound Captain Green, at four o'clock in the morning of March 29th, discovered a sail to windward, and, believing that he might take another prize, tacked in pursuit. At half past eight he came up with the stranger, which proved to be a Portuguese ship from Africa for Maranham, with nearly five hundred slaves aboard. Captain Green took this opportunity of releasing on parole eleven British prisoners who were placed aboard the Portuguese.

Resuming her course northward, the *Grand Turk*, on April 16th, boarded the American schooner *Comet*, from Alexandria for Barbadoes, with a cargo of flour, and learned that peace between the United States and England had been concluded. Captain Green notes that this announcement " produced the greatest rejoicing throughout the ship's company." On Saturday, April 29th, the *Grand Turk* dropped anchor in Salem harbor, cleared decks, and saluted the town, thus completing a cruise of one hundred and eighteen days. This privateer captured, in the course of the war, three ships, twelve brigs, seven schooners, and eight sloops. On May 30, 1815, the *Grand Turk* was sold to William Gray, of Salem, and for some time was employed as a merchantman.

CHAPTER XV.

ESCAPE OF THE IDA.

On the last day of March, 1814, four American captains in the privateer service met at Hôtel des Ambassadeurs in the important seaport town of La Rochelle. They were Jeremiah Mantor, of the Boston privateer *Ida*; David Maffitt, of the *Rattlesnake*, from Philadelphia; George Coggeshall, of the *David Porter*, from New York; and Mr. Brown, of the *Decatur*, from Portsmouth. Thus were four of the principal seaport cities of the United States represented at this meeting. All of these commanders had their ships in La Rochelle excepting Coggeshall, who had come to this place overland looking for means of transportation home for some valuable cargo. There was also in La Rochelle an American merchant brig belonging to New York, which had been laid up there from the beginning of the war. At this time the political situation of France, and of Europe too, was one of great uncertainty and suspense. The allied armies were close upon Paris, if not actually within the city, but as yet the exact state of affairs was not known in La Rochelle. Not the slightest information on the subject could be obtained. All communication between Paris and La Rochelle had been stopped some time before, not a diligence being allowed to run on the road between the two points. Everybody knew that the allied armies were in the neighborhood of Paris, but no one dared to speak on the subject.

This state of anxiety and suspense was rendered
doubly critical to the American officers by the fact
that a powerful British blockading squadron, commanded by Lord Keith in the ship of line *Queen Charlotte*, consisting of five ships of the line, several frigates, and a number of war brigs and schooners, completely blocked the entrance of the harbor, making
it extremely difficult, if not foolhardy, for any of
the four American vessels in that port to attempt to
get to sea. On the other hand, if these vessels remained in port, their commanders had no assurance
whatever that British influence — which in case
Paris fell would be all-powerful in the new Government to be established—would not bring about the
confiscation of their ships and cargoes. In short,
the four Americans, although having entered a
friendly port, suddenly found themselves in a trap
from which there seemed to be not the slightest
prospect of escape. They were menaced both from
the land and sea, and their meeting at Hôtel des
Ambassadeurs was, in fact, a council of war. As
the danger of capture seemed equally imminent
from sea and land, they were not long in deciding
to take their chances on the former as being best
suited to the salty nature of honorable tars.

Captain Maffitt, whose noteworthy career in the
Atlas and *Rattlesnake* we have followed, had recently
arrived from his northern cruise, and, as it had been
one of extraordinary success, the English were particularly anxious to put an end to the cruises of the
mischief-making *Rattlesnake*. Just before entering
this port the privateer had a desperate battle with
the heavily armed British transport *Mary*, the result
of which was highly exasperating to our cousins.
The *Mary* was from Sicily, bound for England, and
had on board as prisoners sixty - two French officers, guarded by several English army officers and
a detachment of soldiers. The two vessels met in
the Bay of Biscay, and immediately engaged in bat-

Entrance to the harbor of La Rochelle, France.

tle at close quarters, the privateer, of course, taking the initiative. In twenty minutes the commander of the transport and two of his seamen were killed and three others were wounded, upon which the survivors hauled down their colors and asked for quarter. The Americans took possession, and, placing a prize crew aboard, ordered her into a French port. In the privateer only one man was wounded. He was a marine officer, " a handsome young man belonging to one of the most respectable families in New York." His injury was in his leg. On reaching La Rochelle he was taken to the hospital and was advised to have the limb taken off, and was warned that there was no time to be lost. He declined to submit to the operation, however, carelessly giving as a reason that it would spoil his dancing. He lingered a few weeks and died, his funeral being attended by all the Americans in the place. The *Mary* subsequently was recaptured and sent to England. The English officers in the transport published letters in their home newspapers exploiting the generous conduct of Captain Maffitt in giving them all their personal property and in his handsome treatment of all the prisoners.

Captain Coggeshall, whose career in the *David Porter* and *Leo* has been detailed in the preceding chapters, had just arrived in La Rochelle overland from l'Ile Yeu, where he had left his ship, the *David Porter*, and, after dispatching her to the United States in charge of her first officer, turned his attention to disposing of cargoes brought from Charleston and prizes taken on the way over. Captains Brown and Mantor, of the *Decatur* and the *Ida*, had entered the port in quest of supplies, when they found themselves blockaded. On April 2d news reached La Rochelle that Paris, on March 30th, had been taken by the allied armies, and on April 3d official orders arrived proclaiming the Government of Louis XVIII. This news spurred the American com-

manders to action, and they resolved to sail their
vessels out of the port at all hazards and make a
bold dash for liberty. All their vessels were swift
craft, designed especially for speed and convenience
in cruising and eluding ships of greater force. The
Ida was a fine, coppered brig of two hundred and
seventy-two tons, mounting eight long 9-pounders
and 12-pounders, with a complement of thirty-five
men.

Early on the morning of April 8th the three
American privateers—the *Rattlesnake*, the *Ida*, and
the *Decatur*—each fully prepared for a race or fight,
tripped anchor and stood down the harbor to run
the blockade if an opportunity should offer. They
stood down with the wind on the north side of l'Ile
de Ré, an island just off the mainland, hoping to
escape through that passage. But unexpectedly
they found a strong English naval force stationed
there, and were compelled to fall back, the *Rattlesnake* and *Decatur* returning to their anchorages.

The *Ida*, however, lay to off the east end of the
island long enough to discharge her pilot, and then
squared away and made a bold dash down the
south side of the island in plain sight of the entire
British fleet at anchor in the roads off La Rochelle.
The English admiral apparently was taken somewhat by surprise by the sudden change of course
made by the *Ida*. In fact, Captain Mantor was taking desperate chances, for he was compelled to pass
within a short distance of the British fleet; and even
if he ran this gantlet in safety he was obliged to
meet a heavy war schooner at the end of the island.
On the other hand, Captain Mantor saw that the
chances of his capture, should he endeavor to regain his anchorage, were great, and observing that,
as the tide was then holding the ponderous ships
of the line at anchor, they could scarcely bring a
gun to bear on the course he proposed to take in his
dash for liberty, he decided on the lesser evil of the

two. The very boldness of his decision was his main reliance in effecting his escape, for, as he rightly conjectured, the English were taken by surprise, and not one of the huge ships of the line was able to give him a shot as he passed them. One of them slipped her cable, however, and soon had settled down to a determined chase.

Just as the little *Ida*, with the gigantic ship of the line tumbling after her, passed the south end of the island, Captain Mantor discovered a war schooner on his starboard side making for him from the cover of the island. If the *Ida* changed her course she would give the huge ship of the line, already uncomfortably close in her wake, a chance to gain a quarter of a mile or more. This was a period of the chase when even such a short distance might turn the balance. On the other hand, if the *Ida* held on her present course she would be compelled to pass within musket shot of the schooner, so that the latter, in all probability, would shoot away some of the privateer's spars, and so cripple her rigging that she would fall an easy prey. Captain Mantor determined to continue on the course he was then holding. In a few minutes he was within musket shot of the schooner, which let go all the guns she could bring to bear, carrying away the *Ida's* studding-sail boom, mainstay, and some running rigging. This damage was anticipated, and the Americans had made every preparation for it, so that in an incredibly short time they had everything tight again and the studding sail reset.

At this time several men-of-war were within gunshot of the *Ida*, and were peppering away at her with all their chase guns. The Americans were too busy, however, looking out for their sails, rigging, and spars to pay any attention to these little pleasantries, and kept on their course in watchful silence. Soon after passing the schooner Captain Mantor discovered another war ship bearing down on his starboard side, and he nerved himself for another broadside. He now determined to put up his helm and bring all his pursuers astern, as that was the only course left to him. This was quickly done, and the *Ida* crossed the bow of the last ship so near that the Americans could distinctly hear her seamen halloo. This ship, as soon as she could get her broadside to bear, let go her compliments at the *Ida*, but fortunately most of the shot went too high. One 32-pound shot passed along the privateer's deck fore and aft, and lodged in the stern. Another carried away the anchor as it hung under her bow ready to let go, and severed the chain. Had not most of the crew of the *Ida* been in her hold at that time, heaving out ballast, many of them would have been killed or wounded.

By lightening his vessel and increasing her speed in every possible way, Captain Mantor gradually drew out of gunshot, although by nightfall as many as ten British war ships were in full chase. The stubbornness of the chase is shown by the fact that when the English lost trace of the *Ida* in the night. they spread out their forces so that some of their ships were sure to be in sight of the audacious privateer on the following morning. How well they made their calculations was shown at daylight, for as soon as the lookout was able to distinguish anything at a distance from the ship he saw two British frigates directly ahead. Captain Mantor quickly hauled up on the wind to avoid them. In doing this he narrowly escaped capsizing his own vessel, for six of the *Ida's* eight long guns had been thrown overboard in the chase, and she had been relieved of so much ballast as to make carrying a press of sail hazardous.

As soon as the two frigates sighted the privateer they were after her, and then began another long chase. All that morning and afternoon the three vessels strained and bowed under clouds of canvas, each doing her utmost to increase speed. As night again approached it was seen that the American had increased his lead some four or five miles, but still he was dangerously near the enemy, who by again dividing their forces in the night stood a tolerably fair chance of sighting the chase at the break of day.

About nine o'clock that night the *Ida* had succeeded in concealing herself from her pursuers. Every light in her had been extinguished save those absolutely necessary for navigating the ship, and these were carefully shielded so as not to be visible to the enemy. Hopes were being entertained by all on board that they would actually make good their escape from La Rochelle, when, most unfortunately, the shutter of the binnacle fell, revealing the light to the Englishmen. At this instant one of the frigates was astern of the privateer and another was on her lee quarter, and the chances were that had they not seen the *Ida's* binnacle light their courses would have diverged so much during the night that by morning the Americans would have been out of sight. As soon as the Englishmen saw the light they signaled each other and changed their courses so as to surround the privateer. As quickly as possible Captain Mantor had the shutter replaced, and again, in total darkness, the three vessels bowled along over the waves under the heaviest press of sail. At daylight, April 10th, Captain Mantor saw the two frigates, hull down, and in the course of the day he ran them out of sight, arriving safely at Boston after a passage of twenty-six days.

Soon after the *Ida* made her marvelous escape from the harbor of La Rochelle the *Decatur* and the *Rattlesnake* seized opportunities for getting to sea. The former was captured September 3, 1814, by the British squadron, and the *Rattlesnake* was taken by the frigate *Hyperion*, June 3, 1814.

CHAPTER XVI.

PRIVATEERS OF SALEM.

THAT Salem holds a unique place in American ship lore must be apparent even to the casual observer. Thomas Wentworth Higginson, writing of the early history of that venerable seaport, says: " Long before the Revolution a plan had been vaguely sketched out by which Salem was to obtain something of that share in the India trade which later events brought to her. In an old letter book containing part of the correspondence that passed in 1669 between Lieutenant-Colonel John Higginson, of Salem, and his brother Nathaniel—a graduate of Harvard College and Governor of the English colony of Madras—the home-keeping brother suggests that the ex-Governor should make the Massachusetts colony the seat of an Oriental commerce by way of London, and thus enumerates the resources of such a traffic: ' All sorts of calicoes, aligers, remwalls, muslin, silks for clothing and linings; all sorts of drugs proper for the apothecaries, and all sorts of spice, are vendible with us, and the prices of them alter much according as they were plenty or scarce. In the late war time all East India goods were extremely dear. Muslins of the best sort, plain, striped, and flowered, were sold for £10 per piece, and some more. Pepper, 3s. per pound; nuts [nutmegs], 10s. per pound; cloves, 20s.; mace, 30s; but now are abated about a quarter part in value. Some of the china ware, toys, and lacquer ware will sell

408

well, but no great quantity. As for ambergris, we often have it from the West Indies, and it is sold for about 3 per ounce, For musk, pearls, and diamonds, I believe some of them may sell well, but I understand not their value.'

"Thus early, it seems, was the taste for Chinese and Japanese goods—germ of future æstheticism—implanted in the American colonies; but when it comes to pearls and diamonds, the quiet Salem burgher, descendant of three generations of devout clergymen, 'understands not their value.' Yet he believes that some of them will sell well, even in 1669!"

During the struggle for American independence Salem sent out one hundred and fifty-eight privateers, carrying about two thousand guns which took in all four hundred and forty-five prizes—more than half the prizes made by our entire maritime forces in this war—only fifty-four of the privateers being lost by capture or shipwreck. In short, when we remember that the important seaports of Boston, Newport, New York, Philadelphia, Charleston, and Savannah were successively in the hands of the enemy during that struggle, it would be difficult to understand how the vast maritime operations of the rebelling colonists could have been effectively carried on had it not been for the open port of Salem.

In the course of the War of 1812 Salem sent forty privateers to sea. A number of these have been noticed in other chapters as being well worthy of extended notice, but many of the others rendered services of value, notwithstanding the fact that usually they were small vessels mounting one to five guns and manned by fewer than forty men. Of this class the 1-gun schooner *Buckskin*, Captain I. Bray, may be taken as an example. In one cruise she took four well-laden schooners, retook a Kennebunk brig, and recaptured the American brig *Hesper*, which had been seized by the British frigate *Maid-*

stone. Among the *Buckskin's* prizes was the schooner *Nelson*, laden with oil, furs, fish, etc., and a schooner from Halifax bound for Quebec, laden with military stores and having on board as passengers Colonel Pearson, of the English army, his wife and family. The *Buckskin* was captured early in the war.

More successful than the *Buckskin* was the ship *John*, Captain J. Crowninshield. This handsome vessel was heavily armed and manned, carrying sixteen guns and a complement of one hundred and sixty men, which made her one of the most formidable privateers afloat at the beginning of the war. After a short cruise of about three weeks, in July, 1812, the *John* returned to port, having captured eleven vessels, of which three were destroyed and one was recaptured. Those that arrived in port were the brig *Ceres*; the schooner *Union*, from Jamaica for Quebec, with one hundred and forty-six puncheons of rum (the vessel and cargo being estimated to be worth thirty thousand dollars); the coppered brig *Elizabeth*, of three hundred tons, from Gibraltar for Quebec, in ballast, carrying four guns and twelve men; the ship *Apollo*, of four hundred tons and mounting eight 18-pounders; and a schooner from Jamaica with one hundred and sixty puncheons of rum. Three brigs, laden with lumber, were captured, but as they were inconvenient to handle they were released. Afterward the *John* captured the valuable brig *Henry*, from Liverpool for Halifax, laden with crates, salt, and coal; the ship *Jane*, of Port Glasgow; the brig *Neptune*, a new, light brig from Gibraltar bound for Halifax; the schooner *Blonde*, from Dominica for St. John's; and a schooner from Jamaica with one hundred and sixty puncheons of rum aboard. All of these prizes reached Salem excepting the new brig from Gibraltar, which was sent into Boston. The *John* shared the fate of the *Buckskin*, being captured by the enemy early in the war.

Crowninshield's Wharf. Salem, Mass.. in 1812.

From a painting in the Essex Institute, Salem.

The career of the *Active*, Captain Patterson, was short, that vessel being captured July 16, 1812, off Cape Sable, by the British 36-gun frigate *Spartan*, Captain Brenton. The *Active* was a schooner carrying only two guns and a complement of twenty men. Two days later the *Spartan* also captured the privateer sloop *Actress*, Captain G. Lumsden, of New Haven. The sloop carried four guns and fifty-three men. She had been in commission only seven days.

The *Alfred*, Captain Williams, was a brig of about the same force as the *John*, mounting sixteen guns and having a complement of one hundred and thirty men. She sailed from Salem on a cruise August 16, 1812, and one of her first prizes was the brig *Diamond*, of two hundred and twenty tons and twelve guns, with a full cargo of cotton and logwood and two thousand five hundred dollars in gold. Another valuable prize was the brig *George*, of two hundred and seventy tons, laden with sugar and cotton. Each of these vessels was from Brazil, and they were valued at one hundred and twenty thousand dollars. The brig *Tercilla* and the *Curfew* also were taken by the *Alfred*; the former, laden with fish, from St. John's bound for Bermuda, was burned at sea, and the latter, from Nova Scotia for St. Lucia, with a cargo of fish and oil, was sent into Marblehead. The *Diamond* and the *George* were sent into Salem. On February 23, 1814, the *Alfred*, when three months out on her last cruise, was captured by the English sloop of war *Épervier* and the frigate *Junon*.

The *Thrasher* and the *Terrible* seem to have been most formidable in their names. The former, commanded by Captain R. Evans, took the brig *Tor Abbey*, laden with dry fish, which was sent into Cape Ann, while the latter, scarcely more than an open boat, captured a schooner laden with a few hogsheads of rum (which was sent into Eastport), two small vessels (which were sent into Salem), and the schooner

Harmony, of Yarmouth, Nova Scotia, which also was brought safely into port. The *Thrasher* also captured the 350-ton ship *Britannia*, mounting six guns, and sent her into port.

One of the smallest of Salem's privateers was the *John and George*, carrying only one 12-pounder and two 3-pounders, with a complement of thirty-eight all told. This little craft made several valuable captures, among them being the ship *Ned*, of Glasgow, carrying ten 9-pounders—sufficient, had they been fully manned and handled, to have blown the puny *John and George* out of water—and a crew of sixteen men. She was laden with timber, and surrendered after a sharp fight. She was sent into Salem.

The privateer schooner *Revenge*, Captain J. Sinclair, sent into Portland the British schooners *Robin* and *Neptune* into Cape Ann, the latter being laden with fish, salt, and oil. The *Revenge* also captured the brig *Bacchus*, of Port Glasgow, and sent her into Salem. In endeavoring to take another schooner the *Revenge* drove her ashore on the coast of Nova Scotia and burned her. Not long after this the *Revenge* was captured by the enemy.

The *Growler*, Captain N. Lindsey, before she was captured by the English, was a fairly successful craft. She sent into New London the ship *Arabella*, from England bound for the West Indies. The *Arabella* was of five hundred tons, coppered, mounted eight guns, and in every respect was a first-class vessel. She was laden with plantation utensils. The *Growler* also took a brig, which was released after every article of value had been taken out of her. Among the privateer's other prizes were the schooner *Prince of Wales* and the brig *Ann*. The schooner was released, after a few pipes of Madeira wine had been taken out of her, as being of more trouble than she was worth, but the brig was sent into Marblehead. She mounted ten guns, and was bound for New Providence from Liverpool with a cargo of drygoods and crates which was valued at one hundred thousand dollars. On July 7, 1813, the *Growler* was captured by the British 18-gun sloop of war *Electra* off St. Peters, after a chase of six hours.

The *Wasp*, Captain E. Ewing (or Ervin), also was a Salem privateer that was captured by an English cruiser, but not until she inflicted some injury on the enemy's commerce. She was a sloop mounting only two guns. After sending a schooner into Machias she was chased July 31 (by another account June 9), 1813, by the British man-of-war *Bream*, mounting ten guns. Realizing the helplessness of giving battle to the cruiser, Captain Ewing made every effort to escape. The *Bream* gave chase, and for nine hours kept the *Wasp* in sight and gained on her. When in easy gunshot the English opened a heavy fire, which the Americans returned as well as they could for forty minutes, when they surrendered. The British lieutenant commanding the *Bream* treated his prisoners with exceptional courtesy.

Among the privateers of Salem lost by shipwreck were the *Gallinipper* and the *Dart*. The former, Captain T. Wellman, captured a schooner, which was released on the payment of ransom. On May 2, 1813, the *Gallinipper* was chased ashore by the English 20-gun sloop of war *Rattler* and destroyed. The *Dart*, Captain William Davis, was little more than an open boat, and was cast away early in the struggle. She had captured the snow *Friends*, a vessel of two hundred and ninety tons, mounting six guns, and a brig laden with rum. The *Dart* also had taken the brigs *Concord*, *Hope*, and *Diana*.

The privateer *Alexander*, Captain Benjamin Crowninshield, was a splendid 18-gun ship with a complement of one hundred and twenty men. She was chased ashore May 19, 1813, by the *Rattler* and *Bream*. Previously she had taken several prizes, one of them the brig *Edward*, mounting eight guns, from

Brazil for London, with one hundred and eighty
bales of cotton. This prize was sent into Salem.
The *Alexander* also seized a brig of sixteen guns,
laden with drygoods and gunpowder, and a schooner,
the latter being released after the valuable portions
of her cargo had been taken out. When chased by
the *Rattler* and *Bream*, the *Alexander* was so hard
pressed that only twenty of her crew were able to
get ashore; most of her other men, however, had
been detailed to man the seven prizes the privateer
had taken, so that the number of prisoners was not
so large as might have been supposed. The *Alexander* had over one hundred prisoners, who were recaptured. The English managed to float the privateer off and carried her into Halifax.

The career of one of the *Alexander's* prizes is especially noteworthy. This was the French privateer
Invincible Napoleon, a vessel mounting sixteen guns.
She had been taken from the French by a British
sloop of war. The *Alexander* fell in with the *Invincible
Napoleon*, under her new masters, in the English
Channel, and captured her after a hard struggle and
sent her into Cape Ann. On the night of May 16,
1813, while lying at her anchorage in this place, the
Invincible Napoleon was re-recaptured by the boats
of the British frigates *Shannon* and *Tenedos*, which
had gallantly pulled into the port, under cover of
night, and attacked her. The vessel was anchored
too far from the fort to receive any assistance from
the garrison, so the British succeeded in carrying
her out. But before the English masters could carry
this unlucky ship to a place of safety she was captured by the American privateer *Young Teazer*, and
arrived at Portland about June 1st. After refitting at this place, the *Invincible Napoleon* put to sea
for a cruise, under Captain P. Desterbecho, with
sixteen guns and sixty men. On August 16, 1814, the
misnamed *Invincible Napoleon* was captured for the
fifth time by the British cruiser *Armide*, after having

thrown overboard ten of her guns in the long chase that preceded the capture.

The Salem privateer *Nancy*, Captain R. Smart, took the brig *Resolution*, laden with flour, and sent her into Portland, while the *Timothy Pickering*, although fitted out for the avowed purpose of seizing vessels evading the Non-importation Law, made several valuable captures. She was a three-masted vessel and well appointed. She took the *Eliza Ann* and sent her into Eastport. The British sloop of war *Martin* appeared of that place soon afterward and threatened to lay the town in ashes if the *Eliza Ann* were not given up. The people of the place were not so easily frightened, and, returning a defiant answer, they awaited the promised attack. The *Martin* soon opened a feeble, ill-directed fire, which the Americans returned with spirit, and after a few shots induced the sloop of war to withdraw. The *Timothy Pickering* also captured the brig *Dart* and sent her into Salem.

In no other privateer from Salem was the command to "sink and destroy" so well carried out as in the *Frolic*, Captain Odiorne. Nearly all of the eleven prizes taken by this fortunate vessel were burned at sea. Some of them were the ship *Reprisal*, from Scotland bound for the Bay of Chaleur; the brig *Friends*, of Bristol (England), for Pictou; the brig *Betsey*; the galliot *Guttle Hoffnung*, of Portsmouth (England); the brig *Jane Gordon*, of London, carrying eight guns and twenty men; and the schooner *Encouragement*, from Antigua for Nova Scotia, having on board twenty hogsheads of sugar, twenty hogshead of molasses, and five of rum. All of these vessels were destroyed after their officers and crews and the most valuable portions of their cargoes had been transferred to the privateer. In this way the *Frolic* soon became dangerously crowded with prisoners, and as a means of getting rid of them they were placed in one of the prizes, the schooner *Hunter*, and sent to England. In the same way the prize schooners *Vigilant* and *Susan* were disposed of. Two of the *Frolic's* prizes were of such value that they were placed in charge of prize crews and sent into port. They were the ship *Grotius*, of London, which was sent into Portland, and the schooner *Traveller*, which put into Squam. The latter had aboard one hundred and nineteen hogs-heads and sixty barrels of sugar, besides a quantity of coffee.

Almost as lucky as the *Frolic* was the *General Stark*, a lugger mounting only two guns and manned by twelve men. One of her first prizes was a one-hundred-and-thirty-ton schooner, from St. John's to the West Indies, which was sent into Machias. The *General Stark* also took the brig *Cossack*, manned by twelve men, bound for Bermuda from Martinique, and having in her hold one hundred and thirty-three hogsheads, two tierces and sixty-eight bar-rels of sugar. When the *General Stark* made this capture she had only eight men aboard, the others being absent in a prize. The crew of the *Cossack* was kept aboard, while three men and a boy were sent to her from the *General Stark* as a prize crew, leaving only four persons in the privateer. In this critical condition the two vessels made for port, the *Cossack* arriving at Georgetown, South Carolina, without mishap. The vessel and her cargo were valued at four thousand dollars. The *Cossack* was purchased for five thousand dollars, and was commissioned as an 8-gun privateer, under Captain J. Nash, May, 1813. The *General Stark* took another prize, a sloop, but she was lost on Cape Cod.

By the close of the year 1813 the receipts from the sale of prizes brought into Salem amounted to $675,695.93. From this time on, however, this port was rigorously blocked by the overwhelming mari-time forces of the enemy. At the beginning of the war the New England ports were peculiarly free from blockades, the English believing that those States were opposed to war, and consequently it was good policy to befriend them. The error was discovered after the war had been in progress a year, and then the British established a rigorous blockade. The list of Salem privateers that had been captured by the enemy down to November, 1813, includes the schooners *Regulator*, *Active*, *Enterprise*, and *Cossack*, and the boat *Owl*. New and better vessels quickly supplied the places of those that were lost or captured, and in spite of the blockade the Salem privateer managed to get to sea.

The *Diomede*, Captain J. Crowninshield, was one of the most successful privateers toward the close of the war. In a short cruise she took six vessels and brought thirty-five prisoners to Salem. Some of her prizes in this and subsequent ventures were the schooners *Mary and Joseph*, *Hope*, *William*, and *Traveller*, the ships *Cod Hook* and *Upton*, and the brigs *Friends*, *Providence*, *Harmony*, and *Recovery*. The *Upton* was not taken without a severe contest. She mounted sixteen guns and had one hundred and four men aboard, and although many of these were passengers they gave a willing hand, and, taken altogether, made a formidable defense. They did not surrender until one man had been killed and one wounded. After making this long list of valuable prizes the *Diomede* herself, while in a fog, on June 25, 1814, was captured by the enemy and sent into Halifax.

The little privateers *Fly*, *Viper*, *Scorpion*, *Leech*, and *General Putnam* also did good service before the war ended. The *Fly*, Captain H. De Koven, took the schooner *George*, laden with drygoods, and sent her into port, and also the sloop *Experiment*, laden with drygoods, hardware, and lumber, which arrived safely in Machias. The *Viper* seized a schooner that pretended to be a Spaniard but was discovered to have a British license. She was sent

into Newport.   The *Viper* also took a schooner
with a cargo of rum and sugar, which reached
Newport, and another schooner laden with drygoods, which was sent into Salem.   The *Scorpion*,
Captain J. Osborn, seized a sloop mounting one gun,
which was sent into Salem, and a schooner, which
was destroyed at sea.   The *Leech*, in 1814, captured
a schooner and ransomed it, and another schooner
which, after being divested of its valuables, was
given up to the prisoners.   The career of the *General
Putnam* was brief, but not without value.   She took
the handsome 380-ton ship *Ocean*, of and for London,
with a cargo of masts, thirty-five bowsprits, and
other timber for the use of the Admiralty.   She was
sent into Salem.   Subsequently the *General Putnam*
herself was captured by the enemy.

The last of the Salem privateers to be noticed
is the *Cadet*.   This was a singularly fortunate vessel.
Among her first captures was the schooner *Betsey and
Jane*, from St. John's for Castine, with one hundred
and nineteen packages of drygoods valued at one
hundred and fifty thousand dollars.   She was sent
into Thomaston.   The *Cadet* also took the schooner
Mary, from St. John's for Castine, having a cargo of
drygoods, with which vessel she had a singular experience.   It seems that the *Mary* was being escorted
by a heavily armed schooner, and she had not been
more than a few hours out of port when the privateer
Charles Stewart, Captain H. Purcell, of Boston, hove
in sight and began an action with the armed
schooner.   Just when the battle was getting critical
a fourth sail appeared on the scene, which the commander of the *Charles Stewart* took to be an English
cruiser and sheered off.   As a matter of fact, it was
the American privateer *Cumberland*, of Portland.   As
the *Charles Stewart* disappeared below the horizon
the *Cumberland* closed with the armed schooner and
took up the battle where the *Charles Stewart* had left
off.   But the Englishman was too heavy for the pri-

vateer, and the latter, after sustaining a loss of one man killed and one wounded, was glad to make her escape. Meantime the *Mary* had become separated from her escort, and it was then that she fell into the clutches of the *Cadet*, and was captured and carried into Thomaston.

CHAPTER XVII.

SOME TYPICAL CRUISES.

ONE of the shortest, and at the same time one of the most successful, cruises made by an American privateer in this war was that of the armed schooner *Kemp*, Captain Jacobs, of Baltimore. This vessel had made two cruises early in 1814, and sailed from Wilmington, North Carolina, November 29, 1814, for the West Indies. Early in the evening of the second day out, while in the Gulf Stream, latitude 32° 32′ north, longitude 77° west, Captain Jacobs descried a number of vessels apparently sailing in company, and from their disposition he was satisfied that they were merchantmen under the convoy of one or two ships of war. For the remainder of that night Captain Jacobs cautiously made his way toward the strangers, and about daylight, December 2d, he was near enough to distinguish eight merchantmen escorted by a frigate. As the *Kemp* showed a disposition to hang on the outskirts of the convoy, the frigate, about noon, gave chase and drove the privateer away.

This was just what the Americans most desired, and making short tacks windward Captain Jacobs drew the frigate away from the merchantmen. The frigate's people evidently thought they had a good chance of overtaking the privateer, notwithstanding her superiority in sailing windward, and they kept up the chase far into the night. Seizing a favorable moment, Captain Jacobs suddenly concealed all

420

his lights, and under cover of darkness gave the enemy the slip and immediately put back for the merchantmen.

At eleven o'clock the next morning, December 3d, the privateer came in sight of the convoy, but nothing could be seen of the frigate. This was the *Kemp's* golden opportunity and she improved it to the fullest extent. Wasting no time with preliminary maneuvering the *Kemp* made straight for the convoy, which Captain Jacobs soon discovered to consist of three ships, three brigs, and two schooners. The English masters of the merchantmen were not slow in recognizing the *Kemp* as the privateer which their protecting man-of-war had chased so furiously and so fruitlessly the day before, and, realizing that they must now rely entirely on their own guns, they prepared to give battle. So far as numbers went the merchantmen had the advantage, for there were eight of them—each armed more or less heavily—against one little schooner.

By the time the *Kemp* was in gunshot she found all the merchantmen close together drawn up in line of battle and presenting a formidable array of black muzzles toward her. Not waiting for the privateer to open the fight the Englishmen, at 2 P. M., bore away for the *Kemp*, and as each ship passed delivered a broadside. Paying no attention to this Captain Jacobs reserved his fire, tacked, and passing directly through the enemy's line delivered both broadsides at close quarters. This had the effect of throwing the enemy into confusion. In their efforts to attack the audacious privateer the merchantmen only succeeded in getting in one another's way, so that only one or two of them could bring their guns to bear. Captain Jacobs was fully alive to his advantage, and skillfully keeping one of the merchantmen between his ship and the others he was in a position to deal with one at a time. At half past two o'clock Captain Jacobs ran alongside one of the brigs, the *Portsea*, carrying eight guns and twenty-six men, being laden with sugar and coffee, and boarded, carrying her without loss, excepting for one seaman wounded.

Half an hour later the *Kemp* ran alongside one of the ships, the *Rosabella*, of sixteen guns and thirty-five men, when First Officer Myers and Sailing-Master Sellers, at the head of eight men, sprang to her deck and carried her after a brief struggle with her men, three of whom were injured. Shortly afterward Captain Jacobs boarded one of the schooners and carried her without opposition. The next vessel to be attacked was the largest of the brigs. Here a more determined opposition was met. The struggle lasted from fifteen to twenty minutes, when this vessel also was captured, making four prizes out of a convoy of eight vessels. Captain Jacobs would have secured the remaining four merchantmen had it not been for the fact that he could not spare another man for a prize crew. As it was, he now had almost as many prisoners as seamen, and, being scattered about in four different vessels, there was danger of their rising and recovering their ships.

Deeming it prudent to return to America Captain Jacobs allowed the rest of the merchantmen to escape, and now gave his attention to getting his prizes into port. Nothing was seen of the frigate that had so furiously chased the *Kemp* when the convoy was first discovered. Her commander probably fell in with the remnant of his convoy a day or so later, and learned, to his sorrow, that while thundering over the ocean waves in chase of the privateer the latter was quietly helping herself to the merchantmen.

The total force of the eight merchant ships the *Kemp* engaged was forty-six guns and one hundred and thirty-four men, as opposed to the privateer's twelve guns and one hundred and thirty men. Captain Jacobs took seventy-one prisoners. The Americans had only one man, John Irwin, killed, and four wounded. The prizes were found to be laden with valuable cargoes, consisting mostly of sugar and coffee. The *Rosabella* and her cargo alone were estimated to be worth three hundred thousand dollars, but unfortunately, while endeavoring to enter Charleston harbor, she grounded on the bar and became a total loss. The wreck afterward was burned by a British war brig. One of the schooners engaged was the *Cossack*, formerly the *O. H. Perry*. The other prizes of the *Kemp* succeeded in reaching Southern ports. In her career in this war the *Kemp* is credited with fifteen prizes.

Another eminently successful privateer was the *Surprise*, Captain Barnes, of Baltimore. This vessel arrived at Newport July 15, 1814, after a cruise of one hundred and three days in the English and Irish Channels and off the Western Isles, in which she had been chased sixteen times and had taken twelve or thirteen British merchantmen. Refitting in Newport, the *Surprise* again made for English waters, and after making a number of prizes she put into Brest, and on December 24, 1814, received a salute of eleven guns from the French admiral. On January 9, 1815, she put to sea on another venture. When five days out she was hotly pursued for several hours by a British war ship, which fired fifty shots at her. Evading the war ship in the night, Captain Barnes, about eleven o'clock on the morning of January 28th, discovered a sail on his lee quarter. As the wind was light he manned his sweeps so as to draw away from the stranger, which had every appearance of being a heavy war vessel. The stranger seemed equally anxious to come to close quarters, and holding a better wind managed to get within gunshot by half past twelve o'clock, at which time she was flying English colors.

Seeing that an action was unavoidable Captain Barnes showed American colors and answered the

Englishman's first broadside with spirit. A heavy cannonading was kept up until a quarter past two o'clock, when Captain Barnes, by the aid of his sweeps, gained a raking position under the enemy's stern, and after pouring in a destructive broadside compelled the ship to surrender. She proved to be the English ship *Star*, carrying eight 12-pounders and a crew of twenty-six men, from Batavia for London, laden with coffee and other valuable East Indies produce. The *Star* had one man killed and one wounded, while several shots had taken effect in her hull, and her sails and rigging were cut to pieces. No one in the *Surprise* was hurt, but some damage was done to her sails, and her foremast and foretopmast were wounded by round shot.

Removing a large portion of the *Star's* cargo to his own ship, Captain Barnes sent eighteen men and a prize master aboard and proceeded with her to the United States. While drawing near the American coast, February 26, 1815, the ships, during a snowstorm, became separated, but they both arrived in New York safely. The entire cargo of the *Star* was estimated to be worth three hundred thousand dollars. It consisted of one thousand one hundred and eighty bags of sugar, five thousand and twenty-one bags of coffee, forty-five tubs of camphor, two hundred and ninety-seven bags of sago, twenty-two bales of nankeens, eighty-three cases of cinnamon, and forty-five cases of tortoise shell. In all, the *Surprise* is credited with thirty-four prizes.

One of the most satisfactory cruises in this war was that in which the privateer *Caroline*, Captain Almeda, of Baltimore, captured two "traitor vessels." On November 20, 1813, this privateer fell in with the American sloop *Osiris*, Captain Driggs, from Martinique for St. Bartholomew, with a cargo of molasses. Driggs, supposing that the *Caroline* was a British war vessel, came aboard and showed his British license, remarking that only recently he had supplied Captain Oliver, of the English man-of-war *Valiant*, with potatoes and apples. Driggs further said that he had received pay for these supplies and added that there would be no doubt of his being hung if he fell in with an American. Captain Almeda promptly seized the *Osiris* and placed Mr. Canoning, with a prize crew, in charge of her, with instructions to make for port. The other " traitor vessel " taken by the *Caroline* was the brig *Criterion*, with eighty hogsheads of rum aboard. She was sent into Stonington, Connecticut, where she was condemned.

The *Caroline* was fortunate in making a number of prizes in the course of the war; but her first, a brig laden with sugar and molasses, was recaptured by the enemy while attempting to enter Charleston harbor. The *Caroline* was more fortunate with her other prizes in this cruise, as she succeeded in sending into a North Carolina port the brig *Abel*, from the West Indies, laden with rum and sugar, and a schooner from Martinique, with one hundred and twenty hogsheads of molasses, into Charleston. The latter had both English and Swedish papers. The *Caroline* also took a brig from St. Lucia, with one hundred and forty hogsheads and two hundred barrels of sugar aboard, and sent her into Elizabeth City, North Carolina. Besides these the *Caroline* captured ten vessels, which were depleted of the most available portions of their cargoes and burned. Captain Almeda returned to Charleston only because his vessel could not hold any more goods. One of his prizes, the schooner *Joseph*, from Surinam, laden with coffee, rum, and sugar, in endeavoring to run into Georgetown, South Carolina, nearly became wrecked, but was saved by the skill of Lieutenant Monk, of the navy.[1]

---

[1] In a subsequent cruise, 1814, the *Caroline* took the brig *Elizabeth*, for Kingston (Jamaica), which was sent into Charleston: the schooner *Jason*, of Nassau, which was destroyed at sea; the brig *Experience*, from Jamaica

Quite as fortunate as the *Caroline* was the *Mammoth*, Captain Rowland, also of Baltimore. Her first prize was the coppered-brig *Camelion*, from the West Indies for New Brunswick, laden with rum and molasses, which was sent into port; and her second was the sloop *Farmer*, with a cargo of provisions, which vessel was sunk. She also took the brig *Britannia*, from St. Andrews for Liverpool, laden with lumber, which was destroyed, and three other brigs in ballast, which also were burned at sea. While off the coast of Newfoundland the *Mammoth* had an action with an English transport having on board between three and four hundred troops. After a severe engagement, in which the privateer had one man wounded, the Americans hauled off for "something that was more valuable to them than mere men."

Later in the war the *Mammoth* took the brig *Ceres*, of Glasgow, laden with brandy, and made a cartel of her. In this cruise of only seven weeks the privateer took sixteen English merchantmen. For seventeen days she hovered off Cape Clear, where most of her captures were made. In all the *Mammoth* took twenty-one vessels and released on parole three hundred prisoners. She arrived at Portsmouth with a full cargo. In her last cruise she was not so fortunate, returning to New York in 1815, after a long and fruitless search for British merchantmen. She was chased several times by the enemy's war ships, and on one occasion, during a calm, she was attacked by their boats, but managed to repel them.

for Gonaives, the last being chased ashore on the island of Cuba by the enemy and was lost. Two other vessels were relieved of the most valuable portions of their cargoes and then burned before the *Caroline* returned to Charleston. In her last cruise she burned the sloop *Eliza* and made a cartel of the schooner *Mariner*, after taking out her cargo of dry-goods. The *Caroline* also made a cartel of the brig *Stephen*, carrying fourteen guns and a crew of thirty men, from St. Thomas for Curaçoa. The *Caroline* returned from this cruise to Wilmington, North Carolina, with a full cargo.

CHAPTER XVIII.

PRIVATEERS AGAINST PRIVATEERS.

A noteworthy feature of the maritime war of 1812–1815 was the number of instances in which our privateers were pitted against British vessels of the same class. When these amateur cruisers of the war met it generally resulted in a hard-fought battle, and in many cases some desperate struggles took place. One of the first actions of this kind occurred August 4, 1812, two weeks before the first frigate engagement of the war, when the American privateer *Shadow*, Captain J. Taylor, of Philadelphia, fought the British letter of marque *May* (or *Nancy*), Captain Affleck. Half an hour after meridian, August 3, 1812, a sail was discovered from the masthead of the *Shadow*, to which the Americans immediately gave chase. The stranger was soon made out to be a large vessel, and Captain Taylor sent all hands to quarters. After a hard run of five hours the *Shadow* came up with the supposed merchantman, but just as they were about to order the stranger to surrender the Americans were unpleasantly surprised to find themselves in the presence of a British man-of-war. No time was lost in taking in the *Shadow's* square sail and staysail and hauling by the wind. The Englishman promptly tacked in pursuit, and opened a brisk fire from his chase guns. Some of his shot came aboard the privateer, but as the damage was speedily repaired it did not cause the Americans to lose ground. Being on her best point of sailing the schooner gradually drew away from the man-of-war, and by eight o'clock that evening lost sight of her.

At 12.30 P. M. on the following day, August 4th, another sail was reported from the privateer's masthead. This stranger was to the east, standing westward. Notwithstanding his narrow escape of the day before, Captain Taylor, on sighting this stranger, made all efforts to overtake her. In their eagerness to come up with the chase, however, the Americans got a greater press of canvas on their vessel than her masts could bear, and at half past five o'clock the square-sail boom was carried away. The wreck was cleared as soon as possible, and by rigging out the lower studding-sail boom, and setting the square sail again, Captain Taylor had the satisfaction of again gaining on the chase.

At six o'clock the vessels were so near that the stranger began firing from her stern guns. Without replying to this Captain Taylor, by seven o'clock, had gained a favorable position and opened from his battery. It was now quite dark, and after the two ships had maintained a running action for half an hour the stranger hoisted a light in her mizzen rigging, to which Captain Taylor responded with a similar signal and at the same time hailed. The reply was that she was from Liverpool. This answer was sufficient to induce the American commander to order the stranger to send a boat aboard with her papers. In a few minutes the boat came alongside and an officer and two men boarded the *Shadow*, but they failed to bring the ship's papers with them. They were detained aboard while an American boat in charge of Third Officer Thomas Yorke put off to the stranger to demand the papers. On gaining the Englishman's deck and making known his errand, Mr. Yorke was curtly informed that the demand would not be complied with. A note addressed to Captain Taylor was then given to him, and Mr. Yorke returned to the ship.

In this note the British commander declared that his ship was the British letter of marque *May* (or *Nancy*), from Liverpool, Captain Affleck, bound for St. Lucia, and carried fourteen guns and a complement of fifty men. Captain Affleck further declared that the Orders in Council had been rescinded and that a change of ministry had taken place in England. Although the *May*, to all appearances, was a formidable vessel, Captain Taylor was determined to have it out with her, and he again sent his boat aboard her with a peremptory demand for her papers. As this was again refused both vessels, at half past eight o'clock, opened a spirited fire. After the action had lasted about an hour a shot wounded the *Shadow's* sailmaker, William Craft. About ten o'clock Captain Taylor dropped astern, intending to remain within gunshot all night and resume the fight at daylight. The weather was very squally and dark, so that in order to make sure that the enemy could not give her the slip under cover of darkness the *Shadow* kept within easy gunshot, and at intervals ran close up to the Englishman and for a few minutes kept up a brisk fire.

On the return of day, having improved the intervening hours in repairing damages, Captain Taylor ran close under the stern of the enemy and began another severe action. It was not long before the *Shadow* received a shot in her starboard bow which shattered the wood ends, started the plank-sheer, and smashed several timbers. At half past seven o'clock she received another shot, almost in the same place but on the port side, which knocked the carriage of the port after gun to pieces, killed six men and wounded three. In spite of these heavy blows the Americans continued the fight for an hour longer, when Captain Taylor was killed by a ball in his left temple. Almost at the same time a shot struck under the port fore chains, between wind and water, which started a dangerous leak. The surviving officers now decided to withdraw from a contest obviously unequal, and with three feet of water in the hold they drew away. The *Shadow* arrived in Philadelphia August 18th. She was refitted, and soon afterward sailed on another cruise.[1]

Later in the war the *Shadow* was captured by the enemy, and, on being refitted, was taken into their service under the name *Fanny*, carrying nine guns. While running from La Guayra to London, in 1815, the *Fanny* was recaptured by the privateer *Lawrence*, of Baltimore, Captain E. Vearey. A prize crew was placed aboard the *Fanny*, but when near the American coasts they were driven into a Cuban port in distress. It is believed that on getting to sea again the *Fanny* was lost, with all hands. The *Lawrence* was one of the successful privateers of the war, taking in all thirteen merchantmen, and on one occasion beating off a British brig of war.

Another action that took place between an American and a British privateer in the summer of 1812 was that between the *Globe*, Captain J. Grant (by some accounts Gavet), of Baltimore, and the *Boyd*, of Liverpool. The *Globe* was one of the first of our privateers to get to sea in this war, and she was generally successful. On July 24, 1812, or a little more than a month after war had been declared, this privateer left the Chesapeake capes in company with the privateer *Cora*. The *Globe* carried a complement of about ninety men and boys. Speaking the ship *Marmion*, of New Orleans for Baltimore, and the ship *South Carolina*, of and for the same ports, on the first and second days out, Captain Grant boarded a number of vessels, but met no ship he could attack until July 31st, when a sail was discovered and chased. In three hours the *Globe* was

---

[1] For action between the privateers *Rossie* and *Jeannie* see page 806.

within gunshot, when she began firing from her long
tom, a 9-pounder amidships. The chase hoisted
English colors and returned the fire with her two
stern guns, 9-pounders. As it was blowing rather
fresh at the time Captain Grant was unable to
bring his broadside guns to bear, and so determined to hold on his present course, notwithstanding the number of guns the enemy could bring into
action.

For forty minutes the unequal contest was main-
tanied, both vessels crowding on canvas, but the
American had a decided advantage in sailing.
At last the *Globe* began to double on the enemy's
quarter, when Captain Grant let go his forward
division of guns, and, as his vessel gradually came
abeam the chase, he opened with his entire broadside guns, which had been carefully loaded with a
double charge of round shot. After the first discharge the American gunners loaded with langrage
and round shot. The Englishman returned the fire
with spirit, answering broadside for broadside, and,
as the vessels gradually edged toward each other,
gave volley for volley of musketry and pistols. For
an hour and a half this contest was kept up, when
the stranger surrendered, announcing herself to be
the *Boyd*, from New Providence for Liverpool, with
a valuable cargo of coffee, dyewoods, and cotton.
The *Boyd* carried two long 9-pounders, two short 12-
pounders, and six long 6-pounders. Both vessels
were very much cut up in sails, rigging, and hull; but,
strange to say, no one had been hurt. Transferring
the crew of the *Boyd*, excepting an officer and two
men, to the *Globe*, Captain Grant placed a prize master and eight men aboard her, with orders to make
the nearest American port. Seven of the English
prisoners entered the *Globe's* crew. On the following day, August 1st, Captain Grant parted company
with the *Boyd* and went in search of two other English vessels, which were expected to pass that way

in a day or two, the *Boyd* arriving in Philadelphia a few days later.

On the day he parted from his prize, August 1st, Captain Grant gave chase to a schooner, but lost her in the night. He saw another sail that evening, but missed her also. At eleven o'clock on the following morning the *Globe* came in sight of Bermuda, and passing with gunshot cruised off the place under English colors. At sunset a sail was discovered directly ahead, but when near enough it was seen to be a British sloop of war. This, of course, was the time for the *Globe* to " show a clean pair of heels; " and that is what Captain Grant proceeded to do, with the Englishman in full chase. In an hour or so, however, the enemy gave up the hopeless endeavor to come up with the swift privateer. On the afternoon of the following day a schooner to windward was discovered and chased. As the wind had almost died away Captain Grant got out his sweeps, and from four to eight o'clock his men exerted themselves to come up with the stranger. The *Globe* slowly overhauled the schooner, but it was night before she was within gunshot, and in the darkness she escaped.

The *Globe* now began to run short of water, and by August 8th both officers and men were placed on an allowance of three quarts a day, the seamen exchanging their liquor, quart for quart, for water. On the 14th the *Globe* chased and captured, without resistance, the English schooner *Ann*, mounting four guns and manned by nine men, from San Domingo for Guernsey, laden with mahogany and logwood. Several of the seamen in the *Ann* enlisted in the *Globe*. Captain Grant now shaped his course homeward, arriving safely at Baltimore with his prize.

Later in the war the *Globe* took a number of prizes, among them being the ship *Sir Simon Clark*, carrying sixteen guns and thirty-nine men, from Jamaica for Leith. She was laden with a cargo of sugar, rum, and coffee, which was computed to be worth anywhere from one hundred thousand to one hundred and fifty thousand dollars. The merchantman was not taken without a severe fight, the Americans finally carrying her by boarding, after a brisk cannon fire, in which four of the English were killed and their commander and three men were severely wounded. The second officer and drummer of the *Globe* were killed and one man was wounded. She was taken into Norfolk by a prize crew. While cruising off the coast of Portugal on another cruise, the *Globe*, then commanded by John Murphy, was attacked by an Algerine sloop of war. The action was continued, off and on, for three hours at half-gunshot distance, when the Algerine drew off, apparently in a bad condition. The privateer received no less than eighty-two shots through her sails, but had only two men wounded.

Three other important prizes taken by the *Globe* in this war were the brig *Kingston Packet*, with a valuable cargo of rum aboard, which was sent into Ocracoke Inlet, North Carolina; the ship *Venus*, carrying fourteen guns, from Cadiz for Newfoundland, with a full cargo of salt; and the ship *Seaton*. The last was captured by the privateer *Paul Jones*, of New York, and was ordered to the United States in charge of a prize crew. The vessel, soon after parting company with the *Paul Jones*, proved unseaworthy, and on meeting with the *Globe* she was burned at the request of her prize master.[1]

Probably no American privateer in this war had such a varied experience as the 11-gun schooner *Matilda*, Captain H. Rantin, of Philadelphia. She got to sea about July 15, 1812, and when a few days out captured a brig from San Domingo for London, which arrived at the *Matilda's* home port, August 10th. A few days after taking this brig the *Matilda*

---

[1] For action between the *Globe* and two packets, see pp. 455–459.

fell in with the English brig *Ranger*, Captain John
Heard, which was taken only after a stubbornly contested action, in which the British commander was
killed. The prize was sent into Philadelphia, and a
newspaper of that city, under date of August 23,
1812, notes: "Yesterday the remains of Captain
Heard, of the British brig *Ranger*, were interred with
the respect which honor and valor, even in an enemy,
can never fail to inspire. Captain Heard was captured, with his brig, by the privateer *Matilda*, of this
port, after a smart action, in which he received a
wound of which he unfortunately died. The funeral
was attended by the officers of the United States
army and navy now in this city and by the uniformed
volunteer corps. The Philadelphia Blues, commanded by Colonel L. Rush, performed the funeral
honors. The war of freemen is not with virtuous
men of any nation, but against the tyranny and op-
pression of rulers, and generosity must even shed
a tear over those whose unhappy lot is to be victims
of their injustice."

In July of 1813 the *Matilda* fell in with a large
ship, which was mistaken by the Americans for a
merchantman. She proved to be the privateer *Lion*,
built as a frigate, to be presented by the English
Government to the Turks, but later converted to
private use. She was pierced for twenty-eight guns,
and at the time she met the *Matilda* was manned by
one hundred and twenty men. Captain Rantin did
not discover the real force of this vessel until he had
boarded her with nearly all his officers; and had
he been promptly followed by his seamen he would
have captured her, for most of the British crew had
run below. A heavy sea, however, carried the two
ships apart, leaving the American officers unsup-
ported by their men. Taking in the situation at a
glance the Englishmen rallied, and, after overpowering the officers of the privateer, made sail for the
Matilda and soon compelled her to surrender. In

this action Captain Rantin and twenty or thirty of his men were killed. The survivors were carried into Bahia, from which place they sailed for New York in the ship *William*, Captain Davis.

The British immediately refitted the *Matilda* and sent her to England, but while in the English Channel she was recaptured by the United States brig of war *Argus*, Master-Commandant William Henry Allen. A few days after taking the *Matilda* the *Argus* was captured by the *Pelican*, Allen dying from injuries he received in the fight.[1] The notice quoted from a Philadelphia newspaper relative to the burial of Captain Heard, of the *Ranger*, will apply to the attention paid to both Rantin and Allen, the English in both cases honoring the American commanders in every possible way. But the *Matilda* was not yet safely " out of the woods," for shortly after her recapture by the *Argus* she was recaptured by a British 74-gun ship of the line. A British prize crew was placed aboard and ordered to England, but before gaining a place of safety the *Matilda* was taken for the fourth time, being seized by the American privateer *General Armstrong*, and was sent into port.

On April 24, 1813, the American privateer *Ned*, Captain J. Dawson, of Baltimore, arrived at New York *via* Long Island Sound from La Teste. She reported that while in latitude 44° 54′ north, longitude 15° west, she fell in with the privateer *Malvina*, from the Mediterranean for London, which vessel mounted ten guns—6- and 9-pounders—and after a close action, lasting fifty-two minutes, captured her. The Americans had seven men badly wounded, while the commander of the *Malvina* was killed and a number of his men wounded. The prize was found to be laden with wine. Mr. Penderson was placed aboard as a prize master, and carried her into a North Carolina port.

---

[1] See Maclay's History of the United States Navy, vol. i, pp. 528–529.

Returning to America the *Ned* endeavored to enter the Chesapeake, but when she came in sight of the Capes, April 18th, she was chased by a 74-gun ship of the line and a frigate. Making her way northward, she tried, on the 19th, to run into the Delaware, but here also she was chased by the English blockading ships, and when off Sandy Hook, on the 20th, she was driven away by a similar force. On April 21st Captain Dawson managed to run the gantlet of four or five British war ships, and touched at New London for a Sound pilot, after which he made his way to New York. The *Ned* sailed again in the summer of 1813, this time under Captain Hackett, but on September 6th she was captured, after a chase of four days, by the British sloop of war *Royalist.*

On December 9, 1812, the privateer *Saratoga*, Captain Charles W. Wooster, of New York, appeared off La Guayra and sent his first officer ashore, who reported to the American consul that his ship was twenty-four days from New York and had met no sail. On the following day Captain Wooster ran down and anchored in the roads, but a few minutes later a messenger hastened aboard with a note from the American consul advising Captain Wooster to weigh anchor and keep out of reach of the batteries, as the commandant had avowed his intention of sinking the privateer if she came to. Captain Wooster acted on the advice and stood off. Shortly afterward he discovered a schooner standing down the coast, some miles to windward of La Guayra. Running down to her he boarded and captured her. Drygoods valued at twenty thousand dollars were found in her hold. Early in the morning of the following day there was a heavy fog along the coast line, but about nine o'clock it lifted, revealing to Captain Wooster a brig some miles seaward endeavoring to make the port. The *Saratoga* stood for the stranger, and two hours later both vessels tacked off shore.

Battle between the schooner Saratoga and the brig Rachel.

To the people on shore it was known that the brig was the English letter of marque *Rachel*, from Greenock, armed with twelve long 9-pounders and carrying a complement of sixty men and boys. She had aboard a cargo valued at fifteen thousand pounds sterling. The news quickly spread that a naval engagement was imminent off the port, and in a short time all business was suspended, everybody hastening to the shore to witness the fight.

After standing off shore some time the two vessels suddenly tacked landward, and when within five miles of the shore the *Saratoga* opened from her starboard bow gun, which was answered by the brig's port quarter guns. The two vessels maintained a heavy cannonading for a few minutes, when the Americans boarded and compelled the enemy to surrender. On the part of the Americans one man was wounded, but in the *Rachel* only the second officer was unhurt, nearly all of her men having been killed or wounded. On December 13th Captain Wooster sent twenty-five prisoners with the second officer of the *Rachel* to La Guayra in the brig's longboat, together with every article belonging to them as personal property.[1]

About this time a small English privateer, name not given, was taken by the privateer *Rapid*, of Charleston. The *Liberty*, of Baltimore, also captured a British privateer, and after divesting her of guns and valuables gave her up to the prisoners. A battle also took place between the privateer *Midas*, Captain Thompson, of Baltimore, and the *Dash*. The *Midas* carried eight guns and thirty-five men, while her opponent mounted five and was manned by forty men. The action took place off Tybee lighthouse, where the *Dash* had captured three coasting vessels from Savannah. Learning the Englishman's whereabouts Captain Thompson put to sea, and coming upon the *Dash* captured her with all her prizes.

---

[1] For action between the *Saratoga* and a packet, see pp. 454–455.

One of the last actions between privateers in this war took place on January 31, 1815. At noon of this day the 16-gun brig *Macdonough*, Captain O. Wilson, of Rhode Island, discovered a large ship to leeward, some six miles off. As the Americans drew nearer it was noticed that she was making signals and apparently had two rows of ports. By 1 P. M Captain Wilson had approached sufficiently near to discover that the lower row of ports was false, upon which he prepared for action. At 2 P. M. he bore up for the stranger's weather quarter and showed his colors, the stranger all this time waiting with his courses up for the attack. By 2.30 P. M. the vessels were within musket shot, when the action became severe. It was now observed that the stranger was using only seven guns to a broadside, but was pouring in a tremendous musketry fire, which led Captain Wilson to believe that she had a large number of soldiers aboard. At 3.30 P. M. the *Macdonough* passed close under the enemy's bow and raked with effect. It was then seen that the enemy's decks were crowded with troops, who were making good use of their small arms. Fifteen minutes later Captain Wilson found that his sails and rigging were seriously injured, while a large number of his men had been killed or wounded, besides which several shot had taken effect near the privateer's water line, which caused her to leak seriously. Seeing little chance of capturing the stranger Captain Wilson sheered off, while the Englishmen, also having had enough of the fight, made away in the direction of Teneriffe. It was noticed that many of her men were slung over her sides, stopping shot holes near her water line. The *Macdonough* arrived at Savannah March 7th, having taken nine prizes in her entire career in this war.

CHAPTER XIX.

NEW YORK PRIVATEERS.

NOTWITHSTANDING the fact that the British maintained a rigorous blockade off Sandy Hook and in Long Island Sound in the course of the war, New York managed to send to sea fifty-five privateers. The careers of many of these have been recorded in other chapters. Of the remaining the *Benjamin Franklin* was one of the first to get to sea, leaving port about July 24, 1812, and returning August 24th, in which time she made seven prizes and twenty-eight prisoners. This privateer was a schooner carrying eight guns and one hundred and twenty men, under the command of Captain J. Ingersoll. Her first prizes were the brigs *Friends* and *Mary*, which arrived safely in Boston, and the sloop *Louisa Ann*. The last was captured in a most daring manner. The sloop was securely anchored in Trinity harbor, Martinique, under the guns of a battery of twelve 18-pounders. She had a valuable cargo of molasses aboard, and was awaiting an opportunity to get to sea. Seven men from the privateer volunteered to take her by surprise, and putting off in a boat they attacked the sloop and captured her. The *Benjamin Franklin* also captured the new and valuable brig *John*, from La Guayra for Gibraltar, armed with ten 12-pounders and laden with coffee and cocoa, which was sent into New York; the brig *Two Brothers*, also sent into New York; and the schooner *Success*, from Newfoundland for New Brunswick,

439

with two hundred and fifty barrels of salmon aboard.

The privateers *Divided We Fall* and *United We Stand*, in keeping with their names, were generally found cruising in company. The former was commanded by Captain J. Cropsy and the latter by Captain W. Storey. One of their prizes was a brig mounting ten guns and having a very valuable cargo, which was sent into Savannah. The *Divided We Fall* also took and ransomed two vessels, sunk another, and gave up three others after the most desirable portions of their cargoes had been removed. Most of these vessels were known as "droghers," or West India trading vessels, which, as a rule, were richly laden.

Of the privateers *Flirt*, *Galloway*, *Hero*, *Henry Guilder*, *Morgiana*, and *Mars* little is recorded. The brig *Flirt*, Captain Storer, is credited with taking the brig *Commerce*, from Martinique for Halifax, laden with rum and molasses, but the prize was partially dismantled, and so badly injured in other respects that she was destroyed. The *Galloway* on her passage to Nantes, April, 1814, captured and sent into that port the brig *Fanny*, of London, laden with fish. The sloop *Hero*, Captain T. Waterman, had an unusual experience with one of her prizes. On her passage to France she took the schooner *Victoria*, which was manned and ordered to an American port. Soon after parting company with the *Hero*, the *Victoria* was recaptured by a British war vessel, and the American prize crew, with the exception of one man, was taken aboard the man-of-war and their places taken by Englishmen. The one American left in the *Victoria*, however, persuaded the new prize crew to run their vessel into an American port. This was done as soon as they had lost sight of the war ship, and the *Victoria* arrived at Charleston. The *Hero*, in 1814, captured the schooner *Robert Hartwell*, from Antigua for Bermuda, with a cargo valued at twenty thousand dollars, which was sent into Newberne; the schooner *Funchall*, sent into the same port; and two vessels which were ransomed. A cutter named *Hero* was manned by volunteers in Stonington, Connecticut, and captured the king's schooner *Fox*, a tender to a ship of the line.

The *Henry Guilder* was fortunate in capturing, in 1814, the schooner *Young Farmer*, from La Guayra, laden with indigo worth forty thousand dollars. The prize arrived in New York. The *Mars* was equally fortunate in capturing the schooner *Susan and Eliza*, of Bermuda, and sending her into Wilmington, with her cargo of one hundred and twenty thousand pounds of coffee. In the same cruise the *Mars* sent into Charleston the brig *Superb*, with a cargo of salt. About February, 1814, this privateer was chased ashore on Rockaway Beach by a British 74-gun ship of the line and a frigate. Forty of the Americans escaped with sixteen thousand dollars in specie, and thirty were captured by the enemy, while forty-three prisoners were recaptured. In this cruise the *Mars* had been chased eleven times. Late in the war the *Morgiana*, Captain G. Fellows, took the schooner *Sultan* and the ship *City of Limerick*, the latter with a very valuable cargo of general merchandise. The *Sultan* was sent into Wilmington, and the *City of Limerick* was ordered into port after the most desirable portion of her cargo had been transferred to the *Morgiana*. The *Morgiana* returned to port with two hundred and fifty thousand dollars' worth of goods.

More distinguished than these privateers were the 18-gun brig *Holkar* and the 10-gun brig *Herald*. The former, commanded by Captain T. Rowland, took the ship *Aurora*, mounting twelve guns, and with a cargo of drygoods worth three hundred thousand dollars, which arrived in Newport. In the same cruise the *Holkar* took the 10-gun brig *Emu*, manned

31

by twenty-five men, from Portsmouth for Botany
Bay. The *Emu* had on board forty-nine women convicts. These were landed on the island of St. Vincent, one of the Cape de Verdes, with provisions
enough for four months. It is recorded that the *Emu*
" was a king's ship carrying twelve guns, and was
provided with a ' patent defense ' surmounting her
bulwarks, composed of spring bayonets, to prevent
boarding. She had a great quantity of ammunition
on board. She was commanded by an arrogant lieutenant of the British navy, who could not persuade
his crew to fight the Yankees." Four other prizes
taken by the *Holkar* were the schooner *Richard*,
which was sent into Savannah; a 14-gun brig, sent
into New York; and two trading vessels.

While in Long Island Sound, endeavoring to
gain her port, the *Holkar* was chased ashore near
New London by the British frigate *Orpheus*. This
cruiser had been very active in harassing our vessels, having taken a number and compelling others
to beach. After running his vessels ashore, Captain
Rowland managed to get all his cargo on land, together with his twenty-five prisoners. Observing
that the *Orpheus* was sending her boats to attack
him, Captain Rowland prepared for a desperate defense and succeeded in repelling the enemy. It is
said that, after the fight, fifteen bodies of the Englishmen were washed ashore, among their killed
being Captain Collins, of the marines. Realizing
that he could not save his vessel, Captain Rowland
escaped with his men, after which the *Orpheus* ran
close in and soon destroyed the privateer.

The *Herald* began her operations later in the war.
She arrived in New York, December 26, 1813, and reported that on her passage from Charleston she had
an action with an English schooner, but after exchanging several broadsides they became separated
by darkness. One of the most important prizes in
the war was made by this privateer. In June or July,

1814, she seized the ship *Friendship*, from London for Lisbon, which was sailing under Swedish colors. Her cargo was believed to be English, however, and as it was invoiced at one hundred thousand pounds she was sent into Wilmington. The *Herald* also took the schooner *Ellen*, from Belfast for Lisbon, laden with beef, pork, and lard, which was sent into Beaufort, and a brig and schooner laden with fish, which were sent into Ocracoke Inlet. Another privateer called *Herald*, a 17-gun schooner commanded by Captain J. Miller, was commissioned from New York. She was captured late in the war, after a chase of four hours by two British frigates. No prizes have been credited to her.

The *Invincible*, the *Jonquille*, and the *Marengo* were privateers that did good service toward the close of the war. The first took a ship in ballast from Liverpool for Antigua, and sent her into Wilmington; the brig *Nimble*, with a cargo of West India produce, sent into Teneriffe; the schooner *Prince Regent*, mounting ten guns, which was given up after her armament had been taken aboard the *Invincible*; the cutter *Lyon*, with drygoods and hardware, divested and released; the brig *Portsea*, carrying eight guns; the brig *Conway*, of ten guns, with a cargo of drygoods, and ordered for the United States; the schooner *Francis and Lucy*, with fish, oil, and lumber, and converted into a cartel; the brig *Margaretta*, laden with wine.

The *Jonquille*, Captain E. Carman, in April, 1814, took the schooner *Cobham*, of Bermuda, and sent her into Wilmington; a brig laden with fish, which was sent into port; the schooner *St. John's*, with coffee, which was ransomed; a schooner, which was turned into a cartel; and the sloop *Trinidad*, laden with coffee, hides, and logwood, which was burned. The *Jonquille* arrived at Beaufort in 1815, nine days from Port-au-Prince, with a full cargo.

The *Marengo*, Captain J. Redois, was one of the

most successful privateers that sailed from New York, taking in all eight merchantmen, seven of which arrived in port and one was burned at sea.

The 16-gun privateer *Orders in Council*, Captain J. Howard, having a complement of one hundred and twenty men, captured the brig *Lady Harriot*, with a cargo of wine, from Cadiz, and sent her into New York, and a brig laden with salt, which she cut out of Turk's Island. On her second cruise this privateer, then on her way to Bordeaux, fell in with the king's cutter *Wellington*, armed with twelve long 12-pounders and manned by fifty-seven men. An action began within musket shot, and was maintained with considerable energy for one hour and twenty-two minutes, when the cutter was compelled to sheer off. The crew of the privateer at this time had been reduced by sickness to fifteen men ready for duty. A few days after her encounter with the *Wellington*, the *Orders in Council* was chased, January 1, 1813, by three English privateers, and in his efforts to get away from them Captain Howard ran under the guns of the British 74-gun line of battle ship *Surveillant*, and was compelled to surrender. In all this privateer had made four prizes.

Several prizes of value were made by the *Rosamond*, Captain J. Campan, and the *Shark*, Captain R. d'Elville. The first took the brig *Roebuck*, with a full cargo of rum, from Grenada for Jersey, which was sent into Norfolk. The *Roebuck* was a splendid vessel, formerly belonging to the United States, but was captured by the *Orders in Council*. The *Rosamond* also took the schooner *Adela*, with a cargo of sugar, from Martinique, sailing under Spanish colors, which was sent into New York; and the schooner *Antelope*, which was sent into Charleston. The *Shark*, in October, 1814, took the schooner *Mary*, with three thousand pounds worth of drygoods, from Jamaica for San Domingo, which was sent into New Orleans; and five vessels off the coast of Portugal, three of which were released and two were ordered to the United States.

The *Young Eagle* at the outset of her career had a spirited engagement with two heavily armed merchantmen, the ship *Grenada* and the schooner *Shaddock*, which were attacked in company. The *Grenada* was a ship of seven hundred tons, mounted eleven guns, and had a crew of thirty men. She was from Guadeloupe bound for London, with a cargo consisting principally of seven hundred hogsheads of sugar and large quantities of cotton and coffee. The *Shaddock* was bound for Liverpool from Antigua, with a cargo of molasses. The *Young Eagle* had only one gun, the unfailing long tom, and was manned by forty-two men. The action lasted one hour and a half when both merchantmen were captured. The master of the *Shaddock* was killed and two of his men were wounded. The *Grenada* had three of her people injured, but no one in the *Young Eagle* was hurt. The *Grenada* was sent into Charleston and the *Shaddock* into New York.

The *Viper*, Captain D. Dithurbide, sailed from Charleston, February 24, 1813, and after a cruise arrived at New Bedford, March 4th. In this time she took three valuable vessels, which realized, on sale, one hundred and fifty thousand dollars. The privateer *Yorktown*, Captain T. W. Story, got to sea early in the war, and by May 30, 1813, she had made eleven prizes. On July 17th of this year she was captured by an English squadron and sent into Halifax.

The peculiar dangers to which the privateersman was exposed are well illustrated in the career of the *Teazer*, of New York. This craft, under the command of Captain F. Johnson, got to sea early in the War of 1812, and among her first prizes were the 10-gun packet *Ann*, which was sent into Portland, and the schooner *Greyhound*. A prize crew was thrown aboard the latter, with orders to make for the most available American port. In carrying out these instructions the prize master of the *Greyhound* was chased and overtaken by the 74-gun ship of the line *La Hague*, Captain Capel. Realizing that resistance was hopeless, the Yankee prize master resorted to a *ruse*. He had preserved the original English papers of the *Greyhound*, and when the boarding officer came these documents were shown to him, with the statement that the *Greyhound* was an English vessel and had a British crew aboard. As all the Americans answered to the names on the shipping papers, the English officer departed and the *Greyhound* gained port in safety.

After taking a few more prizes the *Teazer*, in December, 1812, was captured by the 74-gun ship of the line *San Domingo* and was burned, the crew being released on their promise not to serve against Great Britain again in this war until regularly exchanged. It seems that Johnson, without waiting to be thus exchanged, on his return to the United States entered another privateer, which was called *Young Teazer*, as her first officer, her commander being W. B. Dobson. Dobson was an ideal privateersman. In June, 1813, he appeared off Halifax, where he was chased by the British cruiser *Sir John Sherbroke*. Unfortunately for the Americans they were between the enemy and the harbor, so that it was impossible for them to escape seaward. Taking in the situation at a glance, Dobson pretended to be an English prize master in possession of an American schooner. Hoisting the British flag over American colors, he boldly stood into Halifax harbor. The *Sir John Sherbroke*, to make sure that there was no deception, followed the American until close under the guns of the fort. The garrison, also supposing that the schooner was a British prize, did not fire, and the commander of the cruiser, satisfied as to the *Young Teazer's* pretended character, put to sea again, and in a few hours was out of sight. Under cover of night the *Young Teazer* also got to sea in safety.

Not at all abashed by his narrow escape, Dobson had the audacity, two days after his clever *ruse*, to send into Halifax a proclamation "declaring all Halifax in a state of blockade," and followed this "piece of audacious impudence" with a challenge to Captain Capel to fight the line of battle ship *La Hague* "at any time and place" the British commander might select. In this instance Captain Capel accepted the challenge quicker than the Yankee had anticipated, for on July 13th that ship unexpectedly hove in sight, and again the *Young Teazer* was compelled to run into Halifax harbor. This time, of course, the garrison in the fort knew the schooner, and Dobson took care to keep beyond the reach of their shot. He ran into a small bay near Halifax where the water was too shoal for *La Hague* to follow, but Captain Capel manned his boats and sent one hundred and thirty men against the privateer.

By some means, not fully explained, Dobson managed to get to sea again, with *La Hague* close after him. After a hard run of eighteen hours Dobson realized that he was in such danger of capture that he called his officers in consultation. Escape was impossible, for the enemy's shots were whistling by their ears viciously, and it was only a question of a few minutes when broadsides would be crashing into them. While the American officers were in consultation, Johnson, who knew that, if captured and recognized, he would be promptly hanged at the yardarm for dishonoring his parole, quietly slipped away from the group, and, seizing a live coal, disappeared in the cabin.[1] One of the seamen called Dobson's attention to the strange action of his first officer, but before anything could be done the maga-

---

[1] Private letter from Portland, dated July 24, 1813, to agent of the *Young Teazer*, in New York.

zine was ignited and the ship was blown to pieces. Thirty of her complement of thirty-seven people were killed. "Had he [Johnson] blown his own brains out," says a contemporary newspaper, "or tied a gun around his neck and flung himself over-board, very few would have mourned, and no one would have found fault, as by all accounts he was not the most amiable man living. Indeed, he must have been possessed of the disposition of the devil to plunge such a number of his friends into eternity who had parents, wives, and children to mourn their untimely fate and to suffer for want of protection and assistance."

Dobson was one of the survivors, and it was scarcely two months after the disaster to the *Young Teazer* that he was in a ship that still insisted on having the word "Teazer" in her name—this time it was *Young Teazer's Ghost*. The *Young Teazer's Ghost* had been the British privateer *Liverpool Packet*. This craft had been long cruising off the New England coast, and had occasioned much damage to our commerce. Her presence in these waters was especially obnoxious to the people of Salem, as the English-man made it a point to station himself off that port, where he captured several inward and outward bound ships. His presence was the more exasperat-ing, in view of the great number of American priva-teers that came from Salem, which unfortunately at that time were far away and could not be called upon to chastise the insolent stranger.

Finally, the indignation of the Salem folk became so great that on the morning of November 12, 1812, Captain John Upton declared that he would go out in the merchant schooner *Helen* if sixty-nine men would go with him and give battle to the Britisher. The owners of the *Helen*, the Messrs. J. J. Knapp and White, patriotically loaned the craft for the occa-sion. The sixty-nine men were rapidly secured, and, forming a procession, "preceded by the American flag, and by James McCarthy with his drum and by Henry Hubon with his fife, they marched through the streets of Salem, led by Captain James Fairchild." That same night, at nine o'clock, the *Helen*, with a few cannon hastily thrown aboard and with a small supply of ammunition, was towed out of the harbor, and early on the following morning got under way. Unfortunately for the warlike aspirations of these volunteer sea warriors the *Liverpool Packet* had sailed the day before for St. John's, thereby frustrating the object of the enterprise. This, however, did not prevent the valiant seventy from returning to port with all the honors of war.

It is not unlikely that the people in the privateer had been warned of the proposed attack by some of their allies on shore. It is well known that the English had their "informers" in most of the American seaports. One Samuel Yorke, who acted as pilot of the *Liverpool Packet* while on these coasts, was taken in custody on reaching shore and charged with high treason. He said in his defense, "It was not Englishmen, but his own countrymen who had brought him to this," and stated that the *Liverpool Packet*, "as well as the *Sir John Sherbroke*, belonged in the headquarters of good principles [meaning that they were owned by citizens of the United States], and that several boats were employed in going from Boston to Liverpool and Halifax to give information." Shortly after this the *Liverpool Packet* was captured and taken into the American service under the name of *Young Teazer's Ghost*. She was not very successful, however, and Dobson had to seek another command.

CHAPTER XX.

PRIVATEERS *VERSUS* PACKET SHIPS.

THERE was one class of vessels employed by the British Government in this war that furnished a valuable source of revenue to the owners of American privateers. This was the packet class. These vessels were selected or built especially with a view to speed, and were employed by the enemy in carrying important dispatches, but more frequently in transporting specie. As a rule, they carried formidable armaments and were strongly manned, so that, if attacked, they were in a condition to make a good fight. But as the main object was to reach their destination with all possible speed, they seldom took the initiative in an action, and when chased crowded on all sail to escape, at the same time using their stern guns to injure the enemy's sails and rigging rather than their hulls. If evidence were needed to further demonstrate the superiority of the American-built craft over that of the British at this period, it will be found in the fact that a large number of these British Government packets were captured by American private armed vessels; and, if evidence is needed to show that our privateersmen were as brave as they were skillful in handling their ships, it will be had in the fact that these packets were taken usually only after the most desperate struggles.

One of the first vessels of this class taken from the British by American privateers was the packet

Townsend, from Falmouth for Barbadoes. She was captured by the *Tom*, of Baltimore. Soon after war was declared the *Tom*, Captain T. Wilson, then carrying fourteen guns and one hundred and forty men, got to sea, and about July 26, 1812, fell in with the heavily armed British merchantman *Braganza*, from Port-au-Prince for London, and having on board four hundred thousand pounds of coffee, besides logwood. The *Braganza* was a ship of four hundred tons and carried twelve guns. As soon as he sighted this sail Captain Wilson gave chase, and when within gunshot opened a spirited fire, to which the Englishmen responded with every gun that would bear. After a running fight lasting fifty-five minutes the *Braganza* was surrendered and sent into Baltimore, accompanied by the *Tom*.

Refitting in this port the *Tom* again put to sea, the following notice of her departure appearing in Nile's Register: " The pilot-boat built schooner *Tom* sailed on Sunday last [August 2, 1812] on a cruise. Her burthen is two hundred and eighty-seven tons; she carried sixteen guns and a brave crew of one hundred and forty men, admirably prepared for action. Thus she is able to compete with the smaller national vessels of the enemy, and, we trust, to escape from the larger. The canvas she spreads is truly astonishing."

Captain Wilson had not been on blue water long when he fell in with the packet *Townsend*, the latter being armed with nine guns and carrying twenty-eight men and passengers. True to her character as a " running ship," the *Townsend*, on making out the American, spread all sail in an effort to escape, but the speedy *Tom* was quickly in chase, and after a hard run came within gunshot, when a severe struggle began. The Englishmen fought heroically, and did not yield to the superior armament of the Americans until their commander and four seamen had been killed and a number wounded. The privateer sustained only a trifling injury in her hull and rigging,

while only two of her people were hurt. Taking out
most of the valuables in the packet, Captain Wilson
released the ship on the payment of six thousand dollars. At the height of the action, when the British
saw that they must surrender, they threw overboard
all the mail bags, but as they were not properly
shotted they floated, and afterward were picked up
by the privateer schooner *Bona*, Captain J. Dameron,
of Baltimore, and brought into port. On April 27,
1813, the *Tom* was captured by the British cruiser
Lyra, at which time the privateer's armament had
been reduced to six guns and her complement to
thirty-six men and boys. In her entire career in this
war the *Tom* took two ships and one brig.

Another British packet ship taken by the Americans in the autumn of 1812 was the brig *Burchall*,
having on board an English commissary and his
wife. This vessel was taken by the 5-gun schooner
Highflyer, Captain J. Grant, of Baltimore. The *Highflyer* was one of the first private armed craft to get
to sea from Baltimore in this war. On July 21, 1812,
she took the British merchantman *Jamaica*, Captain
Wells, a ship of seven guns and twenty-one men, and
on the following day she captured the ship *Mary
Ann*, Captain Miller, carrying twelve guns and eighteen men. These vessels were attacked in company,
the *Jamaica* being carried by boarding and the *Mary
Ann* surrendering after Captain Grant had succeeded in getting alongside. The action with the
Jamaica lasted forty minutes, in which time the
Americans had two men wounded. On August 26th
the *Highflyer* sent into Baltimore the schooner *Harriot*, from New Providence for Havana, mounting
four guns. She was in ballast, but had on board several thousand dollars in specie.

It was in this cruise that the *Highflyer* fell in with
the *Burchall*, running from Barbadoes to Demerara,
and captured her. This privateer was singularly
fortunate in securing British officials of high rank;

for, besides seizing a number of the enemy's droghers, or coasting vessels sailing in the West Indies,
she captured another commissary and seventy-two
men, who were sent into Demerara under a flag of
truce.   Governor Carmichael wrote a letter to Captain Grant highly complimenting the latter for his
courtesy in thus accommodating his prisoners.   In
February, 1813, the *Highflyer* was captured by the
74-gun ship of the line *Poictiers*, the privateer having
taken in all eight British vessels.   On securing the
Highflyer the British converted her into a tender, in
charge of a lieutenant and seventy-two men.   On the
night of May 24, 1813, the American privateer *Roger*,
Captain R. Quarles, of fourteen guns and one hundred
and twenty men, slipped past the blockading squadron at Hampton Roads.   Several days before this
the *Highflyer*, under her new flag, had captured the
" lookout boat " *Betsey*, Captain Smith.   This boat
had been very useful to the Americans in eluding
the British blockading ships and getting to sea, so
as to give warning and information to our returning privateers.   The *Highflyer*'s people promptly
burned the *Betsey*, and took her men aboard their
schooner.

At nine o'clock in the evening the *Roger* got to
sea, and soon fell in with the *Highflyer*.   The British
hailed the privateer, and on receiving no answer
hailed again and threatened to fire.   To this the
Americans responded with a broadside, and immediately the two vessels became engaged in a close and
heavy cannonade, which lasted until 11.30 P. M., when
the *Highflyer* sheered off.   The action had been at
such close quarters that words of command in each
ship could be distinctly heard by the opponents.
In the heat of the battle two of the men taken from
the *Betsey* managed to get into a boat and made
their escape to land.   On the following day the British gave Captain Smith and the remaining crew of
the *Betsey* a boat, in which they reached Norfolk.

Afterward it was learned that the enemy had suffered severely in this fight, and had the *Roger* been
able to keep alongside the *Highflyer* the latter undoubtedly would soon have been compelled to surrender. As it was, the British lieutenant, the cook,
and four men were killed, while a midshipman and
nine seamen were wounded.[1] The *Roger* was one of
the most successful private armed craft sailing out
of Norfolk, taking in all seven vessels. One of her
prizes was the English Government packet *Windsor
Castle*, armed with ten guns and having on board
thirty-two seamen and nine passengers. The *Roger*
was at sea at the close of the war. On September
23, 1813, nearly four months after her encounter with
the *Roger*, the *Highflyer*, then under the command
of Lieutenant George Hutchinson, was captured
through a clever stratagem by the United States
44-gun frigate *President*, Captain John Rodgers.[2]

One of the most obstinately contested actions
between an American privateer and a British Government packet occurred in 1813. The English 400-
ton packet ship *Morgiana*, Captain Cunningham,
mounting eighteen guns—9-pounders—and manned
by fifty men, was attacked in September of this
year by the privateer *Saratoga*, Captain Charles W.
Wooster. The latter had left port with sixteen guns,
but shortly before meeting the packet she had been
chased by a frigate, and had been compelled to throw
overboard twelve of her guns. The *Morgiana* did
not surrender until she had two of her men killed
and five wounded, among the latter being her commander, who was badly hurt. The Americans had
three men killed and seven wounded. In her entire
career in this war the *Saratoga* took twenty-two British vessels. In February, 1813, she took, while off
Carácas, a brig from England laden with drygoods.

---

[1] Hampton Compiler.
[2] See Maclay's History of the United States Navy, vol. i, p. 522.

Placing a prize crew aboard, Captain Wooster ordered her to the United States, but being short of water the prize master put into Santa Marta, to leeward of La Guayra, where the vessel and cargo were seized by the Spanish officials and sold to the account of their Government. The prize crew was placed in irons and sent to Havana, where they were compelled to work on the arsenal under the most cruel taskmasters. They were poorly fed, and allowed to go barefooted and almost naked. Several of the men were severely flogged because they refused to enter a Spanish man-of-war.

About a month after the action between the *Saratoga* and *Morgiana*, the armed schooner *Globe*, Captain Richard Moon, of Baltimore, had a desperate engagement with two British packet ships. Earlier in the war Captain Moon had commanded the 1-gun schooner *Sarah Ann*, manned by fifty men. The *Sarah Ann* attacked a British merchantman of ten guns, which resisted until four of her people were wounded. The prize was sent into New Providence, October, 1812. At that port six of the Americans were claimed as British subjects, and were sent to Jamaica. On January 27, 1814, the *Globe* arrived at Wilmington, North Carolina, and reported an action with two British packet ships. It occurred November 3, 1813, while the American privateer was cruising in the vicinity of Madeira. Two days before this Captain Moon discovered a sail leeward, and immediately bore away to ascertain her character. She proved to be a large man-of-war brig, and after exchanging a few shots Captain Moon hauled off. Just before she got out of reach, however, the *Globe* received a 9-pound shot under her quarter, very near the water line, which caused a dangerous leak.

Shaking herself clear of the man-of-war, the *Globe* repaired damages and appeared off the port of Funchal, where two brigs were discovered backing and filling away as if about to leave the Roads. Evidently they observed the approach of the privateer, and were unwilling to leave port until she withdrew. Captain Moon so far accommodated them as to make a feint at sailing southward.   This was sufficient encouragement to induce the brigs to venture out, and Captain Moon, retracing his course shortly after he had run the port out of sight, had the satisfaction of coming upon the brigs just as they were clearing land. He made all sail in chase, but as it soon came on dark and squally he lost sight of them. He continued the chase on a blind course, under easy sail, all that night, and at daylight, November 3d, he saw the brigs bearing away from him to the southwest, some six or eight miles distant. Carrying a press of sail for five hours and a half, the *Globe* came within gunshot of the largest brig, which opened a spirited fire from her stern chasers. The privateer responded with her chase guns, but did not for a moment slacken her speed, as the Americans desired to get at close quarters immediately.

In this manner a running fight was maintained between the two vessels, the American rapidly gaining, until half past twelve, when the *Globe* was fairly alongside and began nudging elbows with the chase. The word was then passed along to board, but unfortunately the privateer fell off a little at that moment, so that only the first and second officers and three seamen of the *Globe* gained the enemy's deck. Cut off from retreat, these men made a heroic fight, but they were set upon by the entire English crew and were soon killed. The first officer's name was John Harrison and that of the second was John Smith, the names of the seamen being Joshua Brown, Richard Blair, and James Thelis.

At this critical period of the fight the second English brig bore up, and passing across the *Globe's* bow gave her a terrible raking fire, which killed or wounded a number of the privateer's people, besides greatly injuring her sails and rigging. This broadside, added to the injuries the privateer already had received, for some time rendered her quite unmanageable. Captain Moon, however, kept his guns going, and made every effort to repair his rigging, hoping to renew the engagement under more favorable circumstances.

Again getting alongside the first brig, he opened a heavy cannon and musketry fire, so that at half past three o'clock she surrendered. All this time the *Globe* had paid little or no attention to the second brig, which had been firing shot after shot at close range into the privateer with impunity and doing great damage. As the first brig had surrendered, Captain Moon was now able to turn his undivided attention upon the other vessel, and this he did with all the zest of long-pent vengeance. The *Globe* was soon got under steerageway, and, running close under the enemy's quarter, the Americans poured in a destructive fire until half past four, when Captain Moon found that his own vessel was in a critical condition.

Seven shot had taken effect between wind and water, which caused her to take in so much water as to endanger the safety of all. Under these circumstances Captain Moon decided to return to the first brig and take possession of her, as the second brig seemed to be undesirous of continuing the battle. When the *Globe* approached the first brig, however, the Americans were surprised to see her rehoist her colors and fire a broadside. Both brigs then set upon the privateer with renewed energy, so that Captain Moon was compelled to haul off to prevent his vessel from sinking. Fortunately the enemy did not seem desirous of following up their advantage, and finding that the privateer was unable to continue the chase they made sail and gradually disappeared below the horizon.

The condition of the *Globe* was critical in the extreme; for, besides the great quantities of water she

32

was taking in, the greater part of her standing and running rigging were shot away, and not a sail was left that had not been riddled with shot. A large number of her officers and men also had been killed or wounded. For some hours after this battle the survivors bent all their energies to keeping their craft afloat and mending the rigging. Having done this, the schooner slowly made her way to the Grand Canary Island for permanent repairs.

Down to this time Captain Moon was ignorant of the names, force, or character of his antagonists, excepting that during the time he was chasing the largest brig he observed that her people were throwing various articles overboard, some of which floated, and when the *Globe* came up to them they were seen to be mail bags. From this circumstance he was led to believe that they were packet vessels. This belief was confirmed when he arrived at the Canary Islands, where he learned, *via* Santa Cruz, Teneriffe, that a British packet brig carrying eighteen guns and another mounting fourteen had recently arrived at that place. They reported that a few days before they had a severe engagement with an American privateer and succeeded in beating her off, but only after great losses to themselves, having twenty-seven men killed or wounded, besides suffering serious injuries in their hulls and rigging. The *Globe*, besides those already mentioned, had Seamen Oliver, Samuel D. Smith, and Sandy Forbes killed, making eight in all killed, and the following men wounded: Captain Moon, Prize-Masters Noah Allen and John Frinck; Seamen Asa Hart, Ab. Kinhart, Fortune, Job E. Wheeler, P. Short, F. Statt, T. Jifford, J. Arnold, J. Beatly, John Wilson, John Mitchell, and Daniel Milton. On this cruise the *Globe* carried her long tom—probably an 18- or 24-pounder—and eight 12-pounder carronades. Her complement of officers, seamen, and marines numbered ninety. After the action Captain Moon found a double-headed shot sticking in the side of his ship which weighed twelve pounds.[1]

So many British vessels of this class were taken by American cruisers and privateers in the early part of the war, and so serious were the losses and inconveniences resulting from these captures, that extraordinary precautions were taken to protect the packet ships. Their time of sailing was purposely made irregular, and, so far as possible, the exact date was kept secret. In some cases war ships accompanied the packet, while, finally, ships of the line and heavy frigates were called upon to perform this service. But even these extreme measures did not prevent our enterprising privateers from continuing their mischievous work of capturing this class of craft.

In September, 1814, the privateer *Harpy*, Captain William Nichols, of Baltimore, fell in with the British packet *Princess Elizabeth* and compelled her to surrender. The English had three men killed and several wounded, while the Americans had one man killed. The packet was armed with eight 12-pounders and two long brass 9-pounders and was manned by a crew of thirty-eight men. The *Harpy* carried fourteen heavy guns and about one hundred men. The prize had on board as passengers the Turkish ambassador to England, an English army officer, an aide to a British general, and the second lieutenant of a 74-gun ship of the line. Taking out of the packet ten thousand dollars in specie, five pipes of Madeira wine, the two brass 9-pounders, and two of the 12-pounders, Captain Nichols threw overboard the remaining guns, and allowed the *Princess Elizabeth* to proceed on her voyage, after paying a ransom of two thousand dollars.

In the following month the *Harpy* sailed from Portsmouth, New Hampshire, and returned to that

---

[1] For other services of the *Globe* in this war, see pp. 430-433.

place, after a cruise of only twenty days, with sixty prisoners, having captured the British transports *Budges* and *Amazon*, from London for Halifax, the first vessel carrying six guns and the second six guns with eighteen men.   Both craft were laden with provisions for the British army in America, the *Budges* having a cargo of rum, brandy, beef, pork, flour, and bread.   They belonged to a fleet that had sailed from Portsmouth, England.   Among the prisoners were two majors and several other officers.   It was estimated that the value of the prizes taken by the *Harpy* in this cruise was at least half a million dollars.   The last cruise made by the *Harpy* in this war was even more remarkable.   She remained at sea eighty-five days, arriving at Salem, April, 1815, with her hold crowded with valuable articles captured in the Bay of Biscay and on the coasts of England, Portugal, and Spain.   The following list will show the variety and exciting nature of her adventures: "One hundred and eighty-eight boxes and trunks, and one hundred and sixteen hogsheads and casks of drygoods, jewelry, plate, women's rich dresses, navy trimmings, fine clothing, etc.   Three hundred and thirty boxes fresh Malaga raisins, sixty-six frails fresh Turkey figs, one hundred and fifty-eight pieces of British manufactured goods, twenty-nine bolts of canvas, a quantity of cordage, ten pipes of sherry wine, three barrels of gunpowder, carronades, muskets, pistols, cutlasses, sails, signal flags, lamps and paint oil, white and patent sheet lead, nautical instruments, cut and other glass, medicines, and upward of one hundred thousand pounds sterling in British treasury notes and bills of exchange."

The following testimonial was written by one of Captain Nichols' prisoners: "Captain William Drysdale, late of the ship *William and Alfred*, captured January 2, 1815, by the brig *Harpy*, returns his grateful acknowledgment to William Nichols, Esq., commander of the said brig, and all his officers for their great civility, indulgent lenity, and humane usage while on board, and generously delivering up all his private property. And should, at any future time, Captain Nichols or any of his officers come to London, Captain Drysdale will be happy to see them at his house, Stepney Green, near London. Given under my hand, on board the *Harpy* at sea, this day, January 6, 1815."

This testimonial was supplemented as follows: " We, the undersigned, feeling congenial sentiments with Captain Drysdale toward Captain Nichols, Lieutenant Place, and the officers on board the *Harpy*, and desirous that such humanity and goodness may be made public, as well in the United States as in England, declare that our treatment is worthy of every praise and encomium, and that all our private property has been held sacred to us and a cartel fitted for us as early as circumstances would permit. George Harrison, W. Newell, J. W. Hall, Andrew McCarthy, late masters of vessels taken by the *Harpy*."

The *William and Alfred* was laden with drygoods and plantation utensils, and was bound for Antigua. Captain Nichols divested her of her drygoods, and, placing her in charge of a prize crew, ordered her to the United States. The ship *Jane*, from London for Antigua, was taken by the *Harpy*. She was laden with provisions for the Government. After taking out a portion of her cargo and destroying the remainder, Captain Nichols placed his prisoners in her, and ordered her to a British port as a cartel. Another prize of the *Harpy* was the ship *Garland*, with a full cargo of rum and sugar. She arrived safely at Salem.

CHAPTER XXI.

BATTLES WITH THE KING'S SHIPS.

A REMARKABLE feature of the maritime War of 1812–1815 was the number of instances in which our privateers gave and received blows from the regular war ships of the British Government. Notable cases, such as the repulse of the English boats in Fayal and the disastrous defeat of the *Endymion's* men in their attack on the *Prince de Neuchâtel*, have been detailed in separate chapters, but those actions are far from completing the list. On September 8, 1812, the American privateer *Diligent*, Captain Grassin, of Philadelphia, fell in with the British 10-gun cruiser *Laura*, Lieutenant Charles Newton Hunter. The *Laura* had taken three American merchantmen, and was in the act of seizing the fourth, when, at three o'clock in the afternoon, she was discovered by the *Diligent*. The Englishman carried ten 18-pounder carronades and two short 9-pounders, and had, according to their accounts, a complement of forty-one men. The *Diligent* was a schooner mounting ten short guns.

As soon as the privateer was made out to be a ship of force, Lieutenant Hunter recalled his boat from the merchantman and made sail for the *Diligent*. From some men captured in his third prize the British commander had learned that the *Diligent* was in the vicinity and was informed as to her force. At 3.55 P. M. the vessels had come within pistol shot, when the *Laura* opened with her guns, to which the

Americans responded with a broadside. Five minutes later the two vessels were fairly side by side, and, while the Americans endeavored to maneuver for a better position, the British attempted to frustrate the effort by taking the wind out of their opponent's sails. At 4.30 P. M. the *Diligent* set her course and tried to tack, upon which the *Laura* put her helm down with the same object in view; but in the failing wind both vessels missed stays, and in paying off they swung round and engaged in a fierce yardarm-and-yardarm fight. At 4.45 P. M. the *Laura*, having had her peak halyards shot away, fell off the wind a little and forereached the privateer, grazing her port quarter. Soon afterward the *Diligent*, dropping astern and catching the breeze, and being the best sailer of the two, drew up on the weather quarter of the *Laura*.

Down to this time, owing to the fact that the men in both vessels were engaged in maneuvering, their fire had not been very effective. The privateer now seized the opportunity to take the wind out of the *Laura's* sails, and running her bowsprit over the starboard taffrail of the Englishman, with her jib boom between the topping lifts and through the mainsail, made fast. The Americans then used their small arms with great effect, and made attempts to board, which at 4.55 P. M. were successful, and soon they had complete possession of the vessel. The English loss was fifteen killed and severely wounded, including Lieutenant Hunter and Midshipman John C. Griffith. The *Diligent* had nine killed and ten wounded. "Captain Grassin," says an English historian, "carried his prize to Philadelphia, and behaved to Lieutenant Hunter in the most honorable and attentive manner. Lieutenant Hunter was landed and taken to the hospital." Afterward the *Laura* was fitted out as a 12-gun privateer and renamed the *Hebe*. In April, 1813, while under the command of Captain J. Picarrere, she was captured by a British squadron.

In February, 1813, the American privateer *Lottery*, Captain John Southcomb, left Baltimore for Bordeaux. While standing down the Chesapeake, at nine o'clock on the morning of the 8th, she was discovered by the British squadron at anchor in Lynnhaven Bay, which consisted of the 36-gun frigate *Maidstone*, Captain George Burdett; the 36-gun frigate *Belvidera*, Captain Richard Byron; the 38-gun frigate *Junon*, Captain James Sanders; and the 38-gun frigate *Statira*, Captain Hassard Stackpole. As soon as the privateer was made out the British sent nine boats, carrying two hundred men, with orders to attack the American. The boats were commanded by Lieutenant Kelly Nazer. Observing the approach of the enemy, Captain Southcomb made all sail to escape, for his vessel carried only six 12-pounder carronades and twenty-eight men. In a few hours, however, the *Lottery* was becalmed, and about one o'clock in the afternoon the British boats came within gunshot, when the Americans opened such a well-directed fire that the advance of the leading craft was checked. Waiting for the other boats, the British got together and made a dash at the privateer, and, notwithstanding a galling fire, succeeded in gaining her deck, where the few Americans were soon overpowered. Captain Southcomb made a superb defense, not surrendering until he was mortally hurt and eighteen of his twenty-eight men were killed or wounded. The British had one man killed and five wounded.

Speaking of Southcomb's heroism, an English historian says: "This was a very gallant resistance on the part of the *Lottery*, and Captain Southcomb, until he died, was treated with the greatest attention by Captain Byron, on board whose frigate he had been brought. Captain Byron then sent the body of the *Lottery's* late commander on shore, with every mark of respect due to the memory of a brave officer, and he afterward received a letter of thanks from Captain Charles Stewart, of the American frigate *Constellation*, at anchor in James River leading to Norfolk, watching an opportunity to put to sea." The *Lottery* measured two hundred and twenty-five tons, and although carrying only six guns was pierced for sixteen. She was taken into the British navy under the name *Canso*.

In the following April, 1813, four American privateers, one of them being the famous *Dolphin*, of Baltimore, were "caught on land" by a British blockading squadron. The *Dolphin*, Captain W. S. Stafford, had put to sea early in the war, and made directly for the coasts of Portugal and Spain. Cruising some time off Cape St. Vincent, the scene of some of England's greatest naval battles, with no success, Captain Stafford had nearly made up his mind to change his cruising ground, when, on February 25, 1813, while in sight of the Cape, a sail was descried from the *Dolphin's* masthead and chase was given to it. Soon afterward another sail, smaller and apparently a consort, was reported. The speedy privateer quickly overhauled the strangers, which were seen to be heavily armed merchantmen, and a severe action took place. In a short time both vessels were surrendered, the larger one proving to be the ship *Hebe* (by some accounts the *John Hamilton*), carrying sixteen guns and twenty-five men, and the smaller vessel, the brig *Three Brothers*, with ten guns and twenty-five men. Captain W. A. Brigham, of the *Hebe*, was badly wounded early in the action by a musket shot, and soon afterward he was severely burned by an explosion of powder. The *Dolphin* carried ten guns and a crew of sixty men, of whom only four were hurt.

Captain Stafford placed prize crews in these vessels, with orders to make for the United States. The *Hebe* was recaptured, but the *Three Brothers* reached

New York. Both vessels were homeward bound from Malta, and were laden with valuable cargoes. Captain Brigham expressed much surprise at meeting an American war craft in that part of the world, and said: "I did not expect to find a d——d Yankee privateer in that place." But Stafford assured him that similar captures might soon be made in the Thames. The British officers, while aboard the *Dolphin*, were handsomely treated, and on her arrival in Baltimore, February 15th, Brigham published the following " card ": " W. A. Brigham, lately captured in the British merchant ship *Hebe*, lately under his command, by the United States privateer *Dolphin*, Captain W. S. Stafford, after a severe contest, begs to make public and gratefully acknowledges the sense he has of the very kind and humane treatment he and his crew experienced on board the *Dolphin* during the passage to this port. All wearing apparel and private property were given up to the prisoners and the wounded (eight in number) most diligently and tenderly attended. W. A. Brigham being badly wounded, experienced a very great share of this attention from Dr. Chidester, the surgeon, which, together with the tender sympathy of goodness of Captain Stafford, added much to his recovery and happiness. Should the fortune of war ever throw Captain Stafford or any of his crew into the hands of the British it is sincerely hoped he will meet a similar treatment. Baltimore, February 16, 1813." This generous wish of Captain Brigham was soon to be granted.

On April 3, 1813, Sir John Warren, having his flag aboard the 74-gun ship of the line *San Domingo*, Captain Charles Gill, with the *Marlborough*, bearing Rear - Admiral Cockburn's flag, Captain Charles Bayne Hodgson Ross, accompanied by the frigates *Maidstone* and *Statira* and the brig-sloops *Fantôme* and *Mohawk*, appeared off the mouth of the Rappahannock, where four American privateers happened to be. They were the schooner *Arab*, of Baltimore, Captain D. Fitch, carrying seven guns and a crew of forty-five men; the *Lynx*, Captain E. Taylor, of six guns and forty men; the *Racer*, Captain D. Chaytor, of six guns and thirty-six men; and the *Dolphin*, Captain W. S. Stafford, carrying twelve guns and one hundred men, then starting out for another cruise.

As soon as these vessels were made out from the enemy's mastheads, the British sent seventeen boats, with a large force of men under the command of Lieutenant James Polkinghorne, against them. Unfortunately for the privateers it was calm at the time, and as their vessels were too far apart to be within supporting distance of each other the British were able to attack them separately. They selected the *Arab* as being farther down stream and made a dash for her. This boat was not surrendered, however, without a desperate struggle, in which both sides sustained the heaviest losses of the day. The British then made for the *Lynx*, whose people, observing the fate of the *Arab*, and seeing that resistance was hopeless, hauled down their colors at the first summons. Some resistance was made in the *Racer*, but that vessel also was carried after a short struggle. There now remained only the *Dolphin*, on which craft the enemy turned the guns of their prizes. For two hours Captain Stafford responded gallantly, but in the final boat attack he was compelled to surrender. In this affair the British admit a loss of two killed and eleven wounded, including Lieutenant Polkinghorne. According to American reports the enemy had fifty killed or wounded, while Stafford places his losses at six killed and ten wounded.

For the part he took in this spirited affair Polkinghorne was promoted to the rank of commander, while the *Dolphin*, the *Racer*, and *Lynx* were taken into the British service, the last two under the names *Shelbourne* and *Musquetobite*. The *Shelbourne* was with the British 36-gun frigate *Orpheus* in 1814 when she captured the new American 18-gun sloop of war *Frolic*. In consideration of his kind treatment of Englishmen who had fallen into his hands earlier in the war, Captain Stafford was cordially received by Sir John Warren, and in a few days was released and sent to Baltimore. Captain George Coggeshall, of the American privateer *David Porter*, who was intimately acquainted with Stafford, describes him as follows: " I always found him a modest, unassuming, gentlemanly man. No one can for a moment doubt his unflinching bravery and gallant bearing when he reflects on the many battles he has gained over the enemies of his country." The *Dolphin*, while under the command of Captain Stafford, had taken in all eleven British vessels, one of them carrying fifteen guns and another twelve. One of these prizes was burned at sea and another was recaptured, while the others—including the schooner *Fanny*, valued at eighteen thousand dollars —were brought safely into port. On November 27, 1813, Captain Stafford, while in command of another privateer, was attacked while off Charleston by five boats from a British brig of war. One of the boats was torn to pieces by the privateer's fire, while the others were compelled to retreat, after having sustained heavy losses. The brig gave the Americans a futile broadside and then drew away.[1]

---

[1] There were five other American vessels engaged in privateering bearing the name *Dolphin*. One of them, carrying five guns and twenty-eight men, under the command of Captain J. Endicott, of Salem, was one of the first to get to sea, and in a cruise of a few weeks captured three ships, seven brigs, and six schooners. One of the ships was armed with fourteen guns and another with twelve. One of the prizes was released, another recaptured. The *Dolphin* herself was captured by a British cruiser, August 12, 1812. Another *Dolphin*, Captain H. Lelar, of Philadelphia, was a ship carrying twelve guns and fifty-six men. She was not very successful, being taken at sea by the English *Colossus*, January 5, 1813. *Dolphin* No. 4 was a two-gun schooner, credited with forty-eight men. Her career was cut short, August 13, 1812, off Cape Sable by the British sloop of war *Colibri*. *Dolphin* No. 5 was a one-gun schooner, carrying twenty men,

A maritime enterprise of a singularly daring nature was undertaken against the king's ships off Sandy Hook, where a British blockading squadron had long been stationed. Some of these vessels had become extremely obnoxious to coast traders. One of the vessels that especially aroused the ire of the Americans was the sloop *Eagle*, a tender to the British 74-gun ship of the line *Poictiers*, the same that captured the United States sloop of war *Wasp* just after her memorable victory over the *Frolic*. The *Eagle* had been cruising off the Hook, and had made herself so offensive to the Americans that they determined to capture her at any cost. On July 5, 1813, a fishing smack, called the *Yankee*, was borrowed of some fishermen at Fly Market, and thirty or forty volunteers, under the command of Sailing-Master Percival, all well armed, were concealed in her cabin and in the fore peak. A calf, a goose, and a sheep were purchased and placed on deck in full view of any pursuing ship. Thus equipped the *Yankee* stood out to sea as if on a fishing trip to the Banks, three men dressed in fishermen's apparel and wearing buff caps being the only persons visible on deck.

Scarcely had the *Yankee* cleared Sandy Hook when the officious *Eagle* espied her and immediately began a chase. Of course the three innocent-looking fishermen obeyed the first summons to heave to, and running alongside the English officers perceived that there was live stock on board—an article greatly in demand by these people, who had been keeping the sea months at a time on dreary blockade duty, having nothing but salt provisions to eat. The Americans were fully alive to this weakness of their

---

under Captain A. Johnson, of Massachusetts. She seems to have accomplished little, and was captured by a British cruiser, December 4, 1814. *Dolphin* No. 6 also was of Massachusetts. She was a mere boat, under the order of Captain P. Moore.

cousins' appetites, and had purposely left the live
stock conspicuously in view. The commander of the
Eagle ordered the *Yankee* to go down to the British
flagship, some five miles distant, thinking that the
live stock would be a treat to the senior officer of
the squadron. Just as the order had been given, the
watchword " Lawrence " was passed, and up rose the
concealed men and fired at the astounded enemy.
The English were driven precipitately below decks,
and did not stop even to haul down their colors.

Observing that the *Eagle's* decks were cleared,
Sailing-Master Percival ordered his men to cease
firing, upon which one of the Englishmen came out
of the hold and hauled down the colors. The Americans then took possession of their prize and carried
her to the Battery, where the prisoners were landed,
amid the cheers of thousands of people. The
Eagle mounted a 32-pounder brass howitzer, which
was loaded with canister, but so complete was the
surprise that the enemy did not have time to discharge it. The *Eagle* was commanded by Master's
Mate H. Morris, of the *Poictiers*, who was killed. Midshipman W. Price and eleven seamen completed her
complement. Mr. Price was mortally wounded and
one of the seamen was killed.

On December 6, 1812, the privateer brig *Montgomery*, Captain Upton, of Boston, made a gallant
defense against the English brig of war *Surinam*, in
the vicinity of the port bearing that name. The
Surinam carried eighteen 32-pounders and two long
9-pounders, while the *Montgomery* mounted only ten
6-pounders and two long 12-pounders. The war brig
gave chase to the privateer, but in the half hour she
was within gunshot the Americans managed to plant
a solid shot in the *Surinam's* foremast, which so weakened the spar that the English were glad to haul off
and permit the privateer to escape. On the 5th of
the following May the *Montgomery*, while returning
from the English Channel, was captured by the Brit-

ish frigate *Nymphe.* In her entire career the *Mont-gomery* took six vessels.

Another instance of an American privateer getting unpleasantly close to a British man-of-war was that of the schooner *Grampus,* Captain John Murphy, of Baltimore. On June 18, 1814, the *Grampus,* in company with the privateer *Patapsco,* of Baltimore, and the *Dash,* of Boston, was chased off Boston Harbor by the 74-gun ship of the line *La Hague,* Captain Capel.[1] The huge ship of the line promptly began a furious chase, but by clever seamanship all the privateers escaped. It is reported on good authority that Captain Capel was so chagrined over this that he snatched the epaulets from his shoulders and threw them to the deck.

Making for the Canary Islands after this escape, Captain Murphy cruised in that vicinity some time with little or no success, taking only the brig *Speculator,* from Lanzarote for London. She proved to be an old and comparatively worthless craft, and Captain Murphy returned her to her people. Not long after this a sail was descried from the *Grampus,* to which chase was given. It was soon discovered that she was a heavily armed merchantman, or, at the most, a letter of marque—so the Americans thought. Acting on this belief Captain Murphy hastened to close, and when near enough he called on the Englishmen to surrender; but by way of answer the stranger triced up a long row of covers, ran out ten or eleven black muzzles and belched forth a broadside that told, plainly enough, that it was not a merchantman or letter of marque speaking, but a full-fledged sloop of war. This broadside killed one man and wounded several others, besides occasioning considerable damage to the privateer's sails and

---

[1] For Captain Capel's connection with the forgery of Sir Philip B. V. Brooke's official report of the *Chesapeake-Shannon* fight, see Maclay's History of the United States Navy, vol. i, pp. xxv-xxvii.

rigging. As soon as the astonished Americans recovered from their surprise they made every exertion to get away from their quarrelsome neighbor.
With colors still flying Captain Murphy gradually
drew away from the sloop of war, and finally made
his escape. In this affair Captain Murphy and one of
his men were mortally wounded. The *Grampus* made
eight prizes in this war.

One of the last engagements between American
privateers and the king's ships took place July 12,
1814, in the English Channel. The 7-gun schooner
privateer *Syren*, Captain J. D. Daniels, of Baltimore,
put to sea in the spring of 1814, and made for British waters. On July 12th she fell in with the cutter *Landrail*, Lieutenant Robert Daniel Lancaster,
mounting four short 12-pounders and manned by
twenty men—thirty-three according to American
accounts. The *Syren* had about fifty men aboard at
this time. As the *Landrail* had important dispatches
aboard, Lieutenant Lancaster made all sail to avoid
a battle. The swift American, however, gradually
overhauled him, and a running fight, lasting one hour
and ten minutes, resulted. At the end of that time
the *Syren* had come to close quarters, and for forty
minutes longer a desperate fight was made on both
sides, when the Englishmen surrendered, having
seven of their number wounded. British accounts
place the casualties in the *Syren* at three killed and
fifteen wounded. Captain Daniels placed a prize
crew aboard the *Landrail*, with others to make an
American port, but before gaining a place of safety
she was recaptured and sent into Halifax. Returning to the United States, the *Syren*, while off the
Delaware, November 16, 1814, was chased by the
English blockading ships, and was compelled to run
ashore, where her people escaped after destroying
their vessel. The *Syren* had made six prizes in this
war.

CHAPTER XXII.

PRIVATEERS OF BALTIMORE.

In point of numbers Baltimore took the lead in sending out privateers in the War of 1812, Boston being credited with thirty-five, Salem with forty, New York with fifty-five to Baltimore's fifty-eight. The exploits of many Baltimore privateers have been set forth in other chapters. Some of the remaining craft fitted out in this port by private enterprise rendered services of great importance.

Among the first to get to sea were the schooner *Revenge*, of fourteen guns, and the *Rolla*, of five guns, the former commanded by Captain R. Miller and the latter by Captain E. W. Dewley, or J. Dooley. The *Revenge* had the good fortune to recapture a prize taken by the famous privateer *General Armstrong*, of New York. This was the brig *Lucy and Alida*, having a desirable cargo of drygoods aboard. Soon after the brig had been taken by the *General Armstrong* she was recaptured by the English letter of marque *Brenton*, of Liverpool. She was again captured by the *Revenge*, and this time arrived safely at Norfolk. Some of the other prizes made by this privateer were the ship *Betsey*, bound for Glasgow and sent into Wilmington, North Carolina; the ship *Manly*, mounting four guns, laden with wine, oil, etc., from the West Indies for Halifax, which was sent into Charleston; the schooner *Fanny*, from Trinidad, laden with sugar, also sent into Charleston; and the schooner *Mary Ann*, which was released, and the prisoners placed aboard with orders to make for the nearest English port. The *Revenge* also captured and destroyed at sea, in July, 1814, the brig *Silena* and the sloop *Friendship* after seven thousand dollars' worth of drygoods had been taken from her.

The *Rolla* was even more successful that the *Revenge*, having made, in one cruise, seven prizes, carrying in all fifty-eight cannon and one hundred and fifty men. The cargoes were invoiced at over two million dollars. These valuable prizes were all made in a few days, December 12–15, 1812, near Madeira, and, although some of the vessels were heavily armed and made resistance, no loss was sustained by the Americans. They belonged to a great fleet that had sailed from Cork with a powerful convoy. The most satisfactory feature of these captures was the fact that soon after the *Rolla* left port she encountered a terrific gale, in which Captain Dewley, in order to keep his vessel from foundering, was compelled to throw overboard all but one of his guns. After the gale was over there seemed nothing to do but to make the best of their way back to port, but the crew of sixty men entreated Captain Dewley to continue the cruise, and the result was that the *Rolla* made one of the richest " hauls " in the war. Besides these more important seizures the *Rolla* burned the schooner *Swift*, of Plymouth (England), from St. Michael, and sent into New Orleans the brig *General Prevost*, from Halifax for Demerara. The *Rolla* was captured, December 10, 1813, off Long Island by the British frigate *Loire*, after one of the privateer's masts had been shot away.

Two other Baltimore private armed vessels that made important captures early in the war were the *Sarah Ann*, Captain Richard Moon, and the schooner *Expedition*, Captain Murray. The former had a sharp action with the heavily armed merchant ship *Elizabeth*, from Jamaica for England. The Englishman carried ten 12-pounders, and was laden with three

hundred and twenty-three hogsheads and some
tierces and barrels of sugar, besides a quantity of
coffee and ginger. The *Elizabeth* did not surrender
until four of her crew had been wounded. The
Americans had two men hurt. In October, 1812, the
Sarah Ann was captured, and was carried into New
Providence.

The first prize taken by the *Expedition* was the
first class schooner *Louisa*, of two hundred and two
tons, carrying one gun, with a crew of twenty-six men.
She was a first-rate vessel, from St. Vincent bound
for St. John's, and had on board one hundred hogsheads of rum and thirty barrels of sugar. She was
sent into Newport, and the bounty allowed on the
vessel, cargo, and prisoners by the Government
amounted to about four thousand dollars. The *Expedition* also recaptured the American schooner *Adeline*. This vessel had sailed from Bordeaux with
dispatches for the American Government and a mail
of over four thousand letters. When four days out
she was captured, after a hard chase; by a British
frigate, in which all the dispatches and letters had
been thrown overboard. Six days later the *Adeline*
was retaken by the *Expedition* and sent into New
York.

The 12-gun schooner *Siro*, Captain D. Gray, was
one of the "re-recaptured" vessels of this war. In
the fall of 1812, the *Siro*, while making a run from
France to the United States, captured the 10-gun
ship *Loyal Sam*, with twenty-three thousand five hundred dollars in specie aboard, and carried her into
Portland. Getting to sea again the *Siro* appeared
off the Irish coast, and on January 13, 1813, was
captured by the English brig of war *Pelican* and sent
into Plymouth. The English refitted their prize and
sent her out under the name *Atlanta*. On September
21, 1814, the *Atlanta* was taken by the United States
sloop of war *Wasp*.

The *Sabine* and the *Baltimore* were two privateers

about which little is known—or, at least, few prizes
are credited to them. The former, Captain J. Barnes,
while on her way to France, captured and destroyed
a brig from Lisbon, while the latter, Captain E.
Veasey, is credited with two prizes—the brig *Point-
Shares*, of St. John's, and the schooner *Dorcas*, which
was relieved of her cargo of drygoods and released.

The 5-gun schooner *Sparrow*, Captain J. Burch,
was captured by the enemy, and recaptured under
singular circumstances. Captain Burch's first prize
was the schooner *Meadow*, out of which he took the
most available articles and then released her. His
second prize was the schooner *Farmer*, of Nassau,
which also was released, the British master highly
complimenting Captain Burch for his liberal conduct,
declaring that he would not even receive some poultry without paying for it. On November 30, 1813, the
Sparrow, while making a run from New Orleans to
New York, with a cargo of sugar and lead, was chased
ashore near Long Branch by the British 74-gun ship
of the line *Plantagenet* and taken possession of by one
hundred men. A detachment of the United States
flotilla stationed at New York, under the command
of Captain Lewis, marched against the enemy, drove
them from the stranded vessel, and took possession
of her in spite of a heavy fire of grape from the
Plantagenet. The whole cargo, together with the
sails, rigging, etc., was saved, and the vessel bilged.

The crew of the sloop *Liberty*, Captain Pratt, had
the satisfaction of enjoying some delicacies intended
for the British admiral on the American station,
John Borlaise Warren. The *Liberty* mounted one
gun, and was manned by forty men. She captured
the schooner *Huzzah*, which had on board a number of
turtle for the British naval officers on the station.
The *Liberty* also captured the schooner *Dorcas*, carrying two guns and thirty men, from Jamaica, having on board sixty thousand dollars' worth of drygoods. The *Liberty* is credited with six prizes in this

war. The little privateer *Wasp*, Captain Taylor, made three prizes.

The *Fox*, Captain Jack, after taking eight British vessels, was chased one hundred miles by an English squadron and captured. A letter dated New London, May 18, 1813, says: "The inspector of New London, on Friday evening last, took charge of a flag with the prisoners taken in the *Fox* and returned on Saturday. He was treated by Commodore Hardy [the British naval commander in these waters] with every attention; waited on by him and the first lieutenant to every part of the ship, even to the berths of the officers. The commodore expressed to the inspector a total disapprobation and abhorrence of their conduct at the southward in burning defenseless towns and villages; and understanding, by the officers who went from New London, that some families were in mourning from these [atrocities] he begged him to assure the ladies that they may rely on his honor that not a shot should be fired at any dwelling—at least while he had command—unless he should receive very positive orders for that purpose, which he had not the most distant idea would be received. He hoped soon to have the pleasure of making New London a visit, not as an enemy, but as a friend. On the whole, Hardy must be a noble fellow."

The *Patapsco*, the *Delila*, the *Fairy*, and the *Tuckahoe* were four Baltimore privateers that were fairly successful. The first, Captain Mortimer, made three prizes. The schooner *Delila*, on her passage from Bordeaux to New Orleans, took a ship filled with drygoods, but the privateer had sent away so many of her crew in prizes that she could not spare a prize crew for her latest capture. The *Fairy*, Captain P. Dickenson, burned the sloop *Active*, and sent into port a schooner, having a valuable cargo of drygoods and provisions. The *Tuckahoe*, in 1814, on her way to France, burned at sea the schooner *Sea Flower*, and after capturing the schooner *Hazard*, from Nassau for San Domingo, and taking what was available, gave her up to her people. The *Tuckahoe* also took another English ship and sent her into port. While on the east end of Long Island the *Tuckahoe* fell in with the British blockading squadron, and was chased for several days. She eluded the enemy, and in March, 1814, got into Boston, having been chased several times by British war ships.

The privateer *York*, Captain E. Staples, began her career under inauspicious circumstances. On April 18, 1814, while off Nova Scotia, she had a severe engagement with the British transport *Lord Somers*. After Captain Staples and five of his men had been killed and twelve were wounded, the *York* hauled off. Soon afterward she fell in with the schooner *Diligence*, from Halifax for St. John's, and burned her. In July or August, 1814, she took the brig *Betsey*, with fish, from Newfoundland for Barbadoes, and sent her into Boston.

The *York* returned to Boston in September, 1814, after a cruise of thirteen weeks, without having lost a man. She had spent most of her time on the coast of Brazil, and the value of her prizes aggregated one million five hundred thousand dollars. The *York's* last cruise in the war, however, was very unsuccessful. She returned to Boston, April, 1815, having taken only one vessel, and that one had been promptly recaptured by the enemy. Throughout the cruise she had experienced a series of heavy gales and four of her crew had been carried overboard and lost, together with several guns and anchors.

The little 6-gun privateer *Perry*, Captain Coleman, sent into the Delaware a schooner laden with rum, cocoa, etc. In 1814 the *Perry* made a cruise of ninety days in which she took twenty-two vessels, of which eighteen were destroyed at sea and four were sent into port. The *Perry* also captured, after a severe action, the British gunboat *Ballahou*, Lieu-

tenant Norfolk King, mounting four 12-pounders and
having a complement of thirty men. On entering
the port of Wilmington the *Ballahou* was chased
ashore by a British brig of war and destroyed.

Almost as successful as the *Perry* was the 8-gun
schooner *Midas*, Captain Thompson. Her first seizure was the schooner *Francis*, taken April, 1814,
which was burned off the French coast, with a cargo
of bullocks intended for the British army. She also
took the schooner *Appallodore*, with four hundred
and fifty boxes of fruit, and sunk her. The *Midas*, in
the course of the war, made fourteen prizes, one of
them being the English privateer *Dash*, of five guns
and forty men. Toward the close of the war President Madison revoked the *Midas'* commission.

The privateers *Delisle*, *Argo*, and *Diamond* did not
become so well known. The first, J. Taylor, made
three prizes; the second, Captain P. Rider, in September, 1814, took the brig *Mary and Eliza*, from Halifax,
in lumber, and ordered her to port, but she was
chased ashore near Barnegat and destroyed. The
Diamond, Captain W. Davidson, in 1815 took the brig
Lord Wellington, from Halifax for Havana, but she
was released, in deference to the wishes of some
Spaniards who were aboard as passengers.

The first prize taken by the xebec *Ultor*, Captain
Mathews, was a brig called the *Robert*, laden with
fish and lumber, from St. John's for Jamaica, which
was sent into Charleston. Her second prize, taken
in April, 1814, was the brig *Swift*, carrying four guns
and fifteen men, from Halifax, with an assorted
cargo, which also was sent into port. While in Long
Island Sound, July, 1814, the xebec *Ultor* was attacked by two English boats, but the Americans
made such good use of their firearms that one boat
was beaten off and the other, with eight men in it,
was captured. The commander of this boat was
killed, and was buried in New London, where the
xebec *Ultor* touched in order to dispose of her pris-

oners. In the course of the war the xebec *Ultor* made fifteen prizes.

The *Pike* and the *Lawrence*, bearing two historic names, got to sea toward the close of the war and were eminently successful. The former, Captain H. Bolton, in May, 1814, captured the schooner *Hope*, the schooner *Pickerel*, from Dartmouth, England, for Quebec, and the ship *Mermaid*, besides twenty other vessels. One of her prizes, the brig *John*, of London, for Teneriffe, was taken and burned within long-shot of an English brig of war that vainly endeavored to come up with the audacious Americans. The *Pike*, about September, 1814, was chased ashore on the Southern coast and seized by British boats. A part of her crew escaped, but forty-three were made prisoners. In her cruise the *Pike* released on parole two hundred and fifty men. One of her prizes, the ship *Samuel Cummings*, of four hundred tons, laden with sugar and coffee, was wrecked on the Southern coast.

The 9-gun schooner *Lawrence*, Captain E. Veasey, arrived at New York, January 25, 1815, and reported having taken thirteen English vessels, eight of which had been manned and ordered to port. She had made one hundred and six prisoners, but only fifteen were brought in. One of her prizes, taken November 11, 1814, was the brig *Eagle*, and was ordered to the United States under Prize-Master John Snow. On December 7th, while the *Eagle* was making for a home port, two Frenchmen—John Secar and Peter Grandjack—and a negro named Manuel, who were among the prisoners, conspired with the former commander of the *Eagle*, and attempted to recover their vessel. Secar stabbed the man at the helm, and, following him below, killed him, together with Prize-Master Snow and one of his men. The prisoners managed to get the hatch covers on, and so confined the remaining Americans below. One of the prize crew, John Hooper, was in the cabin when the attack was first made and received a bad knife wound in his hand. He was then lashed to the deck and kept there three days without drink or food. On the third day after the recapture of the *Eagle*, the surviving Americans succeeded in forcing the hatch covers and gained the deck. They soon overpowered the two Frenchmen, while the negro jumped overboard, cutlass in hand. On January 27, 1815, as the *Eagle* was approaching New York, she was captured by the British frigate *Saturn*. Soon after this the *Eagle* was lost by shipwreck. Early in her cruise the *Lawrence* fell in with the St. Thomas merchant fleet, and, boldly dashing among them, Captain Veasey captured and manned eight large vessels, and actually beat off a brig of war before she could intercept the prizes. Several prizes were made by the privateers *Viper*, Captain T. N. Williams, and *Resolution*.

Of the privateers of Baltimore the 6-gun schooner *Amelia*, Captain A. Adams, was above the average in the number and value of her captures. She arrived in New York after her first cruise with eighty prisoners, having taken one thousand four hundred tons of shipping, valued at one million dollars. In her second cruise the *Amelia* captured two thousand two hundred and seventy tons of shipping and made one hundred and twelve prisoners. She arrived at Philadelphia in April, 1815. At one time she put into L'Orient, where she was well received by the French authorities, but while on her homeward passage she touched at St. Barts for water. The governor would not permit her to take in supplies, and ordered her to leave port at once. The *Amelia*, although frequently chased, always escaped through her superior sailing qualities and the fine seamanship of her officers.

The *Harrison*, the *Syren*, and the *Whig* fully sustained the reputation of the American privateersmen. The first, a schooner commanded by Captain

H. Perry, had a battle with a British sloop of war,
whose commander was killed. The *Harrison* arrived
safely at Savannah, August, 1814.   In her second
venture, made in 1815, she took a brig which was
ransomed and a schooner which was sailing under
Spanish colors, but carrying British goods. After
taking out the cargo the *Harrison* released the
schooner. This privateer is credited with six prizes,
one of them being valued at one hundred thousand
dollars.

The 7-gun schooner *Syren*, Captain J. D. Daniels,
seized two ships on the English coast and destroyed
them. She also took, in December, 1814, the brig
Sir John Sherbroke, mounting twelve guns, from Halifax for Alicant, with fish and oil. This vessel was
manned, but she was chased ashore on Rockaway
Beach by the English blockading squadron off New
York, and burned by her prize crew to prevent her
falling into the hands of the enemy. The *Syren* herself, while returning from a cruise, was chased off
Sandy Hook by the enemy's blockading force. She
then endeavored to make the Delaware, but on November 16, 1814, she was run ashore by the pilot.
While in this position she was attacked by three
barges from an English razee. For two hours the
Americans held the enemy in check, when, finding
that it was hopeless to continue the struggle, they
set fire to the vessel and escaped to the Jersey shore
with their six prisoners. At the time the *Syren* was
attacked she had only twenty of her original
crew. One of her prizes, the ship *Emulation*, put
into the Western Isles and was abandoned by her
crew.[1]

The *Whig*, an 8-gun schooner, under Captain T.
Venice, made thirteen prizes. She arrived in New
York, September or October, 1814, with twenty-three
prisoners. A number of her prisoners had been sent

[1] For action between the *Syren* and the king's cutter, see page 472.

to England in the sloop *Enterprise,* one of her prizes, from Guernsey for Madeira, laden with drygoods and flour. Her prizes, the brigs *Brunswick* and *Race Horse* and the schooner *Britannia,* were burned at sea.

CHAPTER XXIII.

GUY R. CHAMPLIN.

FEW American vessels have had such a distinguished career as the privateer schooner *General Armstrong*, of New York, fitted out, in part, by the shipping firm of Jenkins & Havens. This vessel, named for John Armstrong, in 1813 the Secretary of War, was always fortunate in having an able commander. She was first brought prominently before the public by an action she sustained with a heavy English war ship off Surinam River. On March 11, 1813, this vessel, then commanded by Captain Guy R. Champlin, was cruising in five fathoms of water some thirty miles east of the mouth of the Surinam River. The weather was cloudy, but the wind was light and enabled her to stand closer in shore than usual. At seven o'clock in the morning Captain Champlin, while standing on a tack to the southeast, discovered a sail bearing south-southeast, and half an hour later he observed that she was at anchor under the land.

About 8 A. M. the stranger seemed to have discovered the *General Armstrong*, for at 8.30 A. M. she got under way and stood to the north, firing three shots at the privateer and showing English colors. At 9.10 A. M. the *General Armstrong* hoisted the Stars and Stripes and discharged her long tom. It was apparent, however, that the stranger was far too heavy a vessel for the privateer to attack, so Captain Champlin edged away, ready to lead a long chase

if the stranger seemed disposed to pursue. At 9.50
A. M. the stranger tacked and stood as near the
Americans as the wind would permit, keeping up a
brisk fire from her chase guns. Down to this time
Captain Champlin was under the impression that
he was dealing with a heavy war ship, but by 10.15
A. M. the vessels were near enough for the Americans to get a pretty good view of the stranger. The
opinion was prevalent in the *General Armstrong* that
the stranger was a British privateer, and, yielding
to the desire of his officers, Captain Champlin bore
down to engage, hoping that she might be laden with
a valuable cargo. At 10.30 A. M. he put his helm up,
and, having every gun carefully loaded, came rapidly
down on the stranger, intending to board in the smoke
of his broadsides. As soon as within easy range Captain Champlin poured in his starboard broadside, and,
wearing ship, delivered his port fire also; but when
he endeavored to run alongside the maneuver was
frustrated by the enemy keeping off and continuing the action within musket shot.

Now, for the first time the stranger revealed her
real strength. Port cover after port cover along
her dark sides were triced up in rapid succession,
until the Americans found themselves facing fourteen guns on her main deck, six on the quarter-deck,
and four on the forecastle. It was too late to think
of running away, for in a twinkling the black muzzles began to belch away, carrying death and destruction into the privateer. For ten minutes the
General Armstrong lay like a log on the water, while
the stranger, having her starboard tacks aboard,
managed to keep in range and poured in a rapid fire.

The Americans kept to their guns manfully, and
continued to hammer away at their huge antagonist
with every gun that bore. Fortunately Yankee gunnery was superior to that of the enemy, as it was
shown to have been in so many instances in this
war, which in some degree made up for the great •

disparity of forces. At the first discharge the Englishman's fore-topsail tie and mizzen gaff halyards were shot away, which brought her colors down. Her mizzen and back stays also were carried away. For a moment it was thought in the *General Armstrong* that the enemy had surrendered, but this hope was quickly dispelled by the English renewing their fire and showing their colors again. For some time after this the Englishmen seemed to have lost control of their craft, but they finally got under way and opened viciously from their starboard battery and maintop, evidently thoroughly exasperated at the rough treatment they had received from the audacious American and determined to sink her alongside.

For forty-five minutes the *General Armstrong* remained within pistol shot of the Englishman, maintaining the unequal conflict in the hope that some accident would befall her adversary or some lucky shot would turn the tide in her favor. During this period of the battle Captain Champlin spent most of his time by the long tom, knowing that his main dependence was on this gun. So near were the vessels at times that he fired one of his pistols at the enemy with effect, and was about to discharge another when he was wounded in his left shoulder by a musket ball from the Englishman's maintop. The wound was a painful and dangerous one, but the heroic man, affecting indifference, coolly walked aft and had the hurt attended to by the surgeon. There is a limit, however, to human endurance, and, faint with loss of blood, Captain Champlin was persuaded to retire for a moment into his cabin.

There, while lying on the floor, his hand still nervously clutching a loaded pistol, he overheard some of his men talking about surrender. The words seemed to give him new life, and he exclaimed to the surgeon:

"Tell those fellows that if any one of them dares

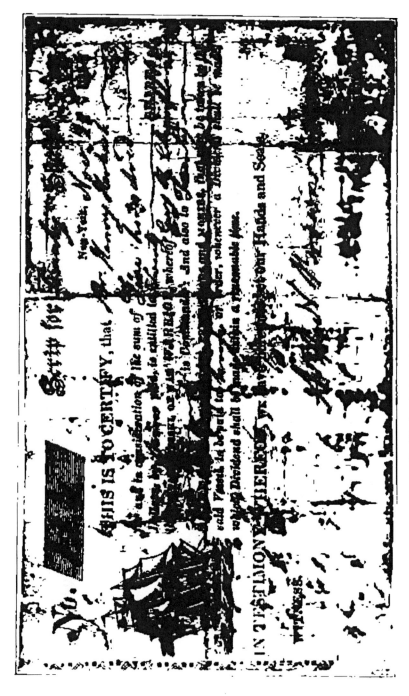

Certificate of shares in the privateer Warrior.

From the original

to strike the colors I will immediately fire into the magazine and blow them all to hell."

The captain's cabin was directly over the magazine, and every man in the ship knew enough of Champlin's character to believe that he meant every word of his threat and all thoughts of hauling down the colors were abandoned.

When the enemy's gaff halyards were shot away and his colors down, the Americans lost an admirable chance to deliver an effective blow. They let slip the opportunity, supposing that the enemy had surrendered. Had it not been for this Captain Champlin could have raked the deck of the Englishmen fore and aft with his long tom, which was loaded with a double charge of round and grape ready for firing, as the muzzle of the gun was within half pistol shot of the enemy's cabin windows. By this time it was seen that the Englishmen had suffered heavily from the privateer's fire, for they replied only at intervals and with poor aim. The Americans then luffed to windward and forereached their antagonist, and by the use of what sails they had left, in making short tacks to windward, and by the use of sweeps, they gradually drew out of gunshot.

In this spirited affair the Americans had six men killed and sixteen wounded. All the halyards and headsails had been shot away, the foremast and bowsprit were cut one quarter through, all the fore and main shrouds excepting one were carried away, both mainstays and running rigging were cut to pieces, and a great number of shot had passed through the sails and the hull, some of them between wind and water, which caused her to leak so much that detachments of men were constantly required at the pump. As soon as possible Captain Champlin got the foresheet aft and set his jib and topgallant sail. During the time the privateer was within reach the English kept up a well-directed fire from one or two guns aimed at the American's foremast and fore gaff, but fortunately without effect.

After running the enemy out of sight Captain Champlin made for a home port, arriving at Charleston, South Carolina, on April 4th. At a meeting of the stockholders of the *General Armstrong*, held in Tammany Hall, April 14, 1813, at which Thomas Farmer presided and Thomas Jenkins was secretary, Captain Champlin, his officers and men, were formally thanked for their gallant defense of the ship and a sword was given to Captain Champlin.

The *General Armstrong* was remarkable both for the value of the prizes she took and for the obstinacy of several of her engagements with heavily armed vessels. At the beginning of her career she had a desperate battle with an English ship carrying twenty-two guns and an unusually large crew. The battle took place at the mouth of the Demerara River and lasted thirty-five minutes, at the end of which time she compelled the enemy to run ashore. On another occasion she had a severe engagement with the English ship *Queen*, carrying sixteen guns and a complement of forty men. The *Queen* was from Liverpool bound for Surinam, with a cargo invoiced at about ninety thousand pounds. Her people made a brave resistance, and did not surrender until their commander, the first officer, and nine of the crew had been killed. This, perhaps, was as valuable a prize as was made in the war. A prize crew was placed aboard, with instructions to make for the United States, but unfortunately, when nearing the coast, the *Queen* was wrecked off Nantucket. Another prize of the *General Armstrong* was the brig *Lucy and Alida*, with a valuable cargo. She was recaptured by the British privateer *Brenton*, and taken again by the privateer *Revenge*, of Norfolk.[1]

---

[1] Other prizes taken by this famous privateer were the 6-gun brig *Union*, from Guernsey for Grenada, in ballast, which was sent into Old

On several occasions later in the war Captain Champlin showed himself to be a commander of no ordinary ability. On December 15, 1814, while in command of the privateer *Warrior*, cruising near Fayal, he made out an English frigate lying at anchor in the harbor just as he was about to enter. Well knowing that the English could not be depended upon to respect the rights of neutral ports, Captain Champlin promptly made sail to escape. This was about eight o'clock in the morning. The frigate's people discovered the privateer about the same time, and, slipping their cables, spread canvas in chase. The frigate proved to be a remarkably fast sailer, and in the run before the wind gained steadily on the American. After a chase of some forty or fifty miles, in a strong breeze and in squally weather, the enemy had got within gunshot, and as there were several hours of daylight left the Americans saw no hope of avoiding capture unless by resorting to some stratagem.

It was not long before the English opened with their chase guns, and the second and third shots told that they were unusually good marksmen for the British of that day. Captain Champlin now luffed to and showed his starboard battery, which maneuver, as he intended, was taken by the enemy as an indication of his willingness to fight. The enemy thereupon shortened sail and prepared to give battle in

---

Town: the brig *Tartar*, laden with one hundred and sixty hogsheads of rum, which was ordered into Georgetown, South Carolina, but unfortunately she was chased by a British war brig and was wrecked on the bar, although her crew and cargo were saved: a brig from the Leeward Islands for Guernsey, carrying six guns, with a full cargo of West India produce, which was sent into Martha's Vineyard; the brig *Harriet*, sent into Porto Rico (being short of water), where she was seized by the Spanish officials and given up to the British; a schooner captured at sea and burned; the brig *Phœbe*, from Ireland for Madeira, laden with butter and potatoes and scuttled; and the sloop *Resolution*, from Jersey for Lisbon, laden with linen, paper, etc., and converted into a cartel after the most valuable portion of her cargo had been taken out of her.

34

due form. Instead of accepting the challenge, however, Captain Champlin threw overboard all his lee
guns, with shot and other heavy articles. All these
things were put over the port side so that the enemy
could not discover what was going on, the starboard
side of the *Warrior* being presented to the foe. As
soon as his ship was relieved of these weights Captain Champlin suddenly made all sail and managed
to keep just beyond the reach of the frigate's bow
chasers until night, when he had little difficulty in
giving the enemy the slip.

The *Warrior* was a beautiful brig of four hundred
and thirty tons, built on the model of a pilot boat.
She mounted twenty-one guns and carried a complement of one hundred and fifty men. On another
occasion she was chased by a ship of the line, from
which she received several shots, but finally escaped
without material injury. Before returning to port
this privateer captured the brig *Hope*, from Glasgow
for Buenos Ayres, which was relieved of a large
quantity of her cargo of English goods, and sent to
the United States in charge of a prize crew; the ship
Francis and Eliza, carrying ten guns and thirty-five
men, from London for New South Wales, having on
board one hundred and twenty-four male and female
convicts, and after taking out of her sundry articles
she was allowed to proceed on her course; the ship
Neptune, from Liverpool for Bahia, carrying eight
guns and fifteen men; the brig *Dundee*, from London
for Bahia, with three hundred and twenty-three
bales of English goods and fifteen thousand dollars
in specie, which was manned for New York. A three-
masted schooner captured by the *Warrior* was lost
on New Inlet bar, North Carolina. In her last cruise
the *Warrior* frequently was chased by the enemy,
and at one time was so closely pursued by an English 74-gun ship that several shots came aboard.

CHAPTER XXIV.

BATTLE OF FAYAL.

WHEN Captain Champlin gave up the command of the privateer *General Armstrong,* as narrated in the preceding chapter, he was succeeded by Captain Samuel Chester Reid, who had been in charge of the 275-ton schooner *Boxer,* carrying six guns and thirty-five men. It does not appear that the *Boxer* had made any prizes. On the evening of September 9, 1814, Captain Reid, availing himself of the cover of night, got under way in the *General Armstrong* and passed Sandy Hook in an effort to evade the blockading squadron and to get to sea. About midnight the dark outlines of a heavy war ship loomed up off the privateer's bow, and shortly afterward another vessel, larger than the first, was reported by the vigilant lookouts. These vessels were soon made out to be a razee and a ship of the line, and as there could be no question of their belonging to Captain John Hayes' blockading force the Americans hastily made preparations for a hard chase. The English discovered the privateer almost as soon as they were made out from the *General Armstrong* and instantly went about in pursuit. Captain Reid quickly got all the canvas on the brig she could carry, and soon the three vessels were bowling eastward over a choppy sea at a lively rate. The privateer continued to increase her lead on her pursuers, and by noon of the following day they gave up the hopeless chase and returned to their station off Sandy Hook.

491

Early on the following morning, September 10th, the lookouts reported another sail, to which chase was promptly given. The stranger, which soon was made out to be a schooner, apparently was anxious to avoid a meeting, and when the *General Armstrong* had come within gunshot she was seen to be relieving herself of heavy articles so as to increase her speed. Notwithstanding these extreme measures, the *General Armstrong*, after an exciting chase of nine hours, held the schooner under her guns. On inquiry she was found to be the 6-gun privateer *Perry*, Captain John Coleman, of Baltimore, and had sailed from Philadelphia only six days before on a general cruise. It seems that the *Perry* had scarcely cleared land when chase was given to her by the enemy, and the little privateer had escaped only by throwing overboard all of her guns. This mishap, however, did not end the *Perry's* usefulness. After her meeting with the *General Armstrong* she returned to port, secured a new battery, and under the command of Captain R. McDonald made a highly successful cruise, taking in all two brigs, four schooners, and sixteen sloops. Eighteen of her prizes, made in the West Indies, were relieved of the most valuable portions of their cargoes and were destroyed, while another prize was given up to the prisoners.

It was the good fortune of the *Perry* in this cruise to render material service to the navy. It will be remembered that the 44-gun frigate *Constitution*, Captain Charles Stewart, sailed from Boston, December 17, 1814, on her most eventful cruise. She made directly for the coasts of Spain and Portugal. The British squadron that had been ordered to keep the dreaded *Constitution* in Boston, when it heard that this frigate had again given them the slip, immediately began a blind chase across the Atlantic after her. On January 4, 1815, while off the Western Isles, they fell in with a brig that had been taken by the *Perry*, which was then in charge of a prize

master. This shrewd man quickly discovered the
true character of the British vessels, but pretending to take them for a part of Captain Stewart's
" squadron "—that commander, in fact, having only
the *Constitution* for his " squadron," though soon
afterward he captured two English war vessels,
which answered the purposes—he misled the Englishmen to such an extent that, when they accidental-
ly came upon *Old Ironsides* in Port Praya, March 10th,
they failed to capture her.[1]

The day after her experience with the *Perry*, the
General Armstrong sighted a British brig of war. Captain Reid, in his official report, briefly notes the occurrence as follows: " On the following day fell in
with an enemy's gun brig; exchanged a few shots
with and left him." [2] The audacity of the American
privateersman in thus deliberately venturing within
reach of a cruiser's guns, and after exchanging a
few tantalizing shots leaving her, is well shown in
the too modest report of Captain Reid. Boarding
a Spanish brig and schooner and a Portuguese ship
bound for Havana, on the 24th, Captain Reid dropped
anchor in Fayal Roads on the afternoon of the 26th
for the purpose of obtaining water and fresh provisions.

Anxious to get to sea early on the following morning, Captain Reid called on the American consul,
John B. Dabney, shortly after anchoring, with a view
of hastening the needed supplies. The consul did
everything in his power to assist the Americans, and
at five o'clock in the afternoon went aboard the
General Armstrong with some other gentlemen. Captain Reid took this opportunity to ask after the
whereabouts of British cruisers in this quarter
of the globe, and was informed that not one Brit-

---

[1] For the details of this extraordinary comedy of nautical errors, see
Maclay's History of the Navy, vol. i, pp. 632–639.

[2] Official report of Captain Reid.

ish war ship had visited these islands in several weeks.

Just as night was beginning to fall and the group of Americans was still on the privateer's quarter-deck discussing these matters, a war brig suddenly hove in sight, close under the northeast head of the harbor, within gunshot. Preparations were hastily begun to get under way, with the idea of dashing past the probable enemy and leading him a long chase to sea; but finding that there was only a little wind where the privateer was, and that the brig had the advantage of a good breeze, Captain Reid changed his plans. Inquiring of Mr. Dabney if the British could be trusted to observe the neutrality of the port, Captain Reid was told that he would not be molested while at anchor. Relying on this assurance Captain Reid remained where he was.

It was not long before a pilot was seen to board the war brig, from whom the English learned the character of the vessel in port, and they promptly hauled close in and anchored within pistol shot of her. About the same time a ship of the line and another frigate hove in sight near the headland, to whom the war brig instantly made signals, and for some time there was a rapid interchange of the code. These vessels were the British 74-gun ship of the line *Plantagenet*, Captain Robert Lloyd; the 38-gun frigate *Rota*, Captain Philip Somerville; and the 18-gun war brig *Carnation*, Captain George Bentham, a part of the fleet having on board the ill-fated New Orleans expedition. The result of the signaling between the British ships was that the *Carnation*

proceeded to get out all her boats and send them to the ship of the line. Having every reason to believe that the enemy intended to make a boat attack upon him that night, Captain Reid cleared for action, got under way, and began to sweep inshore. The moon was nearly full at the time, and as the sky was clear every movement of the vessels could be seen with great distinctness.

When the *Carnation's* people saw the move being made by the privateer they quickly cut their cables and made sail. As the wind was very light, the brig made little or no progress, and, impatient at the delay, her commander lowered four boats, under Lieutenant Robert Faussett, and sent them in pursuit of the *General Armstrong*. It was now about eight in the evening, and as soon as Captain Reid saw the boats coming toward him he dropped anchor with springs on his cable and brought his broadside to bear. He then hailed the boats, warning them to keep off or he would fire. No attention was paid to this summons, and, although it was repeated several times, the English persisted in holding their course, and even increased their efforts to come alongside. Perceiving that the boats were well manned, and apparently heavily armed, Captain Reid could no longer doubt that they intended to attack him, and he ordered his men to open with their small arms and cannon.

The boats promptly returned the fire, but so unexpectedly warm was the reception they got from the privateer that they soon cried for quarter and hauled off in a badly crippled condition. Their loss in this encounter, according to American reports, was upward of twenty killed or wounded. Captain Reid had one man killed and his first officer wounded. Returning to their ships the British could be seen preparing for a more formidable attack. The Americans improved their opportunity to haul close into the beach within half pistol shot of the castle, where they anchored the *General Armstrong* head and stern.

About nine o'clock the *Carnation* was observed towing in a fleet of boats, which, on arriving at a point favorable for their purpose, cast off and took a station in three divisions, under cover of a small reef of rocks, within musket shot of the privateer. For some time the boats kept up a series of maneuvers behind these rocks, evidently preparing to make a dash at the Americans in three separate divisions, the *Carnation* in the meantime assisting the boats in every way she could, and holding herself in readiness to prevent the privateer from making a dash seaward.

By this time the news of the first attack had spread over the town, and the shore in the vicinity of the castle was black with people eager to witness the outcome of the battle. The governor and some of the leading people of the place took up a favorable position in the castle and witnessed the whole affair.

But it was not until midnight that the British boats were in readiness to renew the attack; all the intervening time the Americans were lying at their quarters. At that hour the British boats were observed coming toward the *General Armstrong* in one direct line and keeping close order. Twelve boats were counted, each carrying a gun in the bow and containing in all some four hundred men. As soon as they were within point-blank range the privateer opened fire, the discharge of the long tom doing great execution, and for a time seeming to stagger the enemy. The British responded with their boat carronades and musketry, after which they gave three cheers and made a dash for the privateer.

In a moment their boats were close under the *General Armstrong's* bow and starboard quarter and the command "Board!" was heard. The privateer's long tom and broadside guns, of course, were now useless, but the Americans seized their small arms and prepared to keep the English from gaining their decks. Pikes, cutlasses, pistols, and muskets now came into lively play and with deadly effect. Wherever an Englishman showed his head above the bulwarks it instantly became a target. Time and again the British endeavored to leap over the bulwarks, and as often were they repelled with great slaughter by the vigilant privateersmen.

Not content with keeping the enemy off their decks, the Americans, with every repulse of the British boarders, clambered up their own bulwarks and fired into the crowded boats with deadly effect. After this bloody struggle had lasted some minutes, Captain Reid learned that his second officer, Alexander O. Williams, of New York, had been killed, and soon afterward that his third officer, Robert Johnson, was wounded in the left knee. Mr. Williams was struck on the forehead by a musket ball and died instantly. These two officers had been in charge of the forecastle, and had bravely defended it against the attacks of the enemy. The death of one and the disabling of the other had a noticeable effect, in the diminished fire of the American in that part of the ship. Having effectually repulsed the enemy under the stern of the *General Armstrong*, and fearing that they were gaining a foothold on his forecastle, Captain Reid rallied the whole of the after division around him, and, giving a cheer, rushed forward. The renewed activity of the American fire forward so discouraged the enemy at this end of the fight that they retired with great losses after an action of forty minutes.

Having completely defeated the British, Captain Reid had time to look round him and count his losses and those of the enemy. Two of the *Rota's* boats, literally loaded with dead and dying men, were taken possession of by the Americans. Of the forty or fifty men in these boats only seventeen escaped death, and they by swimming ashore. Another boat was found under the privateer's stern, commanded by one of the *Plantagenet's* lieutenants. All of the men in it were killed save four, the lieutenant himself jumping overboard to save his life.

Among the English killed were First Lieutenant William Matterface, of the *Rota*, who commanded the expedition, and Third Lieutenant Charles R. Norman, of the *Rota*; while Second Lieutenant Richard Rawle, First Lieutenant Thomas Park, and Purser William Benge Basden, all of the *Rota*, were wounded.

From information Captain Reid received some days afterward from the British consul, officers of the fleet, and other sources, he believed that in the last attack the enemy had one hundred and twenty men killed and about one hundred and thirty wounded. On the part of the Americans only two were killed and seven wounded. The killed were Second Officer Williams and Burton Lloyd, a seaman, who was shot through the heart by a musket ball and died instantly. The wounded were First Officer Frederick A. Worth, in the right side; Third Officer Robert Johnson; Quartermaster Razilla Hammond, in the left arm; John Piner, seaman, in the knee; William Castle, in the arm; Nicholas Scalsan, in the arm and leg; and John Harrison, in the arm and face, by the explosion of a gun. The decks of the *General Armstrong*, however, had been thrown into great confusion. The long tom, the main reliance of the ship, was dismounted and several of the broadside guns were disabled. By great exertions the long tom was mounted again, the decks cleared, and preparations made to renew the action should the enemy see fit to attack. But the British did not attempt it that night.

An English eyewitness of this fight says: "The Americans fought with great firmness, but more like bloodthirsty savages than anything else. They

rushed into the boats sword in hand, and put every
soul to death as far as came within their power.
Some of the boats were left without a single man
to row them, others with three or four. The most
that any one returned with was about ten. Several
boats floated ashore full of dead bodies. . . . For
three days after the battle we were employed in
burying the dead that washed on shore in the surf.".

At three o'clock in the morning Captain Reid
received a note from the American consul asking
him to come ashore, as there was important information awaiting him. Captain Reid did as requested,
and going ashore learned that the governor had
sent a note to Captain Lloyd begging him to desist
from further attack, and that the British commander
not only had refused to do so, but had announced
his determination to take the privateer at any cost,
and if the governor should allow the Americans to
destroy the vessel in any way he would consider that
he was in an enemy's port and treat it accordingly.
Satisfied that there was no hope of saving his vessel,
Captain Reid immediately went aboard, ordered all
the dead and wounded to be taken ashore, and the
crew to save whatever of their personal effects they
could. By the time this was done it was daylight
and the *Carnation* was discovered standing close in,
and in a few minutes opened a rapid fire on the
Americans. Captain Reid responded to this fire with
his formidable battery, and soon induced the brig
to haul off, with her rigging much cut, her fore-topmast wounded, and some other injuries.

After repairing these damages the *Carnation*
again came down, and, dropping anchor, opened a
deliberate fire on the *General Armstrong*, which was
intended to destroy her. Captain Reid, with his
men, now abandoned the ship, after scuttling her,
and repaired on shore. English boats then boarded
the privateer, and, setting her on fire, soon had her
completely destroyed. A number of houses in the

town were injured by the Englishmen's fire and
some of the inhabitants were wounded. A woman
sitting in the fourth story of her home had her
thigh shattered and a boy had his arm broken.

For a week the English vessels were detained
in the harbor, burying their dead and attending to
their wounded. Three days after the battle they
were joined by the sloops of war *Thais* and *Calypso*,
which were detailed by Captain Lloyd to take the
wounded to England, the *Calypso* sailing on October
2d and the *Thais* on the 4th. Captain Lloyd's squadron arrived at Jamaica on November 5th, where the
English officers acknowledged a loss of sixty-three
killed and one hundred and ten wounded, among the
former being three lieutenants. On November 3,
1805, Sir Richard Strachan, with four ships of the
line and four frigates, fought a French fleet many
hours, capturing four ships of the largest rates. His
loss was only one hundred and thirty-five killed or
wounded. Captain Lloyd in this affair spent quite
as much time in destroying a single American privateer and lost nearly two hundred men. Such victories, as this Bunker Hill of the ocean, are disastrous to the victors.

The serious nature of this action is better shown
by a comparison of the losses the English sustained
in their frigate actions with the United States in this
war. Taking the losses that the British admit having
sustained in this action, we have:

Comparative English Losses in Frigate Actions.

NAME OF ACTION.	Killed.	Wounded.	Total.
British squadron vs. *Gen. Armstrong*...	63	110	173
Guerrière vs. *Constitution*	15	63	78
Macedonian vs. *United States*	36	68	104
Java vs. *Constitution*	60	101	161
Shannon vs. *Chesapeake*...............	24	59	83
Phœbe and *Cherub* vs. *Essex*..........	5	10	15
Endymion vs. *President*	11	14	25
Cyane and *Levant* vs. *Constitution*	35	42	77

Finding that his conduct in attacking the *General Armstrong* in a neutral port required an explanation, Captain Lloyd declared that the first boats he sent toward the privateer were ordered merely to reconnoiter the Americans, and that Captain Reid took the initiative in hostilities by opening fire on them. The circumstances of the case, however, fully bear out Captain Reid's belief that the boats were sent for the purpose of making an attack upon him. To reconnoiter an enemy's vessel in a neutral port with four boats carrying over one hundred armed men is too suspicious a circumstance to be easily explained away, especially as these boats persisted in drawing nearer and nearer to the privateer, in spite of repeated warnings to keep off. Another circumstance which weighs heavily against Captain Lloyd is the fact that when the *Thais* and *Calypso* sailed for England with the wounded he strictly forbade those vessels to carry any letters or information bearing on the action.

Captain Lloyd still further added to the infamy of his attack on the *General Armstrong* by the methods he employed to seize some of the American seamen when on shore. Under the pretext of searching for deserters he addressed an official letter to the governor, stating that in the crew of the privateer were two deserters from the squadron he commanded while on the American station, and as they were guilty of " high treason " he demanded that the Portuguese authorities produce these men. Rightly judging their man, the Americans, on gaining the shore, fled into the interior, fearful that Captain Lloyd, exasperated at his defeat on water, would follow up his attack on shore. The Portuguese governor, having no force at hand to protect himself, was compelled to obey, and sending a guard into the mountains arrested the seamen, brought them to Fayal, and compelled them to undergo an examination before British officers. The alleged deserters were not found and the seamen were released.

Captain Reid, with his surviving men, retired to an old Gothic convent in the interior, and breaking down the drawbridge prepared to defend himself against any further attacks the British might make. Captain Lloyd did not see fit to resume hostilities, however, and soon afterward Captain Reid returned to the United States and was received with distinction. At Richmond, Virginia, he was the guest of honor at a banquet where the governor and other high officials were present. Some of the toasts were highly characteristic of the feeling of the people toward our maritime forces at that time. They were: "The Navy—whose lightning has struck down the meteor flag of England: they have conquered those who had conquered the world"; "The Private Cruisers of the United States—whose intrepidity has pierced the enemy's channels and bearded the lion in his den"; "Barney, Boyle, and their Compatriots —who have plowed the seas in search of the enemy and hurled retaliation upon his head"; "Neutral Ports—whenever the tyrants of the ocean dare to invade these sanctuaries may they meet with an *Essex* and an *Armstrong*"; "The American Seamen— their achievements form an era in the naval annals of the world: may their brother soldiers emulate their deeds of everlasting renown"; "Captain Reid —his valor has shed a blaze of renown upon the character of our seamen, and won for himself a laurel of eternal bloom."

The United States sailing frigate St. Lawrence sinking the Confederate privateer Petrel.

CHAPTER XXV.

CONCLUSION.

PRIVATEERING, so far as the United States have been engaged in it, has been limited to our two wars with Great Britain. It is true that during our troubles with the French Directory, 1798–1801, letters of marque were issued by the Government; but these were used chiefly by our merchantmen as a license to defend themselves from hostile craft. The few actions that took place in which ships armed at private expense were engaged are notable as being exceptions.

At the time the civil war broke out the commerce of the United States ranked as second in the world, being exceeded only by that of Great Britain. Of our large tonnage at that period, less than one tenth belonged to the seceding States, and that one tenth was quickly drafted into the regular service of the Confederacy or was destroyed by the vigilance of our blockade vessels and cruisers; so that there was, in fact, no field in which Northern privateersmen could engage. The Declaration of Paris in 1856 did much to discredit the practice of privateering. In response to the circular invitation issued by the Powers, Secretary Marcy, in behalf of the United States, proposed an amendment to the rules by which private property on the high seas in time of war would be exempt from seizure. The same proposition was made by the United States delegates to the Peace Conference at The Hague in 1899.

No action was taken on Secretary Marcy's suggestion, and the United States did not become a party to the Declaration. After Lincoln's first inauguration as President, our Government opened negotiations with the Powers, offering to accede to the terms of the Declaration unconditionally, one of which discountenanced privateering; but Great Britain declined to enter upon an agreement which would have been operative in the war then existing between the Northern and Southern States.

On April 17, 1861, Jefferson Davis announced that he would issue letters of marque against the commerce of the United States, and a few vessels sailed from the Southern ports with the license to "burn, sink, and destroy." By the close of May, 1861, some twenty prizes had been brought into New Orleans for adjudication. Most of these privateers were small vessels, old slavers, fishing schooners, revenue cutters, and tugs. Had it not been for the energy with which the blockade was maintained they undoubtedly would have inflicted an enormous amount of damage on Northern commerce. As a rule, these craft concealed themselves in the many inlets along the Southern coast and pounced upon any unsuspecting merchantman that happened along.

A few privateers made bolder ventures. A condemned slaver, renamed *Jeff Davis*, cruised along the New England coast, but after making a few valuable captures she was wrecked on the coast of Florida. A schooner fitted out in Charleston, named *Beauregard*, was captured by the United States bark *W. G. Anderson*, while the privateer schooner *Judah* was destroyed at her moorings in Pensacola by a party of officers and seamen from the frigate *Colorado*, under the command of the late Rear-Admiral John Henry Russell;[1] the present Rear-Ad-

[1] For an account of this handsome exploit, see Maclay's History of the United States Navy, vol. ii, pages 169, 170.

miral John Francis Higginson, receiving a wound in
that gallant affair which he carries to this day. Another privateer from Charleston, the 54-ton pilot
boat *Savannah*, was captured by the United States
brig of war *Perry* and was carried to New York,
where the crew were held on a charge of piracy.
The Southerners met this step with threats of retaliation on the prisoners in their hands, and the charge
was not pressed.

Probably the best-known Southern privateer was
the *Petrel*, a revenue cutter converted to private use,
which was sunk by a shell from the sailing frigate
St. Lawrence. The popular story that the *St. Lawrence* was disguised as a merchantman at the time,
and so decoyed the *Petrel* under her guns, is entirely erroneous, the frigate simply giving chase
to the privateer, and, getting within gunshot, sank
her.

Aside from these few unimportant instances of
Confederate privateering, the South accomplished
little in the line of private enterprise on the ocean.
This was due principally to the rigor with which the
blockade was maintained and to the vigilance of our
cruisers on the high seas. The would-be privateersmen of the Confederacy, therefore, directed their
energies to the more profitable occupation of blockade running, taking out Southern products and
bringing in munitions of war. The better-known
commerce destroyers of the Confederacy, such as the
Sumter, Florida, Alabama, Rappahannock, and *Shenan-
doah*, cannot properly come under the head of privateers, for they were quite as regularly commissioned
naval vessels as were our *Bonhomme Richard, Alliance, Trumbull, Deane*, or any of our other Continental
war ships of the Revolution.[1]

It is believed that all the actions in which Ameri-

---

[1] For an account of these Confederate commerce destroyers, see
Maclay's History of the United States Navy, vol. ii, pages 508–528.

can privateers, both in the Revolution and in the War of 1812, were engaged, as well as all their important captures, have been noted in this work. It is possible that some of the operations of our amateur cruisers have escaped the exhaustive researches of the author. If such is the case he will gladly receive any reliable information on the subject, so that it may be incorporated in future editions. In summing up the record of our armed craft fitted out by private enterprise it will be found that in the struggle for independence one thousand one hundred and fifty-one privateers were commissioned, as follows: Three hundred and seven from Massachusetts, two hundred and eighty-three from Pennsylvania, one hundred and sixty-nine from Maryland, one hundred and forty-two from Connecticut, seventy-eight from New Hampshire, forty-four from Virginia, eighteen from Rhode Island, fifteen from New York, nine from South Carolina, four from New Jersey, and four from North Carolina, while seventy-eight came from ports not designated. These vessels are known to have captured three hundred and forty-three of the enemy's craft, and it is probable that a considerable number of prizes were made of which the record is lost.

In the War of 1812 five hundred and fifteen privateers were commissioned, as follows: One hundred and fifty from Massachusetts, one hundred and twelve from Maryland, one hundred and two from New York, thirty-one from Pennsylvania, sixteen from New Hampshire, fifteen from Maine, eleven from Connecticut, nine from Virginia, seven from Louisiana, and seven from Georgia, while fifty-five were from ports not designated. These vessels are known to have captured one thousand three hundred and forty-five craft of all kinds from the enemy, though, like their brethren of the Revolution, our privateersmen of the later war were careless in matters of record, and it is highly probable that a large

number of seizures were made of which little trace
is left.

After each of these wars the vessels engaged in
the privateer service were laid up, used in commerce,
or were destroyed, while their officers and men were
compelled to seek employment in the more peaceful
pursuits of life. Years after the War of 1812 it was
not unusual to observe men who had once commanded the quarter-deck of an armed vessel, whose
orders meant instant obedience and whose frowns
were more dreaded than the heaviest gales or hostile
cannon, bending over ledgers in the countingrooms
of shipping ports or engaged in menial service.
Finding their calling as sea warriors gone, these
men entered any trade or business offering, where
they soon discovered that the qualifications peculiar
and needful for the successful privateersman were
not only out of place, but a positive hindrance, in
their new fields of activity. As a rule, these mighty
men of the sea rapidly reversed the scale of promotion, and for the rest of their lives ground out an
humble existence as drudging clerks, longshoremen,
or wage earners. Like the noble ships they once
commanded, their occupation was gone, and they
were laid up to rust and wear out the balance of
their days in an inglorious existence, waiting for
Father Time, the conqueror of all, to remove them
to their final haven of rest. They have, however,
left a record in the history of their country which is
well worthy of preservation, and it will stand as
an imperishable monument to the gallant part they
played in the defense of their native land.

INDEX.

509

CPSIA information can be obtained at www.ICGtesting.com
Printed in the USA
235773LV00003B/31/P